THE MYLES HORTON
READER

THE MYLES HORTON
READER

Education for Social Change

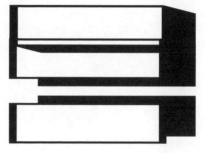

Edited by Dale Jacobs

The University of Tennessee Press
Knoxville

"The Adventures of a Radical Hillbilly, Parts I and II," interview with Bill Moyers reprinted in *Appalachian Journal* (summer 1982): 248–85. "What Is Liberating Education?" an interview by Bingham Graves, appeared in *Radical Teacher* (May 1979): 3–5. "It's a Miracle and I Still Don't Believe It," *Phi Delta Kappan* (May 1966): 490–97. "The Highlander Folk School," *Social Frontier* (Jan. 1936): 117–18. Used by permission of Ayer Company Publishers. "Building in the Democracy Mountains," interview by Danny Collum, from *Sojourners* (April 1986): 26–31. Used by permission of *Sojourners Magazine*. "Highlander," interview of Horton and Claudia Lewis, a chapter in *Roots of Open Education in America,* edited by Ruth Dropkin and Arthur Tobier (New York: City College Workshop Center for Open Education, 1976), 73–90. Used with permission of the City College Workshop Center for Open Education.

All previously unpublished pieces used by permission of Highlander Research and Education Center. All photographs courtesy of Highlander Research and Education Center.

This book is printed on acid-free paper.

Library of Congress Cataloging-in-Publication Data

Horton, Myles, 1905–1990
    The Myles Horton reader : education for social change / edited by Dale Jacobs.— 1st ed.
    p. cm.
Includes bibliographical references and index.
ISBN 1-57233-271-9 (pbk. : alk. paper)
    1. Education—Philosophy.
    2. Social movements—United States.
    3. Horton, Myles, 1905—Views on social action.
    4. Highlander Research and Education Center (Knoxville, Tenn.)
    I. Jacobs, Dale, 1966-
    II. Title.

LB885.H64 M954 2003
370.11'5—dc21   2002155366

Contents

IV. Educational Philosophy

Illustrations

Following Page 138

Horton, 1940s

Horton at Highlander with Labor Group, c. 1940

Zilphia and Myles Horton

Horton, 1940s (two photographs)

Horton, Eleanor Roosevelt, and James Stokely,
Late 1950s

Horton with Calvin Brewer, 1950s

Aimee and Myles Horton, 1964

Esau Jenkins, Charles Gomillion, and Horton, 1964

Horton, early 1950s

Horton, 1950s

Esau Jenkins and Horton, 1950s

Billboard Showing Martin Luther King Jr.
at Highlander, 1957

Horton, 1960s

Paolo Freire and Horton, 1987 (two photographs)

Horton, 1970s

T-Shirt Honoring Horton, 1987

Horton and Rosa Parks, Late 1970s or Early 1980s

Horton, Late 1970s or Early 1980s

Horton, 1984

Acknowledgments

The Myles Horton Reader would not have come to fruition without the assistance of an enormous number of people. I would first like to thank the staff at Highlander and at the State Historical Society of Wisconsin for all their assistance. Special thanks go out to Juanita Householder, Highlander's librarian, for all her patient assistance over the past several years. I would also like to thank my research assistants: at East Carolina University, Missy Pierce and Brandon Wooten; at the University of Windsor, Joy de Bruyn. East Carolina University provided me with two important travel grants to visit the archives, as well as a semester of release time from teaching; without these supports, I would not have been able to complete the project. The staff at Word Processing at the University of Windsor has been invaluable in helping me compile the text. The University of Tennessee Press has been very supportive throughout the project; a special debt of gratitude goes out to Joyce Harrison, the acquisitions editor at the Press, for believing in the importance of the project. In addition, I would like to thank Heidi Jacobs for her support and encouragement throughout the project. Finally, I would like to thank Myles Horton for his words and ideas.

Introduction

So, instead of thinking about having an education program to change society by working with all of its segments, especially with the people in power, so that
change would come from the top, I made a decision to
work with people from the bottom. That is the basis on
which I decided to concentrate on working people, many
of whom were exploited doubly, by class and by race.

MYLES HORTON, *The Long Haul*

[T]he struggle over education is fundamentally linked to
struggles in the larger theater of social and political life.

PETER MCLAREN, *Che Guevera, Paulo Freire,
and the Pedagogy of Revolution*

Finding the Path: Beginning to Walk
with Myles Horton

How often is it that we remember the exact place and time at which
we first encountered the educational ideas and thinkers that
influence and sustain us? It happened for me in the summer of 1996,
at my regular corner table at the Mill, a coffeehouse in Lincoln,
Nebraska. That summer I spent a lot of time in the Mill, a welcome
respite from both my office at the university and from the heat of the
Nebraska summer. On that particular day, I was reading Ira Shor's
Empowering Education, part of a reading project that was helping
me think through issues in my own pedagogical theory and practice.
As I sipped my coffee, I read the section in which Shor briefly mentions Myles Horton and his conversations with Paulo Freire, a dialogue that eventually became *We Make the Road by Walking.* Shor
writes, "regarding the affective side of empowering pedagogy, in
Freire's conversation with Myles Horton, the legendary founder of
the Highlander School in Tennessee, both men insisted on the relationship of play and joy to critical thought and social change" (25).
Throughout my reading that summer, it was the affective—the "play

and joy"—that always seemed to be missing or downplayed. Education, for me, had always been a physical and emotional, as well as an intellectual, experience; critical pedagogy, in opposition to Freire's emphasis on the whole person, often seemed to reduce education to an intellectual exercise of critique. Here, however, on the page in front of me, was the promise of another educational thinker besides Freire who valued holistic education, who spoke to my experience as a student and a teacher and to my own pedagogical ideas.

Later, Shor quotes Horton on holistic education: "We tried to involve everybody in singing and doing drama and dancing and laughing and telling stories because that's a part of their life. It's more of a holistic approach to education, not just a bunch of unrelated segments. The way people live was more important than any class or subject that we were dealing with. . . . They had that learning experience, making decisions, living in an unsegregated fashion, enjoying their senses other than their minds" (25). This kind of educational experience, involving the whole person, emotionally and physically, as well as intellectually, resonated with my own thinking about education at the time. I wanted to learn more; I wanted to know who Horton's "they" were, the people with whom Horton laughed and sang and told stories, the people in whose lives Horton was so invested. Shor didn't supply me with answers to any of those questions, quoting only this brief section from Horton before returning to Freire, a thinker whose influence on adult education cannot be overestimated.[1] Almost all of the educational thinkers I read that summer based their ideas on the teachings of Freire; I was no less influenced by him as I struggled and wrote about my own pedagogical theory and practice. And yet, why had I never heard of Horton, that "legendary founder of the Highlander School in Tennessee"? Why didn't anyone else mention him or discuss his ideas about education? Wasn't anyone else excited about the possibilities that I glimpsed in that brief passage?

Those brief words from Horton sent me in search of *We Make the Road by Walking.* Published in 1990, this book is the textual record of an extended dialog between Horton and Freire that occurred in December of 1987. It is, as Brenda Bell, John Gaventa, and John Peters wrote in their introduction, an encounter between two men who "shared a vision and a history of using participatory education as a crucible for empowerment of the poor and powerless" (xv). As I read, I once again found myself thinking, why isn't Horton cited more often? Why don't his ideas about education and social change have a direct influence on more educational thinkers? Why haven't more people taken up Horton's ideas about education as empowerment? Perhaps it is because of Horton's refusal to separate education from life and life from education, seeing education instead as a lifelong process that involves experience and the whole of person. Perhaps it is because his ideas cannot easily be reduced or summarized. Perhaps it has something to do with Horton's insistence on educational philosophy and process, rather than methodology, making his work even more difficult than Freire's to translate into concrete classroom practice.[2] In his discussion with Freire of educational practice, Horton comments, "I'm less interested in methodology or techniques than I am in a *process* that involves the total person, involves vision, involves total realities" (176). As will be seen in the brief discussion of Horton's life and work later in this introduction, the contexts or "total realities" of his educational work were in an almost constant state of change. Only in looking at Horton's ideas over the entirety of his life, embedded as they are in interviews, speeches, and only occasionally in writing for publication, do we begin to understand the scope of his thinking. Horton is not, in other words, easily reducible to educational aphorisms.

Consequently, when I finished *We Make the Road by Walking* I had the sense that much of Horton's practice and theory remained submerged and that I needed to move beyond this proverbial tip of the iceberg. I next moved on to *The Long Haul,* Horton's autobiography distilled from a series of recorded sessions with Judith and Herb Kohl. *The Long Haul* confirmed my growing sense that Horton's pedagogical theories were inextricably linked to his insistence on equality, social justice, and a radically re-visioned concept of democracy; his pedagogical practice was continually enacted through his work with Highlander, especially in relation to two important social movements, the labor movement and the civil rights movement. At every stage of his work, however, Horton refused to delineate exactly what his vision of the future entailed. Toward the end of *The Long Haul,* he says, "When I speak about a social goal, the goal for society, and for myself, I don't say, 'This is exactly what it's going to be like.' I don't have a blueprint in mind. I'm thinking more of a vision, I'm thinking of direction, I'm thinking of steps. I'm thinking more in terms of signs pointing in the right direction than I am of the shape of future society, because I don't know what that shape is going to be . . ." (226). In this radical openness to possibility, I saw an antidote to what I was coming to see as a misreading of Freire's ideas. Among many educators, Freire's ideas were reduced to little more than a kind of "banking" in which the student will be filled with the correct form of ideology.[3] On the other hand, throughout his essays, speeches, and interviews, Horton is careful to state that while he has always worked for change, he is unwilling to specify what that change might be or how it might come about. This is not to say that Horton existed outside ideology or that he lacked ideas about how he envisioned change, but rather that he refused to impose his ideas on the people with whom he worked, relying instead on a pedagogy of questioning and dialogue. For this reason, just as Horton is difficult to appropriate for a specific methodology, he is equally difficult to appropriate for a specific, sectarian ideology. The following passage from *The Long Haul* is typical of Horton: "I think it's important to understand that the quality of the process you use to get to a place determines the ends, so when you want to build a democratic society, you have to act democratically in every way. If you want love and brotherhood, you've got to incorporate them as you go along, because you can't just expect them to occur in the future without experiencing them before you get there.... A long-range goal for me is a direction that grows out of loving people, and caring for people, and believing in people's capacity to govern themselves" (227). The visionary quality of his work was thus balanced by a democratic desire for input from everyone involved in the educational process; like the pragmatists William James and John Dewey who had influenced his ideas, Horton continually tested his beliefs in action and in dialogue with others. Horton's pedagogical theory and practice, based as they are on love for and faith in people and worked out over a lifetime of teaching and learning, embody both a simplicity and complexity that unfortunately consign him to the status of the legendary, rather than the influential.

As I continued to immerse myself in Horton's life and ideas, I became more and more convinced that he needed to be rescued from the realm of the mythical, that the legend needed to be recontextualized within both his and our educational practice. Reading John Glen's excellent history of Highlander, *Highlander: No Ordinary School,* as well as Frank Adams's *Unearthing Seeds of Fire: The Idea of Highlander,* gave me a further sense of how Horton's ideas were enacted in specific contexts, how he tied "the practical with the visionary" (*We Make the Road by Walking,* 177). Even so, it still seemed that a large part of the iceberg remained submerged. It was at this point—early in the summer of 1998—that I drove across North Carolina and into the Tennessee foothills just outside New Market, the current site of what is now called the Highlander Research and Education Center. In visiting the Highlander archives, I hoped to enlarge my sense of Horton, his ideas, and his practice. However, when I returned to Greenville and began to read the massive amount of material I had collected, I began to see the enormous quantity of Horton's work—speeches, interviews, essays —that was simply not in print or easily accessible. A subsequent trip to Highlander, as well as several days at the State Historical Society of Wisconsin Archives, which houses many of Horton's papers as well as the bulk of the Highlander papers, confirmed this sense. It quickly became apparent to me that Horton's ideas needed to be collected and put into wider circulation. *The Myles Horton Reader* is an attempt to do just that.

From Myth to Reality: Concretizing the Work of Myles Horton

The Myles Horton Reader is a collection of writings, speeches, and interviews. Horton, who died in 1990, and the Highlander Folk School (now called the Highlander Research and Education Center), which he founded, were involved in education in both the labor movement of the 1930s and the Citizenship Schools of the civil rights movement. From its inception, Highlander was controversial because education was seen as a way to understand and change one's world rather than as a way to advance within the existing socioeconomic system. In fact, Horton and Highlander were deeply involved in the project of education for social action long before the academy had articulated this concept and identified it as important. Horton's pedagogy was grassroots, approaching education through action and action through education. At the school's fortieth anniversary in 1972, Horton summed up his philosophy of education in this way: "We believe that education leads to action. If you advocate just one action, you're an organizer. We teach leadership here. Then people go out and do what they want." Horton saw education as a way to foster social action, to promote leadership at the grassroots level, through "trust in people's ability to develop their capacity for working collectively to solve their own problems" (*The Long Haul,* 132). In other words, Horton stressed the importance of always situating education within specific contexts, rather than abstracting theory or methodologies that might not apply to the lived experiences or situations of specific students and teachers. By presenting Horton's ideas in his own words, *The Myles Horton Reader* seeks to give substance to this legendary educator and to situate his ideas within the contexts in which he and Highlander were actually working.

While I recognize that any textual order is necessarily arbitrary and that Horton's work is particularly hard to categorize into neat sections because of the immense overlap in ideas, I nonetheless felt that some form of organization was necessary. Rather than divide the texts into speeches, interviews, and essays, I have decided to group them into three categories that seem to represent Horton's life and career, as well as a fourth section that draws together the strands of his educational thinking that are woven throughout all of his work. The sections, then, are as follows: "The Idea of Highlander," "The Labor Movement," "The Civil Rights Movement," and "Educational Philosophy."

In the first section are texts that discuss Horton's influences, plans for what would become Highlander, and the educational endeavors of the school's first years. I have grouped these texts together because they provide a glimpse into the establishment and early years of Highlander from Horton's perspective; many of these texts have been unavailable in print to this point. In creating two discrete sections about the labor and civil rights movements, I am taking my lead directly from Horton. In *The Long Haul,* Horton says,

> Highlander was involved in two major social movements—the industrial union movement, which was organized by the CIO, and the civil rights movement. They differed structurally but had in common a struggle for justice and human rights. The labor movement was based

on local unions, which were much more than collective bargaining units. They provided a base for political and community activities, cultural and educational programs, and much more.

The civil rights movement was loosely organized, with no fixed structures on the local level to work with. The participants in the Citizenship Schools, voter registration, leadership, and other workshops at Highlander and throughout the South were recruited by staff and community volunteers. (161–62)

Although the two movements shared ethical and philosophical underpinnings, the structural differences meant different approaches for Horton and Highlander. As Horton goes on to say, "The civil rights movement was much more sporadic than the union movement, and we had to think in terms of how to deal with the nuances of particular problems and situations" (164). Thus, it seems prudent to group Horton's writings about these two movements into separate sections as a way to examine how his ideas were situated in specific educational contexts.

As a way to underscore the connectedness of all of Horton's work, the final section, "Educational Philosophy," provides an overview of Horton's educational ideas, emphasizing the philosophical and ethical continuity that runs throughout his work, while maintaining the contextual nature of his approach to education. What follows is some brief background that will set the context for the material in the first three of these sections, as well as a few words about the final section and *The Myles Horton Reader* as a whole.

The Idea of Highlander

Myles Horton was born on July 9, 1905, in Savannah, Tennessee.[4] His mother and father, both sometime schoolteachers, instilled in him the importance of education in the service of a greater social good. As Horton puts it in *The Long Haul,* "From my mother and father I learned the idea of service and the value of education. They taught me by their actions that you are supposed to serve your fellow men, you're supposed to do something worthwhile with your life, and education is meant to help you do something for others" (2–3). The connection between education and service was further infused by the spirit of love in which his mother lived her life and which she passed on to her son. This concept is built around

the principle of trying to serve people and building a loving world. If you believe that people are of worth, you can't treat anybody inhumanely, and that means you not only have to love, but you have to think in terms of building a society that people can profit most from, and that kind of society has to work on the principle of equality. Otherwise somebody's going to be left out.

People always ask, "Can we wait till we have a society that's perfect to have equality?" Well, of course, we'll never achieve it unless we start where we are, so you begin incorporating principles of equality into everything you do. That's complicated, because it's hard to avoid domination or inequality, or paternalism: but the principle itself isn't complicated, it's the application that's complicated. (*The Long Haul,* 7)

For Horton, what is important is the underlying notion of love and the continual process of putting it into practice, a precept that he shares with the Christian socialism that would become increasingly influential for him. This insistence on the loving potential of education for a better society would fuel Horton's restless pursuit of knowledge in the years leading up to the establishment of Highlander and would sustain his lifelong dedication to learning.

Horton attended Cumberland University in Lebanon, Tennessee, graduating in the spring of 1928. Here he began the pattern of eclectic reading and study that would continue as he moved toward and beyond the establishment of Highlander. The process of learning consumed Horton as it became increasingly tied to issues of social justice and equality. "I played football in college," recalled Horton in *The Long Haul,* "but I quit because it was interfering with my reading. In fact, the administration threatened to prevent me from graduating if I left the team, but I went on reading anyway. Learning was more important than graduating" (14).

During the final two summers of his undergraduate years, Horton worked for the Presbyterian Church as a student field representative for their Sunday School and Vacation Bible School programs in the Cumberland Mountains. It was in the second summer of this employment that Horton would begin to think about the possibilities of education among the people of the Cumberland Mountains. That summer, Horton decided to gather the adults of the country around Ozone, Tennessee, for a meeting to discuss the problems of the Great Depression that were already hitting the rural South in 1927. Since the people were expecting a religious meeting, Horton began with a discussion of the daily vacation Bible school. However, Horton soon shifted focus: "I said that I'd been working around this part of the country for the past two years and wondered if we could spend a little time talking about some of the things I'd been seeing ... It was a little awkward for all of us, but the people finally started talking about their problems and what they were up against" (*The Long Haul,* 22). As the people talked, Horton listened, along the way making an important discovery that would sustain him throughout his life: "You don't have to know the answers. The answers come from the people, and when they don't have any answers, then you have another role and you find resources" (23). The meetings continued to be a success throughout the summer, with Horton acting in the role of facilitator and resource person. Although urged to stay on and set up an adult education program, Horton instead returned to Cumberland University. His idea was that he could better serve the community at Ozone by learning more before returning to undertake the kind of adult education program he was beginning to imagine. The idea of Highlander had begun to germinate.

As he moved from Cumberland to Union Theological Seminary in New York to the University of Chicago and finally to a tour of the Danish Folk High Schools, learning continued to take precedence over becoming credentialed. Horton began to work as an educator himself, and he continued to think about learning as a way to collectively change the world rather than as a means for individual advancement, the predominant mode of thinking about education in America today. Horton's commitment to education as an agent of social change allowed him to see himself as both a teacher and a student, as one who could learn from others as he in turn helped them learn. For Horton, the equality engendered by a radical love for humanity also undergirded every aspect of education.

Through his next few years of education, "Ozone became less a location for a school and more a reference point for Horton's elusive educational ideal" (Glen, *Highlander,* 11). As Horton read and studied in various contexts over the next several years, an "O" in his notes came to stand for Ozone,[5] which, as Horton remarked, represented for him not method, "but rootage, that is, it stood for real people" (*The Long Haul,* 24). In *We Make the Road by Walking,* Horton describes it this way: "the circle was Ozone and the circle was these people; it kind of combined everything" (51). Horton knew that there were serious problems in the mountains, and it was through his own further education that he felt he could best help to ameliorate them. With this in mind, and at the urging of his friend, the Reverend Abram Nightingale, Horton enrolled in Union Theological Seminary in New York in the fall of 1929 in order to help him as he thought through issues of community education.

At Union, Horton read widely, familiarizing himself with Karl Marx, V. I. Lenin, William James, and John Dewey, as well as writers such as Harry F. Ward *(Our Economic Morality and the Ethic of Jesus),* Eduard Lindeman *(The Meaning of Adult Education),* and Joseph K. Hart *(Light from the North: Danish Folk Schools and Their Meanings for America).* It was also at Union that Horton met one of his biggest influences, a man destined to become one of his strongest allies in establishing Highlander, Reinhold Niebuhr *(Moral Man and Immoral Society).*[6] As Glen wrote, Horton "was drawn to Niebuhr's attacks on corporate capitalism and the flaccid idealism of the social gospel, his clear commitment to the interests of the working classes, his call for new forms of education, and his concern with the relationship between spiritual values and material welfare" (*Highlander,* 15). Perhaps in Niebuhr's work, Horton saw a way to reconcile the commitment to love that had been instilled in him by his mother with the amelioration of the social conditions that he had seen in Ozone. The potent mix of socialist, theological, pragmatic, and educational ideas at Union percolated in Horton throughout the 1929–30 academic year. His thinking then took him in the fall of 1930 to the graduate program in sociology at the University of Chicago, where he studied with the noted sociologist Robert Park. At Chicago, Horton said he "came to realize that things had to be done through organizations. I knew that people as individuals would remain powerless, but if they could get together in organizations, they could have power, provided they used their organizations instead of being used by them" (*The Long Haul,* 49). Combined with his prior studies at Cumberland and Union, as well as his experiences at Ozone, this insight further helped to develop Horton's thinking about using education to effect social change. As at Union, Horton's commitment was not to personal gain through education, but to social justice and equality, to what he could do to help others, to Ozone and what it had come to mean. Consequently, after one year, Horton left Chicago to pursue what would prove to be his final studies before establishing Highlander in November of 1932.

During the spring of 1931, Horton met a Lutheran minister named Aage Møller. Møller encouraged Horton to go to Denmark to examine the Danish Folk High Schools for what they might teach him about establishing a school in the Tennessee mountains. Having read Joseph K. Hart's *Light from the North: Danish Folk Schools and Their Meaning for America* at Union, Horton had some familiarity with the ideas that underpinned these schools; his discussion with Møller led Horton to delve deeper into what these ideas might mean for his project. He read John C. Campbell's *The Southern Highlander and His Homeland,* and though he would reject "Campbell's romantic view of rural life and social reform, Horton nevertheless thought in mid-1931 that he had discovered in the Danish folk school a first-rate model for his own adult educational program" (Glen, *Highlander,* 17). Never one to accept anything at face value, Horton used the analytical tools he had acquired at Union and the University of Chicago to help him critically assess what the model of the Danish Folk Schools might contribute to his own evolving pedagogical thinking.

In the fall of 1931, Horton used the money he had earned as a research assistant to journey to Denmark. For several months, he traveled around the country, learning Danish, lecturing occasionally on the United States, and, of course, visiting the Folk Schools. Founded by Bishop Nikolai Grundtvig in the nineteenth century, the Danish Folk School movement was an attempt "to awaken and develop patriotism and civic responsibility among the nation's long-oppressed rural peasantry" (Glen, *Highlander,* 16). In a 1983 speech entitled "Influences on Highlander Research and Education Center, New Market, Tennessee, USA" (later reprinted in *Grundtvig's Ideas in North America: Influences and Parallels* and now reprinted in this volume), Horton described what he learned in his travels:

I discovered that the Bishop believed the greatest need of the times to be the enlightenment of the people and he proposed a School for Life to replace lifeless academic schooling. He believed the experience of the students could be awakened by the Living Word and a search for their roots in Danish history and Norse mythology. He believed that people found their identity not within themselves, but in relationship with others. He believed that through songs and poetry, students could grasp truths that might otherwise escape them, and that singing in unison was an effective way of inspiring people and bringing them closer together. His Schools for Life were to be without examination and without rote learning. (27)

However, Horton was less impressed with the contemporary versions of these schools that had either lost their sense of mission or continued to live in a mythical past. The concept of the Living Word, as Horton saw it, was the key: "the process of human interaction that encompassed everything that took place in the life of the school" ("Influences" 28). As Horton came to realize during his time in Denmark, education that emphasized social justice and equality did not just happen but had to be continually made and remade. Without a concrete start, such work would never happen. In notes written on Christmas night of 1931, Horton came to this conclusion: "You know your goal. It will build its own structure and take its own form. You can go to school all your life, you'll never figure it out because you are trying to get an answer that can only come from the people in the life situation" (*The Long Haul,* 55; also reprinted in this volume). Learning, for Horton, was starting to become part of the process of doing, within a larger project of education for social justice.

Upon returning to the United States, Horton persuaded his old teacher, Reinhold Niebuhr, along with four other signatories, including Sherwood Eddy, international president of the YMCA, to send out a fund-raising letter for the as yet unnamed school.[7] The letter in support of the tentatively named Southern Mountains School outlined a plan explicitly based on the Danish Folk School model. In part, the letter stated that "the objective in general is to enable those who otherwise would have no educational advantages whatsoever to learn enough about themselves and society, to have something on which to base their decisions and actions whether in their own community or in an industrial situation into which they may be thrown. . . . We are proposing to use education as one of the instruments for bringing about a new social order" (*The Long Haul,* 62). In the summer of 1932, Horton joined forces with Don West, a young man who had also been to Denmark and wanted to start an adult education center in the Appalachian Mountains. They managed to convince Dr. Lilian Johnson, a longtime educator and community advocate, to let them use her property at Monteagle in Grundy County, Tennessee, for the newly named Highlander Folk

School. She granted use of her property for Horton's and West's venture provided that "they ran it themselves, developed good relations with the community, and achieved tangible results with their programs" (Glen, *Highlander*, 22). By the beginning of November 1932 the Highlander Folk School was up and running.

The Labor Movement

In addition to evening classes in psychology, cultural geography, and economics that arose from outreach discussions with members of the community, Highlander also offered residential education sessions, a practice that would soon form the backbone of the school; these sessions were geared toward rank-and-file union members. In the first residence term at Highlander, scheduled to take place between November 1932 and April 1933, however, only eight students enrolled. What's more, as Horton was the first to admit, neither the community outreach program nor the residential sessions accomplished the goal of linking education to social change. Horton later recalled:

> We ended up doing what most people do when they come to a place like Appalachia: we saw problems that we thought we had answers to, rather than seeing the problems and the answers that the people had themselves. That was our basic mistake. Once you understand that, you don't have to have answers, and you can open up new ways of doing things. . . .
>
> We also found out that our talk about brotherhood and democracy and shared experiences was irrelevant for people in Grundy County in 1932. They were hungry. Their problems had to do with how to get some food in their bellies and how to get a doctor. (*The Long Haul*, 68–69)

Teaching for social change, as they discovered, is not an act that is done *to* students but an act that, along with learning, is done *with* students. Or, as Horton puts it, "we finally understood as long as we kept on learning, we could share that learning. When we stopped learning ourselves, then we could no longer help anyone" (*The Long Haul*, 69).

With that realization, Horton and the others at Highlander began to understand the need to solve what Freire calls the "teacher-student contradiction." Of this contradiction, Freire wrote the following:

> The students, alienated like slaves in the Hegelian dialectic, accept their ignorance as justifying the teacher's existence—but, unlike the slave, they never discover that they educate the teacher.
>
> The *raison d'être* of libertarian education, on the other hand, lies in its drive towards reconciliation. Education must begin with the

solution of the teacher-student contradiction, by reconciling the poles of the contradiction so that both are simultaneously teachers *and* students. (*Pedagogy of the Oppressed,* 53)

As Horton had learned, both at Ozone and again in the first sessions at Highlander, using education to effect social change meant listening as much as or more than speaking. In this way, as Freire articulated just before his death, "the person in charge of education is being formed or re-formed as he/she teaches, and the person who is being taught forms him/herself in the process" (*Pedagogy of Freedom,* 31). In other words, pedagogy involves learning as well as teaching, integrating the two activities into a both/and resolution rather than an either/or contradiction.

At the same time, another event occurred that would have a lasting effect on Highlander and its approach to teaching and learning. In the summer of 1932, the coal miners in Wilder, Tennessee, went on strike to protest a proposed 20 percent cut in wages. By the spring of 1933, the staff at Highlander became involved as relief workers, educators, and resource people for the striking miners.[8] Although the miners were ultimately unsuccessful in their bid to secure higher wages, "the Wilder strike helped shape Highlander's early labor education program, for it presented the sort of 'conflict situation' the HFS [Highlander Folk School] staff thought students needed to understand their own pressing problems" (Glen, *Highlander,* 32). Indeed, such a "conflict situation" embodied the approach to education that Horton had learned from Reinhold Niebuhr. Over the next several years, the Highlander staff continued to take part in strikes throughout the South; several of the staff, including Horton, spent part of their time engaged in organizational work for various unions. However, as Horton came to believe, organizing is not equivalent to educating. In his dialogue with Freire, Horton clarifies this point: "Solving the problem can't be the goal of education. It *can* be the goal of organizations. That's why I don't think organizing and education are the same thing. Organizing implies that there's a specific, limited goal that needs to be achieved, and the purpose is to achieve that goal. Now, if that's it, then the easiest way to get that done solves the problem. But if education is to be part of the process, then you may not actually get that problem solved, but you've educated a lot of people" (*We Make the Road by Walking,* 119). It was, of course, a difficult balancing act to become involved in conflict situations but to emphasize education over successful amelioration of specific conditions. After all, as Horton himself pointed out, these people were hungry. In emphasizing education, however, Horton saw a way to help people with not only the problems that faced them in the present but also those that would arise in the future. Although Highlander's educational methods and growing success were attracting the attention of organized labor, including the Committee for Industrial Organization (CIO)[9], this distinction between organizing and educating would, as will be shown, eventually cause a rift between Highlander and the labor movement of which it was just beginning to become a part.

In 1937, CIO officials asked Highlander to aid in recruiting members and organizing the southern region. Despite the organizational overtones, Horton saw this alliance as a way for the school to become an integral part of the southern labor movement and for workers' education to come to the fore of its concerns. Over the next several years, Highlander continued to engage in extension work with both striking and nonstriking workers,[10] as well as successful residential workshops for rank-and-file union members. As Horton saw it, an educational workshop was "a circle of learners" (*The Long Haul*, 150). He went on to say, "The job of the staff members is to create a relaxed atmosphere in which the participants feel free to share their experiences. Then they are encouraged to analyze, learn from and build on those experiences. . . . Each session had to take its own form and develop according to the students' needs" (150). This philosophy also meant that the students would come to have an increased involvement in the decision-making processes about not only curriculum and subject matter, but also the day-to-day operations of Highlander itself. In the communal living arrangements of the residential workshops, decisions were made democratically so that practice mirrored the underlying theory. At Highlander, teaching democracy, social justice, and equality also meant living it.

By the early 1940s, Highlander had become an important site for labor education in the South. As such, it was increasingly seen as the unofficial education center for the CIO; in 1937, for example, the majority of the students attending winter sessions at Highlander were CIO members. Beginning in 1944, Highlander was named the site for the Southern CIO School, a residential program held in the summer, in addition to other Highlander programs. By all accounts, these sessions, held between 1944 and 1947, were a success. However, the differing opinions held by the CIO and Highlander on the roles of organizing and educating, always a tenuous negotiation at best, would at last come irrevocably between them. As the years passed, the union attempted to assert more control over the Southern CIO sessions by "using the folk school for training sessions on union policy" rather than "allowing the HFS faculty to hold classes on a broad array of economic, political, and social issues" (Glen, *Highlander*, 125). Workers, as well as Highlander staff, were becoming disempowered in the curricular decision-making process; the agenda of each session was no longer shaped by the participants themselves. Clearly, the CIO saw Highlander as serving an organizational, rather than an educational, function. The 1947 session proved to be the last Southern CIO School, and over the next several years, Highlander would have a turbulent relationship with the organized labor in general and the CIO in particular.[11] By 1953, Highlander's role as an educational center within the southern labor movement had effectively ended.

The Civil Rights Movement

To Horton, what mattered was not only class but also race. Since before the creation of Highlander, Horton had been an advocate for desegregation and for civil rights in the South. As early as 1928, as state student YMCA secretary, Horton had managed to engineer an integrated statewide convention, an early effort to "break the pattern of segregation" (*The Long Haul,* 16). At the opening banquet at a whites-only hotel in Knoxville, when the waiters refused to serve the integrated group, Horton convinced the management that the food cooked for 120 people would simply go to waste. They were fed. As Horton later reflected, "I took the gamble of doing something about a moral problem instead of simply talking about it. I just reversed the process that was going on in the universities and churches, and over 120 people learned that they could change things if they wanted to" (*The Long Haul,* 18).

This spirit of action carried over into the educational work of Highlander during its early involvement with the labor movement. From the beginning, Horton and the rest of the staff pressed for integrated residential workshops for union members. Few within the southern industrial labor movement shared their views, however, and with the exception of extension or community work, there was little contact between white and black union members in any of Highlander's programs; even with the official decision to integrate residence terms in 1942, only whites attended any of these workshops until 1944. As Highlander's connection to the industrial unions began to strain in the late 1940s and early 1950s, the Highlander staff focused more of their efforts on working with the farmers' unions, which often included large numbers of black members. As Glen put it, "By 1953 Highlander's teachers had made local and regional leaders of numerous organizations aware that there was a school in the South where blacks and whites could meet to explore their common interests, and they had gained the respect of those pushing for racial equality" (*Highlander,* 155). Highlander's work in one social movement allowed an organic transition into their important work in another. The labor period had ended, and Horton and Highlander were about to enter the civil rights years.

In the spring of 1953, Highlander's executive council decided that the main problem that needed to be addressed in the South was racism. At the same time, the landmark case *Brown* v. *The Board of Education of Topeka, Kansas,* had just reached the Supreme Court. In anticipation of a decision that was far from certain (and was more than a year away), Highlander began to prepare to host two experimental workshops on the subject of school desegregation. The purpose of these workshops was to "prepare representatives of labor, church, interracial, and civic groups to provide leadership during the transition from a segregated to an integrated public school system in the South" (Glen, *Highlander,* 155). A subsequent workshop, "World Problems, the United Nations, and You," was held in 1954, just after the Supreme Court handed down their decision. This workshop was to be an experiment in linking international and local problems, especially the pending issue of school desegregation. At that workshop were two people who would become instrumental in Highlander's involvement in the Civil Rights Movement, especially the Citizenship Schools: Esau Jenkins and Septima Clark.[12] Both of them were from Johns Island in South Carolina and were deeply invested in the specific problems within their community. As Horton later recalled, "Esau said that he wasn't interested in the United Nations, but he was concerned about getting teachers to help people learn to read and write, so that they could vote" (*The Long Haul*, 99). Clark agreed and from those concerns came the first Citizenship School, a community effort supported, but not organized, by Highlander.[13] As Horton stressed throughout his life, education served as the basis for positive social action; people came together to engage in a dialogue about the problems in their communities and were empowered to return to those communities and begin to address those problems.

During the summer of 1955, two more summer workshops were held, both of which again focused on the United Nations as a means of beginning to talk about ideas of integration.[14] One of the participants was Bernice Robinson, Septima Clark's cousin from Charleston, South Carolina, a woman who would become the first teacher in the Citizenship Schools program. As Glen put it, "for black students like Bernice Robinson . . . the mere fact of living with whites at Highlander was far more valuable than the workshops themselves" (*Highlander*, 160). This was also the experience of another participant in that summer's workshops, Rosa Parks. Parks is well known to most people as the courageous woman who refused to move to the back of a bus on a December day in 1955, thereby instigating the Montgomery bus boycott, the first successful peaceful protest of the civil rights era. The myth that has developed is that she was simply tired and that in an act of sheer will and courage, she refused to give up her seat to a white. Given her involvement in these workshops, however, this mythology needs to be revised. That Parks carried through on the act and made the decision on her own is clear, but what has been obscured in the past is that her consciousness had been radicalized in part by her time at Highlander. As Horton himself said in his dialogue with Freire, "Rosa Parks talks about her experience at Highlander, and she doesn't say a thing about anything *factually* that she learned. She doesn't say a thing about any subject that was discussed. She doesn't say a thing about integration. She says the reason Highlander meant something to her and emboldened her to act as she did was that at Highlander she found *respect* as a black person and found white people she could *trust*. So you speak not just by words and discussion but you speak by the way your programs are run" (*We Make the Road by Walking*, 153). As seen here and in the earlier discussion of how the union residence terms were run democratically by the workers, methods and subject matter, theory and practice cannot be separated in education that has as its goals social justice, equality, and democracy.

As an outgrowth of the work at Highlander, the Citizenship Schools were also based on what Lawrence MacKenzie has called a "pedagogy of respect," which emphasizes "believing in the intelligence of students" ("A Pedagogy of Respect," 108). Then, as now, many adult literacy programs were infantilizing exercises, which demeaned students and made them feel inferior and unintelligent because they could not read or write. However, beginning in early 1957 on Johns Island, South Carolina, and eventually spreading throughout the South, the Citizenship Schools provided a model for literacy education that posited respect for each person's intelligence and that moved beyond the acquisition of functional literacy and toward what we now call critical literacy. After all, as Horton said to Freire, why "launch a literacy campaign without having any reason for it except that it'd be a good thing if people could become literate?" (*We Make the Road by Walking,* 93). In *The Long Haul,* Horton expands on this idea: "We weren't thinking of it primarily as a literacy program, because teaching people to read and write was only one step toward their becoming citizens and social activists. The immediate goal was getting the right to vote. Becoming literate was only part of a larger process. We tried to fit literacy into a program that would be clear enough to be effective, and one the people could run themselves" (100). The Citizenship School, then, was not to be a site of rote learning toward the goal of functional literacy. Rather, Bernice Robinson, the first teacher, chose to ask the students themselves what they wanted to learn. She then used the learning of reading and writing as a way to explore and explain their worlds, to become citizens, both in the stricter sense of becoming enfranchised and in the broader sense of being able to act to change their circumstances. To this end, she used the United Nations Declaration of Human Rights as one of the course texts, thus placing the focus of learning not simply on the functional but also on the larger issues of citizenship, social justice, and equality. Because of her respect for these adult learners and her willingness to trust them, Robinson's efforts were successful. As a result, over the next several years Highlander served as a training site for teachers who then conducted Citizenship Schools throughout the South. Through the Citizenship Schools, education worked its way through the community and helped to effect social change as an important component of the civil rights movement.[15]

In addition to helping facilitate the rise of the Citizenship Schools, Highlander continued to serve as an important site for meetings and discussions for people involved in other aspects of the civil rights movement. Beginning in 1954 and lasting until 1961, Highlander hosted annual college workshops that focused on ways in which students could work toward ending racial discrimination. Participants in these sessions came from universities and colleges throughout the South. In April 1960, just two months after the first sit-ins at Greensboro, a college workshop entitled "A New Generation Fights for Equality" was held at Highlander. This workshop proved to be an important venue where students could discuss the purpose of their efforts, the philosophy of nonviolent protest, and the relationships between demonstrators and members of the community, between students and adults, and between black and white activists. Perhaps even more important, this workshop served as the catalyst for a meeting held two weeks later at Shaw University in Raleigh, North Carolina, at which time the Student Nonviolent Coordinating Committee (SNCC) was formed. As it did during the labor movement, Highlander and its staff brought people together, trusted that they knew their own problems and could find many of their own solutions, facilitated necessary dialogue, and acted as a resource. As Horton himself said, "The best educational work at Highlander has always taken place when there is a social movement. We've guessed right on two social movements— the labor movement in the 1930s and 1940s, and the civil rights movement in the 1950s and 1960s. During movement times, the people involved have the same problems and can go from one community to the next, start a conversation in one place and finish it in another" (*The Long Haul*, 54).

Educational Philosophy and *The Myles Horton Reader*

In a 2000 C-SPAN interview, Cornel West was asked to name the white person in the United States who has been the most sympathetic to changing the politics of racial difference in this country. Without hesitation West responded with the name of Myles Horton, who he called "an indescribably courageous and visionary white brother from Tennessee." This statement is indicative of the work that Horton did over the years in the area of race relations, equality, and social justice. At the base of both the pedagogy and life of Myles Horton, a man who was engaged throughout his life in the project of education for social change, are several questions. How do we move toward a more just society? How do we end exploitation based on race, class, and gender? Who decides what such a utopian project will look like? What is the place of education in changing the fabric of society, in remaking the world so that the concept of citizen is reinvested with meaning? What does it mean to link education to "struggles in the larger theater of social and political life"? What does it mean to educate, to change society from the bottom up?

Throughout Highlander's history and Horton's work as a teacher, as seen in his writings, speeches, and interviews, the dialogue never stopped, the people and their concerns never departed from the center of the pedagogical moment, and the commitment to social justice never wavered. As the above discussion demonstrates, that educational legacy is woven throughout his thinking and work leading up to the establishment of Highlander, his work in the labor movement, and his involvement with the struggle for civil rights. His educational philosophy, then, cannot be easily isolated or distilled into a summary methodology but instead suffuses his life and work; education for social change is at the heart of Horton's project. The first three sections of *The Myles Horton Reader* represent the specific enactment of these educational ideas. I have endeavored to choose texts for each of these sections that illustrate those ideas in relation to specific contexts and will help shed more light on Horton's work and thinking within particular situations.

In the final section, I have attempted to collect material that gives a more general overview of Horton's educational philosophy, emphasizing themes that recurred throughout his life and work. That said, it is important to remember, as Horton continually emphasized, that education is not a method but a process that is dynamic, changing with the situation and the participants. In addition, I want to resist the editorial imperative of summary and instead allow each reader to think with Horton's ideas in his or her own way rather than through an outline imposed by an editor's analysis. In the composition of this introduction, I have, of course, contributed ideas to the conversation that I hope will ensue about Horton's educational ideas. By resisting summary, however, my hope is that readers can focus on the complexities and the dynamic and contextual nature of Horton's ideas. Like Horton, I am more interested in "signs pointing in the right direction." In this way, everyone who reads this book and begins to talk about education and social change can become part of what Horton might call "a circle of learners."

By reading Horton's words on the pages of this volume, it is my hope that educators will come away with a fresh perspective on education and its power to change lives, to affect social change, and to move us toward a more just and equal society. It is important to remember that what is presented here represents Horton's perspective on Highlander, the labor movement, the civil rights movement, and education. For other perspectives, see texts such as Glen's *Highlander: No Ordinary School.* I have not attempted to write a history of the events but to reintroduce Horton's ideas into our contemporary context. I hope, as I think Horton would, that his words will start a conversation that we can begin in one place and finish in another.

A Note on the Editing

In editing *The Myles Horton Reader,* I have endeavored to remain true to the syntax and diction of both Horton's written and spoken words. At times, however, I have added words in square brackets for the sake of clarity. As well, in the case of transcriptions of speeches and interviews, I have sometimes altered punctuation to facilitate readability. The reader will also note the places I have indicated a missing section of text; I have most often omitted text for the sake of continuity.

Section I

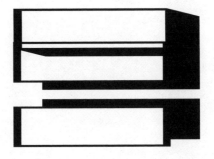

The Idea of Highlander

Christmas Night, 1931, Copenhagen, Denmark

[1931]

Many people are familiar with the version of this text that appeared in
The Long Haul, *which is reprinted below. There is, however, another*
version in the State Historical Society of Wisconsin Archives (also
reprinted below). While the texts are similar, there are also interesting
differences. It is unclear which version was actually written on that
night in 1931, but both represent what Horton was thinking just before
he returned to the United States.

Version from *The Long Haul*

I can't sleep, but there are dreams. What you must do is go back, get a
simple place, move in and you are there. The situation is there. You start
with this and let it grow. You know your goal. It will build its own structure
and take its own form. You can go to school all your life, you'll never figure
it out because you are trying to get an answer that can only come from the
people in the life situation.

Version from the State Historical Society of Wisconsin Archives

I can't sleep but there are dreams—a school where young men and women
can come for a minimum of three months and be inspired by personalities
expressing themselves through teaching (hist. lit.) song and music, arts,
weaving, etc., and by life lived together. These people should be from the
South if possible. Negroes should be among the students. Some students
should be from mountain schools, others from factories.

Such a school should be a stopping place for traveling liberals and a
meeting place for Southern radicals.

In the years to come the whole mountainside should be covered with
visitors who come from all around to have singing or to hear a speaker with
a message.

My idea of a good joke is to help make the mountaineer, who will be
counted on by the industrialists as a potential low-wage worker, danger-
ously individualistic and a threat to the capitalists instead of to organized labor.

How Highlander Differs from a College

[1967]

The following was originally a talk given at the Baptist Student Center, University of Tennessee, November 15, 1967. The text is taken from Horton's notes and the title is derived from internal information/ reference (the original archival version is untitled). As the given title suggests, this piece delineates the differences between Highlander's educational project and methods and those of a college.

I was asked to speak at this center once before, but I think most of you were not students at that time. That was several years ago. I am delighted to be back. It is rather difficult to explain to college students another kind of educational institution entirely different from your own experience. I want to try to help you understand what Highlander is and how it differs from a college.

In the first place, Highlander is an adult education center which conducts short residential sessions or workshops on a wide range of topics in contrast to formal, academic education. This doesn't mean that you aren't adults or the people we deal with are all adults in terms of age. But as we define it, adult education is for people outside regular schools and institutions of learning in this country. Highlander is not a vocational school for adults or a literacy school. Our field is liberal adult education. We teach people how to think, how to work in organizations, and how to deal with their problems. We deal with a wide range of social problems, but we deal with them very intensively in short periods—two weeks or even a long weekend.

It is difficult to explain because the program and way of teaching is purposefully unlike most educational institutions. Programs are designed to help the disadvantaged of all races help themselves, to challenge the status quo in the name of democracy and brotherhood, which has always been the stated purpose of Highlander.

We identify with people who are economically and socially disadvantaged—Negroes in the South, poor people, people in the mountains who haven't had full access to jobs or educational opportunities. Championing the have-nots makes Highlander controversial. The advantaged do not enjoy being reminded of what America should and can be, of the promises withheld or delayed. People who are eating well and making it don't want to be disturbed.

Highlander's aim is not to provide the kind of education I got in college or you probably get at U.T.[1] Both our objective and students are different.

Our way of conducting educational programs flows from our purpose and the starting point and pace is dictated by the problems of the people with whom we work.

For example, we are trying to help people understand how they can go about setting up a community organization in which they are involved. There is not much in textbooks to help local leaders living in impoverished communities. There are theories on organization written for professional community organizers and some written-down experiences of organizational successes. But most of the written materials are so far removed from the life experiences of the men and women who come to Highlander that they are useless.

Consequently, our workshops are not based on subject matter between hard covers—books; we use the experience of the people—verbal subject matter. For example, we had forty people at Highlander a couple of weeks ago from five Appalachian states and the subject matter we dealt with was primarily from their experience. They brought their unwritten "books" with them. Some of these life experiences haven't yet appeared in print and some people don't think of this as education. Recently, a public school teacher who was describing Highlander said, "It's not a school. They don't teach; they just discuss."

What she doesn't realize is what she teaches out of books and is therefore educational was, at one time, only in the mind and experience of the writer and that a lot of the juice of life has been squeezed out. When you talk with a poor person about the problem of raising a big family on a poverty income or a mountain man about the mud that covered his cornfield because of strip-mining, you are talking about a rich experience that someday is going to be subject matter in book form. At Highlander, we accept these experiences now as subject matter. We do deal with these very real facts.

We believe that you can only learn if you are trying to get answers to a problem. You can't learn unless you have a reason for learning and want to learn. I don't mean to say that all our workshops are based entirely on the experiences of the participants or that we do not have workshops based primarily on information and ideas outside the experience of the participants. For example, we have had workshops on how to organize and run a cooperative, how you set up a labor union, how you set up community organizations which have officers and procedures. At such a workshop, people must learn about federal regulations and laws.

For example, last week I was working with a Community Action Program.[2] My job was to train neighborhood workers, most of whom had been recently employed, to get poor people organized to do things for themselves. We started by asking, "What are your problems as you see them? What are you up against? What is going to happen next week when you go back into your communities?" Their answers provided the subject matter.

We took this material as the basis for selecting the most common problems for further discussion.

Among the topics selected were the following: What you do in a situation where you can't get anybody to a meeting; where one person always dominates a meeting—a preacher, a local politician, maybe a strong woman leader; how to find and develop new leadership.

Then, we broke up into small groups and role-played these situations and problems. In role-playing, you get a creative interaction between several people who talk back and forth.

For example, we took a Negro woman who was obviously a strong character for real and had her role-play a strong character and had others deal with her at a meeting. Then the roles were reversed. We had somebody who was shy be the person they were trying to get to conduct the meeting. Pretty soon, we had a half dozen people involved in heated discussion. The neighborhood workers were eager to talk because we were dealing with situations close to them. At times, the teachers would enter in the role-playing and make suggestions about where to get information or attempt to draw a person out who was shy.

Before I left, plans were made for welfare and other governmental agency representatives to come two weeks later and present their program to the neighborhood workers so they, in turn, could acquaint the people in their communities with the services available. At this workshop, the content, as you can readily see, will be quite different. Much of it will be presented in written and audiovisual form. Nevertheless, the emphasis will remain on the neighborhood workers—not the subject matter.

So, what we have to do is think primarily of the person as subject matter. Now, let me say parenthetically here, teachers at Highlander have to know a lot more than they will be able to pass out because there might be four or five things that will come up and the staff has somehow to be prepared to deal with problems raised by the participants. They must be prepared to provide more information than they will have an opportunity to work into the thinking process of the group. Prepared lectures are often discarded because they do not seem appropriate. Consultants who have been brought to Highlander at considerable expense are not allowed to talk because what they have to offer does not provide answers to the problems raised by the participants. Often movies are sent back unopened and pamphlets left undistributed.

So, if you think the people at Highlander are getting shortchanged because of our unconventional approach to education, I would like to remind you that even though we send back unused films and undistributed pamphlets and pay for unconsulted consultants, we provide the world's best teachers along with some of us poorer ones. They aren't people like me or like you—professionals—although we do have them teach at Highlander occasionally. The best teachers of poor people are poor people themselves.

Highlander doesn't attempt to provide the total educational process of people with whom we deal. Our students bring to Highlander their experiences and ways of thinking and doing. We try to stimulate their thinking by exposing them to consultants, books, etc. But more important, they learn how to learn from each other. Then, they go right back into their communities where they keep on learning.

Since our workshops are brief—a couple of weeks or even a long weekend—they must be tied into learning that has already taken place and is in process, the experiences that make up the life of the adult students. We serve as a catalystic agent to hasten the learning process and to provide new information and insights that can be carried over as the men and women continue to learn when they return to their own communities. If we do a good job, we stimulate and enrich this learning process.

It should go without saying that with this conception of education, there are no grades, no examinations or even summaries of what has been discussed—all of which have an element of finality which we seek to avoid.

Highlander claims no neutrality in presenting facts and ideas. We try to teach and practice brotherhood and democracy. Some people seem to have the idea we have a scientific input system at Highlander that pumps ideas into people's heads, but what we actually try to do is set people's thinking apparatus in motion.

I have tried to give you some idea of what Highlander is as we see it. I want to reserve the rest of the time for your questions.

The Roots of Southern Radicalism

[1968]

The following piece was originally published in the December 1968 issue of The New South Student, *the newsletter of the Southern Student Organizing Committee, which was based in Nashville, Tennessee. In it, Horton links the history of Highlander and its involvement in the labor and civil rights movements to the ongoing struggles toward "a true democracy" in the South.*

[Nineteen thirty-two] was a year of crisis in the United States. Millions were unemployed and without hope in the worst year of the depression. Government officials and businessmen stood helplessly and watched the national economy spiral down to ruin.

In the South few escaped the 1929 stock market crash. Farmers clung grimly to their land, tried to eke out a living, and failed. Banks closed down as the archaic banking system collapsed. Credit was destroyed. Textile workers, their lungs full of lint, were laid off as the bottom dropped out of the cotton market. Unemployed coal miners walked through wretched coal camps and waited for the mines to open again. In the cities, bread lines were a familiar sight. Large numbers of working Americans began to realize for the first time that they were only small cogs in a vast inhuman machine they could not influence. The exploitative nature of American capitalism was exposed and people began to talk openly of change.

Highlander Folk School began in 1932 at a small mountain community in Tennessee.[3] From the start it was aimed at reaching southern workers who would be willing to build a new social order. We wanted to use education as a tool to bring about change in the South. Our purpose has not changed over the years.

The problems which the poor faced in 1932 are the same problems the poor face today. Whether they are subsistence farmers, unemployed miners, ghetto residents, southern Negroes or Appalachian whites, the poor of this country have been robbed of their political and economic rights.

Education is a profound political act, especially if education takes place among the poor. But change in the social structure to divert more social productivity to those who have the least can only come about as a result of changes in the political and economic institutions of this country. From the beginning, Highlander was oriented toward social education to be followed immediately by action.

In the early days we worked with people in the local community and in the surrounding mountain counties where the main economy had been mining and lumbering. A woodcutters' strike provided the first opportunity for us to use education in a crisis situation.[4] We found that when people are highly motivated to learn because of problems confronting them every day, a great deal of education can take place fast.

Gradually we expanded our activities and began to help people set up unemployed unions and co-ops. Our approach was to educate these adults who could in turn pass on what they had learned to their neighbors and friends.

With the development of the Committee for Industrial Organization in the mid-thirties,[5] Highlander's programs were directed toward shop stewards and local officials who were not on the payroll of the international unions. These stewards worked in the shop along with the other members. They could put into practice the things they had learned without clearing their decisions through a bureaucracy of higher officials. They were free to experiment with the methods and goals of a democratic union.

Hundreds of union members came to the school for residential workshops in leadership training and returned to their homes to run unions.

These students kept in touch with our staff and there was a constant exchange of ideas and experiences. The exchange not only helped us to evaluate our programs but also gave us an increasing number of friends and contacts in the South.

In the forties, the same approach was used when we began to work with farmers in the development of the National Farmer's Union.[6] Again we were working on a local level with people faced with a common problem— economic deprivation.

Highlander has always practiced integrated living and has worked with the poor of all races. For many years Highlander was the only residential center in the South where interracial groups could meet. For most of our students, Highlander workshops provided their first opportunity in interracial living. It was an experience many did not forget. When we began to work with Negro leaders in community education during the early fifties, some of our former students were ready and willing to help.

Highlander set up Citizenship Training Schools in Negro communities around the South.[7] As always, these schools were aimed at specific problems found in local communities. Most of the people were interested in qualifying to vote so they could wield political power. The workshops concentrated on the goals requested by each group. Emphasis was placed on action, not on learning for learning's sake.

These early Citizenship Schools were later taken over by the Southern Christian Leadership Conference and are still being run successfully today.[8]

When the student sit-ins began around the South, Highlander held a series of workshops for student leaders where they explored possible goals and directions for the emerging civil rights movement. Many of these workshop participants went on to found the Student Nonviolent Coordinating Committee.[9]

During this time, much of our work was with the leaders of the civil rights organizations such as SCLC and SNCC. But as the organizations began field projects for local people, we began once again to work through the SCLC and SNCC organizers to reach local people.

Because of Highlander's work with interracial groups, the Tennessee legislature launched an investigation aimed at driving us out of the state. Police raided our school and arrested several people on trumped-up charges. In 1961 we were taken to court, our nonprofit charter was revoked and property confiscated. The day after Highlander Folk School closed at Monteagle, Tennessee, the Highlander Research and Education Center opened under a new charter in Knoxville, Tennessee, our present location.[10]

We have continued our work with civil rights organizations and most recently ran cultural activities workshops in Resurrection City.[11] Now we are working in Appalachia with the Appalachian Volunteers and other poverty organizations in an attempt to reach local community leaders in the mountains.[12]

Through the years, Highlander has become more than just a small staff training union officials or community leaders. The school has served as a bridge for ideas from the labor struggle to pass on to the civil rights movement and now to poor people in the mountains. In effect, Highlander has become a large group of interested and dedicated people working for democratic progress in the South.

Highlander was developed because we felt that people, especially poor adults, who had been denied opportunities for full development had a capacity that was untapped. If a way could be found to turn people on and give them confidence, we felt they would have something to say about their own lives.

We have found that residential workshops where people can live and work together in a democratic setting provide the best answer for adult education. We have tried to work out an educational program where there is very little difference between students and teachers. The formal and rigid classroom approach used in most academic institutions today simply will not work when people are trying to find democratic solutions to common problems.

Our approach to adult education is based primarily on an attempt to see people as they see themselves and to help generate within them the desires and determination to improve their conditions. We have learned that people often have their own way of dealing with problems, but that they can use educational assistance in realizing their goals and formulating programs of action. Out of this kind of interchange among peers—people who understand and are not intimidated by each other—we found a lot of learning would come.

In so far as Highlander has been able to listen to the people instead of imposing our preconceptions, we have been able to stimulate democratic initiative. We start with people where their recognized needs are and help them solve their problems in the light of Highlander's goal of democracy and brotherhood.

The understanding and appreciation of a cultural heritage is essential if people are to take pride in their community and work toward solving problems. We have used music—the old Southern ballads, spirituals, and working songs—to teach cultural pride and to build a feeling of group unity. "We Shall Overcome" was used as the theme song at Highlander for years before our staff introduced it to demonstrators in the civil rights movement.

Neither the methods used or the institutional form Highlander takes is as significant as the spirit in which the educational program is carried out day by day. Unless a teacher can convince students that he recognizes their individual worth, the best methods will [be] inadequate.

The developing and spreading of nonprofessional community leadership is essential to a democracy. There can never be enough full-time professional teachers and workers to release the energies and stimulate the ideas needed to make democracy a reality. By teaching people to teach others, we are spreading leadership and reaching our goal in a manner that would be otherwise impossible.

The challenge to people in the South has not changed. At a time when we are faced with the results of four hundred years of racism and the continued exploitation of the working man, there is a greater need than ever to search out new and better ways for a true democracy. For too long in this country, people have given personal loyalty to institutions which are outdated and do not meet the needs of people. Only when people are able to get their minds off survival will they be able to concern themselves with the reason for living and for a humane society. Living and not working for a living should be our goal.

Highlander

[1976]

The following is an excerpt of an interview of Horton and Claudia Lewis that was conducted for a 1976 book titled The Roots of Open Education in America, *edited by Ruth Dropkin and Arthur Tobier. Lewis was involved from early on with nursery and children's programs at Highlander, a role Horton alludes to early on in his discussion. In order to keep the focus on Horton's words, however, the sections of the interview with Lewis have been omitted. The text that remains represents Horton's retrospective connections between people's learning processes, decision making, residential programs, and the early history of Highlander.*

MYLES HORTON: The idea of the Highlander Folk School, which grew out of the early years of the Great Depression, was to try to use adult education as one of the main mechanisms for changing society. I had come to see that it was wrong for adults to always say: "The younger generation is going to change society," and then for them to go ahead and fix it so that it would be impossible for the young to do just that. I decided if you're going to do anything about changing society—through education —it has to be with adults. And I still believe that that's the only way educators can make a contribution, if at all, to change society.

We decided to move into a mountain area and establish a regional base to deal with adult problems, whatever those problems were perceived as by the people in the area. That doesn't mean we didn't have certain values of our own, certain ideas of our own. We did and do. We wanted to have a place where people could come freely regardless of sex or race. In fact, we had a combination of all ages because of the connection we had with community programs and extension programs. One way or another, we reached everyone, starting with Claudia Lewis's kindergarten kids, and even before that, and all the way through the span 'til we buried our neighbors. In fact, all the tools for the funeral were kept at the school. So we took care of the birth and the burial. I guess that's a good way to describe it. The school hasn't changed a great deal since that time. It did move from one county to another, but we're still in the East Tennessee mountains. And we're still trying to do something to help the workers in that region.

As in the past, our efforts overflowed. They overflowed from that county to neighboring counties, to working essentially with the industrial union movement of the South—the CIO and the emergent labor unions.[13] Later on, our work overflowed beyond the boundaries in connection with a kind of pre–civil rights program, one of the programs being discussed at this conference, the Citizenship Education programs that Martin Luther King's Southern Christian Leadership Conference took over from us.[14] Then during the civil rights period, we got pretty deeply involved, like many of the people who were active at the Highlander School.

That's the fairly recent phase of the civil rights movement. I think there's always been a movement, but I think the one that we're most familiar with was sparked by Mrs. Parks,[15] who came to Highlander about three months before she refused to move to the rear of the bus in Montgomery, Alabama, and by a lot of the people who became leaders in SNCC or SCLC or one of the organizations in the South connected with Highlander.[16] Highlander was the only integrated place in the entire South, you know; we had a kind of a monopoly. We knew practically everybody who was doing anything. They asked us why we were integrated. We told them we were too poor to be segregated. We couldn't afford two toilets, two rooms, two tables. We were poor. So we just had to mix everybody up. By that time, a lot of people knew about Highlander and when things started moving they came to where they were free enough to have solidarity with people, instead of trying to figure out the people.

So we became involved with the civil rights period, after which we tried to get back to where we started, to our own region, tried to do something there with the people. We think of our people as being a kind of subculture. Appalachia is the biggest gathering of poor white people in the United States. We feel we have a lot of kinship with the other poor peoples around the country—blacks, the Indians, the Chicanos—as well as with people in other parts of the world. We maintain relations with other parts of the world. I think one of the important things to tell about is a Tanzanian workshop we had down there recently. We try to keep the people in our region informed of what's going on in other places, everywhere from New York to China, and we do it in workshops.

I can tell you briefly what a workshop is: It is a residential coming together of people, who live together for three or four days, or for two or three weeks. They include adults who are already active in their community, emerging as leaders; not top leaders, not official leaders, but emerging leaders. Many of them are functionally illiterate, but wise, experienced. They choose a topic or subject they want to deal with—it might have to do with welfare problems, strip mining, black lung, education, health, unions, co-ops—and then they select participants from their own people, the people they think will benefit from this, and these come to Highlander. In a real sense, they bring not only their subject with them, but they bring their curriculum. That curriculum is their experience. We do what, I guess, you would think of as peer learning. We think the best teachers of poor people are the poor people themselves. The best teachers about black problems are the black people. The best teachers about Appalachian problems are Appalachians, and so on.

We say we're going to have an educational experience, a learning experience, where people can learn from each other. There's some cross-fertilization occasionally, some mixing of the groups, but that's always by choice of the people who have asked for the workshop. Most of our workshops are on request. If the Indians want to have a workshop there and they don't want to have anyone but Indians there, we say okay. If they want to get somebody else, we say okay. We'll have to do whatever they want to do. The same with any other group.

These programs are worked out in a rather informal way. At present, our board of directors is made up of a majority of Appalachian poor. During the civil rights period, the majority were southern blacks. During the labor period, they were labor unionists. The board and staff kind of move along with whatever the major program is. And the board and staff and the people at Highlander help to kind of create the program. The program is an interchange between the people who come to Highlander, whether they work in the field or in the classroom. We don't make any distinctions. Staff members work both places. We think the educational program is a continuing start for poor people who come to get a little shot in the arm and then go right back to their communities and continue their learning.

At Highlander, people sit down and learn from each other. We are not into individual action. We discourage people from trying to improve themselves as individuals at the expense of other people. We value interdependent, rather than independent, learning. And we believe in groups working together, not only with their own neighbors but with all kinds of people, all over the world, who have something in common. The idea of interdependence, too, is based on what people can bring to the sessions themselves. We don't have legal information, or technical information, but we provide the person, the materials, movies, or something. We say we'll help you do what you want. If you ask for it, we'll provide it. But basically, you have to learn from one another, because that's where the real learning takes place. Learn so that when you get back to where you live, you'll continue to learn. That's the nature of the program.

[Text omitted]

INTERVIEWER: How did you deal with the problem, or challenge, of talking to the larger community so that they would understand what you were up to, so that, at least, they'd allow you to go ahead with what you were trying to do, or, still better, support what you were trying to do? I know the survival of Highlander was often involved, having been burned down many times.

HORTON: How did we cope with the problem of communications in the community? What we did was uneven. In the early days down there, we didn't have opposition from the local people. People were very poor and we identified with them. Actually, we went through a period of making a lot of academic mistakes, until we started learning about the people. Then we all got on a good basis and started relating. We helped them with their problems, we identified with them in their struggle. For about fifteen or twenty years, we helped build a base of local strength. We built an independent political group that took over the county government.[17] We organized unions and cooperatives—all kinds of programs. It frightened the coal companies and state authorities. They got busy about us and they got scared, and the burnings started. The white/black situation at the school was aggravating some people, not so much the local community as the people outside. So you make enemies, but you build friends, you build support.

Highlander always had the support of the community. Highlander was never done in by the community. It was pressure from outside forces. In fact, Highlander was confiscated at one time,[18] the whole town was confiscated. Governors of five states got together and ganged up on Highlander. And they had to bribe every local person to testify against us. They didn't have a single person that they didn't bribe, not a one. They couldn't get any one to just volunteer. They had to threaten to put them in jail or something. So we started with a welfare community and drew on power from outside. That's how you start. Then you build a broad base. We felt we had to start building a base among black people and labor. They were the ones we worked with. You build friendships and you make enemies as you go along. There's always opposition from people who don't like what you're doing.

We had enemies, but there was nothing they could do about it. They burned us down, investigated us, they even put us out of business—they thought. And we just kept going. They don't bother us much now. You'll find that after forty-five years, you wear them down. It doesn't bother me that we have enemies; it bothers me that they get so powerful and put us out of business temporarily. But I think if you're going to deal with social issues, you're going to be unpopular. And interestingly enough, the things that we were unpopular about are now accepted. They've become the law.

If you wait long enough to avoid getting people enraged or something—if everybody waits—nothing would happen. And, of course, you wouldn't have any problems. But that's not the kind of education we're interested in. We're interested in cutting into education. And I don't want to give you the impression that we don't deal with a lot of very practical sorts of problems. But we are dealing with people, unlike some schools that I know about. We say our job is to get people moving and to get out of the way before they run over us—to start working with some other groups when we are no longer needed. We're kind of always on the borderline. And, of course, we've learned from the people we've worked with. That's a hard thing. You know, you get preconceived ideas, composed by people who get in the way of education, and that's their training, I guess. It's hard to get people to understand that we really want them to run their own program and do their own thinking, because all the education in this country—and I don't mean just schooling, but all kinds of education—sell people on the idea of fitting into a groove and being useful, turning out a product that can be labeled and certified and passed on. So we've had the problem of getting people to know that we really mean for them to run the program.

At Highlander, the students run everything—and have been doing it for, well, not the first two years, we didn't know that then, but actually by about 1934 we were turning everything over to every group that came to Highlander, and they ran everything from the minute they got there until the time they left. We insisted they do it. They didn't like to do it, they didn't want to do it. And we didn't do a great deal of talking about things. For example, we were interested in cooperatives, to get people together, and instead of talking about it, we'd say, set one up and run it from the beginning, organize it and run it, keep the records, go broke, whatever happens. If anything would happen, they'd say, "This person's a troublemaker what do you do? What do you do with it?" We'd say make that your problem. We turned everything over to them at the very beginning. That's the way Highlander has been running since 1934. We leave the decision making to the people involved—and it still is as difficult as it was in the early days to get people willing to make decisions. Problem is they aren't allowed to make decisions, going into this playpen sort of thing we call schools to get certified.

We put our kids in the playpen or a crib and we haven't got the nerve to say to the little devils, if you get in our way, we'll lock you up: call it a playpen; it sounds better than saying crib. That's why I use that figure of speech. But it's really college graduates in a little more active playpen. You're never let loose until you get that top certification. But now you're an adult, now you're educated, now you can start making decisions. You never made one in your life about anything important, and now you make real decisions. How can people do that? So we have got to kind of undo, in our own way, our two cents worth, all this stuff that comes down on us from the outside.

Highlander, as I said at the beginning, is an adult school with the major emphasis on residential adult education. That's the main focus. We don't have any high school graduates and things like that. But when we're working in a community, we try to serve the community, the total community, and in the effort to serve that community, of which Highlander is a part, we had a nursery school and we had co-ops, we had gardens, and we had all kinds of things, including credit unions. We dealt with all the ages of that community. We had camps in the summer. We dealt with people outside the regular schooling system always. So, it's been an adult place primarily, but we've never drawn the line about who's supposed to be there.

We just tried to influence the educational systems in our region, developing and encouraging outlets and study groups. Last year, there were forty common universities in our region that sent people to Highlander. We find that that is one of the ways of getting in—through the student—and counteracting all the mischief done by all the so-called good schools in the South you hear about, and read about, and send money to, which just package people for export—wrap them in cellophane and label them, and ship them off, get them ready to be useful to make some money, operate some program. We try to get the younger people and some of the more imaginative teachers whom you always find in any school—a small number, but they are always there—and kind of get in there and change things around. All the people on our staff come from the region, went to school in that region. We have got to be working on the inside. So we try to work on the colleges problem and make a little headway there. Then we're on the other end with open schools, free schools, experimental schools. We try to encourage the development of all kinds of schools, in the hope of bringing to bear some of our influence on education. We've been part of some pretty good tussles down there. Some of our ideas are rubbing off in those places.

We believe that the boundaries people accept are always unnecessarily restrictive. We think everybody can push the boundaries out far, far further than they ever dreamed of. People who live too limited a life don't dare do things, they don't dare think or stand up for their rights, they don't dare explore, be creative, or not conform. We encourage people: if they want to sit on the front porch and whittle the rest of their life, I think that's a good thing; they might come up with some good ideas. And if you want to work hard, as long as you don't exploit anybody, that's fine with us. If you want to work part time and live on a subsistence basis—that's your lifestyle—we think it's fine. We try to encourage people to do what they themselves want to do and not let other people influence them so much and that includes us. We say, don't pay any attention to anybody, including me. Start doing your own thinking.

I remember in pre–civil rights days, Hosea Williams,[19] who was in SCLC for some time, was running this little program down in Atlanta, Georgia, and he invited me down to speak to the farmers. At first, I turned him down, and then he said if he couldn't get me, he would get somebody else. So I went down—I knew I was as good as anybody else he could get—and I got up before these black people, country people from seven or eight counties around Georgia, and I started out by saying, "I hope I'm the last white man you ever ask to give you advice." That was in 1950. "I hope that you never ask another white man to come down here to give you advice. That's what you asked me to do. The advice I'm going to give you is not to take any more advice from a white man. Get busy and start making your own decisions and start thinking for yourselves, and while I'm here, since I took the trouble to get down here, I'll discuss how you go about making decisions, but I'm not going to help you make decisions, and if I ever find out you asked another person to come to tell you what to do, I'm going to sabotage you."

I went all over the South telling people just that. I'd tell white mountain people, tell black people, tell anybody I talked to. I'd tell them, make up your own minds, make your own decisions, start learning to run your own lives and work out your own educational program. I wrote a little script, or an article, or something, in which I responded to the question: "What do you do about schools today?" I said, "Close all the schools down in the United States and take all the teachers that know anything about education, and get them out to educate the people about how to make decisions, any kind of decisions. Spend about two years learning to make decisions, here, there, and everywhere, and then come and tell your congressmen the kinds of schools you would like to have. That's what I would like to see happening."

Poor people know that school certificates have to do with jobs. If you get a certificate that says you went through grammar school, you get a certain level job. If you've been through high school, you get a certain level job. If you've been through college, you get a certain level job. They also know that it has nothing to do with the quality of the education. They know that a Harvard Business School graduate who can barely get by gets the same job as the one who can, and they know it from their own experience. They know it has nothing to do with the quality of the education; it has to do with certification. So they want certification. And they want less "schooling" and fewer tests. The schools have the power to certify people as being educated. Poor people want their kids to get out of the poverty they've had—and they know that the certification is necessary. They want their children to go to school whether they learn anything or not. They want that certification, and if they could find somebody to give it to them without their going to school, they wouldn't be interested in going to school, they wouldn't be interested in education—the kind we have now. Then we could start over again and get some real education.

About thirty-five years ago, I proposed that everybody should be given a Ph.D. at birth and get rid of that problem right then. Then you'd spend your life getting educated. You wouldn't have to worry about grades or tests because you've already got that degree. It'd solve all the problems. Then you could get on with education.

[Text omitted]

Television may have brought in some images of the outside world, but I don't know how to analyze that. The people in Appalachia somehow have lost their pride—the poverty is there—but I don't think it's because of television. I think it's because, strangely enough, they're better off than they've ever been before. They have nicer houses. They have welfare. But the nature of the way the welfare is delivered, the nature of the way they are treated, demeans people and takes the heart out of them. Materially they're better off, but spiritually, they've been exploited by the very people—social workers, administrators, teachers, preachers—all the people who live off of them, or live on the basis of service; they have exploited and demeaned them and it causes real degradation. When the black people finally could stand up against whitey and spit in his face if he got in the way, even the poor took pride in being part of a people. But we haven't had anything like that since. That's what I'm working on now, building pride on a basis of interdependence, not independence—that's outmoded. By working together, you help give the individual strength to stand up and believe in something bigger than himself, strength to try to get away from the business of loss of pride. A lot of that's been achieved since then.

The younger generation, the kids who have been to college, and who have been away at work, have decided to come back to Appalachia and live, to work hard, perhaps not to eat so well, but to live. A lot of the people have done that; the wheels have turned. For the first time in thirty-five years, there's an immigration in middle Kentucky, the coal mine area; that's not too well known. It's not too well populated either, but it will be as the people begin to try to make their lives there—the young people particularly. We had a workshop a couple of weeks ago; it started out to be a creative writing workshop. The people involved, though, wanted to turn it into a storytelling session—telling folktales and making up stories. They might be writing whole new stories now. I just got some stuff—two completely new stories about strip-mining and the war; old jack tales. They're getting back into something that's maybe very alive. This is the turn—something that looks pretty good. But the older people—they've had it beaten out of them. It's the price of having more material things; you get caught up with getting it until it degenerates the spirit. And they had to take it. I guess that was the nature of the pride. Now a lot of the people have to learn to dish it out.

What I think is wrong with the regular decision-making processes is that they're all so rarefied and stratified. You know, you say, "Here is an area where you can make a decision, here's one in which you can't." People are boxed in. After a while their heart isn't in it. They say, "What the hell, it doesn't make any difference." And they're absolutely right. So they don't do it. If they do it, it's because they have a purpose in doing it. What seems to me crucial here—what it has to do with—is getting people used to making decisions: short-range decisions, long-range decisions, important decisions. Say we're going to decide something. I want to come into this room and make a decision during this session. Then I'm not going to get involved in making decisions about tomorrow and about running this place. If somebody else wants to get involved with long-range decisions, well and good; let people make any kind of decision they want to make, any time they want to make them, for as long as they want to make them. In other words, get people into making decisions, and set up processes in which this is possible.

A good example of how this works is what happened in the mountains in eastern Kentucky recently. A little community burned down and the school authorities tried to consolidate it in a school forty miles away; they put the kids in with 1,100 people, and trucked them forty miles to do it. And the people put up a fight—they always do. They opened up a storefront and got some old building, including the church, and ran it for three or four years—and they ran it themselves. It was fine, you know, they were using state money to pay teachers, but they were financing everything else. The state wouldn't build them a new building, said what they were doing was illegal (finally, you can't even educate people), you got to truck them over to this other place. Those people put up a fight for a couple of years and the experience educated the whole area around there as to how to run the school, how much it cost, how to deal with the board. They might have lost. Battles were lost on education before. But that community is a good community, a live community, a vital community, involved with something that means something to people, and they got the education, even with lost causes.

What Highlander has always said is that the power is in the people. Nothing new about that idea, nothing original about it, but the practice of it is kind of rare. We say *go to the people*. Like Claudia said, people came and wouldn't let them move her out. The people did that, they didn't have lawyers. They just had people who sat there; that's progress. If you get people involved, then creativity comes out of people; it helps the "leaders" get things done. The power comes from the bottom instead of the top. Then people start educating each other, they don't have to expend their energy competing for power, trying to be manipulative. That's when you're going to get things moving. And that's what Highlander's done.

Influences on Highlander Research and Education Center, New Market, Tennessee, USA

[1983]

The following was originally given by Horton as a speech at the Grundtvig's Ideas in North America Conference, which was sponsored by the Scandinavian Seminar College, June 16–19, 1983, at Holte, Denmark. It was later reprinted in the conference proceedings, published by the Danish Institute under the title Grundtvig's Ideas in North America: Influences and Parallels. *In it, Horton outlines the work of Highlander and connects that work to the fundamental ideas of Bishop Grundtvig, especially the concept of the Living Word, and the rise of the Folk High Schools in Denmark.*

I appreciate the invitation to participate in this celebration and to speak on the influences of Bishop Grundtvig on Highlander.[20]

So that you will be in a position to make your own judgment, I will tell you about Highlander. Then I will describe the search that started in the United States and brought me to Denmark and what I learned that I believe influenced my contribution to Highlander. Other teachers, of course, made similar contributions. Lastly, I will cite the less subjective opinions of others.

Highlander is a residential education and research center located on a Tennessee mountain farm, where most of the members of our small staff live. There is a meeting room, a library–resource center, and residential accommodations for students. In addition to the residential sessions, our principal means of education, there are research, cultural, and follow-up programs.

Our major programs have always been tied to the history of the South and the Appalachian mountains, where Highlander is located. The first program was shaped by the Great Depression of the 1930s, a turbulent period of despair and creativity. The major program thrusts have changed about every ten years to fit the times and have been determined by the situations and the problems of the people we work with.

Our goal, a truly democratic society, has remained the same as has our attitude toward people we work with. We have respect, trust, and faith in our students and love for all humanity. We try to embody our purpose, beliefs, and examples of a just and creative society in the structures and programs of Highlander.

Since our major programs lasted for a decade or more, some observers have mistakenly, in my opinion, concluded that Highlander has been a series of schools. In the depression era, we worked in our community and county with the unemployed miners, striking woodcutters, and desperately poor people. With the sporadic organization of industrial workers, our community program merged into a labor program. We became known at that time as a labor school, and still later, we were known as a farmer-labor school.

Beginning in the '50s, we became active in a pre–civil rights movement and were later known as a civil rights school. And in the '70s, we were again working in Appalachia; and in recent years we have expanded our program to again include the entire South. Later I will describe these programs in more detail.

Since Highlander has received a degree of recognition, some educators are beginning to take a look at our educational process. It was not always worth learning from. For example, during the early period, we believed that subject matter imaginatively presented could be used to radicalize the students. It took only a few months to learn that we weren't communicating. The academic ways we had learned were not the ways the people who came from the community, the factories and the mines, learned. Also, our perception of their problems differed from their perception. We were imagining problems for which we had solutions and answering questions that were not being asked, trying to make their practices fit our theories.

We discovered that we had been miseducated for the job we were undertaking and had much to unlearn. What we needed was a schooling by the people we were trying to teach, so we could understand how they learned and how they perceived their problems. After learning from the people with little book background, we came to value their primary method of learning, experiential learning. The application of what we had learned required a different educational process and a fresh source of subject matter. We had discovered that the students could bring their curriculum with them and that the starting point of the educational process should be their life experience and perceptions, not ours.

With our reeducation, and new understanding, we set about reconstructing Highlander. There was less teaching and more learning from action. While a class on co-ops was in progress, cooperative gardens, canneries, and buying co-ops were started in the county and surrounding areas.[21] A class in labor history grew out of a local woodcutters strike.[22] During a class on economic problems of workers, students helped to organize unions for the unemployed coal miners and the timber workers.[23] Classes at Highlander and at union halls led to the formation of an independent political party in our county which elected a majority of the officials.[24]

The principles and values we had tried unsuccessfully to teach were practiced and discussed as part of life situations and struggles. The democratic principles we advocated were tested in the cooperatives and unions and in political action. Brotherhood and solidarity had become more than a classroom topic. The people were hewing out building stones for a more democratic society.

Having demonstrated some understanding of people's problems and our solidarity with them, they were open to listening to our ideas and what we had learned from books. Many students at Highlander and in the coal mining and factory areas around learned to appreciate books; and meeting places for miners and the unemployed became depositories for books from our traveling library.

In addition to coming to respect experiential ways of learning and discovering that democracy and brotherhood could be learned best in practice, we discovered that life at Highlander could also provide an opportunity for practicing and demonstrating our principles, if they were incorporated in the structure of Highlander, and in our personal behavior and relationships. This concept of sharing values and making them part of the educational process was done best by working with no more than thirty students at a time in a relaxed, friendly atmosphere. We found that Highlander's residential setting, away from distractions of the everyday world, was ideal for this purpose.

As more industrial unions were organized in the South, we developed a major program of week- or month-long labor education sessions for workers selected by their unions for their leadership potential.

In addition to classes, provision was made for students to learn by practice. In their cultural activities, they learned to make decisions as well as analyze their problems. They had the full responsibility for every phase of their life at Highlander and were divided into committees for planning and decision making. They published their own school paper, issued press releases, wrote and acted in labor plays, made up songs and put out songbooks, and ran their own consumers co-op. These responsibilities helped them to realize the value of learning from practice and also from the staff, visiting speakers and consultants, from audiovisuals, and from printed matter. In the process of trying to carry out their responsibilities, they often made use of role-playing and the use of cultural activities. For example, drama was utilized to give a better understanding of their problems or subject matter and to provide practicing problem solving. Group singing was not only for pleasure and inspiration but thought of by the students as a way of enlivening their own local union meetings and some took classes in song leading.

I have given you one staff member's view of what took place during the earlier years. For an assessment of the results, I will quote from a labor leader and an educator.

Ralph Helstein, former president of the United Packing House Workers' Union of the CIO describes Highlander as a place where people came,[25]

> without regard to their race or color, their religion or politics, workers came from the plants, fields and mills, particularly from the South but many from other parts of the nation, and Highlander asked that they bring their own agenda. The things that they were to discuss and learn from each other were to be based on their own experience, their own pain and anger.

Adolph Meyer in his book on *Development of Education in the Twentieth Century*, published in 1939, writes,

> For many the Highlander Folk School has come to symbolize the spirit behind the movement of the American working people. Yet it is much more than a shining ideal. Through it countless men and women have learned how to work and live cooperatively. Characterized as "a focal point for the new labor forces gathered in the South," the school has reached thousands of unionists of all colors and creeds—a rarity in the South. To many thousands more it has given training for some form of leadership in the labor movement. A large proportion of its students hold important offices in their local unions.

In the 1950s, we developed a program which we hoped would lead to a farmer-labor political alliance. We began with organizing and educating small farmers affiliated with the National Farmers Union.[26] In working with cooperatives and other concerns of the small farmers, we discovered the same problem that had limited the democratizing of the industrial unions: legally enforced and traditionally honored racism. Racism was an inhuman barrier that had thwarted every effort to create a truly democratic society.

At Highlander we practiced social equality, although that required an act of civil disobedience, but we realized that much more was necessary. The aim of our program against racism was to strengthen black leadership and to be supportive of their activities. We rejected the popular notion of shared leadership between blacks and whites. Our residential workshops brought together concerned leaders of both races to discuss strategy and discuss such topics as integration of public facilities.

At Highlander after group analysis of situations described by the students, it was a practice to have them commit themselves to actions in their communities or workplaces. It was the commitment of Esau Jenkins to teach his neighbors to pass the South Carolina literacy test required for voting that initiated a literacy program that eventually reached thousands of southern blacks.[27]

As was our custom, we responded to his request for assistance, and in 1957 the Citizenship School Literacy Program was developed.[28] The curriculum was built from the expressed needs of men and women who wanted to become full citizens. They chose the United Nations Declaration of Human Rights as their primer. For three months between farming seasons they gathered in the rear of a cooperative store twice a week. Their teacher had been urged to volunteer because she had no teaching experience and was unlikely to be judgmental.[29] Two-thirds of her forty-nine students passed the voter registration test and some played active roles in the formation of the civil rights movement.

This literacy program for blacks taught by blacks spread rapidly, and Citizenship School teachers themselves staffed a training program to meet the demand for more teachers. When the program became South-wide, it was transferred to the Southern Christian Leadership Conference, where it became the educational arm of the growing civil rights movement. One student's dream had become a reality with thousands and thousands of blacks becoming active citizens.

The executive directors of both the Southern Christian Leadership Conference and the Student Nonviolent Coordinating Committee have stated that the Citizenship School Program and other programs related to Highlander were the base upon which the whole civil rights movement's success was built.

Following the pre–civil rights period, Highlander became the gathering place for civil rights activists, both young and old, and continued to work with the movement people in voter registration campaigns and in protest activities. Music played a very important part in the movement, as it had in the residential programs at Highlander.

Civil rights leader Dr. Martin Luther King, speaking at Highlander's twenty-fifth anniversary, said, "You have given the South some of its most responsible lenders." Since the late '60s, we have been working primarily in southern Appalachia[30]—made up of mountainous regions of seven states with the greatest concentration of white poor in America, with people and resources exploited by the absentee owners of 80 percent of the region. Many of our programs have had to do with environmental issues such as strip mining that destroyed the land, hazards to communities from poisonous chemical dump sites, and atomic energy plants, and with exploitation of miners and natural resources.

There are now more people's organizations working together than ever before. Included are music, poetry, and theater cooperatives, which often grew out of Highlander workshops. Former students and staff participated in the formation of the Appalachian Alliance, now composed of thirty-two regional organizations.[31]

Recently the land study commission of the alliance conducted a massive survey of who owns the land. Some ninety people, few with previous research training, came together at Highlander in preparation for the participatory research project. The land study has been acknowledged as being one of the most significant land ownership surveys of the country. But more important from Highlander's point of view was the empowerment of the people who took part in studying their own region. A number of new organizations have sprung up as the result of actions based on the study.

Betty Jean Hall, director of Women's Coal Employment Project,[32] writes:

> As a native Appalachian who has always cared about peace and fairness, I have been involved in the work of many grassroots organizations that focus primarily on social and economic justice issues. The one thing that practically all these groups have in common is a backbone of learning and understanding that has come directly or indirectly from the educational process at the Highlander Center.
>
> Highlander is much more than a place or an institution. It is a process which enables people from tiny communities who have important ideas about how to make their communities, the nation, and the world a peaceful and humane home for mankind to translate those ideas into action. Nothing is as powerful as an idea whose time has come, and Highlander enables us to translate those ideas into reality.

A beginning has been made in linking up Appalachia with the rest of the South. We are now working with a number of labor unions and with organizations that grew out of the civil rights movement.

We have become increasingly concerned that better ways must be worked out to relate to international problems. Plans have been made for a South-North gathering of popular educators to meet in Nicaragua at the invitation of the minister of adult education.[33] Facilitating the exchange of international visits among workers who face common problems is high on the agenda.

I have sketched the major program thrusts over the past fifty years. What these major programs have been were determined by the staff and board, and as Mike Clark,[34] former director, pointed out:

The choice is based in many ways on the ability of the people on the staff at a particular time to perceive what is happening around them and react to it. It is necessary to be politically literate and judge both what is happening and what is possible and to relate the educational program to the reality.

We realized that understanding the past and analyzing the present was essential to changing society. Andrew Young,[35] former united ambassador to the United Nations, would say that, "For fifty years the Highlander Center has produced leadership ideas, and a spirit of freedom that changed the course of history."

Our most effective education was done when we were involved in the industrial union and the civil rights movement, which brought masses of people together around challenging goals. Dedicated leadership multiplied until thousands of poor and disinherited men, women, and children were actively involved. During the movement periods, Highlander was on the cutting edge of social change and shared in the victories and punishment of those with whom we had solidarity. It was a peak time for education. Out of the struggles came a consciousness of the people's power and visions of goals that might ultimately be reached. When the people have mountaintop experiences, we can struggle and celebrate with them, but if we are not to be separated from them we must stay by when they are in the valley. We must relate our programs to the working people and the unemployed in the non as well as in the movement periods.

When there is no social movement for structural reform, Highlander is not on the cutting edge of social change as we would like to be. In such times we work to democratize community, labor, and other organizations that have a potential for becoming more responsive to the needs of the people and could contribute to the building of a social movement in the future. During nonmovement periods, workshops often build on conflict situations or crises which provide opportunities for growth. This could not be done if we became involved in the operation of the organization with which we are cooperating. Our aim is to develop people, not organizations, and we chose to use education to that end.

During the nonmovement period, many of the organizations are limited to nonstructural reforms or to immediate problems of their members. The grassroots leaders they send to Highlander, however, are in a position to contribute toward the enlargement of the vision of the organization.

I would like to call attention to the common threads that run through the major programs I have described. All have been primarily for the workers, the unemployed, and minorities, who have been socialized to blame themselves for their plight, and to discount their experience as being of no worth. It is the experts and authorities that are supposed to have knowledge, not the common people.

Consequently, they mistrust themselves and their fellow workers and defer to the self-proclaimed experts. Our students are painfully aware of their problems but not aware that, as a group, they can figure out most of the answers. They have been discouraged from making use of their experience and consider it of little educational value. Consequently, they have not deemed it worthwhile to analyze the one field of learning where they are the true experts. They tend to look outside themselves, not only for answers, but also for motivation and empowerment, which can only come from within.

Education at Highlander is based on the student's experience. We try to set in motion an organic educational process—a continuum that begins with what is brought by the students and extends beyond Highlander. Our role is more than that of a catalyst, stimulating interaction. Hopefully, we enlighten and inform the before and after process. Needless to say, what we do at Highlander can never be enough to bring about fundamental social change, but we try to stimulate and enhance and set in motion a yeasty, self-multiplying process.

If students have been convinced of the necessity of collective action, gained self-respect and respect for their peers, they will have a message that they can use and will want to spread. The Highlander process of learning from analyzing experience is in itself a form of self- and peer education. It affirms our faith in working people's capacity to become their own experts and take control of their lives. We not only provide practice in analyzing experiences, but give students a glimpse of a more humane society and urge them to push back the boundaries that inhibit them.

I have come to think of the educational process as symbolized by a circle. The circle as a symbol has a Highlander history. From the earliest days, following the Indian Council example, we sat in a circle, in nonhierarchical fashion.

Gathering in a circle, students and teachers can share what they know as equals, provided the teachers are perceived as having respect for the students' way of learning and having solidarity with them. Like others in the circle, teachers are expected to share what they have learned. We have two roles—one to introduce the process and keep it on course and the other to be one of the learners and sharers. However, care must be taken not to manipulate or introduce unrelatable information or ideas outside the collective experience of the group. We should not allow techniques or preconceived solutions to distract from building on the group learning process. This is not to suggest that use cannot be made of appropriate methods and information from consultations, books, or audiovisuals. For example, role-playing of real situations is enhanced when videotapes can be played back for self-criticism.

Highlander does not have a neat, predictable pattern of activities. We have not moved in a straight line toward our goal. We have been more like the Tennessee River, which starts nearby on its journey to the ocean. We zig and zag to get around obstacles to take advantage of an easier route, and like the winding river, we are not self-sufficient, but constantly being reinforced, refreshed, and nurtured by students, new teachers, and coworkers. It is fitting that I can share this journey with you here in Denmark, where influences originated that merged with other influences to affect Highlander's course.

Now, I would like to describe a pre-Highlander search for educational ideas in which Bishop Grundtvig and the Folk High Schools played an important role.

I had planned to teach in the Appalachian mountains but discovered that our schools and colleges were not meeting the needs of students of the region. Obviously a different type of school was needed if I was to teach what I believed in. My search, beyond the mountains, for a model school was unsuccessful and was extended to books, investigations of abandoned Utopian colonies, and American Indian customs. I found exciting ideas in books and from my investigations, but they were for other times and under circumstances that made them inappropriate. While I was searching, I had in the back of my head memories of an experience during my college days of mountain men and women around Ozone, Tennessee, walking for miles to evening meetings.[36] They were burdened with problems and disappointed when I could not provide answers, but they soon learned that by pooling what they knew from their own experiences, they could figure out most of the answers themselves. When they could not, I brought in people who could supply additional information and suggestions. Aside from using "O" or a circle as shorthand for Ozone on notes I made as a reminder to keep my search rooted in reality, I put the Ozone experience aside. My academic training had conditioned me to look elsewhere for educational ideas.

I was getting frustrated when two Danish-born Lutheran ministers, Enok Mortensen and Aage Møller, told me that what I had in mind was a Folk High School.[37] I was interested and read all the books on the subject I could find in the library of the University of Chicago, where I was a student, but was unable to reconcile the contribution to the democratization of Denmark attributed to the folk schools with the explanations of how it was done. I could not understand how the achievements resulted from the methods that were described, and I decided to make an on-site investigation.

I had been questioning the concept of a model, but became convinced that looking for a school to imitate was the wrong road to travel when I learned of the noble failures of Danish Americans to transplant Danish Folk High Schools to North America.[38] By the time I had worked my way to Denmark in 1931, my search was no longer for a model school. However, I was still trying to map out the details of what form a school should take and how to get started.

While I wanted to absorb all of Denmark's life and history that I could soak up, my quest was single-purposed. I wanted answers to the educational problems I had been struggling with. Like the early Folk High School students, I mainly wanted to learn what was of use and what would give me pleasure.

Understandably, what I would find would be colored by my preconceptions and the intellectual and cultural baggage I had brought along. I was admittedly biased, and neutrality to me meant support of the status quo. I was not interested in doing scholarly research. Facts and fiction, stories and songs, ancient myths and the folklore that had grown up around Grundtvig and the Folk High School all were grist to my mill. Fortunately, there are scholars on the program who can separate the facts from fiction for us.

For a while after coming to Denmark, I lived with a helpful family in Copenhagen and studied the language at Borups Folk High School. When I started visiting Folk High Schools for a few days or a week at a time I received a warm welcome and found the visits enjoyable and instructive. The schools had the form of the earlier Folk High Schools, but some less of the spirit. There appeared to be little discussion in class or informal interaction between teachers and students, and some of the schools seemed to have adjusted to the complacency of the times. The earlier schools, that were part of the mid-nineteenth-century ferment, seemed more relevant to my need and I sought out retired and older teachers with memories of the past. This is when the Living Word I had learned about from reading came alive for me.[39] My original impression was that the Living Word was primarily lecturing, which I considered authoritarian and held in low esteem. Only after hearing explanations in Danish did I begin to comprehend the scope and richness of the concept and understand why it had been so central. I was told that the Living Word was not only an inspired message, but whatever went on in the schools encompassed the past, the present, and the dream of the future; and the merging of spiritual and physical, the intellect and emotional. I found the totalness of the concept shockingly and refreshingly unacademic and was reminded of the holistic philosophy of the Hopi Indians in America.

Although the limitation of book learning was demonstrated by the way I had learned, so was the value of books, for it was from books that I had learned to ask questions that would stir sparks from the banked fires, arouse memories, and send the older teachers scurrying for their records. With these new insights from firsthand contact with informed and inspired teachers, I found books more useful than ever and new questions were suggested.

I wanted to know more about the first schools and about Bishop Grundtvig. I discovered that the Bishop believed the greatest need of the times to be the enlightenment of the people and he proposed a School for Life to replace lifeless academic schooling. He believed the experience of the students could be awakened by the Living Word and a search for their roots in Danish history and Norse mythology. He believed that people found their identity not within themselves but in relationship with others. He believed that through songs and poetry, students could grasp truths that might otherwise escape them, and that singing in unison was an effective way of inspiring people and bringing them closer together. His Schools for Life were to be without examination and without rote learning.[40]

But it was not only his educational ideas, but Bishop Grundtvig himself that attracted me. I saw him a rebel with prophetic insights; a champion and inspirer of the poor and voiceless. I imagine the terrible depression which he experienced at the age of twenty-seven, about my age, must have affected him just as the depression then paralyzing the United States was affecting me.

His many poems and songs carried messages of hope and joy and expressed confidence that the Danish people, once enlivened and enlightened, would act to shape the emerging democratic society. I admired his ability to change and to learn from others.

His willingness to break with traditional and conventional wisdom was illustrated by the shockingly unconventional imagery in his hymns and poems which were, contrary to the traditions of the times, written in language the people could understand and enjoy. He must have had a sense of humor. Nevertheless, he reflected his conservative times politically but not all together. He was moving in a democratic direction and had faith in the common people's ability to govern themselves. Even though he was far ahead of his times, viewed from my times, he seemed to me paternalistic and elitist. Nevertheless, his ideas were in many important ways similar to my own, and I was anxious to learn more about the Folk High School movement he had inspired and how his educational ideas had been put into practice.

It became obvious that the early schools could only be understood in their historic setting, marked by the end of absolute monarchy and the beginning of constitutional government.[41] Social movements of farmers and laborers and the culture movement of folk songs and ballads, all were part of the national revival. I learned that the Folk High Schools were shaped by and helped shape these movements.

I was eager to learn how the Living Word and Grundtvig's educational ideas had been adapted or changed by the first Folk High School founder. I learned that each founder was dedicated to an overall spiritually inspired purpose—a *forkyndelse*—that was communicated through the Living Word.

They had thoroughly analyzed their situation and specified what they were for and what against, what obstacles stood in their way and had to be overcome. In one school, for example, the landlord and noblemen were named the oppressors of the small farmers. All recognized that poverty and voicelessness was not basically due to lack of opportunity. Consequently, it was social education, not technical instruction, that was required at that time.

I came to interpret the Living Word as [the] process of human interaction that encompassed everything that took place in the life of the school: the inspired lectures, peer learning, and search for roots.

Such an educational process would have been impossible, in my judgment, if teachers and students had not been living together in an atmosphere made possible by freedom from examinations. Students were free to learn what they deemed useful and "gave them joy."

Although the founding fathers constantly quoted the revered Bishop Grundtvig, they interpreted his words in all manner of imaginative ways. However, they honored him by faithfully following his example of originality and creativity.

I was significantly influenced by both Bishop Grundtvig and the Folk High School Movement. All I had lived and learned became a part of me, but some specifics can be identified. Among them are:

Students and teachers living together
Peer learning
Group singing
Freedom from state regulation
Nonvocational education
Freedom from examinations
Social interaction in nonformal setting
A highly motivating purpose
Clarity in what for and what against

There were less tangible insights regarding the interacting with social movements and the imagination and creativeness exhibited by the early schools and by Bishop Grundtvig. Both the schools and the bishop were originals, providing no encouragement for imitation or for discipleship.

Other insights came from the schools I visited. From the teachers I learned that many schools had adjusted uncritically to the times. For me, what these helpful teachers had enabled me to learn was in part what to avoid.

But from other schools I learned how institutionalization had been avoided. The International People's College at Elsinore,[42] where I was a student, and the Folk High School for Workers of Esbjerg[43] were excellent examples of both the spirit and form of the earlier schools. They seemed to be breaking new ground and were relevant to the needs of their time. They did a lot of singing and had made study circles and discussion part of the Living Word. Their directors were men of vision. Peter Manniche sought to build a bridge between nations.[44] Poul Hansen at his workers school was preparing students to live in a new society which they were helping to build and, in his words, to "enlighten and meet the workers where their greatest problems lie."

On returning to Tennessee, I wrote Poul Hansen:

The successful adaptation of the Folk High School idea to the needs of a labor school suggests many possibilities for work of a similar nature in other countries. It was instructive to learn that the most desirable features of the older type of folk schools could be retained. In the transition you have not lost the emotional warmth made possible by intimate personal contact, nor have you discarded the idea that each school should have a purpose or mission.

I rode from school to school on my bicycle; I made the following notes:

Lyngby,[45] December 1931: The job is to organize a school just well enough to get teachers and students together *and see that it gets no better organized.*

Other notes:

The school will be for young men and women of the mountains and workers from the factories. Negroes would be among the students who will live in close personal contact with the teacher. Out of their experiential learning through living, working and studying together could come an understanding of how to take their place intelligently in the changing world.

I wrote my last note in Copenhagen after I had gone to bed Christmas night, 1931:

I can't sleep but there are dreams. What you must do is go back, get a simple place, move in and you are there. The situation is there. You start with this and let it grow. You know your goal. It will build its own structure and take its own form. You can go to school all your life, you'll never figure it out because you are trying to get an answer that can only come from the people in the life situation.[46]

I still remember that night. It was the sweetest feeling, a five-year burden had rolled away, and I went to sleep wondering why it had taken so long. It all seemed so clear and simple—the way to get started was to start. That Christmas night I had rediscovered Ozone.

[Text omitted]

Building in the Democracy Mountains: The Legacy of the Highlander Center

[1986]

This interview originally appeared in the April 1986 issue of Sojourn-ers. *In it, the interviewer (Danny Collum) and Horton discuss the way in which Highlander has been and is currently involved in social change. The following is the original prefatory material.*

In 1932 theologian Reinhold Niebuhr wrote an initial fund-raising letter for something called the Southern Mountain School, a project initiated by his former student Myles Horton. After a few years of study at Union Theo-logical Seminary and the University of Chicago, Horton, a native Ten-nessean, had become inspired to return to Tennessee and begin an experimental school specializing in education for fundamental social change. That idea developed into the Highlander Folk School, now called the Highlander Research and Education Center.

In the ensuing fifty-four years, Highlander has served as a meeting place, training center, and catalyst for the movements of poor people, workers, and minorities throughout the South. In the 1930s and 1940s, Highlander was an integral part of efforts—especially by the newly founded Congress of Indus-trial Organizations (CIO)—to organize Southern workers.

In the 1950s Highlander became a center for the then-embryonic civil rights movement. Rosa Parks, who helped spark the civil rights explosion by refusing to yield her seat on a segregated Montgomery, Alabama, bus, was one of the hundreds of black southerners who were inspired and prepared to act by their experiences at Highlander.

In the 1970s and early 1980s, Highlander became identified with the struggles of the Appalachian people around issues such as land rights, toxic wastes, and strip-mining. Today, while the engagement with Appalachian struggles continues, Highlander is turning its attention back to the rest of the South as well.

Myles Horton served as Highlander's director from its founding until 1973. Since stepping down from that post, Horton has continued to travel, speak, and teach throughout the world. Within the last year, at eighty years of age, Horton has visited Nicaragua, South Africa, and the Philippines, spreading the Highlander philosophy. He was interviewed at the High-lander Center by Danny Collum.

SOJOURNERS: In 1932 you started what was then called the Highlander Folk School. What was the dream for it?

MYLES HORTON: We were interested in building a democratic society and were going to use education as one of the means to changing society. We were openly out to change society and have what we called a second American revolution that would be an economic democracy as well as a political democracy. The purpose of Highlander has always been the same: to try to contribute toward a genuine democratic society through radical social, economic, political, and cultural change in this country.

When I'm talking about democracy, I mean it in the full philosophical sense of people governing themselves and working out the systems that make that kind of relationship possible. Capitalism certainly isn't democratic. If you put things before people, there's nothing democratic about that.

One of the things that we felt was very important was to have a new type of labor movement, because at that time the American labor movement was at a very low ebb. We advocated that there should be a democratic, industrial-type union and we hoped to get people in the mountains interested in unions and cooperatives and things of that kind as one of the means of building a democratic society. So that was a specific statement of purpose that more or less outlined the program of the school.

SOJOURNERS: What do you mean when you talk about education? I'm not sure it's what people usually associate with that word.

HORTON: Several years ago I was speaking at an alternative school conference. One of the people explained that Highlander was not a school in the sense of a college or any other kind of school because we didn't have classes, we didn't have credits, we didn't have this, that, and the other thing, and that we built on people's experiences instead of teaching them things they needed to know. And that's true. Highlander is not a school. But it is educational in the traditional meaning of the word "educate," which is to draw out instead of pour in.

We think people become educated by analyzing their experience and learning from other people's experiences, rather than saying there's a certain body of knowledge that we need to give them.

SOJOURNERS: How did you see the religious impulse that was present when you started on this project being tied in with the kind of work that has happened at Highlander?

HORTON: Well, we were not considered religious by most people because we decided early on that we were going to stay away from all kinds of sectarianism—religious, political, or otherwise. So we didn't have any church or religious affiliation of any kind, which was their way of deciding whether people are religious or not.

But we tried to work with the local community church and did, up until the time that we started getting a number of black students. The church people refused to let them come to the church, and we couldn't very well go without them. We couldn't tell the students that we had to go and worship the Lord but they weren't allowed to go along. We said we wouldn't go without them, so we dropped out of that. We still said that we'd be delighted to take part in any church service or religious service that would allow us to bring our students, but we got no offers.

If you think of religion as having something to do with morals, or ethics, or, as Paul Tillich said,[47] the search for truth as a religion, then we never said we weren't religious. We just said we weren't church-related.

SOJOURNERS: The philosophy of Highlander fits in well with the notion of a gospel that is good news to the poor and gives liberty to the captives.

HORTON: You're absolutely right. We decided not to try to deal with all of society. We tried to carve out a segment of society to deal with that we thought was the most important—the poor, the working people, and the minorities.

If you say religion is to be judged by the way it treats the poor, then Highlander would qualify as religious. But we do that primarily out of an analysis of society. We want to bring about a fundamental change in society, and we think it has to come from the bottom up—it can't come from the top down. Anything that's given to people can be taken away. So we try to help people struggle to gain their own freedom.

That doesn't mean that we think it's our job, or could be the job of any institution, to make overall programs and analysis for minority people. What we do say is, "You decide what you want to do." As we said before civil rights times, back in the '50s, we think that blacks are going to have to liberate themselves, and however they go about it we'll offer to help.

SOJOURNERS: One of the things that people always say about Highlander is that back in the '30s, '40s, '50s, and even into the '60s, it was one of the few places in the South where black and white people could get together as equals and get to know each other in a new way.

HORTON: Well, there was a Catholic school down in Mobile, Alabama, that quietly, off the record so to speak, had some black and white people. They tried to keep it kind of quiet, for good reasons. They would have been run out of town if they hadn't. Then there were other places where people would quietly get together. But Highlander was the place where people knew you could openly have social equality, and they knew it because Highlander brought down the wrath of the opposition. And since we were the only place that was attacked at that time for doing it, we were practically the only place that was known. That opened up the opportunity for us to work with black people and was well worth all the harassment and trouble.

Besides, it was a matter of principle with us. If we had denied that, then we would have had no reason for existence. If you don't practice the things you advocate, you're losing your greatest opportunity to educate people. It's the experience, the action, that educates much more than words or pronouncements. We were living out what we believed in, and that was the message. By the way we lived and the kind of policies we had, we thought of Highlander as a place to give people a glimpse of the kind of society you could have.

SOJOURNERS: It's interesting that with all the supposedly radical labor activities and all the alleged notorious Communists who came through here, or didn't, what ended up getting you in trouble with the law had as much to do with how you sat down to eat supper.

HORTON: Yes, it had more to do with that. The worst thing that could happen in the South at that time, as you know, was intermarriage between blacks and whites. The next-worst thing was eating together, because that was a social ritual. So we defied the social ritual, which scared people more than anything else we could have done except get married.

SOJOURNERS: How did this work out back in those days when the focus was on the labor movement? I assume that the white workers were white southerners who had been socialized with all the racist mythology that white people were taught then. How did you bring black and white people together?

HORTON: At first we had great difficulty getting blacks. We could occasionally find whites who would live with black people, but we couldn't find many blacks who would take the chance of getting lynched. So we used to have to bring people here for short periods. But gradually we got to the place where we could have a minority of blacks, and then we would try to get the students who had that experience at Highlander to go back and translate that immediately into their local unions. And to a very surprising degree that worked.

By actually living on the basis of equality together, the whites were easily persuaded that their union would be stronger and more democratic and they would become better leaders and have more influence in the union if they made that alliance with blacks. So a lot of our students went back and started working with blacks. Then they started sending whites and blacks together from those local unions. And so it spread.

Now all this was taking place before the civil rights movement. It wasn't framed as a civil rights issue because we put it all together on the basis of having a strong union, a democratic union, a union that could stand up and fight the bosses and get some benefits. And we said, "It doesn't matter whether you like it or not. You've got to take the women in. You've got to get old and young together. You've got to get everybody working together in a democratic set-up, or you won't have any strength." That was the angle we used. So the groundwork was laid, and although we weren't dealing with civil rights on a daily basis, a lot of black people and white people whom we worked with later became leaders of the civil rights movement.

SOJOURNERS: How did what started as an economic struggle during the depression evolve into a civil rights movement?

HORTON: We finally came to the conclusion that we couldn't go any further in terms of economic, political, or cultural changes until we dealt head-on with this business of racism. We'd get so far, and then racism would be used against us. So in the early 1950s, around 1952 or 1953—before the Supreme Court decision on *Brown* vs. *Board of Education*[48]—we decided that we were going to have to consciously concentrate on dealing with the public aspects of segregation.

That's when we came to the policy of saying to black people: "OK, we'll work with you. You decide what to do, and we'll be supportive. We think that's the most important single thing we can do now, because we can't move on social life or anything else, until we crack that." Then we started trying to pull together people who would talk about racism, both white and black, and the basis for this was our old trade union people.

You see, to the labor people we added black people who, for economic reasons, were freed of influence from whites—preachers from black churches, beauticians, morticians, and other business people who only worked with other black people. A few people in education were involved, along with private people, black and white, who were more independent. But the basis for this was the labor people.

SOJOURNERS: I understand that one of the first things to come from that work was the Citizenship Schools. How did that come about?

HORTON: I guess that's what you'd call one of the Highlander success stories. Our policy has always been not to go out and do anything anywhere unless we have students who start something and then ask us to come and help. The Citizenship School program is a typical example of that. A fellow named Esau Jenkins had come to a workshop at Highlander,[49] and he was trying to get people registered to vote in Johns Island, South Carolina, when he asked if we could help. After doing some real analyzing and thinking about the situation, we came up with a very simple idea that the black people there called the Citizenship School.

The law required blacks to read part of the U.S. Constitution before they could register, and so it ruled out illiterates. If you had a certain amount of property or wealth, and you were white, you didn't have to be able to read to vote. But if you were black, you did. So our program was really a way to help people get to be citizens. That's why they called it Citizenship School.

Out of that program grew a lot of leadership for the civil rights movement. Some people credit the Citizenship School program for being one of the bases of the civil rights movement. It was simply black people teaching black people in a system of adult education based on what's called popular education now, especially in Latin America. It was based on the fact that if you know just a little bit more than the people you're teaching, you are closer to them and you can help them. You don't need to have expertise to do it, but you have to respect the people you're dealing with.

That program spread, and later on Martin Luther King Jr. asked me if I would work out an educational program for SCLC (Southern Christian Leadership Conference), which didn't have an educational program.[50] After spending a month or so thinking about it and visiting some of their programs, I came to the conclusion that the Citizenship School program was ideal for them. They accepted the program, and that became the official program of SCLC. It became a big program, but it started out in the back of a little co-op which we'd helped set up.

SOJOURNERS: You mentioned Highlander's relationship to SCLC and Dr. King. What is the story about Highlander's role in the explosion that began in 1956 in Montgomery, Alabama?

HORTON: Well, we were bringing people together to discuss the problem of segregation. Rosa Parks had been active in the NAACP (National Association for the Advancement of Colored People) as a secretary,[51] and a fellow named E. D. Nixon,[52] who was a Pullman Porters Union organizer, was head of the NAACP in Montgomery. Nixon and two white Alabama civil rights movement sympathizers, Cliff and Virginia Durr,[53] decided that if Highlander could get Rosa a scholarship, they'd provide bus fare to send her up, because they thought it would be nice for her to come to Highlander.

When Rosa got here, she sat very quietly through the session, and she didn't take much part in the discussion. When it came to the end of the session where we'd ask people to make a commitment of what they were going to do about segregation when they got back to their home communities, Rosa said, "I really can't say that I'll do anything because I just don't see anything that can be done." Well, everyone knows what she, in fact, did do just a short time after she got back to Montgomery.

SOJOURNERS: Was it during the period of involvement with the civil rights movement that Highlander really faced enormous persecution?

HORTON: If you're not facing some kind of resistance from the people in power, then you must be a traitor to your cause. So you can be sure that if you're accepted by people who are struggling, then you're going to be harassed by people who want to keep the status quo. So in a way it's a measure of your involvement.

SOJOURNERS: What form did that harassment take for you?

HORTON: Well, I've had ribs broken and my skull fractured. I've still got a crack in it. I had teeth knocked out, collarbone broken, arms slashed, but all of it short of death. Now, I had to go to jail like everybody else, but that was no problem—you got a little rest. So on a personal level you had to take punishment.

One thing a lot of white people don't understand is that we have a certain advantage in the fact that we are white. They'd beat me senseless. But they'd kill a black person. They didn't quite dare kill me. That would have been embarrassing. In fact there were instructions in writing by the FBI to the officers in Mississippi when I was there not to kill me. There weren't any such instructions not to kill black people.

As far as Highlander itself was concerned, they tried every way in the world to harass us. They tried to have vigilantes come and run us off and try to burn the place, but our neighbors protected us.[54] Then they had a state investigation to try to put us out of business, and that didn't work.[55] Sen. James Eastland's Internal Security Subcommittee came,[56] but that didn't work. Finally they raided the school and set up a case over a two-year period during which they bribed local people to testify; but even after all that, most of them got mixed up and said the wrong things. They finally found a technical way of getting us by charging us with selling liquor without a license for having a cooler of beer with a collection cup beside it.

The one thing we pleaded guilty to was the one thing they were concerned about—running an integrated place. We very proudly said we'd been doing that for years and were going to continue to do it. And it was that issue that got us in trouble.

SOJOURNERS: And you were raising a family during the worst of those times?

HORTON: Yeah, I was raising two kids. My wife died when my kids were ten and twelve.[57] All their childhood lives, they lived in this period of harassment during which I had to send them to a neighbor's house when we'd be attacked. And they used to hear all this hate stuff on television and radio and from the preachers and read about it in the paper. So they grew up knowing all about that, and they'd just kind of bear with it.

My daughter was going to a local school, and the teacher would say, "Comrade Charis, will you read?" And then the teachers would say, "Well, you better get back out there with those little nigger kids you live with." So the kids didn't have an easy time, but it was more than made up for by their growing up knowing wonderful people. They knew Rosa Parks just like family.

SOJOURNERS: That's important because, as you said, when you take certain stands about how you're going to live your life, you can expect the things you experienced at Highlander. People may not fear that for themselves, but they fear that for their families.

HORTON: I was asked at one of the state investigations of Highlander if I felt like I had some obligations to live a more normal life and assume my responsibility as a parent for my children. I was also asked what kind of heritage did I think I was leaving them. I said I thought I was leaving them the best heritage that I could. I thought it was important to leave them a heritage that they wouldn't be ashamed of. I thought that was much more important than playing Little League baseball with them or doing some of the things that the investigators thought were part of a parent's duty.

So I don't feel that you neglect your kids when you do something that they can be proud of. I'm happier now that my kids are not ashamed of Highlander, not ashamed of me, and not sorry about their own lives, than I would be if I'd left them conventional sorts of memories and money and things of that sort. And they're better off.

SOJOURNERS: One thing that is pretty unique about Highlander over the whole span of the last fifty-four years is the role of culture, especially music, in the education and agitation work that's been done here.

HORTON: Even before Highlander started, I was making notes on some ideas that I'd like to see incorporated into it. One of them was the use of culture, music, and drama as a way of saying things that you can't say otherwise. You can say things in music and in dance and drama and poetry that are not exactly the rational step-by-step sort of things. I always conceived of that being important.

"We Shall Overcome" was just one of the many songs that were brought to Highlander. It came from Charleston, South Carolina, where the American Tobacco workers were on strike.[58] Like a lot of people, they made up songs based on their hymns. And they brought to Highlander a pretty rough-hewn song they'd made up. With my wife Zilphia's encouragement, that song grew. It had something to it that people just kept singing it. When Martin Luther King Jr. heard it, he said, "This has got to be the hymn of the civil rights movement." Zilphia collected such songs and put out music books that spread all over the South and were used during the civil rights movement and the labor period.[59]

SOJOURNERS: There's a story that one of the verses for "We Shall Overcome" came into being much later at Highlander.

HORTON: There was a black Baptist church youth choir from Montgomery, Alabama, and Septima Clark,[60] a black woman on our staff, had made arrangements for them to come up. While they were eating and looking at a film, there was a raid.

People came in with guns and demanded that they put on the lights. But nobody would put on the lights. The people had flashlights and showed their guns and kept demanding that they turn the movie off and put on the lights. No one knew whether they were vigilantes or the law. It turned out that they were deputies and people who'd been deputized for this raid. Soon the kids started singing "We Shall Overcome," and they added that verse "We are not afraid." And Septima said it just infuriated those people, the whites, to have these black kids sing "We are not afraid."

I have only one musical credit in the world. I can't play or sing, but as we were making up verses for songs, like we always do, I had a feeling that there was a lot of uncritical thinking going on about some of the hard issues of civil rights. I was trying to think up a verse that would say that we have to keep searching for the truth and not just assume that we have it.

So I finally said, "I haven't been able to figure out any line that fits this idea, but maybe somebody else can help. It's the search for truth that will make us free, not the struggle." So they immediately started singing, "The truth will make us free," and I said, "No, no, that's not what I mean," but it was too late. From that night on, "the truth will make us free" has been a part of that song. And that's the only contribution from my musical career.

SOJOURNERS: During the past several months, there has been a lot of talk about what Dr. King meant in our nation's history. What do you remember about him, and what do you think should be remembered about him?

HORTON: We used to talk about the need for industrial democracy, the need for getting people in unions, and the need for dealing with the economic problems. Martin knew you to have both economic democracy and political democracy. But he had to deal with the political first. As soon as he got the Voting Rights Act,[61] he turned his attention to two things. One was the 1968 Poor People's Campaign to work with the other minority groups.[62] Martin had set up a committee to work on bringing together the Indians, the Chicanos, the Appalachians, and all the poor people of this country. They included white Appalachia as part of the poor. And it was in that capacity that I was involved, as a representative or spokesperson for Appalachia on the planning of the campaign and the setting up of Resurrection City.[63] So I know a lot about his contribution that never got out in the public because he died right before it happened.

He also, as the record shows, was moving toward doing something about unions. He was publicly saying that it wasn't good enough to have the right to go in someplace to eat, you had to have the money to buy something. He was beginning to move toward combining economic and political democracy and working with other minority groups. So what Martin would have done had he lived and what he would have stood for was an expansion of the civil rights efforts. As important as they were, the voting rights victories by themselves could never succeed in making enough of a difference. The blacks didn't have that great a percentage of votes, and he knew he had to have allies. He learned you had to have allies and that you had to deal with economic problems. He was moving in that direction when he died.

SOJOURNERS: You said there was a shift at Highlander from working primarily on labor issues to working more on racial and civil rights issues. But then there was another shift when the Highlander Center again became very much identified with Appalachia.

HORTON: Well, first of all, we started out working in Appalachia, and worked here for the first four or five years, and that established the idea that we were Appalachia-based. And then in the '60s, after working on racism and civil rights issues, we switched and started back to working on Appalachia, as part of the Poor People's Campaign.

One of the reasons we concentrated on Appalachia was we thought there was a possibility of building that alliance among all the groups of poor people. If we were going to be part of that coalition, we would do it as part of Appalachia.

About four years ago, we decided we'd gone as far as we should go in working on Appalachia, and we announced that we would open up the workshops to folks in the Deep South again.

In the South we're working on some basic civil rights issues through cultural programs, voter registration, and our work with the Federation of Southern Co-ops in Alabama. Here in Appalachia, the women's movement is important right now. Women are beginning to make demands and make some headway, and women miners are getting organized. A lot of that work is connected with people at Highlander.

SOJOURNERS: After decades of social struggle, what perspective can you offer to people who are involved now but haven't been at it for so long?

HORTON: One of the ways it seems to me that people can keep going is to have a moral conviction about what they're doing, not just a rational analysis of society. However, you do need your rational analysis to size up the situation, because you've got to start where the people are. So you've got to be very firm about your convictions and very analytical about the situation.

If you're going to get ready for the long haul, you've got to be able to look down the road a ways and decide where you're going. You've got to make up your mind about the way, or the path, or the process you're going to use in getting there so you aren't always trying to rethink everything every Monday morning.

If you're going to think in terms of staying with something until you get it done, you've got to have a vision that's worth spending a lifetime on. The strength to stay with it comes from two sources. One is the people you're working with. We choose to work with Third World–type people. You get inspiration from them when you see them struggling and thinking and developing their ability to analyze their situations and build on their experiences.

But you also need the support and help of coworkers who supplement your limited abilities. It seems to me you have to think in terms of some kind of collective effort from the very beginning, not some individual effort. Highlander has tried to put together the creativity of individuals and the creativity that grows out of a collective effort.

SOJOURNERS: You said that at Highlander fundamental social change is the objective and that at different times Highlander may work on toxic

THE IDEA OF HIGHLANDER

wastes or union rights or civil rights. How does your work on the specific issues, some of which you may win and others you may lose, relate to the larger objective?

HORTON: I think there are two things involved. One is that what results in a revolution is a culmination of a lot of things that have their fruition at a certain time. But the revolution is being built all along.

What you do is build little cells of decency, little cells of democracy, little experiences of people making decisions for themselves, little philosophical discussions about civil rights and human rights. All of those get built into what's going to happen later on.

So you're really building for the revolution when you do something to develop local leadership. You get some satisfaction out of seeing steps as you go along, even though you don't get all the way.

Then, if you're around long enough, you see things like the industrial union movement, the civil rights movement, the antiwar movement, and other movements that seem to get something done. So you know people can do things. A lot of people today have never seen anything succeed.

I've seen things succeed. I know people can do things. I've seen the complete labor movement restructured; I've seen the civil rights movement. I know people can make changes. They're not making them now, but they're building things. The time is not being wasted. But it's not being fully occupied either.

The purpose of Highlander is not to solve problems but to use problems and crises as the basis for educating people about a democratic society. To make them want more, and make them understand they can do more.

SOJOURNERS: A lot of people in the movement these days are starting to suffer from a kind of crisis-to-crisis, issue-to-issue burnout.

HORTON: Don't tell me. I don't understand this kind of thinking, you know. I get the impression that the organizers have reduced the people they're working with to their own level of expectation. But these people are used to tough problems; they're used to defeat.

I think you need to challenge people. I think you stretch them as far as you can. I think you have expectations that you share with them and you give them hope.

If you believe in certain principles, you practice them. If you believe that people can learn, then you learn. If you stop learning, you'd have no way to help other people learn. You have to go through life sharing your own enthusiasm for your beliefs and trusting people and having a love for people so it can be understood by others. You help them understand that within them is the possibility of accomplishing things. You do nothing to limit people.

I feel very strongly that people have the capacity to go further. You've got to deal with people's self-interest, some say. Well, I agree with that, but their interests are much broader than most people think. Their personal interest includes a willingness to struggle, a love for their country, a love for humanity. Those are personal interests too. It isn't just feeding your belly and getting some clothes on and getting a little security. Those are personal interests, they're valid and they're important. But these other things are personal interests too. And you can challenge people, you can build with people on those things. And if you don't, it seems to me you're minimizing the humanity of people.

Ideas That Have Withstood the Test of Time

[1986]

This interview was conducted by Gary J. Conti and Robert A. Fellenz and originally appeared in the journal Adult Literacy and Basic Education *in 1986 under the title "Myles Horton: Ideas That Have Withstood the Test of Time." This interview, while rather far ranging, focuses mainly on the core ideas that make Highlander what it is. As Conti and Fellenz put it in the abstract that originally appeared with this interview, "This record of an informal conversation with Horton contains a discussion of his views on many topics such as current social issues, staffing at Highlander, the role of trust and experience in the educational process, Paulo Freire and Saul Alinsky, teaching methods, and sensing social change."*

GARY J. CONTI AND ROBERT A. FELLENZ: With what kind of issues are you now dealing?

MYLES HORTON: We have been doing a lot on toxics lately because that is the problem that fits the responses and needs of the people as they feel those needs, as they perceive them, and not as we perceive them. We try to see what their perceptions are and how we can latch onto that. So whatever the people are struggling with, that seems to be the flow at Highlander.

CONTI AND FELLENZ: Can you give an example of such a project?

HORTON: Probably the most successful project in terms of organization is at Middlesburg, Kentucky, which is across the line up here.[64] Those people started fighting the tannery that dumped its waste in Yellow Creek. This polluted the area water supply that they used to water their stock, they swam in, and they washed their clothes in. They started fighting that. They were kind of country folks, miners and ex-miners. They all live in Yellow Creek about fifteen to twenty miles outside city limits. They did not have much clout, but they stuck together. They finally started coming into the city, picketing, and taking over the city council meeting. They came in and sat there for a week. They did things like that to build up their strength.

These are not voters in the city; they are people who live out on Yellow Creek, but they have organized the people in town. They told them this is your problem too. They parlayed this into a political organization. Unlike most people who get into politics who have to run somebody to get in and represent them, they are too smart for this. They have been in mines and organizations. They know you don't have a token person in some place [and then] you have power. So the first time they ran, they ran five people. They asked people to vote for all of them. They said, "It won't help to just vote for me. But if you vote for all five of us, we'll have enough to do something." They had that kind of savvy that a lot of people don't have. Darn if they didn't win all five of the council seats. Last time they won three more. Now they have eight. They want complete control because there are some things that the mayor can veto if the vote is not unanimous.

But there are some things that they are able to do. The person who fought them the hardest was the lawyer for the city, and he just made his living fighting these people down the creek. They didn't have the power to hire or fire him, but they fixed salaries. So they cut his salary down from $75,000 per year to $50 per month. They can't fire him but they can say how much he can make. They don't quite have control, but they are really throwing their weight around now.

CONTI AND FELLENZ: How did Highlander get involved in helping the people of Yellow Creek?

HORTON: Ed, who had been at Highlander several years ago, helped organize the people in Yellow Creek.[65] They were having all kinds of trouble. So Ed brought four or five people down here. We started working with them, working out ideas, and putting them in contact with people. We got people to go up and take some pictures, but mainly it was getting them to think about how you build an organization. It's more than just a short-range, single-purpose reform organization. Most organizations are based on the theory that people are so stupid that they have to win everything or the people will lose interest. That's more the mentality of organizers than it is of the rank and file. They think that the people are a reflection of them, but that is not true at all. They are much more cautious and less imaginative than the people. We tried to get the people to use their own resources and to do their own thinking.

They really have done a terrific job of running their organization. They have financed it completely themselves. They pay dues to themselves. They do a tremendous job. Right now they need some legal help because they have gone as far as they can in terms of protesting political actions in the South. It's out of their hands. They had to do something to get the company to deal with them. They had kept control in their hands. They agree with Highlander that they are their own experts and don't want anyone else to do their thinking. But the company has lawyers so we need lawyers that know how to deal with them. But the lawyers think we don't know anything even though we pay them. We want to be in a position to give them the information we have and make the lawyers use that. In this way, we can keep control of the situation.

We have a person, John, who is very good at research and knows how to use computers.[66] The people from Yellow Creek came down, and they said, "We have all of this information, but it is just stacked up in people's barns and everything. We don't know how to use it." John suggested that the only way that they could keep up with all of this information was to put it on a computer. They knew that the lawyer was going to call down and ask for information on this subject or that. Even after you run around and get it, it's too late. John went up and worked with them for a few days. They set up a program where everybody is getting their stuff and where they are coding it themselves. They have all the facts— thousands of items by date on this computer now. Press a button and they have it. It forced them to get all of their stuff together and reevaluate what they have. They are probably the most sophisticated bunch of creek people in all of Appalachia. They know what they know, and they know how to get what they know. That is a pretty sophisticated example. John suggested the computer because they wouldn't have known it was possible. But they did the work. He did not do any of the work.

CONTI AND FELLENZ: How do you go about identifying the staff for Highlander? Do they come to you?

HORTON: That's right. Basically that is what happened once we got started. The board and staff has functioned the same since 1935. People start working with Highlander. They might come as a visitor or to a workshop. They keep coming back. Or they might be working with an organization. Or they might be involved in a student program. One got involved in a Vanderbilt program to help people set up community controlled clinics. Through that he got interested in the mountain area. In working with the Vanderbilt group, he had a relationship with Highlander and found that they overlapped. After he got a Fulbright, went to

Oxford, and wrote a dissertation that won lots of awards, he came back. He had been Vanderbilt's student representative on the board. Others had thought that he would come back and get a job at Vanderbilt. But John had a mind of his own; he had an idea of what he wanted to do with his research. He wanted to do what is now labeled "participatory research." At that time it did not have a name—it existed without a name. It existed at Highlander all along. So it is now named. He wanted not to do research for people but rather to empower people to do their own research. Then they would not have to depend on [a] researcher because that is manipulative. The researcher can take knowledge away from people and give it to someone else to use against them.

CONTI AND FELLENZ: Many of Highlander's staff members are very talented individuals. What motivates them to remain a part of the staff?

HORTON: Most are here because they are interested in a certain thing that Highlander gives them a chance to do. They bring a lot to Highlander in terms of ideas. They think of Highlander as a base in which they will have the freedom to operate. So you have little principalities—cultural research, working toxics, music. It used to be labor and civil rights; now it is political action. Each has a little area where they can try their wings. Others respect them because that is not their area. They each have their own thing. It gives them a lot of freedom, and at the same time they have the support of everybody. You get backing from others because they want you to back them in what they are doing. It is a mutual kind of support. But it is not run from the top. It is not someone telling you what to do and them getting a staff person to do a preconceived program.

Everyone comes to Highlander to do a new program. That keeps it alive. They do it in the Highlander way with the Highlander ideas of participation and democracy; the Highlander ideas of giving power to the people; the Highlander ideas of making people their own experts; and the Highlander ideas of basing it on their own interests. They come because they think it is a good way to work because it has been working for fifty years. They think, "Hell—maybe my something will work." Somebody like John has made participatory research as kosher a Highlander approach to education as you can have. That is why he came here—because he liked that idea. We didn't have a program. He made the program; he fits it in.

All the people at Highlander appreciate the Highlander history. They are proud of it and are proud to be a part of it. They want to extend it and contribute to it. So it is part a brand new something and part something old. It's that combination that makes it work. So that is how people come.

CONTI AND FELLENZ: Is Highlander a center which people come to, or do the Highlander staff members go out and do the training?

HORTON: Well, we don't so much do the workshops away from here. The last one we did was in Mississippi. We had deep-South people from Louisiana, Mississippi, Georgia, and Alabama at a four-day culture workshop. When I say culture, we are talking about politics, economic struggles, civil rights, and international problems. But that is not the usual pattern even though there might be a half dozen things like that a year. What we mean primarily by field-work extension or getting out in the field is visiting with former students, who have started programs, who need help. Highlander does not go out and do things. Our policy is to find people who have already begun to provide some social leadership and to bring them here. Our contribution is to help them because they are already there. They have their roots. Now if they say they need some help to do what they want to do (what we decided that we want to do and what they had decided to do before they contacted Highlander), we would have someone come down and take a look and see if there is anything we can do. So that is the relationship that we have. It's following up on the people who have been to Highlander. That way we know the field. That is extremely important at Highlander because a high percentage of what success we have at Highlander is due to the selectivity of the people we work with. We work with those people in a situation that we think has some social potential, a potential for some structural changes more than just little reforms—fundamental change. We work with those people, have them go back to where they are from, and continue to be supportive of them. To do this you have to know something of the community; you have to know about the area that you are going to be working in, or you wouldn't know how to select people. It is particularly true since the flashy people, the ones who look good, are seldom worth working with. So the kind of people that most people know about, that most people relate to, that most foundations give money to, and that most organizations work with are the ones that we don't work with. We found that they are mostly conservative. They know how to be glib, they know how to write proposals, they know how to get publicity, but they don't know how to work with the people. So you get a little bureaucracy set up that is very glib and scintillating; it looks very good, but it doesn't have any roots. If we see something that is shiny and looks good, we all take a real hard look at it. That's a no-no for us; we look behind it.

CONTI AND FELLENZ: Yes, that is fine to go out to people, but how do you find out what they are really thinking?

HORTON: To do this we have to be out in the field and talk and listen to people. Listening to them is important. You see people generally have a preconception of what they are looking for. So they look around until they find someone to fit that preconception, and the glib will know that game. What we try to do is to find out what the grassroots people's perceptions are. We ask what their perceptions are of themselves and their situation and not what our perceptions are. To do this, you have to get out and talk to them, to get out and live with them, and to ask them question[s]. Look around—see if they are telling you the truth; check with someone else; dig in. You have to know people to get in a community at this level. You can't go into anybody's community on that level unless you know someone. You have to have a door-opener for you; you need someone that vouches for you. Otherwise you stay on the surface.

So we try to cultivate where we have students, and by now we have thousands of them scattered around. There is usually someone around who knows Highlander, knows who we are, and gets us an introduction. Highlander is a good password in most of the rural areas of the South. People may not know all the ideas, but when they mention Highlander, it is as something good. They know that somebody in the labor movement or in the civil rights movement has been to Highlander. So they say it must be ok. That is why it is so important to get out into the field. Who comes is important because they are going to do whatever is done. We can only strengthen them, and maybe we can enlarge their vision, encourage them, or help them learn how to analyze.

CONTI AND FELLENZ: A lot has been written about what goes on at Highlander, but what do you think is the most important thing you do for people?

HORTON: Probably the most important thing that we do for people is to have them participate in an actual democratic experience—a ripe experience where people are free to talk and make decisions, where there is no discrimination, and where their experience is valued. If you don't value a person's experiences, I don't know how you can value them as a person. Poor people know that; sometimes academicians don't know that, but poor people do. When you value their experiences, then they recognize that you respect them. That attitude and atmosphere is as important as any other thing. It is an extension of the idea of helping people value their own experiences so they can be something to learn from. An unexamined experience is just a happening; it is just something you know. Experiences don't educate, but you can tear experiences apart and try to figure out all that is in there. Then it becomes the best educational experience, and it's their experience. It is rooted in them. If you can get them to value their peers' experiences, then this can be extended to their peers, their past, and other countries. People don't understand that when you get people appreciating themselves and their peers in Hardin County, then they can appreciate what is going on in Nicaragua and South Africa because those are poor working people too. It is an extension of their experiences. It is not something that is happening to poor people in a different part of the country. You can talk to them about their peers and their past. So it is not a limiting concept; it is a liberating concept! But it is basic. When you do that with people, they have something they can take back with them. They can do that when they get home. They can go back and do the same thing. When they leave Highlander, they do not need to come back for another shot later on. They take the ideas with them.

CONTI AND FELLENZ: How important are the physical arrangements for the educational setting?

HORTON: What we have always done, I got from the Indians. They always sit around in circles so that there is nothing hierarchical. They did have a chief, but he was on the same level. What I always tried to do was to break the hierarchical situation so that everyone was a part of the learning circle. If we are part of the same circle, we are all learning. Our experiences may be different, but we all are learning. It was just a way of having everyone equal, and so they could see each other. The comfort is in the rocking chairs we use.

Physical is important: sleeping together, having people together, having people eat together, and having people talk together. Togetherness is important. The residentialness of it is important. You couldn't go to a hotel and have a Highlander workshop. You couldn't go to a college and have a Highlander workshop. You couldn't go to a place where you have a big building with several other groups meeting and where you meet in one corner. It has to be contained, unified, concentrated to get the sense of the people who are there. We get them physically away from their everyday life so they can begin to think about something that is terribly important. Actually, our staff a month ago rented a place in North Carolina and went over there to have a residential staff meeting. Here they can't get away from the phone; here they can't get away from the baby or whatever; they have their jobs here. To have a residential workshop, our staff has to get away from here. It's really very important if you are going to concentrate.

CONTI AND FELLENZ: How important is documenting with pictures what goes on at Highlander?

HORTON: We do a lot of this. In the early days at Highlander, we started working with labor unions getting the people to tell their stories. Many of them couldn't write at that time. We would get them to write the little stories of their lives and how they got interested in the union movement. Since we didn't have any recording machines there, those who could not write would dictate to somebody. We would write it down and read it to them. We would put out books of people telling their stories. We would just keep collecting that information. We always felt that anything you can get people to say about themselves is meaningful. It also shows that you honor and respect them by putting it down and keeping it. Now that was a very simple thing compared to what has happened now as we get more sophisticated [with] the kind of equipment we have today. We are able to do videotapes of this timeframe and world histories. There are all kinds of angles to that. We have hundreds of hours of videotapes and interviews, and then we have movies based on interviews. We have a book based on interviews.[67]

We do a tremendous amount of oral history, but we are doing more of it now because of the resources. It has to do with the same thing I talked about earlier—the perceptions. You have to ask people what their perceptions are before you can find out. You can't guess at it. If you ask people to tell you their story, you're getting their perception of things. It is an extension of this idea that if you want to know what people think, you have to ask them. We are getting back to what we did in the early days at Highlander; we are getting the ordinary rank-and-file people telling their stories. We don't get many named people here. Some of them later become named people, but when they came here, they weren't named people—just people. Somebody said that for our fiftieth anniversary that we needed to get a big speaker like when we got Martin Luther King on our twenty-fifth anniversary. I said you wouldn't have much trouble getting as big a speaker as he was now. He wasn't a big speaker at the time we got him. We didn't have any trouble getting him. He was delighted. He was just getting known out of the South.

CONTI AND FELLENZ: How did you get a feel for the culture, the music, and the heart of the people that has become such a part of Highlander?

HORTON: If you grew up poor like I did in the mountains and the rural South, you tend to think of the totality of things that make up life. Everybody struggled to make a living. Most people in my culture went to church; there wasn't much else to do. When I was growing up there were only two places that kids could meet people, school or church. Activities had to do with either of these. If you weren't in school or church, then you didn't have any social life. So it wasn't a matter of making some decision about this. It is like having some food on the table, you don't make a decision about if you're going to eat it. You just eat it. The church is there, and the school is there. You don't make a decision particularly, you just do it. So I grew up thinking of those things being integral—all part of life. The singing, the square dancing, and the fights— all were part of life. It wasn't as segmented as in more civilized or advanced society. So I always thought more holistically. Culture is what I always thought was the underlying category that took everything that was not pulled out and called education, or religion, or what. It is the base. The other things you pull out so that you can look at them, but they are like a rubber band that slips back down in there. You pull them out to look at them, but to me they were all part of the same ball of wax. It was the culture that tied them all together. I never thought of culture as being limited to the fine arts although they are part of culture.

Music was a part of everything. Music was always a very important part of things. In my life pictures, not art but pictures such as calendars or any kinds of picture, were important. They enriched life. A picture was something important. I'm not saying that I like now the things that I liked then; I don't. But then it had a meaning. I like poetry for reasons that I don't know. Poetry was always important to me. I don't want to leave any of those things out. That's why I want to include them at Highlander. Without culture in its broader sense, you have a tendency to make intellectualization a bloodless kind of exercise. It becomes a kind of a gymnastic exercise. It has very little to do with life. You have to keep it tied in with the cultural side to have meaning. The intellectual part should serve the cultural; not the cultural serve the intellectual. The culture is a totality.

CONTI AND FELLENZ: How is success judged at Highlander? Who decides if things are going well?

HORTON: We all have to have someone who judges us. If you are at a college, it is by your peers. At Highlander it's the people you work with who decide if you are doing a good job and if you are effective. You need to learn to be valued by the people you work with. Success at Highlander is not what your peers think but rather what the people we work with think. Success is if they want you to come back. Our judges are the people we work with because if they stop coming to Highlander and stop supporting our program, we can get all the money in the world, all the acclaim, and all the awards, but we'll just be sitting up here doing nothing. Just looking at a beautiful sunset. If you want to work, you have to have people to work with. It is terribly important that the people we work with find us useful. So that's who you should be judged by.

It's always more fun to be judged by the people you are trying to work with because that is why you did it. People in education are not in it to get rich. Yet we don't have the opportunity to be judged for the very reason that we got into education. There is something wrong with that system. Those most concerned about the school system are educators. Yet we can't get the privilege of being judged by those we are trying to serve.

CONTI AND FELLENZ: It seems that many are frightened by change. Are they afraid to seek solutions to today's problems?

HORTON: The old pressures are for a person to accept the preconceived path that others have laid out for them, and that is what schooling is pretty much about. It's comforting if you don't want to make up your own mind. We go through that system without thinking about it because it is socially approved system and we might be unhappy with it if we examined it. But it is an extension of the family; you have a little nest. It's a little bigger nest, but you can fit into it. Your peers all agree with you, and there is a little comfort there. The trouble there is that when you get out of it and get certified as being educated, you no longer have a nest. What you do then is join a nest that someone else makes for you. You fit into whatever society tells you to do. People who are unhappy have not stopped to think that they have been nesting all their lives and have been afraid to try their wings. They have never been allowed to test their experiences because that was a no-no. Other people know what is good for you, and the whole educational and societal system is to fit you into that pattern. You are never supposed to know from your experience if that is good or bad. When you start doing that, you are bucking a lifetime of conditioning.

CONTI AND FELLENZ: The questions are usually more interesting and important than the answers. Are they not?

HORTON: Yes, that is absolutely right. You see the answer is not really important. Answers get back to someone saying that this is the right thing. This is the authoritative answer. This is what is right. Answers are tricky. I don't care much for answers. People at Highlander will never tell you what to do. I don't tell them what to do because I don't know what to tell them, and I'm not about to lie to them. They want you to pretend that you know. They come here for answers like they go someplace else for answers, but you are letting them down if you give them answers. Most of those people who give those answers know less than I do, but they are very glib at giving people answers. The tragedy is that this is what people want, and they will take them even if they don't fit. Giving answers is not as good a way of education as asking questions and making people face up and think through things for themselves.

When you can get people to think about the process that they are going through, this is the beginning of their education. They don't have to have a classroom, a teacher, or book of instructions to do that. They just do it wherever they are. When you get people to value their own experience and learn how to learn from and do thinking for themselves, they can practice in the toilet, in their walking, in the car, or anywhere. It is the best system that I could ever come up with—giving people practice in educational processes. It is a process. That is what education is about. Educators come to Highlander and ask what is your method; what is your technique; what is your gimmick? They believe that you have to have a gimmick. We had a very important person in Esau Jenkins, who worked in the Sea Islands.[68] People would come up to him and say, "What is your root?" Like a rabbit foot, they thought that he had gotten the right charm. What's your root; what's your gimmick; what's your magic. That is exactly what they are asking when they ask about our method and techniques. To get people to understand that education is a process and that whatever method or technique seems best in that given situation is the best one to use. This is better than a method that you clamp onto every situation and force people into it like you are torturing them. If they are not long enough, stretch them; if they are too long, cramp them up so they will fit your methods! Deform them anyway you can so they fit your methods. I was on a panel with Paulo Freire at the Riverside Church recently in New York.[69] The topic was methods; what's the best method for education. I thought, my God, this is going to be short! The moderator introduced the subject and asked me first. I said I can answer that rather briefly. "The best method is the method that works best by the person in a given situation." I didn't say anything else. Then he asked Paulo. He said in very erudite academic terms exactly the same thing. The third person on the panel said, "It looks like neither of these people are going to talk about it, so I will talk about it." Well, I thought that I had talked about it. I had said all there was to be said. The reason the moderator asked that question was that he had worked with both of us before and he knew that most people think that Freire has a gimmick. Most people reduce him to a gimmicker. Of course, he has been fighting that all of this life. He just wanted to give him a chance to say, "I don't have any gimmicks."

CONTI AND FELLENZ: How do you compare what you try to do at Highlander in this cultural setting with what Freire is trying to do in his?

HORTON: Freire and I have talked several times, and we have talked a little about this. He is at a great disadvantage. While we have had fifty years to experiment and work in the same place, he was put in jail after a couple of years, exiled, and never allowed to get back in the rural areas. He has never had the opportunity that we have had to be in one place and to work it out. He is extremely aware of that and unhappy about it. He would have liked to do the same thing. Instead he is forced to go to Harvard, forced to go to go to Geneva, and forced to work in a country that he didn't know anything about. He has had a terribly disadvantaged opportunity to do things. I would think that we would do pretty much the same thing if we had the same circumstances because of our thinking. He has a kind of liberation theology which is a type of Marxist social gospel.[70] He is a Christian socialist.[71] I've always been religious; I've tried to do a Marxist analysis. So the goals that we believe in are quite similar. He didn't have time before he was put in jail, and the situation that he thought was developing didn't develop. He never had time to test out ideas like we did so he has to theorize about them more. He has to do it more academically because he had less opportunities to experiment. That does not mean that one is better or worse than the other. It just means that it is of describing what he is thinking and what we are presented in different language.

Freire never had what they called a kind of democratic opening that he thought was taking place at the time he was teaching the peasants in Brazil to read and write so that they could organize and do something. It turned out not to be an opening at all. They put him in jail. But here with all the weaknesses of this country, we have opportunities that make Highlander possible. They have tried to put us out of business, but they didn't succeed. People ask why should I say that the United States has more freedom when what has happened to you. Well look what has happened to me. Here I am. Highlander is right there. It could happen in other countries, but it could not happen in Brazil. It could happen here. We have certain traditions, freedom of speech, civil rights, and human rights. They are most often not honored, but they are here. If you force them, if you push the boundaries, and if you insist on them, you can exercise them. They may stop you for a time. They may beat you over the head, put you in jail, or take your property away. But Highlander is proof that you can do it if you maneuver and don't quit and still survive. There are differences but the differences are slight.

There is one thing that is kind of interesting. We were talking about it the last time we had breakfast in New York. Somebody in Germany had written a book on Freire. They spent some time here and asked me what I thought Freire's greatest contribution to adult education. I said that the significant one that has benefited the rest of us the most was the fact that he got academicians to read something that is based on the study of people. Few of them had ever done it before. It became respectable academically to talk about the kind of education that he was talking about. Up to that time, it could not be done. Now people think that Highlander is not so strange. People used to say that Highlander is not educational, that it's a propaganda place, that they just get up there and talk, and that they never do anything. After Freire, people began to say maybe they do something.

CONTI AND FELLENZ: Can people misuse Freire's and your ideas?

HORTON: His methods have been distorted and used against him. It is used by the military in Brazil, which disturbs him very much. He told me that. It is also used with Wall Street bankers. He said, "Oh, my God." I said, "Well it's not as bad as the military!" His ideas can be taken and used against what he believed because he presented so much of it as a methodology. It's almost a technique in the way the Japanese use quality group things to make people think that they are part of industry without allowing them to do it. It's like the old group dynamics training used by industry to make workers think that they had some say. All of those things get distorted and turned around, caricatured and turned around. Freire's is easier to lend itself to that kind of thing. As far as I know, we haven't helped people because ours is so undefined and hard to figure out. It never has been described step by step. Although we have never hesitated to describe it to other people, others have described it. It's no secret. We try to tell people if they ask us how we run a workshop, we tell them that this is how we run a workshop. So it's not a secret. Yet it has not been used as far as we know by our opposition. People just can't figure out what is going on.

CONTI AND FELLENZ: Isn't the problem that they don't believe in people the way you do?

HORTON: The reason the workshops at Highlander work is that you have to trust the people, you have to love the people, and you have to care for people. You have to practice what you preach with people. That is the methodology. That puts the finger on the reason why we cannot be imitated by the oppressor very effectively. How people learn is a miracle. I don't understand how it takes place. I have seen people change scores of time and I have seen those people change scores of people. The multiplication of this is the thing. I can do it but really don't understand what happens. I have known Klansman who come to Highlander. They say, "I will eat with these niggers, but I want you to know that I am a Klansman." I have had them leave changed, and they are still changed today. By changed I mean they were going in this direction and now they are going in this direction. Now they haven't gone very far, but they have all their life in the other direction. I have not been concerned with how far but rather in the direction. I have seen that happen, I know it has happened. I knew at the time it was happening but was in awe of how it happened and why it happened. Yet it was happening. To make it happen is easier than to understand it. Human beings are so darn sensitive and complicated. There is still that great mystery there.

CONTI AND FELLENZ: How do you get your sense of what the important social issues are going to be?

HORTON: There is [a] combination of things. I talk to the people and get a feel of it—their unspoken sense of it. Before we started the Citizenship School program, I went down to the Sea Islands and stayed with Esau. It was all a blur. Yet I was determined to find a way to help Esau because it was a real problem. If you are going to have a democracy, people have a right to vote. If they are required to read and write to vote, then you are going to have to teach them to read and write so they can vote. That is aside from being interested in education for education's sake. It is kind of a moral imperative to me. But I couldn't figure it out. I stayed off and on for a couple of months and talked to the people out in the rice fields, watched them fish, went out and helped them with the work, got out to visit, and went to their churches. Gradually, I got to understand them. They got used to me because I was a friend of Esau. I finally got the sense of people. Then I saw why it is that they didn't want to read and write. My first understanding was that they never had a need to read and write to vote because they never had anyone to vote for and never thought that made any difference. Esau ran for office to give black people a person to vote for. That heighten[ed] their image. That made sense to me, so I could now see the motivation. Lots of people learn to read and write because it's a good thing, but that didn't work. So I thought that well maybe there is no opportunity. But there [was] unspent money for teachers for literacy, and there were teachers who had not had a student for two or three years. I had to find out why. I started to try to analyze the situation and came up with this whole bit of dignity. They didn't treat them with respect; they didn't treat them with dignity. They treated them like little kids. They were contemptuous of them. They actually put them in seats for children; they called them daddy longlegs, these big old lanky people sitting in a chair for first graders. They just treated them like dirt. So that became obvious that you have to treat people with respect. The reverse of this might mean success: How could I design a program to treat them with respect and to cash in on the fact that they were beginning to be interested in politics but that they couldn't vote because of the laws that said you had to read and write? It was a law which was designed to keep them from voting. I finally put it together. I got a cultural feel. That is very important. How can you tie into that?

What I am trying to say is that I don't sit down and try to figure the thing out in my head. I try to get in and get a sense of it. Now I use the same kind of sensing and feeling about the other problems. Are people ready to move on something, or have they gotten their head beat in every time they tried to move? When preachers started to try to agitate back in slavery days, they made it illegal for them to preach. They put all the blacks in the backs of the white churches where they could keep an eye on them and wouldn't let them have their own churches. Now they have their own churches. What is the significance that they have them? Is this something new? Then I began to realize that the churches are the whole basis of the black community. It was the religious life with all of the singing. Down there they had all the stomping with the shout. Those are the guts of the people. Then I used to go out on the farm where the people worked, and where there was the "man." I saw that they couldn't watch the scales; they couldn't figure anything, they knew they were being gypped. I was beginning to see some of the conflict situations and to see some of the points where you could stir them up, get them angry, and get them to see the injustices. You have to find points of injustice that people will recognize as injustice. Finally, I began to think that I must begin to think like they must think. How do these people think? I tried to put myself as far as I could in their situation. I parlayed that kind of being sensitive to what is the climate everywhere. I felt that uneasiness. I supposed that people could be moved because I had experience in organizing people. I helped the CIO (Congress of Industrial Organizations)[72] organize the first textile workers in the South. I know how people work. I had that experience from before from the mountains and the coal mines. We organized 80 percent of the unemployed in our county. We elected our people to every office in the county on an independent political ticket back in the '50s. So I had some experience working with masses of people. I knew a little bit about how they moved or how they could move if you got the grassroots leaders going. Using education as a means instead of organizing them is a big difference. Through some of my contacts and because of Highlander's history, I had access to information that most people did not have. Then I had contact with the bottom and most people didn't have. So I had two avenues of information that most people didn't have.

CONTI AND FELLENZ: Did you know Saul Alinsky?[73] What do you have in common with him?

HORTON: Yes, very well. I knew Saul when he was working in the prisons. We were good friends for many, many years. We were good personal friends.

I think you use organizations to educate people and use them consciously. I am less concerned about whether you win in your goal. If you don't educate people regardless of how many little victories you have, nothing is ever going to happen. To me organizations are for the primary purpose of educating people because most of them do not bring about any kind of changes that are significant anyway. So you might as well use them for something worthwhile. That is my line. Saul takes the line that the organization itself educates. The mere fact of organization educates. It's a fine line. I remember one time we were supposed to be debating. Saul said, "Myles has never been able to explain Highlander. Let me explain it!" So he did. He did a better job of explaining Highlander than I did. He was a staunch supporter of Highlander and helped us raise a tremendous amount of money. He used to be a fund-raising rabble-rousing speaker of Chicago. Saul and I worked differently, but basically we had the same ideas. We were always posed as being different, but I had no trouble doing it his way and him my way.

CONTI AND FELLENZ: Do you go out much to speak to share the ideas of Highlander?

HORTON: I only go to those places where somebody invites me who has been or worked at Highlander and knows what Highlander is. I have found some really embarrassing situations for people who thought they knew about Highlander and asked me to come and set up a whole series of programs. Their perceptions of Highlander were not at all correct. So it wasn't very fruitful. So I made a determination as a result of that to never go anywhere unless the people who asked me really knew what I was going to say anyway and wanted it. I don't want to go anywhere unless I can help somebody who is there do what they want to do and unless they think I can help them.

A Different Kettle of Fish

[1989]

This piece is an excerpt from an unpublished interview that Horton conducted with Susan Walker and Ike Coleman in 1989; there is no evidence of the occasion or purpose of this interview. The title is taken from a quotation from the interview that was used as an epigraph in the original archived manuscript. In this interview, Horton critiques the educational system and offers a set of alternative perspectives on education as illustrated by his experience with Highlander.

IKE COLEMAN: How did you end up starting Highlander? What led you that way?

MYLES HORTON: I answer that question in a book that's coming out in February with Doubleday,[74] a book on how I learned things and why I did what I did. It takes a little while to explain. Briefly, I was interested in education. I thought I'd be a teacher of some kind, and I had a religious background, and I knew a lot about schooling in Appalachia. And I thought, well, I'll just get a job teaching in school. And as I explored the possibility I found out I didn't want to teach in any of them. None of them. The religious schools were too sectarian; they were proselytizing and competing for the same members. Then I looked at the other schools and they were all practical vocational schools preparing people for the labor market, which didn't exist at that time but they were still doing that. There was very little of what I call education going on. So I decided there ought to be some better way of doing it and in the process of trying to figure out the answer to that question I got to make a real analysis of society. *[Text of paragraph is incomplete]*

I grew up during the depression. The depression started early in the South, so I knew what poverty was. I thought in order to have a better society, a more decent society, the only people who could change it were adults. We're always telling people we're preparing them for the future, and I discovered something. I discovered they made the same speeches when I graduated from grammar school, high school, and college. They always said when you get out of school then you can use what you've learned and the world will be yours and the future is for the young people. The same speech. And when I got out of college, out of graduate school, and everything I tried to do they said no, no, you can't do that. That's a wild idea. We know how to do it—"customs" and so and so and so. So I thought the job of school was to fit people into the existing, to pass on the past and fit people into the existing system, and that's all the schools could be in our society because they are an agent of the parent organization like the United States is an agent of the capitalist system. As the head of the state commission on [education] said a few years ago,[75] "Schools should be a microcosm of the profit system, it should be a little imitation of the profit system, preparing people. It should be run like a profit system to prepare people for the system." So I decided I didn't want to work in that system at all; I wanted to work with people who had a chance to change the system.

And then I started looking around, thinking, well, you can't work with everybody, it's impossible. There are limitations on what you can do. Whether you're one person or a group of people, there's only so much you can do in a lifetime. So I said what's the leverage? The way to change society is quite obvious; in history it's the working people, the poor people, the dispossessed people who want to change things because they're unhappy with it. I decided to work with adults old enough to be in the system, voters, and poor or disadvantaged because of race or being in a Third World country or a poor section of the United States, like here in Appalachia. There would be the people who most likely would have complaints, who'd want to do something about it. So I wouldn't try to think in terms of an educational approach to everybody, but a specified segment of society. And not try to appeal to society as a whole but to try to deal with a segment. So it was to find/define my search, and it was to find how you work out a program for adults who are in a position to do something.

A school is an extension of the playpen. It's still a contained situation where you don't have much leeway to think; you aren't allowed to think. You're not allowed to think for a very good reason. If the school system is an agent of the state, it's controlled by state levels, federal levels, county levels, or in a private school by boards, by the president, faculty. By the time it gets down to the student at the bottom of the ladder, there's not much leeway left for the student or the teacher to have much leeway. There's very little left for the teacher by the time it gets that far down. So I tried to work with adults outside the schooling system. Now that didn't mean age, that means anybody who's still in school I don't want to work with, because they weren't free to do what they wanted to do and weren't free to put into practice the things they learned. And they couldn't practice until later. As Paulo Freire says,[76] they've got a banking system of education to store up goodies for the future. They never use them, but they can. It's like you build this chimney. If you should find that pretty upper left-hand rock there with that moss on it and [I] said I want that to go in that corner here, and you just stuck it up in the air, as if it could stay there until you could build up under it. Ideas that you give people out of context [are] just like putting that rock up there. It's gonna come tumbling down. There's no way for it to build on. The way we learn is by adding stuff onto what we already know. Learn.

COLEMAN: It's got to be connected.

HORTON: It's got to be connected to what you already know. You build on what you know. You perceive something to be of value, of use, because something else tells you that other things like that have been of value or use. One thing is built on another. Knowledge is built on previous knowledge. Unattached facts are not knowledge, they're just facts. So I wanted to get out of the schooling system where you can try to work out a system of education where you build on people's experience, using people's experience. Then I started looking around for ways to do this. That's how I got interested in this whole business. Trying to figure out a way to do that kind of educational approach. It was never supposed to be a school. It was never in competition with schools. It never was supposed to demonstrate what could be done in a school. It's a different kettle of fish.

COLEMAN: I've never done anything with adult education, so I don't even know what to ask, but—

HORTON: Adult education, in this country, is not what I'm talking about. Adult education is training, it's technical training. It's skill training, what we used to call vocational training. In fact, most colleges are now vocational training. Or they're not education, in the old sense of education. The word *educate* means drawing out. Education today means pouring in—

COLEMAN: Pouring in, yes. Exactly.

HORTON: So it has nothing to do with what was originally education. Highlander's idea is still in the old sense of education, that there's already things in people you build on, you draw out. The idea of building on something. You build on what's in people to start with. And most of the theorizing and stuff to come out of Highlander has had to do with empowering people by building on what's already there. The potential's in everyone. I've got two good eyes. I use both of my eyes. I use one to look at people where they are, at what is. And what's observable. That's the starting point. You've got to start at the bottom. You can't start up there. You've got to start at the foundation, not halfway up. You start with people's experience. That's one unique thing—the only unique thing—in the world, I guess, is individual experience. Your experience is unique to you, and mine is unique to me. So that's a sound basis on which to build, and it shows respect for the person. We talk about respect for individuals and yet we don't respect their experience. In school you have no respect for people's experience. The guy who says that the schooling system should be a replica of the capitalist system didn't say we ought to help people develop what's inside them. They say this is what we're gonna teach them, get a captive audience, and reward and punish them so that they fit into that situation. And you have to do [it] if you're going to use that kind of education because there's no reason for anybody to learn anything except because they were told to or promised some benefit from it. There's not much pleasure—in fact, schooling kills the pleasure of learning for most. But if you start the other way, with people's experience, one eye looks at what people are, and the other eye is their potential. You look at them simultaneously.

If you were coming to a Highlander workshop I would look at you and I'd say where is this guy? I've got to get him to talk and find out where he is, find out something about his experience, what kind of person he is. I already know your background in general, because I grew up in the region, or a similar region, so I know some things about you already, but I don't know much. So my job is to try to size you up as a starting point, because I've got to start with you. You cannot move from where you ain't. You've got to move from where you are. If you want to get out that door, and I tell you to start from over at the TV, you can't start with the TV, you've got to start where you are. You have to start from where you are. That's the one eye that does that. Then you have to see the potential. There's a potential in everyone, and my job is to have the imagination, as you talk and I get to know you, [of] seeing these little sprouts of interest, the seeds in there and understand a little bit more about you by using my imagination, from what I know about myself and about other people, so I can see some of your potential and start encouraging you to develop those potentials.

And a lot of my encouragement depends on my genuine attitude toward you, my genuine respect for you as a human being and my faith that you have a potential to learn and to do things, my belief in you. And I have to demonstrate that not by telling you that [or] by making a speech about it but by the way I treat you. My attitude toward you has to be expressed in my actions. Because you can't learn anything about my attitude, you can only look and learn about my actions. My actions have got to be such that I say to you by my actions, I have confidence in you. I enjoy reading poetry, I enjoy looking at the mountains, I enjoy learning, it's a lot of fun, now you do that too—you may not enjoy a book right now, you may not enjoy poetry, but you enjoy fishing—you enjoy something, you enjoy eating, or something. And you can get joy out of learning, and the reason I know that is because I do. Now you can object to that, but if you see me get excited about the things I'm learning, my action then says to you, I want to share this enthusiasm for learning. In other words, your action has to be the thing that tells where you're coming from in terms of that second eye that looks at the future. It's not too easy. Because half that tree's underground, half of all plants are underground, half of anything practically is underground. And half of what people are is hidden inside, and you can't see it.

I just read the other day that somebody is trying to work out scientifically a way to use sound waves and computer images to look underground and see the roots without having to dig them up. Now that would be a step forward because up to now you have to dig them up to see them and when you dig them up you destroy the hair roots, and you can't ever see those without a microscope. And people have those microscopic roots too. Then they have sprouts, and seeds, and they have all levels, and that imagery helps me see what's inside people. And my job is to nourish them and water them and encourage them and give people hope and give them the fun of learning and the fun of developing. It's painful for people to grow. Growth is painful. It's painful for a seed to break out of the ground, and it's painful for a person to grow. And people have got to be introduced to the pain of growth, and not shy away from it, not be afraid of the pain, not be afraid to be unhappy, not be afraid to be stretched out, not be afraid to be laughed at, not be afraid to grow. Because that's part of growth. That's the way I kind of see education, that's my way of thinking about education. As kind of a natural, holistic way of looking at it. And the whole idea at Highlander is built around that theoretical concept, of the growth inside. And that means you can't try to shape people's lives, make them all alike. People grow at different speeds, have different interests, so you've got to take that into consideration, and you can't impose your ideas on people.

Now I've got very strong convictions about what I think about society, what I believe. Philosophically, it'd be a socialist concept of society instead of a capitalist one, where instead of [being] based on profit it would be based on people. But I don't see any examples of the kind of socialism that I think would lead to a democratic world. My goal is democracy, not capitalism, or socialism, or communism or something else, but democracy. A real democracy, where people control their lives. And I can see the possibility of some kind of combination of socialism and capitalism or something we don't even know about leading in that direction, but I don't have any blueprints of this or that. People have to shape that, just like you have to shape your own goals, society has to shape theirs. It's not up to me to try to mastermind that. I think it's up to all of us to share our hopes and our dreams and our ideas as far as we can. But it's not something you try to impose on people. I'm very glad to tell you what I believe about, though. But if people don't ask me, I don't tell 'em. But I hope they'll ask me.

SUSAN WALKER: You have worked with so many different kinds of people who have come here from other places to work with you. What have you learned about how people grow or change? What do they get from it? Starting from wherever they are to wherever it is they want to get to. What happens in people as they go through that process?

HORTON: We all accept imaginary limits to what we can do and learn and be. You know, customs, traditions. [We've] got a lot of baggage to carry along that we never look at. And that's a limiting factor in trying to develop our potential because our potential is inhibited by or being held captive by these things. Another thing is equally persuasive to persons, and that is their peers, what people think of them, not society as a whole, but the people they like. Whoever you run around with. That's why people are not going to get anywhere with the drug problem in cities because peer groups are into selling crack, say, and it's the only thing they're allowed to do, they've been forced out of legitimate ways of making a livelihood. They've been told there's no legitimate way they can make a livelihood, so they find an illegitimate of making a livelihood. And within that, they build a structure of philosophy. Death is not important, going to jail is not important—

COLEMAN: Being tough is important—

HORTON: Being tough is important and having your peer group like you is important and being accepted is important.

WALKER: And money is power—

HORTON: And they say that's what capitalists taught us is that money is power, and they crook it, and lie and steal, and we do it too. They don't see themselves as being any different from being a shyster or somebody that takes over a big company, except that they deal in smaller cash. Now the way that this affects education is that if you're in grammar school or high school, say, in a city like Washington or New York or Chicago, and your peer group says we're not gonna have these people who won't let us make an honest living, who won't give us a future, educate us the way they want to educate us. We're gonna show them they can't teach us to read, they can't teach us anything. And they deliberately set out to try not to learn. And the teachers work out all kind of gimmicks, thinking the problem is gimmickry or bribery or something, to try and get them to learn, and that's not it [at] all and they're sitting there laughing at them all the time. Because if [you] learn they say you're a traitor, that woman, boy she got next to you, or you really let that teacher get next to you, so they shame [you]. So peer pressure [at] that level is rather obvious, but it's equally pressured on all levels, social levels, economic levels, religious levels, political levels; people have those peer pressures. So we're limited by those customs, by those peers. But education helps people break through that, liberates them from that, so they can begin to do things that aren't popular, that might get them in trouble, will get them in trouble if they do it. Democracy is the most radical idea that has ever been conceived by man. Communism is a conservative program compared to that. Democracy really says that people can learn to govern themselves in every aspect of their lives.

I've often been asked and been concerned about—I don't know anything firsthand about schooling—what people could do within the system. I said what people have to do who don't like the system is to bootleg the kind of education they believe in. You know, do it illegitimately outside the system. And I don't mean to get out of the school system, but don't follow the lesson plans, so to speak, the schooling plans any more than they have to hold their jobs. To do just enough of it to hold their jobs, and to spend the rest of the time trying to figure out a way to create an education while doing that.

[Text omitted]

I think that people should do what Paulo Freire calls "invading the system." He says that his job is to invade the educational system and try to change it. He does it from the outside, and I think you can do it from the inside. I think you can find ways to better it. But I don't think anybody can defy the system. You can't say I refuse to do this, or I'm not going to teach this, or I'm not going to use this textbook, I'm not going to have grades. I have a friend at University of California, Berkeley, and he doesn't believe in grades, but they have to have grades. So he lets his students grade themselves, and then he turns that into an educational experience. His students grade themselves and then the class discusses it, so it isn't just an exercise. He takes care of the technicality, but he does more. They discuss the basis they grade themselves on. So sometimes as a result of discussion the class says you've got to up the grade, sometimes they say you have to lower it. It has nothing to do with the system. It's part of the educational program. He's turned something he just doesn't do into a something they can learn from instead of just doing it as a technicality. And he has to do that.

WALKER: Otherwise you have to leave the system. If you're good that's a shame, it hurts the system.

HORTON: I'm suggesting that people try to stay in the system, not leave the system.

WALKER: That's a problem I think that some Bread Loaf[77] teachers have found is that very often when they leave in the summer they've been exposed to ideas about teaching that are so new and fresh and they go back to an institution that's rigid and doesn't particularly care and they respond in various ways. One way is to go at it tooth and nail and fight the system, completely up front, not in a guerrilla way, and get so burned out that they feel like leaving. And then you've lost a really good teacher.

HORTON: It's like the weather. Now you can have all kind of ideas about defying the weather, but it doesn't make a bit of difference to the weather.

WALKER: God knows.

HORTON: Defying the schooling system is almost like defying the weather. What you need to do is to learn to live with it, learn to get out of the rain, or enjoy it, or make something out of it. You can't change it. That's there. The only way you can change the schools is to change the system. The system has to be changed before its instrument, the school, is going to be changed. It's impossible to conceive of having a democratic schooling system without a democratic economic system. But in the meantime we've got to live with it, try to use the school to change the system, and to do that you've got to use guerilla tactics. You can't defy it, and you can't pretend it doesn't exist. To change things you have to understand it. And if you don't understand how the system works, you can't go about changing it. But you better respect it. I don't mean to respect it in the sense you're agreeing with it, but to respect its power and its existence.

[Text omitted]

Section II

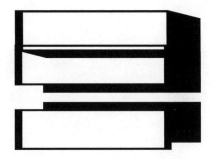

The Labor Movement

Notes on Worker Education

[Early 1930s]

The following piece was taken from the Highlander archives. These "Notes on Worker Education," as they are titled in the original manuscript, represent unpublished ideas written by Horton sometime in the 1930s. In the following, Horton outlines the relationship between the individual and the social and stresses the necessary link between theory and practice in worker education.

Perhaps the best way to make clear the relationship of Worker Education to organized labor will be to discuss the aim, method of teaching, and general approach to Worker Education. It can be readily understood that institutionalized education, as carried on in our regular school system, has almost nothing in common with Worker Education. The same can be said for vocational training. But Adult Education is often, and justifiably, confused with Worker Education. They have much in common but the differences are fundamental. Adult Education appeals to the individual while Worker Education, without losing sight of the individual, seeks to enlighten and liberate a group or class. The first is individualistic, the second is social. The primary concern of Adult Education is to hand on culture and knowledge, but it shortsightedly ignores the class nature of society which makes culture and knowledge a monopoly of the few. On the other hand, Worker Education makes an effort to understand the class conflict so as to be able to educate for a more democratic society, and carries with it the conviction that the producers, of hand and brain, have a mission to reconstruct society, to break the monopoly so that the good things of life can be shared by all. Worker Education aims at a classless society, and in so doing represents the finest elements in our American tradition.

Another important distinction between Adult and Worker Education is that Worker Education includes a program of education for children as well as for adults.

What has been said concerning Worker Education applies to all countries; while the aim is international, it takes different forms in different countries. In general, however, mass education is carried on by means of single lectures, debates, the press, films, radio, libraries, and by the use of dramatics. Other forms of education are study groups, week-end conferences, such as the LID,[1] forums, evening classes, and residence schools. It will be necessary to limit our discussion to one form of Worker Education, and since workers' schools should become centers from which other forms of education emanate, we will discuss resident schools for workers.

Worker Education has not reached the advanced stage in this country that it has in Europe, where it is largely an outgrowth of the trade union and cooperative movements. In contrast to the situation in America, the European workers are conscious of class distinctions, and workers' schools are conducted primarily along class distinctions, and workers' schools are conducted primarily along class lines. Our approach, however, must be worked out in terms of our own situation. In the United States less than one-sixth of the thirty-odd millions of workers are organized. 3,045,000 are affiliated with the AF of L^2 and approximately 1,000,000 are in unaffiliated unions and brotherhoods. Only a few thousand are members of consumers' cooperatives. In the south the percentage is even less than that in the country as a whole. Many union and cooperative members themselves do not understand the nature and possibilities of their organizations. Consequently, the task of Worker Education, in relation to the labor movement, is twofold: to help organized workers take a more intelligent part in their unions and cooperatives, and to interest the unorganized in the labor movement as their most effective means of raising their standard of living, and their most powerful method of bettering society as a whole. But in addition to meeting the needs of organized and unorganized workers in industry and in rural areas, a constructive and effective program of Workers' Education should appeal to many of the middle class, in fact all the 85 percent of our population who earn their living by hand and brain. But before discussing an approach to this problem let us examine briefly the method of teaching, or the tools to be used.

Theory and practice must be united if the purpose of Worker Education is to be realized. An objective or aim, however rational and just, that cannot be linked in a practical manner with the everyday lives and aspirations of the working people will forever remain an objective. It's alright to hitch our wagon to a star, but the wheels must be on the ground if we want to haul stove wood. Theories may be accepted, but until they are made to live and can be translated into action they are of little value. An understanding of society is not enough; we must change it.

Only by testing theories on the firing line of everyday life can their validity be determined. If theories cannot stand the test, even though sanctified by authority and tradition, they must be discarded. Those that prove worthy should be made the basis for new theories, and can give meaning to experiences both old and new.

An insistence on combining theory with practice will necessarily influence our approach to Worker Education. A school using this method must necessarily operate in the realm of everyday life and, consequently, have its rootage in the existing labor movement, in a particular locality.

Otherwise its efforts will be largely confined to speculation. Students must be drawn from an area in which the problems are similar, and from which common experiences can be drawn upon for teaching purposes.

It would be difficult to build a curriculum (and a Jerry built curriculum doesn't go with workers) around the experiences of a student group composed of midwestern farmers, industrial workers of foreign parentage from New England, and textile workers from the towns and cities skirting the southern mountains. Their immediate problems and backgrounds are far too diversified. But by limiting the area, a course of study can be based upon common problems and similar backgrounds.

Many problems, however, are so basic that they cut across regional boundaries, but even these problems, which are usually of a political nature, can only be understood when they are related to individual or group experiences. For further study along these lines students should attend schools which exist for that specific purpose.

It should be borne in mind that we are talking about an approach and not a well-developed system of Worker Education. None exists in America and the form which such a system will take remains to be seen. Schools will no doubt develop that have a particular emphasis, i.e. for trade union officials, cooperative managers, etc. We now have party schools, but their emphasis is too specific to serve the broader purpose of Worker Education. The more basic regional schools should be independent of political and economic control. They must maintain their freedom to teach unmolested by party discipline and especially by antilabor organizations.

The problem of Worker Education can only be successfully approached by starting where people are and building on their experiences. That is, by basing a program of education on the interests of workers in a given area. The labor movement has not yet caught their imagination to the extent that it can become the sole basis for Worker Education. What then are most workers interested in? Generally speaking, they are interested in making a living and having some pleasure; in wishing for, but not knowing how to get, cultural, social and intellectual opportunities; and [in] a better life for themselves and their children. These are some of the things people everywhere are conscious that they desire and here is where Worker Education, or any kind of education, must begin. It should be noted that with such a basis, rooted as it is in everyday life, emotional energy is generated, without which a sustained effort to reconstruct society is impossible. Worker Education must have heat as well as light.

By starting where the interests of people lie, not only industrial and rural workers but many of the middle class can be appealed to. For lack of a more accurate term we have called this the Folk approach to Worker Education. Such an approach can be adapted to any region and places no limitations whatsoever on Worker Education.

The Highlander Folk School

[1936]

The following essay was originally published in the January 1936 issue of The Social Frontier: A Journal of Educational Criticism and Reconstruction, *edited by George S. Counts, a prominent American educator of the period and one of the signatories of Reinhold Niebuhr's original letter supporting the Southern Mountains School. Other members of the Board of Contributors included John Dewey and Joseph K. Hart. In this essay, Horton outlines the conditions for workers in the Tennessee mountains at the time Highlander was founded and Highlander's use of residence courses, extension programs, and community activities to help workers intervene in these conditions.*

I watched my friends leave their mountain homes in response to agents' stories of mill villages, and return a few months later broken in spirit and health. The industrialists, not satisfied with grinding profits out of those who left their homes to take jobs in cotton mill towns, built branch mills in the mountains. There was no escape. In the name of progress exploitation followed the valleys back into the hills. Moral and physical disintegration was the price that young and old alike were forced to pay for life's necessities. The whip of poverty and lure of shabby mill life combined to make a death trap which sucked in bright-eyed girls in their teens and strong men who loved freedom and the out-of-doors. Some returned to their hillside farms to spend the remainder of their broken lives coughing up lint. But most of the families stayed in the mill villages. They had sold their homes and, unable to get away, were forced to send their children into the mills to help support the family.

Economic conditions were little better back in the mountains. With the coal and timber almost gone, they had turned to farming. But poor land and inexperience produced only enough to make a miserable existence possible. Though trapped, exploitation was not accepted as a necessary part of life. Here in the mountains, should the economic situation become pressing enough, the people could be made to understand that the socialization of property would give them more personal freedom than would ever again be possible under the existing profit system.

The lack of industrial progress and education among the people in the mountains and neighboring mill towns has served as a protection against their acceptance of wage slavery. Workers in the South, especially those not more than two generations removed from the mountains, are willing to fight for the American ideals of "life, liberty, and the pursuit of happiness." Here was an opportunity to direct the American revolutionary tradition toward a cooperative society operated by and for the workers. Ideas of revolt run through many of the songs written by workers, some of which are sung as ballads. Many strike songs are as class-conscious as the writings of Karl Marx, and much simpler.

Having decided to concentrate on the farmers and industrial workers in the southern mountains, the problem arose of how to go about the job. Mountain schools and colleges gave no clue. They were educating people out of their class or giving them vocational training. The people need to be awakened and enlightened as to their place in society as a class, not trained to do better work for the industrialists. The problem of influencing the existing schools to change their aims seemed more difficult than working out a new approach. While working on an educational setup that would meet people where their interests are and lead them to envision a new society, my attention was drawn to the work of the Danish Folk High Schools which furnish an excellent example of purposive education.[3]

The Highlander Folk School, located on a mountain farm, within five hours' drive of a number of industrial centers, was opened November, 1932, to provide an educational center for southern workers, for the purpose of educating rural and industrial leaders for a new social order. It was not our desire to create another institution, but to develop a natural approach to workers' education. We were fortunate in securing for our advisory committee Reinhold Niebuhr,[4] George S. Counts,[5] Norman Thomas,[6] Mary Nail Kleeck,[7] and other outstanding social educators. At first the school was only a large farm house and an idea. It was two months before any students came. During that time we cut wood and worked on the farm. The first resident student was the son of an Alabama coal miner. There was no curriculum. One evening, while visiting a neighbor, we started to discuss psychology. The farmer, his wife, and the resident student wanted to continue the discussion, so we met at the school the following evening and held our first class. Soon we had a class of twenty-five, including farmers, miners, unemployed, college graduates, and one minister. Their ages ranged from eighteen to eighty. No classes were started that were not asked for or that did not grow out of some life situation. A class in cultural geography followed the neighbors' interest in some snapshots taken in Europe. Stories of a miners' strike brought back by teachers who had visited the coal camp at Wilder, Tennessee, raised problems that led to a class in economics.[8] Another class grew out of discussions of the presidential campaign. Most of the students were neighbors. Only three were full-time resident students.

One of the students who came for the special course brought a basket of onions, bacon, and canned fruit to pay her expenses. She had worked in a hosiery mill, but at the time was living way back in the mountains. In an economics class held in the kitchen where the student cook could keep an eye on the stove, the group had been asked to explain a number of theories that they had been studying. One used a small blackboard propped above the sink. A neighbor who had dropped in for the class said he would never forget the illustration of surplus value given by the girl who had brought the basket of food.

"When I was working at the hosiery mill in Chattanooga," she said, "we were told that we would have to take a wage-cut or the mill would go out of business. Of course, we took the cut. About two weeks later I read in the paper that the daughter of the mill owner was sailing for Europe to spend the winter. I suppose it was the surplus value we had produced that paid her way."

There are three phases of our program: residence courses, extension work, and community activities. Workers who show promise of becoming active in the labor movement as organizers or as local leaders are selected as residence students. Last summer we had an enrollment of nineteen regular resident students for a six weeks' course. The majority were from the mills, mines, and farms but a few were college graduates interested in workers' education. Courses were given in economics, labor history and tactics, workers' problems, public speaking, dramatics, and labor journalism. In each class an effort was made to stay within the experience of the students.

An example of capitalistic tactics was furnished the students when a gunman hired by the Fentress Coal and Coke Company at Wilder, Tennessee, attempted to dynamite the school.[9] Teachers and students of the Highlander Folk School had helped in a United Mine Workers strike the year before. After threats of death were made to any striker who housed or gave us a meal, we withdrew from Wilder, but arrangements had been made for three students to study in the school. For two weeks, students and teachers guarded the school night and day. It was not necessary to stress the class nature of society to students who had to do guard duty all night for the privilege of studying at a workers' school.

An extension program is carried on throughout the year in connection with unions and farmers' organizations. Some of this work is done by teachers and students who lend assistance to workers during organization campaigns and in strikes. The more systematic work is done through study groups set up by the extension director and by former students. Our activities of this nature keep us in close touch with the labor movement and enable us to help students after they have left school. Most of our new students are recruited through the extension work.

The community activities also continue the year round and are of a cultural as well as educational nature. Piano lessons are provided for anyone in the community. As many as twenty children and young people have been taking music lessons at one time. Old and young take part in dramatics and folk dancing. A few adults attend regular morning classes during our residence courses but all our special lectures are given at night so that a larger number from the community can attend. An average of twenty books are checked out of our library each week by people in the neighborhood. The library also serves dozens of workers' groups throughout the South.

It is the policy of the school to work through the existing organizations whenever possible. Last year the woodcutters in our community struck with the slogan "It takes a strong back, a sharp ax, and a weak mind to cut bugwood at 75 cents a cord." A Workers' League was organized to carry on the strike.[10] Practically every worker in the community joined, including the staff and students at the school. Repeated failure to get government officials to oppose the wealthy Tennessee Products Corporation we were fighting taught the entire community that working people must depend upon themselves. They decided to start a cooperative cannery and later a cooperative store. At the request of the community a ten weeks' course in the history and management of cooperatives was given. A small but successful cooperative cannery was operated last summer. Plans for a consumer-producer cooperative to take in most of the community are under way.

The three approaches merge when workers from a union or farm community where we are carrying on extension work come for a residence course and for a time become part of the community. During our short residence courses, farmers and millworkers find that their interests are basically the same. Their problems are discussed with the neighbors, with visiting organizers, and with teachers. New social theories are discussed naturally by the neighbors who drop in for classes or for an evening visit. The students are stimulated and eagerly attend classes where they hope to learn more about these new ideas. They see the need for fundamental social change and become interested in the means for bringing about a new social order. Once students see the economic necessity for organizing and the justice a workers' society alone will make possible, their hearts as well as their heads are won to the cause of labor. Workers' education must furnish heat as well as light, for there is no time to waste.

Our place is with the working class. We must not cut ourselves off from them by proclaiming social theories for which they have not been prepared by experience to understand. We are working primarily with the American Federation of Labor unions.[11] The southern workers have asked for our assistance. National officials of three unions have asked the Highlander Folk School to train organizers and local leaders for them.[12] Education for workers must be financed by organized labor so that they can have full control. At the beginning, this calls for low-cost workers' education. The absence of salaries and the supply of food stuff grown on our farm enables us to run the school, exclusive of our extension work, on a yearly budget of $4,800, which maintains a regular teaching staff of six members.[13] It is up to the Highlander Folk School to demonstrate to organized labor in this part of the South that workers' education is necessary.

In an effort to help build a militant labor movement and to give experience to our students, the school moved from Monteagle and is stationed for a week in a mill town near Chattanooga. Teachers and students are scattered in the homes of striking hosiery workers. We meet one hour each day for discussion. The remainder of the time is spent at union meetings or on the picket line. A Washington's Birthday parade, which we helped organize, led by the local High School band, ended as a mass picket line in front of Daisy Hosiery Mill. Four hundred shots were fired into the unarmed paraders by armed guards inside the mill. Our librarian and four other men and women were shot. As a result of the parade, the three Richmond Hosiery Mills were forced to deal with the union officials. Aside from the educational value to our students, we were able to broaden the outlook of the strikers. The school has been asked to do educational work for the American Federation of Hosiery Workers in Tennessee and neighboring states.[14]

We are becoming accepted as a part of the southern labor movement. The Highlander Folk School's most important contribution will be to help the workers to envision their role in society and in so doing, make the labor movement the basis for a fundamental social change.

The Community Folk School

[1938]

This piece was originally written for a 1938 collection titled The Community School, *edited by Samuel Everett. It was later reprinted in the November 1976 issue of* New Schools Exchange Newsletter. *Like "Notes on Worker Education" and "The Highlander Folk School," "The Community Folk School" represents Horton's understanding of the links between education, workers, and Highlander at the time that he was deeply engaged in the labor movement.*

Public schools should be one of the most important agencies for the dissemination of useful information and the shaping of attitudes necessary for the achievement of a democratic society. In so far as they fail to do this, schools are not adequate to the needs of the masses of the people in whose interest they were established.

Unfortunately, the transition from the private to the public school failed to carry with it a corresponding change in philosophy. The point of view which still dominates in public education is better suited to private schools for the favored few than to public education. Great areas of life having to do with the welfare of the masses are not properly dealt with. Although organized labor, as Beard points out, took "a lead in demanding, from the legislators the establishment of free and equal schools," the part these organizations played in American life is either ignored or misrepresented in the great majority of textbooks from which children of workers are taught (*The Rise of American Civilization* 810). The facts selected for teaching do not include those that would give children a just pride in the workers' struggle to better society through their own organizations. Instead, it is the individuals who have gained power through ownership and the generals of armies who are pictured as citizens worthy of emulation.

The need for clarity was never so urgent as today. Productive capacities have been developed, making possible a future of plenty for all. At the same time, control of our natural resources and means of production is becoming centered in fewer and fewer hands. Our economic life, on the side of production at least, is rapidly shifting, from an individual to a collective basis. The fundamental question is: "In whose interest is it to be operated?" Will our human and material resources be organized in the interest of the few, or for all? If the public school sides with private interests, the working out of an educational philosophy will be only a harmless form of mental gymnastics. If, on the other hand, the public school is to champion the cause of the masses, a clear-cut and positive educational philosophy is essential.

The philosophy of individualism which attempted to give meaning to the period of economic expansion from which the nation has emerged must be discarded. New attitudes and new institutions must be developed in keeping with our shifting economic foundations. If the public schools are to be a factor in the reconstruction of society, they must be guided by a philosophy of economic democracy.

The acceptance of such a philosophy would mean that teachers would no longer uncritically proclaim the virtues of existing customs, practices, and institutions as though we lived in a static society. The untenable policy of pseudo-impartiality must be rejected. One who teaches cannot avoid laying some social emphasis. A personal bias either consciously or unconsciously influences the selection of facts to be taught and the emphasis which is to be made. A preference for certain values determines what is good and what is bad in the eyes of the teacher. So-called neutrality is, therefore, a surrender of the status quo.

All education is a form of action based on some kind of social philosophy. Dignity will only come to the teaching profession when this guiding philosophy becomes intelligent and can be honestly proclaimed.

A Community Approach

With the broad orientation of education outlined, we turn to the approach. The nature of the educative process makes it necessary to begin with things as they are, however far removed they may be from the desired goal. We must deal with people in relation to specific problems at specific times and places. Knowledge is not of such an unchanging nature that it is the same at all times and in all situations. Attitudes formed in a school insulated from life are not transferable to normal relationships. It should be realized that experience is given meaning not only by the point of view taught at school but also by the attitudes learned at home, in the church, in community organizations and associations, and from life in general. The school which is not a natural part of this educative process can play only a minor role in shaping social attitudes.

Life educates. Schools can give direction to the educative process not by presuming to educate for life but by becoming an organic part of life itself. Both children and adults live in a world where needs and wants are bound together. Schools must combine the economic, social, intellectual, esthetic, and moral elements of our culture, just as ordinary people combine them in everyday life. Organized education must move in from the periphery of life where the school has formed an artificial society and become a part of the struggles and dreams of the masses. Life, for the most part, is organized into communities, and the community must be the basis for social education.

Our educational system must undergo drastic changes. The reshaping of an institution, with its traditions and vested interests, is a difficult task. Complete freedom to carry on democratic education can hardly be expected short of a new social order. Nevertheless, constructive changes are being made in our public schools, and in certain communities even more fundamental changes could be made. These advances are coming, in the face of attacks on public education by predatory interests. The general public accepts the public school and will defend it. Sumner's statement, although made soon after the turn of the century, applies today.

> Popular education and certain faiths about popular education are in the mores of our time. We regard illiteracy as an abomination. We ascribe to elementary book learning power to farm character, make good citizens, keep family mores pure, elevate morals, establish individual character, civilize barbarians, and cure social vice and disease. We apply schooling as a remedy for every social phenomenon which we do not like. (628–29)

The public school must accept the responsibility such faith places upon it.

The experience of the writer has been largely in connection with an educational program independent of the public-school system. There is something to be said in favor of the freedom for experimentation that is made possible by independent schools. In other countries, programs of workers' education especially have served as a demonstration ground for methods later used in schools and universities.

Community Analysis

The curriculum to be outlined is based on a specific community in which the writer lives. A description of the community as it was four years ago and as it is at present, and an explanation of how community education has been a factor in the change, should make the proposed curriculum more intelligible. A program for a living community cannot be based upon a picture of still life.

The community of Summerfield is located on the Cumberland Mountain, an elevated tableland with an area of five thousand square miles. It borders on the larger community of Monteagle, where the nearest post office and stores are located. Nevertheless, Summerfield has a distinct community life. The United States census classifies the population as "rural nonfarming." In this respect it is typical of a majority of the mountain communities. Agricultural experts attribute the failure of the early settlers to make a success of farming to the lack of phosphate and lime in the scanty soil. Instead of farming they turned to the coal mines and the timber industry. These natural resources have been ruthlessly exploited, and now, with the timber gone and only a few mines in operation, the problem of earning a living is acute.

Grundy County, in which Summerfield is located, well illustrates the problem. Even though one of the largest mines in operation on the mountain is to be found here, most of the men are ex-miners. As to agriculture, 314 of the 625 small farms fail to provide subsistence. Most of the women are as inexperienced in handicrafts and providing for home needs as the men are at farming. It has been necessary for a majority of the people to turn to government agencies for support.

The people in this community are, with few exceptions, descendants of the early settlers. They are racially and culturally homogenous. All are working people. Thus, their economic interests are basically the same. However, four years ago there was little unity and practically no native leadership. Suspicion and jealousy encouraged individualism. Memories of feuds and bitter strikes were still fresh. The few jobs that were available, from the summer tourists at a nearby resort, were not enough to go around and increased the tension. The organized social life of the community centered around the elementary school and three churches, the latter run by nonresident ministers or student pastors. Recreation for adults consisted largely in playing or watching baseball games during the summer. The native square dancing had been banned as irreligious. Fortunately, the young people fared better. Social evenings and Sunday afternoon games were being encouraged by one church leader.

The efforts of the elementary-school teachers to cope with community problems [are] enlightening. For about sixteen years semiphilanthropic work had been carried on in the community under very able leadership, the most tangible result being the establishment of the elementary school and the securing of exceptional teachers. Children, not subjects, had been taught, and the job had been done with understanding and ability. Nevertheless, the teachers watched a discouraging proportion of these children, for whom they had the highest hopes, being swallowed up by the indifferent life of the community. Each year three or four pupils started to the county high school, four miles away, but only one or two of them graduated. The five or six who had gone away to college furnished little community leadership on returning and, with one exception, were less able to adjust to life than those who had remained at home. The prevalent attitude toward education was that children should learn reading, writing, and arithmetic, and then do as they pleased about continuing school.

The community is not isolated. Good roads and newspapers make possible daily contacts with the world. Some people had never been off the mountain although it is only a two-hour drive to Chattanooga, the nearest city. But members of many families had worked in nearby industrial cities, and some had gone as far away as Chicago and Detroit in search of jobs.

The problems confronting such a community were complex. Old customs and new experiences were in conflict. Here were people living in a rural area whose experiences had been primarily those of industrial wage earners. Which way were they to turn? Cities could not absorb their own surplus labor. Farming was unprofitable even in more fertile areas. Yet it is evident that the answer could not be found in the community alone. Basically the problems were the same as the problems of working people everywhere. A program of folk education was therefore planned with the aim of facing, with the local people, their fundamental problems, which extended far beyond the boundary lines of the community.

The Highlander Folk School

The Highlander Folk School was guided by the belief that our economy, which is rapidly becoming collectivized, can be made the basis for a genuine democracy, and that the final attainment and protection of the fullest rights of the masses can come only through their own economic and political organizations. Further, we held that the new society must be built upon the best elements of our present social order. With this goal constantly in mind we set to work. A large house, in which the founder of the elementary school had lived and worked, served as a community center and residence for two teachers. Social evenings, when young and old gathered to sing familiar songs and to talk and play games, were the first organized activities of the school. Only one student from outside the community had come to attend the resident term for workers. Later he was joined by others. There were no scheduled classes for weeks after the students arrived.

The wife of a neighboring farmer, in remarking about her unruly child, started a discussion about psychology with one of the students and a teacher. Returning from his evening chores, the farmer, in whose home the conversation was taking place, joined in the discussion, which lasted until bedtime. The next evening the discussion was continued at the school, and at the request of neighbors and students, a class in psychology for adults was announced. The following week our first class was held.

Soon afterward, a class in cultural geography grew out of an evening around the open fire looking at pictures taken of Europe. Conditions and customs of people in other lands were contrasted with our own. Reports by students and teachers who had visited a coal miners' strike led to a class in economics. It was election year, and the political platforms of the various presidential candidates were analyzed and compared. During this first winter four evening classes were conducted weekly with an average attendance of twenty men and women whose ages ranged from eighteen to eighty.

The residence students attended the classes and were given individual instruction in the use of source material, in writing, and in speaking. In addition, each selected a community activity. A young woman who could play the piano started a girls' club which developed into a music class. So many children wanted lessons that arrangements were made with the local schoolteacher for the music lessons to be given during school hours. Another student organized a dramatics club for all who were interested, regardless of age. Plays written about local situations were produced for the entertainment and education of the community. A young man held educational meetings among the miners and relief workers in neighboring communities.

Out of this first year's experience grew a threefold program consisting, first, of community work; second, of a residence program of short courses and weekend conferences; and third, of extension work. Members of the community participate as students and coworkers in all phases of the program.[15]

A Community Program Develops

The community program of classes, lectures, discussions, and social and cultural activities has been given additional meaning and direction by a number of activities.

A little less than a year after the school opened, the first economic organization in the community was formed. A majority of the employed men were cutting what remained of a once valuable forest. The shoddy timber, called *bugwood,* was used for its chemical content. A woodcutter who had calculated that he was making only two and one-half cents per meal for each member of his family went to the other workers.[16] He told them, "It takes a sharp axe, a strong back, and a weak mind to cut bugwood at seventy-five cents a day. Let's strike." Soon the woods were deserted. A moonlight meeting was held in front of the school, and the Cumberland Mountain Workers' League was organized.[17] Within a week a majority of the adult population of the community had taken an obligation "to be loyal to one another and to the purpose of the organization, which is: 1. To prevent the wholesale destruction of our forests and 2. To better the condition of the community by raising wages."

Men, women, and children picketed the woods for miles around to prevent "people who didn't understand" from taking the jobs of the woodcutters. Section 7A of the N.I.R.A.[18] was memorized and quoted to every one who questioned the strike, including the representative of the corporation, who had said, "It's against the law to strike. You will all be in jail by the weekend."

At a meeting, the apparent contradiction between community support of striking woodcutters and community interest in preserving the forests brought the following comment from one of the strikers:

We really don't want to cut down the trees at all, but on the other hand there isn't any other work to do. It looks strange to me that the government would be paying C.C.C.[19] boys a dollar a day for planting trees at the other end of the county while we are cutting them down around here for seventy-five cents a day.

Although such a program of the faraway but potent agency called the government failed to make sense, the community had boundless faith in government willingness and ability to assist in a struggle against a rich and powerful corporation. After half a year of fruitless correspondence with various government agencies, a committee was sent to Washington with affidavits showing living conditions and instances of discrimination by the local relief officials. Two thousand striking coal miners and textile workers in the area learned of the proposed trip and asked the committee to represent them also. A letter was sent to the Secretary of Labor[20] asking for an opportunity to present their problems. Arriving in Washington, they were informed by a secretary "the Secretary of Labor is in conference with some important industrial leaders and cannot be expected to give her personal attention to every delegation of workers that comes to see her."

After three days of waiting, part of the time without food, the woodcutters' committee returned home, their report adding the final word to a severe but practical course in community problems. The knowledge that their strike had been effective in saving the remnants of the forest did not buy shoes or feed hungry children.

Many of the people were discouraged, but others turned their attention to cooperatives as a solution to their problems. Fifteen men and women requested a class in the history and organization of cooperatives, which they attended two hours daily for two weeks. A number of possibilities were discussed. Seven families offered to pool their resources, totaling eleven scattered acres of poor land and two worn-out horses. It was decided that they would be only pooling their poverty. The only good farm in the community was for sale and, encouraged by a visiting government representative, a request was made to the F.E.R.A.[21] for a grant to finance a cooperative program. Not being certain of government aid and desiring to start a part of the cooperative program immediately, plans were made for a cannery. A large outdoor furnace and vat were made by the men. A sealer was purchased, and cans were obtained from a state relief agency. Each family grew what vegetables their land would produce and brought them to a central place where the canning equipment, which they owned in common, was located. Those who brought vegetables worked until all the canning was done. The produce was divided according to the amount each family brought. A total of one seventh was given to the democratically elected manager for central expenses.

Finally, the F.E.R.A. made a grant of $7,000 for purchasing land and getting equipment for a producer-consumer cooperative. Protests were made that the funds would be used by the Highlander Folk School "for the teaching of anti-American doctrines," by the president of the Southern States' Industrial Council[22] and others who opposed the organization of workers. The grant was withdrawn.

Still determined to experiment with producers' cooperatives, as well as to develop the buying club which had previously been started into a cooperative store, the members rented a plot of land and grew enough tomatoes for everyone. A record was kept of the work time, and after expenses had been deducted, the tomatoes were divided according to the amount of work done. The following summer a larger plot was rented. A mule had been contributed to the cooperative, and the members expected to grow and can surplus products for which they had already found a market. A prolonged drought destroyed everything that had been planted, leaving the members of the cooperative in debt.

The strike and cooperative ventures could have led to a spirit of futility on the part of those involved, but instead these experiences became the basis for a new approach. Discussion and analysis supplemented practical experience, and the community leaders whom the strike had developed arrived at three conclusions:

1. Their experience and the results of surveys made by government agencies, especially the T.V.A.,[23] offered convincing evidence that the natural resources of their own and numerous other mountain communities could not provide subsistence. Nevertheless, the problem of national unemployment forced them to remain where they were.
2. They assumed that the present form of government, local and national, could be counted on to do nothing objectionable to the owning class.
3. Their request for a cooperative grant had brought about a lining up of interest groups in which the only organizations to side with them had been the labor unions. The support of organized labor,

liberal ministers, and professors had encouraged them in their efforts to better their conditions. Uncritically they concluded that by joining hands with such friends immediate demands could be obtained, and political steps could soon be taken toward placing the national government under the control of the masses.

In effect, the community had swung from implicit faith in the government, through a period of lifting itself by its rotten boot straps, to a romantic conception of radical political action. Already, however, the pendulum had begun to settle somewhere between disillusionment and expectation of not-far-distant fundamental change. A $19.20 monthly wage rate for W.P.A.[24] work and a corrupt county relief administration, supported by a self-perpetuating and equally corrupt county political administration, had made organization for immediate protection a necessity for the relief workers.

Community students took the lead in organizing the relief workers into bona fide labor unions which received the support of organized labor elsewhere. As a result there are at present in the county three Common Laborers' Union locals made up of unskilled and semiskilled workers in W.P.A. and in private industry, and a local of the American Federation of Teachers. In addition to the unions organized by students and teachers of Highlander Folk School there are two locals of the United Mine Workers. The joint action of these unions, backed by the Chattanooga Central Labor Union and the Tennessee Federation of Labor, has resulted in improved working conditions and a slight increase in wages. Plans are being made, well in advance of the county elections, to replace county politicians with members qualified to serve the people.

Along with the growth of the unions, plans have developed for starting cooperative stores, and the people in the community still have hopes of working out a successful producer-consumer cooperative. The desire for fundamental economic change has not lessened; however, there is a growing realization that unions and cooperatives not only afford an answer to immediate problems but are also the schools in which they as workers are being trained for the new society.

In addition to this type of community education the school has provided music lessons for as many as twenty children and young people at a time. There are games on the recreation ground and in the school, and in the summer the community gathers to see plays on the outdoor stage. One year an active librarian created such an interest in reading that many more books than formerly were checked out of the school library weekly. Visiting lecturers join with the teachers in presenting social, economic, and political problems. There have been courses on war, race problems, the social teachings of the Bible, old and modern Russia, social developments in Scandinavian countries, and the labor movement in the South.

An evening is set aside each week for a community gathering. Usually the programs are informal and consist of singing and dancing and occasional discussions. A recent "community night" was devoted to a program on Germany. The young people had learned some native folk-songs, one of them in German, for the occasion. A representative of a local young people's organization reported on the plight of youth under fascism. A mother spoke on the position of women in modern Germany. A visiting speaker compared conditions in the South with conditions in Germany, pointing out the necessity for defending and extending democracy in America as a bulwark against fascism. The program ended with a German movie which had been banned by Hitler.

Square dancing has been revived and is the most popular form of entertainment. Young and old join in traditional mountain dances. An interest has been aroused in collecting and singing almost forgotten ballads and workers' songs of today. In addition to writing new songs, usually in ballad form, neighbors and students often reinterpret familiar songs to conform to their own experiences. Many of these songs have become popular and are being used by labor groups in neighboring states. Recently a program of ballads, workers songs, and native folk dances was broadcast from the Highlander Folk School to England by the British Broadcasting Corporation.

There is a growing respect for local history as well as an increasing interest in the cultural heritage of songs and dances. Old-timers are searching about in their memories for stories of the early settlers and are recalling their own experiences as striking miners, back in the days of the Knights of Labor.[25] Young people bring bits of information or clues to old records for a history of the county.

Residence Term

In contrast to the community program, the residence term for adult workers is a more extensive period of study lasting six weeks to two months. A majority of the students are sent by a union or cooperative, and they are expected to return better prepared to deal with the problems of their organizations. They are usually poorly equipped to study but are eager to learn. Education almost inevitably means academic training to them. The courses are made somewhat formal partially to meet their expectations. Yet the major part of our program is designed to encourage students to become a part of the community and to relate themselves to situations similar to those to which they will then return. As a part of their preparation, students attend union meetings in neighboring communities and assist in organizing campaigns in industrial communities and assist in organizing cooperative stores. The students go on weekly trips to out-of-the-way places where the school is helping to make local union meetings the centers of social and cultural activity.

Much of the formal teaching must be done by lectures and discussion or through graphic forms. Teaching is related to the experiences of the students.

There are classes in labor history and economics, workers' problems, tactics, current events, public speaking, parliamentary law, and labor dramatics. Students learn to write by putting out a weekly news bulletin, to speak simply by speaking at the school and in union meetings and by analyzing and criticizing their own efforts. In the same manner, parliamentary law is learned by practice. Much of this practical training is unified in a mock American Federation of Labor convention, regularly held at the end of each term. Here, students discuss in dramatic fashion the current issues confronting the labor movement. At all times teachers are available to supply help when needed. The teacher's job is to speed up the natural learning process, not to warp it by becoming academic.

Students learn to work together creatively. During one term the teacher in charge of dramatics guided them in writing and producing a short play about the union struggles of sharecroppers.[26] Factual material and union songs (all of which are spirituals reinterpreted by sharecroppers) were supplied by sharecropper students from Arkansas. Another song, both words and music, was created out of the spontaneous effort of the group for use in the play. Songs and play expressed the spirit of the union struggle against arrogant and brutal planters. The play was received with enthusiasm by people on the mountain and in nearby cities.

Life at the school is democratically managed by students and teachers who share the necessary routine work and make all plans relating to the welfare of the group. This experience in working out the practical problems of cooperative living is by no means a small part of the educational program.

In addition to the residence terms, held twice a year, there are informal weekend conferences. Usually only a few people attend these conferences, but occasionally the group is larger. Once, seventy people gathered from four states to discuss new methods of workers' education. At weekend gatherings of this type much of the time is given to recreation in the form of singing, outdoor games, and hiking on the mountain. Sometimes the school is reserved by one group which combines business and recreation. With the growth of the labor movement in the South, the school is being used more frequently for specializ[ed] purposes. For example, one labor union has requested that a two weeks' course be planned for its members alone. Preparations are being made for a special labor-cooperative institute.

Extension Work

The seven regular staff members spend part of their time in the field as union organizers and in extending workers' education into areas where our program is requested.[27] Many of these field contacts involve working with former students in their own communities and organizations. One student living in a rural section has for three years maintained an extensive library. Other students are active labor organizers and teachers in local workers' education programs. Teachers are available for schools organized by unions for the training of their members. Indeed, a staff member recently taught in two such schools for union sharecroppers.[28]

The Highlander Program and the Community

The community has taken part in all phases of the Highlander Folk School program, and this common interest has created a spirit of solidarity. The tension growing out of deep-rooted feuds and the rivalry for jobs is being relieved as people are brought together by the economic and social activities of the school. The people think of the school as their own and are willing to defend it. They have had occasion to do so. When the school had been in existence only a few months, there was strong evidence for believing that the officials of a mining company and a hosiery mill whose workers had been helped in a strike by staff members and students, had jointly hired a gunman to dynamite the school.[29] The neighbors volunteered to help guard the school day and night for several weeks. Two years later, people from the community stood guard when the press reported that a group of delegates from a state convention of the American Legion, meeting two miles away at Monteagle, threatened to "march on the school."[30]

More recently, an effort was made by the chairman of the Chattanooga Americanization Committee of the American Legion to discredit the school. Immediately a vigorous defense was made in a public statement signed by most of the people in the community. Resolutions of confidence in the school were passed by local unions in the county. The Chattanooga Central Labor Union joined the local protest with a resolution "condemning such attacks on the Highlander Folk School as an indirect attack on the Chattanooga labor movement and the organized labor movement in general," and expressing confidence in the conduct of the school and the character of its work.

The cultural program of the school has given the people a taste of the advantages life holds just beyond their reach and has been one of the factors creating a desire for a just and rational social order. A knowledge that such a society is possible through their efforts has added purpose and dignity to life. Economic problems are no less pressing, but they are being faced more intelligently and courageously in the knowledge that other workers are also looking toward the new day.

A Suggested Community-School Curriculum for Summerfield

The Highlander Folk School program, the community analysis, and the educational philosophy previously indicated provide a basis for the following outline of a community-school curriculum. Such an outline should be considered a starting point rather than a rigid plan and would be subject to constant revision. It should be noted that the curriculum is planned for a period of social transition. Under a genuine democracy the emphasis would necessarily be different.

Purposive education rooted in a community calls for a new type of curriculum. The community is composed of persons of all ages working and living together. Therefore, the community school should be a place where persons of all ages can get the kind of education they need. Like other educative forces, the school must educate from childhood throughout life. Times change, and unless education is continuous, people will become uneducated as they grow older. Also, the curriculum must be developed along unified lines to meet the needs of the various age groups. The departmentalized curriculum is foreign to the life of the child or adult and to the organization of the community.

Starting with the resources at hand in Summerfield, the first step would be to coordinate the work of the elementary school and the Highlander Folk School. A nursery school should be added at once. A neighborhood school, replacing the conventional junior and senior high schools, would complete the framework. At first, greater liberties would be taken with the spirit of the education than with the form. Changes that might prove too disturbing could be made slowly. Children might for a time still be allowed to take home grade cards marked with ABCs and perhaps for a few years they would be allowed to pass from one grade to the next, and even to graduate. However, as soon as public support could be gained, a unified program of community education extending from the nursery school throughout life would be developed.

Nursery School

A nursery school would be welcomed especially by the mothers, many of whom work away from home and are forced to leave the older children in charge of their younger brothers and sisters. Parents would cooperate in running the nursery school by taking turns at assisting the teacher in charge. Parent and child education would thus go hand in hand. As the children grew older, a pre-elementary school would be established to continue the educational process. The first children to enter the nursery school would not profit as much from the experience as those who follow them whose parents have learned that education begins when the child is introduced to its first group, the family.

Just as the family life is a powerful factor in determining the social attitudes of the child, the community life or membership in a larger group chiefly determines the attitudes of the youth and adult population. On the whole, it is the way people live in the community that is the dominant factor in shaping attitudes. Therefore, education from nursery school on should have for its primary objective the transformation of the community.

Elementary School

Elementary education would start with the interests of the individual and relate them to the life of the community. Reading, writing, and arithmetic would be introduced as the children became conscious of the need for them. This would call for individual work. As common interests develop, group teaching would be added. However, a period would not be set aside each day for a lesson in drawing or reading. A child cannot piece together and retain bits of information given in scheduled doses. Group teaching must be based on group interests and lead to group experience. Given the proper environment in the form of a schoolroom with the atmosphere of a workshop and a teacher whose enthusiasm is contagious, interests can always be discovered or created. Tool subjects would be taught in connection with activities.

For example, assisting in putting on a community fair and carnival could be the basis for active learning experiences in the first years of elementary education. Children would be stimulated to print, draw, read, and write simple plots in which they would be the actors. The desire for group approval and admiration of adults would make them more sensitive to poor painting, misspelled words, and inability to draw, than would numerous corrections from the teacher. In addition to awakening an interest in basic subject matter, such an activity would give the children an experience in which plans would be made and carried out. They would get a sense of accomplishment and an opportunity to evaluate their work by comparing the results with better examples of similar work done by other pupils or exhibited by the teacher.

An interest in our own and foreign countries could be aroused by comparing and contrasting social conditions and customs in foreign lands with those which can be seen in the community. Life beyond the borders of the immediate community could be made real by stories, pictures, maps, songs, dances, and dramatics. Likewise, the past should be brought to life. In early childhood the world is a dim and confused pattern. Gradually the home and the neighborhood begin to take shape. A trip to a neighboring community or a visit to a city enlarges the pattern. Graphic information and stories add other countries and ages to the pattern. The surface picture of the world grows less confusing, but the underlying forces and conflicts will be understood only by looking at society over and over until it is possible to see beneath the surface. But even looking beneath the surface is not enough.

Too many histories focus the child's attention on wars of acquisition and on presidents. Instead, the struggle of the masses for democracy must be made central. The economic background and social consequences of the American and French Revolutions would be studied and contrasted with the causes and results of the Russian Revolution.

Attention should be given to the struggles of American workers for the legal right to organize. Their daring and eventually successful efforts to gain shorter working hours, higher wages, and public education would be considered as milestones along the pathway to a democratic society.

If we desire robust thought and action from children, their emotions must be educated. Dramatics is perhaps the best medium for reaching the child's emotions. This is especially true when music and dancing are included. Children, and adults too, need to visualize human situations to be able fully to comprehend them.

Handicraft and artwork should be represented in such a way that beautiful things would not be thought as unattainable luxury but as necessary parts of life. Beautiful things would be made for use in home and school. Considerable time would be spent outside of the schoolroom, studying natural history, observing the life of the community, and in recreation. Useful work for the community would be a part of the curriculum. It should be carried on where practicable with both young people and adults.

Surveys could be made of living standards and working conditions, and of the attitude of voters on important questions. The cooperation of the entire community should be enlisted in bringing about the desired improvements. Surveys could be made of local trees, flowers, herbs, and wildlife. Far too little is known about fruit and nut-bearing trees and the various uses of timber for making furniture. A program of reforestation and preservation of animal and plant life would be of great social value. In connection with a general health program the young people could make a vital contribution to community life by demanding and helping provide for fresh fruits, vegetables, eggs, and milk to be produced and distributed cooperatively.

Group activities, both inside the school room and in the larger community, afford an excellent training in democratic behavior. Social and creative rather than competitive and possessive tendencies should be encouraged. The experiences from which children learn most are those in which there is a natural interest in the outcome. This fact, and the knowledge that standards and actions are strongly influenced by the desire to belong, and to win status by doing the things approved by the group, should make the directing of natural groups, such as gangs, an important item in the curriculum.

Neighborhood School

A natural transition could be provided from the elementary to the neighborhood school. Individuals or groups should be advanced as soon as they are prepared to understand the larger problems and to participate in more mature activity. Records of individual and group work would be used to determine such readiness.

Workshops supplied with books, periodicals, newspapers, maps, charts, mimeograph, and typewriter would furnish the basis of operation. The number of such workshops should depend upon the number of the children and teachers. It would be desirable to have a teacher directing the activities of each shop, assisted, when necessary, by other members of the community-school staff.

Vocational training of a specialized nature would not be included in the curriculum. The mechanization of industry and the uncertainty of securing the job prepared for limits its value. Agricultural training, sewing and cooking, health, and sanitation education would be planned for the entire community. For practical results in these fields the cooperation of adults is, of course, essential. Handicraft, artwork, dramatics, and community singing would be continued from the elementary school. Individual study in art, voice, and instrumental music would be encouraged for the enrichment of individual and community life. Natural and physical sciences would be taught. Learning in the natural sciences, for example, would be carried on largely by means of field trips. Plant and animal life in the neighborhood of the school would be examined. This type of education would give the students an appreciation of their natural surroundings. Provision would be made for those interested in pursuing a more systematic study of these subjects. The social sciences, however, should form the basis for the community-school curriculum and will be discussed more in detail as an example of the emphasis and method advocated by the writer.

Material found in separate fields of social science should be unified around activities related to community needs and problems such as the improvement of economic and cultural organizations, elevating health standards, enriching home life, and preserving and extending an appreciation of natural and cultural surroundings. The necessity for a great deal of information would lead to a study of history, economics, cultural and physical geography, civics, sociology, and psychology. Students would be assisted in following their interests into related fields of knowledge such as philosophy, ethics, and religions. Systematic study would be expected, but carefully selected historical novels, biographies, and other worthwhile literature should replace the usual textbook, with its presentation of stereotyped events and facts.

In general, the struggle for democracy would be enlarged upon and critically examined. Society should be pictured as ever changing. Students would study tribal society, chattel slavery, serfdom, and the various stages of capitalism. Emphasis would be placed not on wars, kings, and those who have acquired great fortunes, but on the way people earn their living and on their struggles for freedom. Revolutionary changes would be traced to their economic roots, but would not be dehumanized by ignoring the heroic men and women who have made history live. Understanding, will not come simply by presenting historical facts in chronological order. It comes only by shuttling back and forth from present to past situations.

Democratic ideals should be contrasted with infringements of civil liberties familiar to the children of world people. Denial of the right of free speech to minority groups such as Communists, and in some places to labor organizers, would be discussed. A study would be made of the extralegal functions of vigilante organizations which openly and secretly commit acts of violence against union organizers and radical political leaders. Thus segregation, inequality of opportunity, and lynching of Negroes would be analyzed. Other infringements considered might be the herding of unorganized industrial workers, farm laborers, and the sharecroppers to the polls by their employers. Such studies should lead to a critical attitude toward political democracy and the knowledge of its limitations without a basis in economic democracy.

Social theories such as socialism, communism, and fascism would be discussed freely. Countries where these theories are being tried would be examined in the light of democratic ideals. Capitalism as we know it in America would be studied at length. Starting with the local situation, a study would be made of poverty, insecurity, depressions, the relationship of the rural to the industrial worker, our political parties, and organized interest groups. The relation of economics to imperialistic war would be dealt with. The potentialities of our country would be investigated. A study would be made of our natural resources, the emerging power age, and our engineering and managerial ability. Students would learn how goods are produced and distributed. Stock would be taken of the trends in our economic life and of the interest groups which are endeavoring to direct or obstruct the trends. An appraisal of their activities would be made in terms of our democratic ideals. Youth would be dismayed by the magnitude of such problems were it not for the fact that they would also be taught that human organizations can translate the ideals of democracy into reality.

An important phase of community activity would center in the enrichment of the social and cultural life and the elevation of the standard of living by means of cooperatives, unions, and youth organizations. Out of the union and cooperative activity would grow an interest in the theories back of these organizations and the labor movement in general. Youth would be given instruction in the function and structure of economic and political organizations of wage earners.

Adult Program

The working-class nature of the community would suggest that the adult program of the school consist primarily of workers' education. Adult education, concerned as it usually is with passing on traditional information, would contribute little to community transformation. Workers' education, like all organized education, is too often stripped of emotional content. This could be avoided by a folk approach to workers' education which would root it in the everyday lives and dreams of the people. Without emotional energy thus generated, a sustained effort against overwhelming odds is impossible. Description and analysis and practical training are not enough. There must be a dynamic for social change.

The adult needs of the present generation are somewhat different from the needs of a generation which will have received the schooling outlined. A generation having been influenced by the community school from childhood should approach maturity with some understanding of the class nature of capitalistic society and the problems brought about by the exploitation of human and natural resources. It will be familiar with the background and some of the practical problems of cultural, economic, and political organizations of the working class. It will have had training in public speaking, writing, and parliamentary law. Youth, having already become intelligently active in community affairs, would be ready for organized adult action. A greater part of the curriculum for adult groups would then be devoted to activities, discussions, tactics, current events, and lectures. If the community school is to succeed, we cannot wait for a new generation to grow up. We must face present adult problems. The educational attack on community backwardness and indifference for adults must be based not so much on the fact that adults can learn as on the encouraging discovery that they can unlearn.

Evenings in the community school would be used by the adults for informal gatherings, organized meetings, classes, and lectures. One evening each week could be set aside for a social occasion where all ages would join in square dances, group singing, and other forms of self-entertainment. The nature of the classes would depend upon problems or interests. Whatever the subject, the teaching would be informal, simple, and graphic. Ample time would be allowed for discussion. Day classes would be conducted when requested or found necessary to meet specific situations.

All adult members of the community would be encouraged to attend a two months' session for more intensive education, spending all possible time at the school. It has been found that people from Summerfield and other communities are delighted to have such an opportunity. Neighbors and unions join in supporting the families of such students when it is otherwise impossible for them to attend. Provision should be made for students outside the community to live at the new community school. Resident students will be one means of spreading the idea of a community school to other localities. Intimate association with workers from nearby rural and industrial centers will, moreover, broaden the outlook of the local people.

The life of adults at such a combination residence and day school would be carried on cooperatively. The school would in no sense, however, be a utopian colony cut off from the community. Cooperative living would be considered an educational activity and would be used as a basis for an analysis of democracy. Students would share in making the curriculum, which would include planning and doing the work necessary for orderly existence, group living, and the carrying on of classes. The first few days of any session would be devoted to the pooling of individual statements by the students, covering their background, problems, community and labor experience, and what each wants to get from the school. This information and past experience with similar student groups would serve as the basis for the curriculum. Recommendations by the teachers would be made subject to the student approval. The curriculum would remain flexible.

Judging from past experience, it would be necessary to approach the problems and needs of the adult group from various angles. Labor history, economics, and political science would be unified and made the basis of one approach. There would be a class in tactics, which would include union organization and strikes, rural-urban sociology, and problems peculiar to the region. Visitors with practical experience would be utilized in such a class. The history and organization of cooperatives would be taught. There would be instruction in public speaking and parliamentary law carried on in connection with actual experience in speaking and conducting meetings. Labor journalism and dramatics would be other approaches. Personal problems would be given individual attention. Capable students would assist the teachers in tutoring those who find it difficult to read or write well.

Theory and practice would be combined in all educational work. The starting point in a labor-history course would be the economic problems familiar to the group. The desire and necessity of organized action should be one of the results of a properly planned survey of labor history and the phases of political science bearing directly on the workers' struggles. Visual-education methods and experience in a social-science workshop doing simple research and organizing the findings in graphic form would supplement lectures and discussion. Journalism would consist of editing and mimeographing daily bulletins and a weekly bulletin to be distributed in the communities represented and to former students. Dramatics would consist of writing and producing plays based on familiar and significant experiences. Fieldwork with nearby unions and cooperatives, and participation in community life would keep such a program realistic and enable the students to work out methods and test ideas in relation to actual situations similar to the ones to which they will return.

Community-School Teachers

The success of the community school will depend on the teachers. Specialists in imparting information must be replaced by teachers who have an understanding of individual personalities and their relationship to the community and to society as a whole. Learning must not be meager, but must supplement practical experience. Teachers must live in the community and take active part in community life. They should seek to coordinate the most advanced thinking and become identified with progressive influences. It is not sufficient to advocate abstract principles. Human organizations are the sole means of transforming ideals into action. Both as citizens and educators, teachers belong with the working class. The struggle for academic freedom and for adequate financial support makes it necessary for teachers to unite with other workers to protect the public schools and the ideals for which the masses of the people are striving.

Administration

The most democratic aspect of community life should be found in the administration and methods of the school, which should exemplify ideals diametrically opposed to the undemocratic administration of big business. The master and servant relationship between teachers and administrators is foreign to the spirit of a community school. Every interest in the community should be represented. The school should be administered by representatives of parents, students, teachers, unions, cooperatives, and of the community as a whole. A democratically selected director or coordinator would be charged with the responsibility of keeping the whole group unified. Once a policy was decided upon, it would be the director's responsibility to see that it was efficiently executed. A maximum of responsibility and freedom would be delegated to the individual teachers who would be encouraged to use their initiative in putting policies into effect.

Summary

The development of many educational programs seeking to transform community living would contribute to the improvement of the present standard of living throughout the United States by introducing more effective methods of developing and utilizing natural and human resources. The benefits of such efforts would be safeguarded and extended by membership in cooperatives and unions and by organized political action. At the same time it must be recognized that, regardless of skill and organization, there are limitations set to progress by local natural resources and by our present economic system. The thwarting of desires created by the cultural activities of a community school would lead to a spirit of futility if these limitations were accepted as permanent. But by thinking of community education as a part of the age-old struggle of the masses for democracy, what would otherwise be hopeless drudgery is turned into a preliminary battle and becomes a meaningful part of the fight for a better society.

The Layman's Stake in Education: As a Member of Organized Labor Views It

[1952]

The following was originally presented as a speech at the April 2, 1952, meeting of the North Central Association of Colleges and Secondary Schools in Chicago, Illinois. It was later reprinted in the October 1952 North Central Association Quarterly, from which the text for this edition is taken. In the original printed version, Horton is identified as the "Educational Director of the United Packing House Workers Union, Monteagle, Tennessee," a post he occupied from 1951 to 1953 while directing a specific education program for the union. In this talk, one of his last as an active participant in the labor movement, Horton emphasizes the importance of the link between public education and the work of unions, especially with regard to the promotion of education for citizenship and democracy.

We have a way of making dreams come true and one of our great American dreams was of a free and universal system of education. Our forefathers dreamed of education that would provide for all people the enlightenment necessary for citizenship, "Free to the children of rich and poor alike."

Labor joined with other advocates of public education in launching a movement rooted in the needs and dreams of the people. "The vitality of the movement for tax supported schools was derived," said a historian of this period, "not from humanitarian leaders, but from the growing class of wage earners." Later, Beard was to state that organized labor took a lead "in demanding from the legislator the establishment of free and equal schools."[31]

Labor people seldom attend a convention without being reminded of organized labor's role in establishing free schools in the face of opposition from the more respectable elements. The feeling is generally conveyed that public education is a dream come true, that public schools are a cure-all for whatever ails us. Labor, however, is not altogether uncritical. An effort was made to recapture some of the dreams of splendor by advocating vocational training of children of workers, a poor substitute for education for citizenship. On the whole, labor's role has been too much that of an outsider. This has certainly been true regarding participation in secondary education.

Let us take a look at the development of high schools and of labor's passive role in their development. The high school is a young institution in American educational history and was not an immediate outgrowth of the movement for mass education. In fact, the early high schools prepared students for college and did little else. Even today most high schools are better fitted for educating the one out of five students who go to college than for educating the majority who go out to earn a living. The fact that most students go to work and not to college has had too little influence on the high school program.

Vocational education attempted to remedy this situation. It not only fails to give the student an understanding of the world in which he will have to live but does not even provide the training needed for a livelihood. Vocational training has never been more than a patchwork affair.

It is also worthy of note that the high schools became institutionalized and got set in their ways during a period when our philosophy was that of individualism, when education was keyed to getting ahead.

The high school was naturally a product of its time, tailored to meet certain limited needs of the day. But times have changed. The early program has lost much of its meaning. Today, students must be taught to unite with others in a common struggle for a decent standard of living and to stand together against bigotry and war. Only by working together can the individual become a worthwhile part of society.

High schools, your association declares, "must promote the principles and spirit of American democracy." This forthright statement of purpose has a tug to it but not enough of a tug to offset the force of practices that run contrary to the purpose.

What of the practices in high schools? Are the schools set up from top to bottom on a democratic basis? Are the policy-making bodies representative of the people in the community? Is the relationship of administrator to teacher and teacher to student democratic? Do all have a voice in policy making?

High purposes can be nullified by the manner in which the school is organized and administered. Democratic principles must be incorporated into the structure and conduct of every facet of school life. Gandhi said it this way, "The value we seek in the goals must appear in the means we employ."[32]

The average school board members, for example, come from business and the professions. However, most students come from working families and homes of white-collar employees. There are few children of employers simply because there are few employers. The presence of one or two labor people on a school board may be a friendly gesture or it may be window dressing, but it can hardly be considered representative, especially in cities where about four-fifths of the children come from homes of workers.

If the administrator's primary concern is with buildings and budgets rather than with the democratic organization of people, there will not be the kind of cooperation which is essential. Genuine cooperation is possible only when all affected by a policy share in making it.

The professional relationships of teachers must be democratic. They should have a union so they can practice the democracy they teach. "Our whole educational system suffers," says John Dewey, "from the divorce between head and hand, between work and books, between action and ideas, a divorce which symbolizes the segregation of teachers from the rest of the workers who form the great mass of the community."[33]

Students must be given the opportunity to learn from experience how the democratic process works. Teaching about democratic goals is not enough. Students learn far more from what they see and do, from the way they live, than from all the verbalizing to which they are exposed. The democratic principles should apply to the relationship of students one to another and with teachers and administrators. Students should certainly take part in making and carrying out school policies.

The high schools in many instances fall far short of the dream of democratic education.

What happened to labor? Why hasn't something been done about the situation? When the dream became a movement, labor was in the forefront, but when the victorious movement resulted in the establishment of institutions, organized workers took a backseat. The infant's upbringing was left to the teachers and to the better-educated citizenry. The high school teachers brought over their ideas from the private school, the only school they knew; and the better educated, being also the better off financially, shaped the schools to their own interest.

Labor, poorly organized and trustful, allowed the schools to drift into an alliance with the privileged. Labor's failure to follow through was not due to a lack of interest. Labor had failed to grasp the nature of institutions.

Labor's role in the movement for public education cannot be disputed, but labor's failure to follow through and guide the destiny of the schools that it helped make possible is a different and less commendable story. Labor is becoming aware of this weakness but has not fully accepted the responsibility for doing a proper share of the day-by-day chores. Labor must help put life and vision in the institutional framework.

While labor must accept its share of the blame, what of those to whom labor looked for guidance? The institutional side of the school which they neglected has absorbed too much of the attention of the school people. Too much time has been devoted to keeping the machinery of the institutions oiled and running. Too often sight has been lost of public education as a democratic movement. Spirit and purpose has been subordinated to framework.

Perhaps labor needs schools today less than the schools need labor. If the schools are to halt the present retreat and become truly democratic, understanding and constant support of labor is necessary. In the long run no other groups will have the will to fight off encroachments on democratic education. The basic interest of labor and the schools is the same. Educators should make it clear that the school needs labor's democratic strength that labor should share in the policymaking and running of the schools.

"A school system," says the National Education Association, "which uses all the means at its command to create an understanding of the school's program and which invites the close cooperation of parents and other citizens in educational planning, will build a community-school relationship in which the popular mode of behavior is to support and befriend the schools, not attack them."[34]

With organized labor and public education united in vision and in daily operations we would be in a position to make democracy a reality. No longer would distinction of class, of race, and of religion be tolerated. The schools could rise to the challenge of the day and help in the creation of an army of democracy rooted in the struggles and traditions of the American people, an army so vast and do determined that nothing undemocratic could stand in its path.

Study the Power Structure

[1968]

This talk was originally presented at the Consultation on Appalachia–Rural Poverty in North America, which was sponsored by the Commission on Youth Service Projects in Berea, Kentucky, February 26–29, 1968. The text printed here is derived from a transcript of the proceedings and includes the speech only and not the question-and-answer period that followed. In this speech, Horton makes connections between Highlander's previous work with the labor movement and civil rights movement and its then current work with the Appalachian program by emphasizing the necessity of working with, rather than on behalf of, people. In doing so, he warns against coming into a situation as any kind of missionary who will "save the people" from whatever oppression they supposedly face.

The Highlander Folk School started back in 1932, before there was any talk of the industrial union movement in this country. We spent the first few years doing what we're trying to do now—find a way to organize the poor people of Appalachia, most of them unemployed.[35] My credentials for speaking to you tonight can, perhaps, be based primarily on that early experience when we had to improvise and try to do things without any formal structure.

When you talk about who runs Appalachia, or who runs America, and when you talk about how you're going to research, you find that we can take two approaches: one, the academic—where you work out questionnaires and you ask the people who are supposed to be running the country what they do, starting with the justice of the peace and [the] county court and the county judge. Or, you can take another approach: you can try to work with the disinherited, the poor, and you can learn that way what the power structure is. I don't want to depreciate the more academic approach. In fact, I kind of worked my way through graduate school doing this kind of thing and I know something about questionnaires, something about interviewing. I know that, within limits, they tell you *something* about the power structure. But, I don't think this is applicable to most of the people who are here tonight and who will be working out in Appalachia. I think the better way to learn about the power structure and to investigate it is to try to do something in a local way which will illuminate the problem for you.

Now, just let me cite an experience we had in Grundy County, Tennessee, which sounds very much like a lot of Appalachia today. Grundy County was one of the eleven poorest counties in Appalachia in the early thirties. It was a coal mine area; there was strip mining then, not much but a little. The union, which had been organized several years ago, had been broken and the people were in a very discouraged, despondent state. The Highlander Folk School started, not [as] an organizing program, but [as] an educational program—an educational program based on the idea that the best way to serve people is to find out what their needs are and what kind of service they want. A rather radical idea, even today. And, we moved into a little house in this rural area and we said to the people, "What can we do as a group of people who want to do something educationally to help you with your problems?" And they said "nothing," because education to them meant reading, writing, arithmetic, or doing a little something else.

We sat long enough and finally started talking about the problems. We sat and listened and learned and we started working with very nonacademic problems like "How can people eat during a depression?" "What do you do if your child needs to got to the hospital?" "What do you do in a situation there the whole town is controlled by the people who own the mines and the timberlands which has been cut off?" I don't want to go into the history of the Highlander Folk School, but I want to suggest that this enabled us to reach people on their own terms.

The first thing that happened is something very unspectacular; people were cutting pulpwood, called bugwood, and they were getting fifty cents a day. They were working very hard, and a fellow named Henry Thomas, a mountaineer, who had been a bit disturbed about that after some meetings where we talked, not about organizing, but about people, said, "It takes a strong back, and a weak mind, a sharp axe to cut bug wood at fifty cents a day, so, let's strike."[36] Well, this threw the whole area into pandemonium—

hungry people striking for what? It wasn't a terribly important strike in the sense that there were any great issues involved. In fact, the demands were contradictory: they want a dollar a day and they wanted to stop cutting wood. Those were their written demands, and they carried those demands to Washington to Madam Perkins.[37] They did a lot of things to get those demands carried out. They were not bothered about contradictions—only intellectuals worry about contradictions. They knew what they wanted, they wanted to live and they also didn't want to spoil their forests, like the people in Appalachia today want to live and they don't want to have the strip miners tear off the land.

This [was] the beginning of something, something that they themselves brought to us, not what we brought to them. Well, as a result of this beginning, we started talking about cooperatives, we also started talking about meeting with other organizations around the country. We started talking about trying to get private industry into the country. We started talking about government help. And, pretty soon the people found out that they had a source of energy, a tremendous source of energy, that had been created by this organization around bugwood with the contradictory purpose, which was unused, [under]utilized, and undirected. And they started to ask "What can we do further?" They found, after talking about the matter, that they could start some co-ops. They worked that for a while, [but] it didn't bring in any special amount of money; it was kind of like swappin' poverty. Then they decided they needed to do something politically because county officials were not too sympathetic about their problems when they were talking about organizing politically.

They set up ten or twelve unions in that little community, just the bugwood cutters and the miners, and they got confidence they didn't know they had. Then they said, "let's run our own candidates for office. Let's not try to fight the thing through the regular machinery. Let's name our own people as candidates and elect them." And they [developed] their own strategy, meeting after meeting, discussion after discussion. All of which had an educational value to us.

We were more concerned about people getting educated, thinking for themselves, acting for themselves, than anybody taking power. We hadn't thought in terms of today when you say that you are going to "take over a country" or have political action. We were thinking in terms of people developing, and understanding their problems and doing what they themselves thought they wanted to and could do. Well, as a result of this kind of approach, furnishing educational services and encouraging people to think through their problems on their own, they worked out a very sophisticated strategy. I had the advantage of going to some good schools, studied political science and I was also an avid reader. I read practically everything I could find on political action. But, gee, these people in the mountains, they figured out some strategy that works. They won every post in the county.[38]

Every one! They carried eleven offices. You talk about independent action by working people. There it was, they had it.

I hear people talking today about independent political action. They are going to start a campaign to start talking about it. Well, these people did it. This was about 1936. Now what happened? I don't want to discourage you, I just want you to get a kind of picture of them before we talk about it. The state of Tennessee, my state, just thought that this was an unheard-of thing. Working people, poor people, unemployed people electing all of the officers! And what did they do? They said, "We will not recognize them." Not that the election was illegal, not that they didn't win. But, you know, "we just can't tolerate this kind of thing." So when you talk about the power structure, you start telling people who come into Appalachia to study what happens in the county seat as if just knowing what is going on is going to make any great difference. I would like to remind you that here was a group of people who had the sheriff, the county judge, the school superintendent, and everybody else, and the state says "Fooey on you!" And, they cut off the revenue from the county which paid the sheriff's salary, for example. We had to pass the hat and raise some money to pay our officers. But we did it, you know, by having a lot of publicity and demonstrations and so on to take over their rightful responsibilities. I'm telling you this to say that this is a tough problem we talk about when we talk about dealing with the power structure. It isn't just enough to survey it or it isn't enough to think it over. You have got to think in terms of a large enough unit where you can have power.

As a result of that, we got together and decided that we would organize a four county area and maybe there could do it.[39] And then we thought maybe we would organize a state and we could do it. But, in the meantime, the momentum was lost, and business-as-usual took precedence. We never got anywhere, but, as I said, I'm not telling you this to discourage you, but to point out how difficult it is to do, anything with studying the power structure. You need to do a little advance thinking and not think that a bunch of questionnaires, a bunch of interviews are going to tell you anything.

Now let me start over in another way. When I was in school I learned in some civics classes, and later on in political science courses in college and universities, that there is a structure—city, county, and federal government and so on. And I kind of believed these things—that they were operated by the people who were elected in the democratic way. That these people took these offices where they performed certain functions and that was our government. I believed that. That was one part of my training. And another part of my training was that people have motivations, they have values, they are supposed to live a certain kind of life. And, I was taught to believe that if a person was a good person, went to church, and didn't beat his wife, did all the things that he is supposed to do, that if this person got elected to one of these offices which I had learned about in civics, then he'd be good, he'd do good things.

Now, let me just tell you something. I've learned that there is no connection, absolutely none, between these two ideas. So when you talk about researching the power structure, you have to have two tabulation sheets. Now, if you want to keep records on who is going to heaven, then you've got one tabulation sheet. He is a good man—he does this, he pays his bills, goes to church, good to his neighbors, he even does good things for people he doesn't know! He gives money to the church for missionaries in Africa. You know he is interested in people and he wants to help them, and some of them are so sophisticated, so enlightened, that they even give money to send a Mississippi Negro to school. You see they are good people. Now, you take score high "A" for this man. That is, he rates high on the going-to-heaven sheet. Or, you know, the conventional what's good sheet.

Now you elect this good man to office, and, parenthetically, I have to say here that I'm drawing on my relatives. I grew [up] in a family where my father was a circuit court clerk, and I kind of grew up in a courthouse, where I knew all these good people. Now if these good people, "A" rating people, and heaven people, if they get into office, what do they do? Well, then you have to switch to another kind of sheet. That sheet says "how do they perform?" Not "are they good people?" "How do they perform? How do they perform in terms of doing things for people, all people, because when you get in the political arena you can't say "he gives money for missions in Africa," or that "he helps some poor Appalachian or some poor Negro." You've got to say "what is the result of his vote?" His action? So you have another tabulation sheet.

Now, I just say that there is no correlation between the two sheets because this man, this good man gets into office, and for some reasons which I have never been able to figure out—I have tried because I don't quite understand this yet—he gets into office, and he becomes a different person. He is an official person in office, and as an official person his concerns have not been the people, but money. He doesn't have any money, but he is concerned about money, saving taxes, for some strange reason.

A metamorphosis takes place and this person-oriented "good man" suddenly becomes the custodian of property of people very much unlike himself. He doesn't have any, but for some reason he wants to protect the property of other people, in the name of what's good-and-holy. Then, he spends the rest of his life trying to see that taxes are low, services are reduced to the minimum, and that the poor people are "put in their place."

Now, this happens. If you don't believe it, just go into your own county and look around. You will find that this is what happens. Why? I don't know. I can't even give you a clue to it. For example, recently, in Knoxville I had some work done at my house and I had a Negro carpenter there, a good, honest workman, tin-skilled, who had a hard time getting a job. We had an election in Knoxville just recently, and just to make conversation I asked him who he is going to vote for, and he said that he was going to vote for a certain candidate. Some of you people in that area know this one. This man is a merchant there, who is a type of demagogue.[40] He has a radio program in the early morning in which he talks to the country people and he makes fun of rich people, and Jews, and Negroes, and college people, and then when he gets on the radio in the afternoon he tells what wonderful people they are. He is a real operator. Well, this man has a paper which he puts out called the *Watch Dog*.[41] The *Watch Dog* takes care of the "people's interests." He spends a lot of his time attacking Highlander, but the real objective of the paper is attacking the mayor. He doesn't like the mayor because the mayor won't do what he wants him to do. But he always talks about "protecting the people against tax-gouges." He is a Watch Dog and the Watch Dog primarily means that he is going to keep us "Communists" quieted down. He is going to keep the mayor under control and he is going to keep people's taxes low. So this Negro said, "I'm gonna vote for this man," and I said, "Why?" He said, "He is our Watch Dog." What does that mean? He said, "Well, he keeps us, well, you know, if it wasn't for him we'd have to pay high taxes." And I said, "Now, that is interesting, how much taxes do you pay?" He said, "None." "Ever pay any taxes?" He said, "Never." "Ever expect to pay any?" "Never." And, I said. "Why are you so much concerned about the taxes?" He said, "Well, if taxes get high they will rob people and then the people will be unhappy and you know, you shouldn't just ask for too much taxes."

So, here is a poor Negro, who never paid any taxes, voting for a demagogue who is keeping the taxes low. He is just like most people in office. He thinks that for some mystic reason if you keep taxes low, that is a good thing.

Now, if you are going to do research on power structures, you've not only got this problem of having two tally sheets. Don't be thrown off by how pious and good the man is, because he is going to be a good person. My father was a good man, you know, all of my relatives who hold offices are good people, but they do the wrong thing when they get into office for reasons which I am not attempting to explain. You not only have that problem of good people doing bad things because they become public people, for some strange reason they don't carry this thing over.

But, you have another problem, which makes me a little leery of any kind of research on the power structure. My relatives, and other people like them, don't even know they really have been manipulated by somebody who has interest, behind the scenes, and whose name you will never find out, regardless [of] how much research you do. So you've got that problem, as well. Well in brief, if you are going to try to find out who runs

Appalachia, I would suggest that unless you've got at least ten years to stay in Appalachia, you skip it. That doesn't mean to say that I don't think that it isn't important. That doesn't mean to say that you couldn't help somebody who has been here long enough who could dig in deep enough to get some facts and work as a secretary for them or as a tabulator for them. But don't kid yourself that any of you could come down for three months or a year's time and even get beyond the heaven-keeping record. You know that is about as far as you would get—three states removed from the real source of power.

I think the important thing is to do the kind of things which we did in the earlier days of Highlander—to help people to get organized to the place where they expose the power structure. They can learn from their own experiences how it works. This is much more important than trying to make an academic analysis of what goes on. In fact, if I was in the seat of power, back behind the politicians, I would love nothing better than to have people focus endless hours and ergs of energy on investigating the structure of the county in which I operated. They would be completely useless for a period of years.

This may sound discouraging to people who somehow think of research as a contribution to make to Appalachia. I have been appalled at people who come down without any research experience. Research is a technical job. You have to know your business to do it properly. People come down and say, "I can't organize, I don't know enough, but I'm going to do research." Research meaning, "I'm going to look around and see what miscellaneous, unsupported facts I can get together and put on a piece off paper."

I'm against it unalterably. I think we have got to drop this whole concept of people doing research (except people who are capable of doing research) and have people come down to Appalachia and work with people. Work with people, develop the people to the place [where] they themselves want to know the difference between the good men and the politician and the man behind. This is the important thing because, let us just assume for a minute that this thing could be found out. So what! Unless the people in the region could understand it, and it means something to them, it has no value. Because you can't transfer this information from research sheet to people. So, I'm all for doing what I could call a "Horton kind of research." I would like to see people come down to Appalachia (and this is a hard thing to expect) under the guidance of people who have already been here and know something and do what would seem to be routine work (but which is very important) to help build up a body of information that would stay with the people and would help them understand what is going on. But that body of information would only be meaningful as it was related to the struggles of the people themselves and the questions coming from the people themselves.

I think that we are mixed up at one point here, and in the academic world, I think we are mixed up on this point too. There may be some very strong reactions to what I'm about to say. Many people think there is a transference, a transference of information in a usable form, from somebody who does it in a kind of vacuum to somebody who is working in the real situation. I do not believe that this is true.

I challenge anybody to give me any evidence that any research, or that any information which I have, will be accepted by any of you in an actual situation if you don't understand it and if it doesn't relate to what you know yourself. To accumulate information per se is not a contribution. But to accumulate information which helps people's problems and helps people do what they want to do is a tremendous contribution. I think that it is in this area where people with academic training can be helpful, but not if you say that information per se has any value. I feel very deeply about that because I think tremendous energy is wasted in this country. People are thinking that the accumulation of a lot of miscellaneous information is going to do us a lot of good, except that to be relatable and usable means that it has got to be worked out with the people who are going to use it.

I know what kind of meeting this is, or is supposed to be. It is a meeting of people who want to help in Appalachia on a short and longer term basis and people in Appalachia who have apprehensions about how they can be helped by those people. This is what this meeting is. I'm in the middle of this thing. Now, I'm in the middle because my experiences have been that some people—whatever their motivation to come to work in Appalachia, [be it the] civil rights movement or work with the poor (which has been my interest throughout my adult life)—some of the people have become our most effective educators and organizers. And I'm not willing to say that because the majority of the people do more harm than good that the doors be locked and the people be excluded. This is a personal experience of mine, and I have probably sweated through as many volunteers who have gummed up the works as anybody in this room. Hundreds, literally, hundreds of them, so you see I'm not naive about this problem. On the other hand, I could list scores of these people who have made a tremendous contribution. Now, [I] think that this whole business of research and studying the power structure has been used as a gimmick by people in the mountains to put off to the side people who are coming in, and who they don't know how to handle otherwise. And I'm against it. I don't think that it makes any contribution for the reasons I've stated, and I think that we need to lay it on the line and approach this problem honestly and say that people aren't capable of making any contribution by doing what is called research of the power structure. We don't need that kind of help. To do that kind of a thing, you need much more skilled people, people who stay longer. On the other hand, we do need to figure out a way to strain out the people who have staying power and ability, and utilize them in Appalachia. And, I say this because I have a strong conviction (as I told one of the smaller groups), I have a strong conviction that now that the Negroes have decided that they can manage without us (white people) and now that there is a degree of nationalism developing in some of the foreign missionary fields, the only place which is open for people to come to "save the world" is Appalachia.

I think that we are "in for it," and I think we need to face the fact that there [are] gonna be waves and waves of Saviors coming into Appalachia in the next few years.

And we are gonna have to figure out a way to make something of this. Now, I think something can be made of it, you see. I can talk this way, quite frankly, because I started out as a missionary to Appalachia back when I was a college student. I went to little Cumberland University in Lebanon, Tennessee. In my junior and senior year I came surging into Appalachia, where my ancestors had lived. I came surging in to save Appalachia for the Presbyterian Church.[42] I was very sincere and very intelligent. My motives were good so I'm not casting a reflection on all of the people who, like me, are also fairly intelligent, have good motives, and so on. I am only commenting on the fact that I didn't do any good. And I would like for the people who come later to do some good. And I think I now know more than I did then about how I could have been more effective, and I would like to share that with people. But I'm not making my comments with any feeling of superiority, rather on the basis of being one of the missionaries to Appalachia. I was a consultant for the Appalachian Volunteers here a couple of years ago.[43] I horrified them all by addressing them as "fellow missionaries."

You see, the problem is that we have to have enough confidence in the people in Appalachia to believe that our job is to help them save themselves. Instead of for us to save people. And I think that we have a role there. I think that my relatives, who haven't had the opportunities that I had to go on to school, travel around a little bit, know many things that I don't know. But I know some things that they don't know. Now, if I can respect what they know that I don't know, maybe they will respect what I know that they don't know. But, when I went in, the trouble with me was that I didn't know that they knew anything, and I didn't think that there was anything that I could learn from them. Well, I'm making up for that deficiency ever since, and I'm beginning to feel that there is a tremendous lot that can be learned. My suggestion to people who come to work in Appalachia is that they be aware of the fact that they can learn more than they can teach in this kind of experience.

Now, this brings me to the last point that I want to make. If you are going to talk about understanding the people in Appalachia, understanding the whole system, the power structure, the people and everything, then I think you have got to face one very simple fact. And that is that attitude of learning from people who have a different kind of experience, maybe a richer experience, maybe fuller experience, rather than teaching the experience that we have had, which is primarily a middle class, highly structured cellophaned package sort of deal which we could impose on people. And, I think if we could get straight that one simple idea, we could cut through a lot of things and begin to learn something.

I spoke to a group of people in Boone State College in North Carolina last year,[44] and I'm using this as an illustration because I don't want to give you any impression that I'm talking about any other college. But if you want to apply it you can! I said, "You know what is happening to you mountaineers here?" They talked about people from their regions going to schools which they say deal with the people in the mountain regions and educate them to serve the region. I said, "This is not true, you know that it's not true." "What they are doing is packaging you for export." Now, what's happening in Appalachia is that years ago they came in and exported the timber and then they started exporting the coal. And this is done primarily by absentee owners who, for a pittance, got control of the land. The one thing which is ordained by God is property rights. Not people rights, property rights. So, they simply had the property rights. They could take the coal, take the timber, and now all that is left in Appalachia are the people. Now as I said to this college, and of course it doesn't apply to any other colleges, "What this college is doing is preparing you for export. They are going to export you." The only thing that we have got left is the people and the brain and our human power is now being prepared for export. They put you in little packages, they wrap you up neatly, tie a ribbon around you, and they say, "this is a female export or male export." I said that the more advanced colleges have a few Negroes and I said this is a black export. But, they all prepare to export. And that's education in this college.

I think we can do better than that, and I think that we need—since our colleges are exporting our brain power and our people—we need to have people from the outside. (Lord knows the colleges who are on the inside won't do it.) We need people from the outside to come in and say there is something of value here that we need to keep and to help, not to impose outside values on Appalachia (because it won't work even if it is a good idea, which I doubt), but to enhance the native resources of what we have left, and that's the people. Appalachia has one thing and that's people. So, if you are going to come to Appalachia, build on the people. Try to help us develop the people in Appalachia and try to understand that the people have something worth developing. Then, I think that we can begin to move and you will end up understanding all about Appalachia if you get with the people.

So, I guess that I would like to close by saying that despite some efforts to label me I would, if I choose a label, say "I was a people's people." And particularly an Appalachian people's people.

On Building a Social Movement

[1968]

The following text is taken from a talk given at a workshop with Mrs. Easterling and the staff of the Marrowbone Folk School, held at Highlander, July 24–26, 1968. The Marrowbone Folk School was founded in 1967 by Edith and Jake Easterling, who brought other coal-mining families like themselves together to discuss what they could do about strip mining, polluted water, black lung disease, poor schooling, and other issues that faced them. In this speech, which has been edited for the sake of continuity, Horton explores the connections between education and social change and attempts to define social movements.

Yesterday, I had been giving a little thought to what we talked about. We discussed, among other things, this idea of there being a difference. I think when you can get some kind of understanding of how you have to work out an educational program, what's involved in it, a kind of a theory (I guess you'd say background), it's easier to make your own educational program work. Sometimes, people just think you do this, you do that, you do this, and then you don't know why you're doing it—it isn't very helpful. I'm much more concerned in you knowing *why* you do something, and you can work out *how* you do it, if you understand why you do it. Yesterday, we talked about the differences between nation and the people in a nation; for example, we said the kind of educational programs that seem to be worked out to keep poor people in their place don't appeal to poor people. Your reaction was that you felt this wasn't appropriate to your needs.

Now, one of the ways of finding out (this isn't just theory) whether you can transfer an educational program from one group to another is to try; you can test it out that way and find out what works and what doesn't. Now, some teachers say, "This is the way to do it, and whether it works or not isn't my problem—of course we're not interested in that kind of education; we're interested in the kind of education that works—if it doesn't work, you have to take a look at it. There's what you call social or cultural differences [which] means you have to have an educational program that's adapted to the needs of the people. One way we found at Highlander to do that is not to sit and talk about it, but to find out what it was the people were doing, what it was they were interested in; to try to understand that and try to help them.

Now, I used one example of the early bugwood strike,[45] and I think I brought an article over that tells about the early bugwood strike. Now, the thing that that did, as I indicated yesterday, for us, was to get us away from our academic, our educational, college classroom type approach to a people approach. In other words, that forced us to take this step, that I'm talking about, and deal with people where they were, not where we wanted to or expected them to be. Now, Highlander discovered that that not only was a good way to carry on education (and for lack of a better term, we talked about "dealing with a crisis"—something in people's lives which was pretty important to them), not only a good way to educate people, because when people are excited they learn faster, their minds are open, they want to answer problems that they have, and they know what their problems are. About the only time people learn to get information to help solve their problems is when they're interested. And sometimes they don't know what their problems are. This list here (of FCCA demands)[46] of so many things suggests that the people aren't yet ready to decide what their main problems are and to think through their problems—they put everything down. Sometimes people are that way not because they don't have problems, it's simply because they never focused on one problem. Now, the bugwood strike—they found out what their problem was. As Henry Thomas says, "It takes a sharp axe, a strong back and a weak mind to cut bugwood for 75 cents a day, let's strike." He knew what the problem was, others knew what the problem was. And Highlander could find out how to deal with people in terms of their problems because there was a focal point. Now, taking that clue, we decided that what we needed to do, instead of reading books and thinking about how to work out an educational program, was to get out with the people, not only people who are known in the community, but people in other parts of the mountains.

One of the first things we did was to start going around where there was (that was in the thirties before the CIO started their own labor organization among poultry workers, and textile workers and miners), and I read about a strike over in Wilder, Tennessee (this is in a movie some of you have seen—*People of the Cumberland*),[47] and went over there just to see what was going on, and I found out, as I told you yesterday. That was the first time I was called a Communist—I came back and talked in a church about what I saw. Incidentally, I was arrested over there (I didn't tell you that) for getting information and going back and teaching it—that was the official charge. Well, they were right, that's really what I was doing; I was trying to find out where people were and what we could do in relation to where they were. Soon after that, there was a textile strike in Georgia, and a man named T. C. Walker was killed.[48] Well, this focused a lot of attention of most people on that problem. We went down and worked out an educational program in connection with that strike, and then we brought back a couple of students to Highlander for training so they could go back in that situation. We were learning fast that the way to find out where people are was to get with them.

A little later on, we had some hosiery workers from a place called Stye, Tennessee, not far from Chattanooga—a sit-down strike for awhile and they came to us and asked us if we could give them some help. Well, we didn't know enough to help them. So what we decided to do instead of saying, Yeah, we know the answers, was to move the school down there. So we took the whole student body, everybody we had (about thirty or forty people), the whole staff, a mimeograph machine, the typewriters, loaded up and went down. We had a friend there, a preacher named Dejarnet; he had been fired because of his interest in unions, and he had a big house, and a vacant community building. He just let us move in, so Highlander moved into the situation—we didn't bring people to us, we went there. We started talking to people and finally decided that we needed to have a Fourth of July parade and end up as a kind of mass picket line around the plant, and we started working out posters, and plans, and songs and plays, and get[ing] people ready for that. Then after, we had the march (incidentally, it was a little rough on teachers sometimes, because people were so scared of this mass of people going around singing, and we had a band that day, that the guards of the company shot into us, and they shot our librarian in the leg. Now, librarians usually sit back in the library, they don't get out and get shot in the leg, but our librarian got an education fast and became very much interested in this kind of thing, and it changed her whole life. I don't mean it crippled her, it shot some ideas into her). So we went back after that. Not back to the mountains, where the school was located; we went back right there and talked about what happened, how could it have happened better. So we were using a real situation, a problem that was clear cut in the minds of the people, as a means of not only our running an educational program, but trying to help ourselves learn where the people were.

Now, I'm going ahead with some more illustrations, because I want to give you a variety of illustrations, but first I'd like to stop for a minute and say something else I'd like you to keep in mind. Now I think you can already see that this kind of education helps you to understand where people are and gets you off this business of not meeting the people as they are, and trying to impose your own ideas and methods on them. But if all you did was to go into a crisis wherever you found them, every time there's a hot spot, every time there was trouble, every time there were people excited, then you know, you might spend all your life just going around in a circle. You'd learn a lot about people, you'd know how to deal with people, but it wouldn't add up to anything very important in terms of bringing about social change, and that's what we're really interested in.

There's another idea that I'd like to introduce to you, and that's an idea of what someone once called a "social movement." Now that means a movement of people that is openly and honestly dedicated to bringing about basic social changes. It isn't just people just doing anything they want to do. It's truly trying to change society, trying to challenge the establishment, as we said yesterday. A social movement is really a movement of social change. Now a social movement not only has to be a movement aimed at change but has to involve a lot of people. You couldn't have a social movement in Pike County, anymore than you could have a social movement back when I told you in Grundy County we were able to elect every office.[49] But you could have a social movement in Appalachia, you see, because it would deal with a big enough hunk of the problems in the country, and it would have enough people involved and, as we indicated yesterday, you might change Appalachia if you could get enough people. So a social movement involves not just a good cause or a small number of people who are dedicated to something, but it has to be significant enough in size and scope to bring about change.

For example, the beginning of the industrial union movement was considered a social movement, because here we were talking about getting away from craft unions and really organizing the masses of workers to change society. Now this didn't turn out too well, as some of us know, but the purpose was a good purpose—to change society. Now the civil rights movement is a social movement. It set out to change society. Now if we could have something of that size in Appalachia, we could have a social movement.

How do we know whether you're dealing with a social movement or not? How do you know whether in doing what you're doing in Pike County you can think in terms of a social movement? Well, you can't, except in the sense that you know it would be a good thing, and you know other people are stirring all over Appalachia. You know they need to be stirring, and you know that the purpose is to bring about some pretty basic changes. So you can say that if you could really get something going that would spread, then it would be a social movement for change. So you can't wait until you find out what it's going to be; you've got to take advantage of every little opportunity, but after awhile, when it doesn't seem to be moving in that direction, then you say, well, maybe this is a limited thing, it's a good thing, but it's not part of a social movement.

Now we started working in the poverty program at Highlander in the early thirties in the hope of building a social movement out of the unemployed and the poor. It didn't gel, there wasn't any basis for it. But later on, we felt that the beginnings of the industrial union movement, which then became the CIO, did provide the basis. Now how did we deal with that problem? Well, we dealt with it not by waiting, but by taking the position that we thought it would be a good idea to kind of get in on the ground floor so that by the time the CIO got started in the South, Highlander had been, as I've already indicated, working with every group around the country and people knew about us, and they came flocking into Highlander because we were the one group that they knew about that was interested in their problems and could talk to them. Now, at that time, it looked like we had guessed right, so to speak, that this was an emerging social movement, in which we could fit all these pieces. Now, the civil rights movement, I won't analyze that, but it happened the same way—we guessed that there would be a movement among Negroes to get more rights, because it seemed like the time had come for that, and we started working with people in '48. And there again, we guessed right. When the civil rights movement started going, people started flocking to Highlander because that was the one place they knew and the place where we could talk their language, because we learned how to talk the language of the people who . . . *[Text missing in original]*

Now right now, what we should really be trying to do is, how do we really deal with Appalachian problems; how do we find out the things that are happening that can be parlayed into a movement later on, or maybe not, but at least we get to start doing things that might or might not. We can't lose, in the sense that what else would we do that's as important [as] trying to get people excited and stirred up, and educating as many people as we can to their problems, and what they can do about them. Well, if you deal with a social movement, then you've got a lot of things going for you. All of these little pieces begin to fit together in a pattern and using an illustration, if you learn how to deal with southern workers in hosiery and mines, textiles, lumber, then you know how to help these people about their problems, and then, as the movement starts, it adds momentum and it all kind of adds up, and you begin to deal with something that's very important. And your education takes on more value, not only because it's good education, but because it is tied into something that does things that you don't do. You know, sometimes much more important than what you do is things that other people do, things that happen as a result of the opposition, the international situation, or something of that kind [that you could] tie the educational program into. So, think of [the larger context when] you're dealing with a crisis; then you're dealing with a social movement, and then you begin to get what Highlander's all about.

How do you relate education to people's groups or people's needs, that have more than just an immediate need? I could go on to use other illustrations; I don't want to use too many because I think I want to discuss it in another way later on. I'd just like to point out how important this is by saying that in '37, when it became apparent that the industrial union movement was going to get under way, and that Highlander was being asked to train a lot of leaders, that I took seven months off, a leave of absence from the school, and went out as an organizer to learn firsthand more about the problems than I could learn just going out for a week or ten days at a time.[50] I wanted to learn from the inside so I could be in a better position to shape up an educational program. And I found that as an organizer, I was more successful when I used the educational method to organize. I'm basically an educator, and I found that you needed education to organize, and I still think that is a sound way to organize. But the main reason for doing that was to learn what was going on.

I don't want to spend too much time on this one area of experience, but we had a variation of this over here at Lafollette, Tennessee, not very far from here, where one of our students organized shirt workers, with the help of the miners, and we went over to do another kind of an educational program.[51] That is, to run an educational program to help establish a whole community around a labor organization. At that time, we thought of labor organizations providing the base for a broader social movement—not just trade unionism, pure and simple, but a broader base. And we tried to involve the whole town of Lafollette, and succeeded pretty well in getting all the people—the merchants and everyone together. We set up an educational program right there in Lafollette. We sent staff members there, ended up having a Labor Day rally which was also in the movie *People of the Cumberland* (those of you that haven't seen it I'd like for you to see. It tells some early stories of what we were doing.). Well, later on, we decided that in addition to working with what we call a strike situation, we would be able to run educational programs in the field in terms of actual situations, so we started running programs in the field; we sent staff members out to New Orleans, to Knoxville, to Louisville, to Memphis, to Charleston, and they would actually work right in the field, there again, keeping in close touch with the people. They fed that back in to Highlander, so we got the benefit of all their experiences.

We didn't stop with working with working people in industry; later on, we were asked to set up an educational program [for] the farmers. The Farmers Union asked us to organize and develop a cooperative educational program, and we used the same method, getting out and living with farmers, we lived with farmers in Greene County, Tennessee, in Huntington and West Tennessee, in Andalusia, Alabama. We went out and stayed with people until we learned how to talk their language and made their program our program.

Later on, I've already mentioned a connection with the civil rights movement. Before that time, we used to go into Negro communities and get acquainted with people there and then we'd bring them into Highlander. When they'd go back, we'd follow them up. And one [of] the programs, the program I gave you yesterday, the Citizenship School program, grew out of going and living in a community long enough to listen to people, so we could hear what they were saying, and find out what their problems were and work out a program that was appropriate to their needs—to skip all this business of doing things from the top down way—to find out just what it is that these people need (we spoke about this, yesterday). In the meantime we were trying to find out what was going on in communities in other parts of the South; so when the sit-ins started in '60,[52] Highlander was the place to which students came, labor came, SNCC, people from Martin Luther King's organization came, and [we] were able to work out programs for these organizations.

The last thing like that I did was when I took the job as the Educational Program Coordinator for SNCC—for a couple of years, I was their consultant on education. There again, we went right into Mississippi, right into the places where we were working, dealt with the people, dealt with their problems. All this was to enable us to do two things: to deal with people where they were, in terms of their own interests (not to impose the top-down idea on people). Well, this sounds very farfetched, I think, to you, but I'm going through these steps because I want you to understand that if you're going to have a real vital program at Marrowbone, and I think you will, or anywhere else, it can't be something that you cook up in your head, that you think is good for people. You have to find out what it is the people are doing, and you can't [neglect their experience]; you've got to really tie into it.

[Text omitted]

Another thing we talked about yesterday, you just have to understand that you can't play two games at once—you can't do the kind of thing that an ordinary educational institution—that a government program does, that is, play along the Establishment, and run the kind of a program that you want to run. And you're going to find that people are going to be your enemies, because you challenge the way things are run. Now, if you know that, you don't worry about their running you off. You try to find a way to get around them and get to the people. You don't get impressed because you talked to them, you see. You understand, we told you yesterday, that they really don't represent anything. There are so many illustrations of this that we think of; we know to talk to the right men. Now in the cities, they say that if you can get a Negro policemen, then there won't be riots, because the Negro policemen will know how to deal with the problem. The first question you have to ask is, who tells the Negro policeman what to do. They're part of the system of white policemen, and you know even if they're black, Negroes would have no more to settle for than they would a white policeman. You have to get behind this and find out what it is behind them.

[Text omitted]

It's been my experience that, to get started, you have to have unannounced meetings or you can't have a meeting. What you've got to do is to find a man back there that'll get a few people together at his house, back in the hollow, and talk to one or two people, when there's not anybody around. You have to build it up, in little house meetings. You don't have a meeting; meetings are the worst way in the world, because that's an open invitation to the politicians to come in and take over. That's their meat, that's their game. Don't play their game. You know, set up your own rules of the game. You know, when you were talking about one community wanting a school? Now, what you've got to find is somebody needs to go in to a place like that, somebody that's preferably a native, or known to these people, or somebody that's related to them, even better; and go in and talk to somebody until they tell you the truth of the situation. And then, you win their confidence, and say, well, you get three or four other people together, and they'll say, maybe these people are afraid to talk to a stranger, but I'll see. You finally get through, and you meet two or three more people, and you build up very slowly, and these people are the people you want to reach. And then they begin, and if they're doing something, and they ask for your help, you give help to them—then you've got it made. But you have to keep it kind of underground, not too open, and that's for two reasons. One was the reason you gave where they come and take over. And the other is, these people aren't going to talk if those people are around. So you've got to work with the people you're dealing with.

[Text omitted]

If you're going to use this as an adult educational program, you don't go in there and help solve their problems and tell them how to do it and what to do and who'll do it for them; what you do is try to get them together to try to discuss it, to try to decide what it is they really want. Now, in this bugwood strike that you'll read about, these people were able, by having meetings and discussing it, to do something that was contradictory. They wanted to get more paper cut in the timber, and then, the next paragraph in there said that they wanted to preserve the timber, they don't want to cut it all. Now, a lot of people said, well, you can't have it both ways, but people can have anything they want. If that's the way they wanted [it], that's the way it was. That was a very profound understanding of the situation, you see. They knew they had to live, they knew they had to eat. They really didn't want to have to eat off the forest and be a firetrap. So they were really doing two things at once. They really were saying, if we have to cut these things, we want more money, but we'd rather not cut them, we'd rather find some other way to work. Now, they didn't say that they wanted to save the trees at first, nobody told them to do that, they just finally figured this out, themselves, and discussed it, but that didn't keep them from going ahead and demanding more money. So if you can work with people long enough, they'll begin to talk about these problems and begin to think through things themselves.

I have an illustration right here in Knoxville; we were asked to come to Knoxville and set up classes on a picket line of a hosiery mill here where they had a long drawn-out strike to take advantage of the fact that people were unemployed—to run educational programs.[53] We had a lot of teachers from the TVA[54] and the university[55] that we trained at Highlander go out every morning at 4, 5 o'clock or in the evenings, after they came from work and have classes. Now, as a result of these discussions they had (and they discussed the contract), they decided that they shouldn't have struck. A lot of the union representatives got worried and said, oh, you're going to confuse these people. You don't confuse good, honest poor people. They will think for themselves, they don't have any problems about that. So they made a public statement that, after having studied their contract, they decided that they made a mistake, but since they did it, they would stay out, anyway, and they were going to force them to go along with their original decision. And the newspapers screamed, and everybody screamed. It didn't bother them; they could still say, we saw that we were wrong, but we aren't quitting, anyway, because the boss has done so many wrongs, that we can have one wrong. In other words, if you deal with people long enough in an educational relationship, you talk to them, they can work out all these things that they have confidence in themselves to contradict themselves. Now if you're working with these people, some of the people might decide that maybe the price is right, others wouldn't, but that wouldn't mean that you didn't do a good job of getting the people. And remember, the reason for getting people together is not to solve that problem anyway; you get people together so that they can educate themselves so they can solve [problems] in any way they want to do it. Never try to use education to solve the problem, then you lose the people, because then you become a functionary, an organizer, doing things for people, and a very poor organizer at that. You don't want to do things for them, you want to get them together. You don't say, well, we failed, because we got them together and they decided that they didn't want what they started with. You succeeded if you got people together and worked through them. See what I'm talking about? You use the situation to get at the people, not to solve their problems. It gives you a chance to deal with real people in a real situation, that's what I'm talking about. *[The final portion of the text, involving a more general discussion, has been omitted.]*

The Adventures of a Radical Hillbilly, Part 1

[1981]

The following interview with Bill Moyers was originally aired on PBS in two parts on June 5 and June 11, 1981. It was subsequently reprinted in the summer 1982 issue of Appalachian Journal, *from which the text reprinted below has been taken. The second part of this interview appears in section III. In this wide-ranging interview, Horton discusses, among other things, his influences, ideas about education, and his recollections of his experiences in the labor movement. Moyers's original headnote follows:*

Few people I know have seen as much change in the American South, or helped to bring it about, as Myles Horton. He's been beaten up, locked up, put upon, and railed against by racists, toughs, demagogues, and governors. But for almost fifty years now, he has gone on with his special kind of teaching—helping people to discover within themselves the courage and ability to confront reality and change. Myles Horton came to his mission from a childhood among the mountain people of Appalachia, a land rich in beauty but a colony of poverty. "Nothing will change," said Horton to himself, "until we change—until we throw off our dependence and act for ourselves." So in 1932, in the mountains west of Chattanooga, in one of America's poorest counties, Myles Horton founded the Highlander Folk School, dedicated to the belief that poor working-class people—adults— could learn to take charge of their lives and circumstance. At first he ran workshops to train organizers for the CIO. Jim Crow laws forbade integration, but Horton invited blacks and whites alike, and Highlander became one of the few places in the South where the two races could meet under the same roof. In the early 1950s, Horton turned the emphasis of his workshops from union organization to civil rights. Highlander was now a principal gathering place of the moving forces of the black revolution. Martin Luther King came; so did Rosa Parks, Andrew Young, Julian Bond, Stokely Carmichael, and scores of unsung foot soldiers in the long march of southern blacks toward equality. The state tried to close it down; the Klan harassed it; state troopers raided it. But Highlander seemed indestructible. He's now seventy-five, and his school, from which he has stepped aside as leader in favor of younger colleagues, is preparing to celebrate its fiftieth anniversary this year. I thought it a good time to pay a visit to Myles Horton at Highlander, now located on a farm near Knoxville.

BILL MOYERS: Myles, you've upset a lot of people down here over the years. The Mill Owner said that Highlander was about the boldest and most insulting thing in an Anglo-Saxon South that has yet been done; one Georgia governor said that you were a cancerous group spreading throughout the South;[56] the state of Tennessee closed you down, confiscated your property, sold it at auction;[57] the Ku Klux Klan beat up your staff and burned your buildings;[58] a United States senator had you ejected from his hearings.[59] Now what's a nice man like you doing upsetting all those people?

MYLES HORTON: Well, I don't try to upset people. I try to help people grow and be creative, and fulfill themselves as people. And in the process of doing that, they upset a lot of people.

MOYERS: How do you mean?

HORTON: Well, they start doing things, asserting their rights, for example, working people asserting their rights to have a union, asserting their rights to be treated decently, people in the mountains assert their rights to be left alone to live their own way if they want to without having the absentee landowners run them out of their holdings, their heritage. And we try to help people, you know, stand up against this kind of thing. We try to help people become empowered so they themselves can do things, and that's very irritating. One of the reasons they confiscated Highlander was because the charge was made by the governor of Georgia that this cancerous growth was spreading over the South and that the civil rights movement came out of Highlander. And only a, you know, only a racist white person could make that assumption that some white people had to be doing that kind of thing. So they assumed that since a lot of the black[s] had been at Highlander long before the civil rights movement and during the civil rights movement—blacks couldn't do anything themselves, so it had to be some white people. So they got four or five of the governors together and closed Highlander. And it was only after they closed it they found out that they, you know, didn't have anything with the civil rights movement, but the blacks were doing the civil rights movement.

MOYERS: I think that's what really upset a lot of people.

HORTON: And they got upset, I think, when they found out they couldn't— they couldn't stop it by confiscating Highlander. When they first came, they came and padlocked the building, and some of the news reporters that were there said, "What are you laughing about?" I was standing outside laughing, and they took a picture of me standing there laughing. And the sheriff padlocked the building. I said, "My friend here, you know, he thinks he's padlocking Highlander," and, but I said, you know, "Highlander is an idea—you can't padlock an idea."

MOYERS: You say Highlander is an idea. What's the idea?

HORTON: Well, we have a philosophy, that we know, that we can identify. We believe that—we believe in people. Our loyalty is to people, not situations, structures. And we try to translate that belief and trust in people's ability to learn into facilitating people's learning. Now you don't teach people things, since they're adults; you help them learn. And insofar as you learn how people learn, you can help. And that's a powerful dynamic force, when you realize that people themselves in these hollows, and these factories and these mines, you know, can take much more control of their lives than they themselves realize.

MOYERS: How does it work, I mean, how do you teach—how do you help people learn something like that?

HORTON: Well, first thing you have to clarify is that—you have to understand, you have to know that people—working people, common people, the uncommon common people—they're the most uncommon people in the world, the common people have mainly a past, they're adults. Unlike children in the regular school system, who have practically no past and are told by the schools that their present isn't worth anything, are taught, you know, they are taught about the future, they're prepared for the future. Adults are—come out of the past with their experiences. So you run a program at Highlander based on their experiences, their experience in learning—from which they may not have learned very much, because they haven't learned how to analyze it, but it's there, and the grist for the mill is there. And our job is to help them understand that they can analyze their experiences and build on those experiences and maybe transform those experiences even. Then they have a power that they're comfortable with. See people—first I should tell you that not only are people adults with a past, with experiences, but they are leaders in their communities. I don't mean official leaders, but grassroots leaders.

MOYERS: You mean, not bankers and—

HORTON: No, they are the people in the people's organizations, like labor unions or community organizations of various kinds. Well, those people come and we say, "Okay, what are your experiences that relate to this topic—not all your experiences, but your experiences that relate to this topic?" Now they hadn't considered those experiences too important— they hadn't thought of them being very important. We say, this is very important because that's the curriculum, that's the building stones that we're going to use here. And it's something you can take back with you, because you, you know, you brought it here. So we start out—

MOYERS: They didn't know it, when they got there.

HORTON: They don't—they hadn't learned to analyze those experiences so they could learn from them. You know, people say you learn from experiences—you only learn from experiences that you learn from, you know. That's not all experiences. And we try to help them learn from their experiences in such a way that when they go back they'll continue to learn. But we have to also learn from our experiences. And one of the things we have to do in addition to what they have to do, is to learn how to relate our experiences to theirs. And you do analogy, you know, you do it by storytelling. You don't get up and say, "Look, here are some facts we want to dump on you." We say, "Well, you might consider this. Now this happened to somebody kind of like you in a different situation." So we get them doing the same thing with each other. You get peer teaching going, where everybody that's in the circle is part of a peer teaching group.

MOYERS: What's radical about that? What was radical about that back in 1930?

HORTON: Well, it's terribly radical, because education, it goes against what education is supposed—Education is supposed to prepare people to live in whatever system the education school system is about. Like in our system it's to prepare people to live under capitalism and be—you know, fit into that system. In the Soviet Union, it's to prepare people to live in that system, and fit in that system. And that's what education, official education, is all about, to prepare people to fit into the system, and support the system.

MOYERS: And Highlander?

HORTON: And turn them—really, it's to turn them into nuts and bolts to keep the system together, you see, whatever kind of system it is. Highlander says, No. You can't use people that way. People are, you know, creative, you've got to allow them to do a lot of things that don't fit any kind of systems, and you've got to have a lot of deviations, to have a lot of pluralism. We believe in people keeping a lot of their old customs, and adding new ones. And we said, that's what enriches life. So we're going to focus on that, and there's a lot of dynamics and a lot of power in that, that scares people. When people in the South, before the civil rights were started, began to feel that they could do something, in spite of the laws, in spite of tradition, and started doing it, then you know, all hell broke loose. We had that experience earlier, in the '30s. We started back in the depression, in the preindustrial union movement in this country, before the CIO was started.[60] And many of our students who had been at Highlander before, you know, became leaders in the unions in the early days when it was rough. When we first started organizing it was illegal to have a picket line, and a lot of our activities were illegal. Highlander itself was illegal up until about four years ago. We defied the state law on segregation in public—in private schools, which stayed on the books long after the public schools were integrated. You know, we had to work that way to live up to our principles. So, to get off the subject a little bit, but the people have all this power, but it's suppressed by the public school system and the institutions. We, having loyalty [to] people and not the institutions, you know, always try to throw our weight on the side of the people, and help them do things that are right. Now you can't get people to do something they think is wrong. You know, you can't—you know, people say Highlander is a propaganda nest, you get all these ideas in people's heads and they go out and do things they learned at Highlander. Well, you know, that's not the way things are.

MOYERS: They were in their minds.

HORTON: They were in their minds; they're seeds. What you do, you develop those seeds. They're crusted over, you know, with all kinds of things and the people don't even know they're there. We know they're there, we dig for them, and we cultivate those seeds. We help prepare the ground for them to grow, and we help people learn, they can learn from each other that they're stronger. Individualism is enhanced by being part of a group, you know, individuality, I guess would be a better way of saying it, is enhanced by being part of a group, instead of telling people they should go it alone, they should be competitive, they should, you know, compete with their fellow man. We say, work together and you'll be a better person.

MOYERS: What started you thinking radical thoughts a long time ago?

HORTON: Well, Bill, I was asked that story by—asked that question by a priest back in the CIO days when there were a lot of efforts to have labor schools. And Highlander was—we were officially designated as *the* CIO school of the South.[61] And we had more programs than anybody else. So they had Communist-sponsored labor schools, Catholic-sponsored labor schools, and some independent schools like Highlander. And a priest in Nashville, who was trying to start a Catholic school, kept coming to Highlander and he says, "I did—I go back, I do everything I learned at Highlander, I go back and I just imitate everything I learned. It doesn't work, doesn't work." And he said, "It doesn't do—it's no good just to look at it, but it's something I don't understand. Maybe I can get at it by asking you what books influenced your life most. Because I got to understand this," he said. And I said, "Well, I can tell you, but it won't help you any, because, you know, like all people I got my own track of development, and my own background is a part of it." And I said, "I grew up in a religious family, like most people in the South," and I said, "Undoubtedly the first book that influenced my life was the Bible, there's no question about that. All my early influences came from the Bible and things like that, you know, not an ultra religious family, but a conventionally religious family, and that was the values in little country towns, you know. You went to church and you went to school. There wasn't anything else to do." So I said, "There's no question, and I still, the values of the Bible I still hold dear," I said, and he said, "Well, what in particular?" And I said, "Well, okay, there's two—there's the New Testament and the Old Testament. In the New Testament we learned about love," and I said, "You can't be a revolutionary, you can't want to change society if you don't love people, there's no point in it. So you know, love people, that's right out of the Bible. And another thing is, the Old Testament tells primarily about the Creation. God was a creator. If you're going to be with people, born in God's image, then you've got to be creators, you can't be followers, you know, or puppets, you've got to be creators. So from the Bible, I guess, people ought to be creative, or love people, people ought to be creative." Well, he thought that was rather skimpy theological background, but anyway, I was trying to tell him the things that affected me, and then I said I got so discouraged by seeing the people in the church and politicians and all being hypocritical, that well, I almost got very cynical about society. And the way I knew this [was] because I used to work in a store and I used to do things where I knew people, when I was growing up. And I just found that the leaders, you know, these were all hypocrites. So, I said, that's the way people are. So I was getting very cynical, and I decided, well, you know, what's it all about, the business of loving people and sharing with people in this cynical world. So at that time, I always loved poetry, I always read a lot of poetry. And I ran into Shelley.[62]

MOYERS: Shelley?

HORTON: Shelley. And he said the same thing. He said, "Shelley!" like you did. *[Laughs.]*

MOYERS: It's been a long time since I read any.

HORTON: He said, "What has Shelley got to do?" Well, Shelley was a young rebel, he died young, same age Christ died, but he wrote some wonderful poems, about, you know, defying all authority if it's wrong to obey authority, and living your own life. And you do things without fear of punishment or for rewards, you know, and somehow I—

MOYERS: You do it for the good—

HORTON: You do it because they're right. And Shelley just hit me at the right time, he gave me a feeling that I wasn't going to get cynical, I was going to live my own life. And it made me think independently and say, well, I'm going to create my own life, I'm not going to play the games of other people if I don't believe in them. I'm going to find a way to survive and live my own life. Shelley did that for me. Then I realized that what's good for me is not—if I just want to live my own life, you see, I've got to think everybody should have the same rights I have, a universality of rights. If they're right for me, then I've got to work for them to be right for everybody else, or they're not—I have no right to them.

MOYERS: You do believe there are certain truths and rights self-evident?

HORTON: Yes, and those have to be shared. It can't be for me—I can't have something that isn't for you, or for the poorest person, you know, in the world. And I believe that, and I believe you've got to work for that. Well, I had nothing in my background that prepared me to work for things like that. You know, I didn't have any understanding, I'd gone to a little liberal Presbyterian college,[63] and I had only the kind of academic background that anybody would have and I—so there's nothing in my schooling that would help me on that, nothing in my background, nothing in the Bible, nothing in Shelley. And it was then that I discovered about Marxism and analysis of society on a class basis. I discovered that first, not by knowing about Marx, but by the *Federalist Papers,* when Hamilton talked about classes, that's when I first got to understand classes, from Alexander Hamilton, when he said that the, you know, that the workers would vote their interests, the farmers their interests, and the merchants their interests. That was the first insight I had, and then I found Marx said the same thing, a little more elaborately. So I found out from Marx I could get tools, not blueprints, tools that I could use for analyzing society. That helped me analyze. Then I had to get a synthesis of my religious background and my understanding of economic forces. And then I started trying to work on a synthesis. And that's how I got a—And those are the things that helped kind of get me to think and gave me some kind of guidance. Now I've never been a doctrinaire, you know, religious person, or a doctrinaire Shelley advocate, or a doctrinaire Marxist, but you know I got from all those things—ideas—that helped me.

MOYERS: I thought you might have become a Christian-poet-activist.

HORTON: Well, I did a lot of poetry in life. I think that somebody said, you know, Highlander is a myth. And I said, well, you know, it's a poem, too, it's a picture. It's because it's not anything that any of us here have done, but the people have come here have made a mosaic out of Highlander. And it's a—poetry's a beautiful thing, you know.

MOYERS: The segregationists, and the Klanners, and the politicians were fond, in the old days, of calling Highlander Communistic, and calling you a Communist. Were you ever a Communist?

HORTON: I was never a member of the Communist Party, and I was invited to be a member of the Communist Party, and then I was told two years later that I couldn't be a member of the Communist Party by the head of the Communist Party.

MOYERS: Why?

HORTON: Well, I asked him the same question. And he said, well when we first wanted you to be a member of the Communist Party, you know, you were a radical activist—I was active in college—and we thought, you know, you'd be a good Communist, but you started Highlander and began to get ideas of your own, you know, you wouldn't be trustworthy. Because you'd want to do things, you wouldn't follow discipline.

MOYERS: And you couldn't accept any system without challenging it, any doctrinaire—

HORTON: I said, you know, when they first talked to me, I said, well, I like a lot of the things that Communists believe in, just like I like a lot of things that a lot of groups believe in, I like what Christianity's supposed to be. Those things are not practiced, but I like the ideals. But I said, you know, I come from down the southern mountains, and the, you know, I guess it's part of my background, I couldn't take any kind of authoritarian—nobody could, I couldn't say to any group, any organization, I will do what you want me to do. I'll have to do what I want to do, my conscience has to be my guide. That's what I told Senator Eastland—

MOYERS: Senator Eastland?

HORTON: Senator Eastland, he was, I was investigated by the Senate Internal Security committee, by Eastland. And Eastland says, "If you're not going to answer these questions," he says, you know, "you can just take Fourth Amendment, you know, and protect yourself."[64]

MOYERS: Fifth Amendment.[65]

HORTON: Fifth Amendment. You see, I was advised, I said I've got good legal advice, I've been advised by all the lawyers that I could do that. But I said that's not my way to work. I'll always talk about what I want to talk about and if I don't want to talk about it, I don't want to talk about it. And I'll do that right here. And he said, "Well, you can't do that." And I said, well, I believe I can because in the beginning of this country there was a revolution, and people had all their rights. And they delegated rights to the states, and they delegated rights to the federal government, but they reserved unto themselves one right: that's freedom of speech. Well, that's still reserved, I'm part of the people, and that's reserved. I use it the way I please, and nobody can tell me how to use my right to speak or not to speak. He tried—he wanted me to talk about other people.

MOYERS: He wanted you to name some other people who—

HORTON: He said, you know, he said that he wanted to ask if certain people had been at Highlander, and certain people were—if I knew certain people. And I said, "I speak for myself. I choose to say what I believe. You ask questions about me you want, I'll answer you. But I will not answer any questions about anybody else—they have to answer for themselves, just like I answer for myself. So I will answer no question about anybody." The first person he asked about was my wife.[66] I said, "I can't speak for her, I speak for nobody but myself." And then he gave me this song and dance I just told you, and I said, "Nope. Ask me about me. I love to talk about what I believe in—that's what I've been doing all my adult life." And he said, "Throw him out! Throw him out!" And he had the guards take me and throw me out. It was the only time I ever made the front page of the *New York Times*.[67]

MOYERS: Look, Myles, if everyone made a private heresy out of challenging the system, how would society function?

HORTON: I believe in laws, but I know that the only way that laws can have any meaning, they have to be just laws. For just laws to have a meaning, and to have a society of laws, you've got to challenge unjust laws. This concept was provided for by an amendment to the Constitution, you know, our trials where you can appeal—this is not as kind of outside of reality as it seems to people.

MOYERS: You think that's what Jefferson might have meant when he said that every generation ought to entertain the possibility of its own revolution?

HORTON: That's right, that's right. I've quoted that many times, I've said, you know, I started out I thought there ought to be a revolution in this country, I mean a revolution that, you know, is run democratically, because I believe in democracy—we don't have it, and none of the countries that I know of and I know practically all of them—

MOYERS: We don't have it? We hear all these salutes to democracy on Inaugural Day and—

HORTON: No, we don't have it. We have some trimmings of democracy. We have some of—like the parliament electoral system, which might have worked in the early days when you had a handful of people, but, you know, people don't have anything to say about the people they elect today, you know that. That's why only a small percentage of people vote.

They know that the thing is set up—it's so—too far away from them. We have to really examine all of our structures in this country, to make them more democratic. You can't have democracy in the workplace, when the system is run for the benefit or the profit of somebody instead of for the benefit of all the people. You know, so we can't have economic democracy under a profit-taking system, we can't have political democracy when we don't have some kind of decentralization that brings government closer to the people. That sounds like Reagan,[68] you know, but you do have to have—you do have to break the system down to where people could have more say about their own lives. I mean that's efficient, that's more creative. I believe in a kind of pluralistic sort of society. We've never—no country, no system has to my mind, you know, thought too seriously about how you do this, and I think it's one of the things we ought to be about in this country.

MOYERS: On your journey to Highlander, you were studying in New York at Union Theological Seminary, under Reinhold Niebuhr.[69]

HORTON: I went up there, I'll tell you what happened. I was—I used to stay with a preacher over at Crossville, Tennessee, named Nightingale,[70] he was as near a saint as I ever ran into. Instead of just preaching on a Sunday, he'd go out and help people. He'd go to a hospital and empty bedpans, you know, he was a worker, he identified with people. And I liked him and I used to stay with him when I was bumming around the mountains. I worked for—I was state student YMCA secretary for a while and then I worked for the Presbyterian Church in the mountains, so I used to know him quite well. So the year after I finished college I was kind of flipping around, trying to figure out what I was going to do. And by that time I had discovered that my dream to be at a job teaching in a college or a high school in the mountains wouldn't be realized, because I found that those schools were not all I thought they were, or what I imagined them to be. I found they were all indoctrinating people, all building people into the status quo, they were all, you know, doing kind of molding people instead of liberating people. There was nothing creative about it. So I decided I couldn't do that, so I was trying to figure out what I wanted to do. I wanted to work educationally, in terms of my values, but I didn't know how. And this preacher says, "You ought to go to—" you know, he said, "you don't know enough, you're too ignorant." And he said, you know, "You ought to go to Union Theological Seminary, someplace like that where, you know, you'd like the intellectual atmosphere and so on." And I said, "Never heard of it." But he wrote and got an application. And one day he said, you know, "You don't have to go, you fill it out," he said. "They won't accept you, they're pretty—it's hard to get into, it's a kind of intellectual place, you don't have enough—such a good education, but it won't hurt to just fill it out and even if they accept you, you don't have to go." And to get him off my neck, I signed that application and sent it in. Well, the reason I was accepted, not because I was academically, you know, trained for it—they did have, they picked the best in the country—but because they wanted somebody from the South from the mountains, and somebody who played football, and somebody who was a hillbilly. You know, that's how I got into Union.

MOYERS: *[Laughs.]* Token hillbilly.

HORTON: I know that, I know I was a token, otherwise I could have never gotten in, because everybody there, they were all, you know, smart, academically smart. But Niebuhr was there for the first year, and he was a flaming Socialist, a pacifist, with a lot of qualifications, and [had] explored. But most of all, he'd run a workers' church in Detroit,[71] and he was—

MOYERS: He had just come from that church.

HORTON: Just come from there, and he was—

MOYERS: What he had seen with the workers and the Ford, and the industry—

HORTON: Yes, he was exploring these other things. So he was just made for me, and he took me under his wing—not as a token person, but somebody—

MOYERS: You became friends, didn't you?

HORTON: And we became very good friends, after you know, and I spent the—I put in a lot of time with him. And he, in fact, he moved me way ahead of myself. He put me in a seminar with the graduate students and professors and priests and people like that, and I couldn't understand a word he was saying.

MOYERS: Did you think about dropping out?

HORTON: Hell, I told him I was—We had a break, I went through one whole two-hour session of the seminar, two periods, and I kept thinking, well, you know, it's over my head, I don't have the conceptual background, I don't understand these things, but, you know, I'm trying to learn, and it was nice. But then I went to the first of the other one, and after the first one, I said, I can't cut it, you know, I knew it was not for me. So I walked out and said, "I'm not going back in, Reinhold, I appreciate your inviting me, but I can't, I don't understand what's going on. I can go to the library and if I can't read one book I can read another." I said, "I know how to read, I know how to learn, but I can't understand what you're talking about. I don't have enough background." And we were out in the quadrangle—he's a smoker, and you had to go outside to smoke—and we're standing there, and he said, "Now don't do that Myles, don't." And he turned around to these people, and he said, "Now this fellow, he can't understand what I'm saying. He should be able to understand, and I want to talk to people like him, because he's got a good mind." And—but he says, "What about the rest of you?" And do you know they admitted to the man that they didn't understand it, and they didn't have the nerve to tell him about it? Then they all said, "No, no."

MOYERS: "We don't understand it."

HORTON: "We don't understand it"—every one of them said it. And there was a judge there who said, "Yep, he's right. We were too embarrassed to do it." Rein says, "Myles, you've got to stay in, because you're the only one to tell me the truth." And he said, "Any time in the middle of something, you just hold up your hand, and tell me what's wrong, and I'll listen." Well, that's the kind of relationship I had with Rein.

MOYERS: There was a story about your attending a parade there.

HORTON: Yeah, oh yeah, what happened was I had played football in college, and I'd a big maroon sweater, I had taken the letter "C" off of it for Cumberland University, and I just wore it to keep warm. You know, I didn't have any money. I hitchhiked to New York to go to school, I waited on tables, you know—I was just a poor guy trying to go to school. I started out doing it when I was fifteen, so I was pretty good at it by then. And I was—it was a May Day parade—May Day was big then, and I had never seen a May Day parade. May Day, in my background, was when you went around and decorated the graves in the cemeteries, you know. So there was a big May Day parade up there, so I said, well, I'll go to the parade, you know. So I went down and there was a tremendous lot of people there—they had all these banners, and people marching, and unions and lots of organizations, and some religious organizations, and I was standing there, just watching.

MOYERS: Just a bystander.

HORTON: Oh, yeah, I was on the sidewalk, I didn't even know what the parade was all about. So the police—they had what they called the Cossacks, and it was a good name for them, police rode horses, and they rode between the bystanders on the sidewalk, and the paraders, you know, I guess to keep them separated, and this cop on a horse leaned over and said, "There's a red son of a bitch," and just Wham! right on top of my head. You see, I got a red sweater on. But the amusing part of that was, I used to try to tell it to explain my confusion about the initials they used for the Communist Party, the C.P. And I grew up in the Cumberland Presbyterian church, and that was C.P. And all my life, C.P. meant Cumberland Presbyterian. And that sweater came from a Cumberland Presbyterian college, that marked me as a red, you see.

MOYERS: Was it a radicalizing moment?

HORTON: Oh, man, it moved me—you know, like Castro said the Bay of Pigs made a Communist country out of Cuba, this moved me into thinking very fast, you know, about what's it all about, what's the police power. That was my first run-in with police. I lived in small towns, I'd never lived in the city. I'd had trouble, but I'd never had been beaten up. So I saw the police as part of the establishment, part of the oppressive something. It—

MOYERS: And that explosive power—

HORTON: At that time I was beginning to try to understand Karl Marx, just theoretically. Most of my background was a religious background, mountain background. I had a little working, but not—it had no radical influence.

MOYERS: What did you see in the South in those days that made you believe there was a need for a school like Highlander?

HORTON: Well, the need for it was the poverty that I grew up knowing about and being a part of. See, I started making my own living when I was fifteen, so I could go to school, so I knew—I didn't read about it, I knew it, I lived it. And I knew all my people and you know, all the people I grew up with, my relatives and all. I knew the poverty, and I knew that people were shut in, you know, they couldn't—their life was too narrow, and there ought to be some way, you know, to get something more creative going. And I also knew that industry was going to come in, you know, you can make an analysis of that kind very simply. And that industry was going to come in to exploit the people, and I didn't want them to be exploited, I wanted them to learn how to organize, so they could, you know, take care of their interests. One of the chief purposes we had in mind was to try to—we said we try to change society by understanding it so we'd have a decent society, but one of the immediate things was to help people understand union, labor and political strategy for working people.

MOYERS: You really wanted to try to organize the workers?

HORTON: Oh, we weren't going to organize. Highlander is not an organization school. Fact is, we've had hundreds and hundreds of people at Highlander who've been organizers, but we don't—we say to do a good educational job, to teach people how to think and how to analyze, they can become organizers, we don't train them to become organizers. I don't agree with this training people to do things. You liberate them and they train themselves.

MOYERS: So what was the germ of your idea?

HORTON: We did want to help develop leadership for unions, and leadership for—a tremendous lot of leadership in the South came out of Highlander, through Highlander.

MOYERS: Why unions? Why did that appeal to you?

HORTON: Well, the basis of economic democracy. I don't believe you can have democracy with just political democracy. I used to talk to Martin Luther King a lot about that, and he agreed theoretically, but it was only later on that he started putting into practice the idea that you had to—[it] wasn't enough as he says to be able to eat a hamburger with a white person, you had to have the money to be able to buy it. And he got killed when he did that, you see, trying to organize the garbage workers. So I thought— I knew from the beginning economic democracy had to go hand in hand with political democracy, so I was always keyed into that.

MOYERS: Can you describe for me what conditions were like for the workers in this part of the country in those days?

HORTON: Well, they tried to organize Elizabethton up here,[72] where my ancestors came from, Watauga settlement,[73] and that was in the late '20s, and they brought troops there to break the strike and run people back into the hills until they behaved themselves, and all they were doing was trying to cut down on the twelve-hour workday and get more than eight dollars a week for working. And you know, they beat them into submission.

MOYERS: They?

HORTON: I mean, the company, it was the first multinational, it was—it came here in the '20s.

MOYERS: What was it?

HORTON: It was a Bimberg rayon plant. It was a multinational plant—of course, we didn't know that then. But that's what it was that I'm talking about.

MOYERS: And the workers tried to organize?

HORTON: They tried to organize. And that plant was built on the land that one of my ancestors got the first land grant in Tennessee, that's where that plant was built, right on that spot. And—but those people were just being pushed around. Now, those people had a background like my background, they came out of a good tradition and so on.

MOYERS: Mountain people are supposed to be pretty tough, pretty independent, they could take care of themselves.

HORTON: Well, tough, till you know you bring these troops in, tough, you don't stand up against hard gun thugs, and police, and troops.

MOYERS: Well, given that reality, why did you think that a bunch of teachers at a seclusive place like this could identify with men in circumstances as painful as those?

HORTON: Okay, now, I believe that it had to be done. And I was determined to try to do it. And I was determined to identify, to be—have these people perceive that I had solidarity with them. I knew that had to be.

MOYERS: Here you were—Union Theological Seminary, Chicago University—

HORTON: A year ago up in West Virginia they got to arguing about people who had come down, these experts would come in from these universities, and somebody says, "Well, you know, your friend Myles Horton is one of them." "The hell he is," he says, "he's never been to school. We know him." You know?

MOYERS: *[Laughs.]* But why did you think—

HORTON: So I knew it was a handicap, but I thought I could overcome it somehow. Well, I tell you, it's very interesting. We did make a terrible lot of mistakes the first year because of that. We thought what we had learned we could apply pretty much like you were taught it would apply. So we fell flat on our face, we weren't getting through to the people. So we had a little self-criticism, and we said, what we know, the solutions we have are for the problems the people don't have. And we're trying to solve their problems by saying they have the problems that we have the solutions for. That's academia, so it won't work. So what we've got to do is to unlearn much of what we've learned, and then try to learn how to learn from the people. In other words, instead of learning from what we learned academically, we've got to learn how to relate to their experiences.

MOYERS: Well, how did you do that?

HORTON: Well, we did that by very strict censorship on ourselves to try to quit talking the jargon, to quit trying to use educational terminology, and go out and listen to the people. Now you listen to the people, not just words but by their emotions, or what you see around, by the children, by the surroundings, there's a lot of ways of communications. We had to learn a whole new way of communicating.

MOYERS: Did you have to ask them what they wanted to learn?

HORTON: No, you don't ask them, you just go around and get to know them well enough that you could figure it out. You go around, and one of the first things I figured out was all of my interest in democracy and brotherhood, all of which I think is sound, it was that they didn't want to talk about democracy and brotherhood, they wanted something in their bellies. You know, they wanted some clothes on their backs. And they weren't listening to anything we said about that. So we had to learn, we had to help them with our programs—we had to start cooperatives, we help[ed] organizing unions, we had to fight for them, to, you know, get surplus food—we had to identify with them in the economic struggles—

MOYERS: The realities.

HORTON: The realities that they perceived as the important thing before they would—we could share the things that we perceived. That was the kind of learning we had to go through.

MOYERS: But tell me specifically, Myles, what did you do to these workers when they came here in the early days?

HORTON: Okay. In the first place, you had to have their confidence, because by helping them with their problems, like I said earlier, you had to learn from people, you had to start where they were and deal with their problems. And we say, "Look. Who's been telling you what to do—teachers, preachers, politicians—and did it work? Was it good advice, did it work for you? I don't know, but you wouldn't be here if that worked. Because you've had plenty of advice, you've had plenty of people telling you what to do. So we're not going to do that, we're not going to compound that. We're going to try something else—we're going to try to build on what you know, and your experiences, and help you understand that your neighbors have some experiences, and that other people in another place, maybe in another country, have some experiences that relate to this problem. I remember one fellow that came from over here in the mountains, up near the North Carolina line. He said, "When I came here, I had one little piece of pie that had all of the answers. Pie has all of the answers." He said, "I had a little slice of that pie. And Joe here, he had a little slice, somebody else had a little slice. And Myles told us about some other people that had a little slice, and he contributed to that slice. So now we got the whole pie and now I know everything, I got the whole pie, and I'm going to take the whole pie back home instead of my little slice." Well, he was proud of the fact that he contributed a slice, you know, he didn't then just learn from other people. Well, that's what happens.

MOYERS: You didn't—

HORTON: But in addition to getting that information, you got to get motivation. And motivation comes from within, not from outside in something, you don't motivate somebody, you help them to learn to motivate themselves. So what you do is to try to get people to have more confidence in themselves and their peers, and to understand it's up to them, there's nobody else can do it.

MOYERS: Many of these people would go back and put their heads in front of a billy club, wouldn't they?

HORTON: Yes, and then they'd get in jail and so on, and they'd yell for help and we'd [go] to help them, but we'd never show our faces, you know, we'd work behind the scenes with them.

MOYERS: And yet you were arrested several times.

HORTON: Oh, well, we're—well, you know, if you are perceived by the enemy of working people, or enemy of blacks, to have solidarity with them, if that's their perception of you, then they're going to treat you like they treat them. In other words, you're one of them, so they'll beat you up or jail you just like them. That's not the price you pay, that's the privilege you have.

MOYERS: When was the first time you were arrested?

HORTON: Oh, the first time I was arrested was in the second year of Highlander, in '33. There was a strike at Wilder, Tennessee.[74]

MOYERS: That's in one of—that was one of the poorest—

HORTON: Yes, well, we were living in—Highlander was located in one of the eleven poorest counties in the United States.[75] There was a higher percentage of people on welfare in that county. And there were only eleven, I don't know how it rated among the eleven, but it was among the eleven. Wilder was another one of the counties—another one of the counties in the mountains in Tennessee. So, they had a strike. And they'd had a strike for some time, and some of the people came over and asked if we'd come—if we could help them somehow with that strike. And I said, "I don't know enough about it," and they said well—I said I'll go over, you know, go over and visit. I went over there and I was trying to get some of them to come to Highlander, because that's the way we worked—don't go in and do it, you get—pull them out and then send them back in to do it. They go back to where they came from to do it, it's their base. And they—word got around that I was—folks, outsiders were around stirring up trouble, and the National Guard—there was a lot of young National Guard people over there, the governor had sent the National Guard in to protect the property,[76] there had been some violence—and they arrested me. And I said, "You can't arrest me, you got to give a charge." And they had these bayonets punching in my belly and my backbone, so I wasn't arguing with them much, I was kind of gently suggesting, you know, that they ought to have a charge. So they had a little huddle over to the side, one guy said, "You're arrested for coming over here and getting information and going back and teaching it."

MOYERS: And that was a crime.

HORTON: And that was what I was arrested for. So I always said this was the only time I was ever arrested where the charge was accurate. That's exactly what I was doing.

MOYERS: What was it like for those men in Wilder when they went on strike? It was a company town, wasn't it?

HORTON: It was a company town, and the company was determined to break the union, and during the depression, and lot of people wanting jobs, so it was fairly easy. But the people wouldn't, you know, they just wouldn't give up. So they brought the troops in to protect the property. And they were—there was no welfare programs there, and the Red Cross was in existence, but the head of the Red Cross was the wife of the superintendent of the mines, and she gave Red Cross flour to the scabs, not to the union people, not to the strikers. No strikers could get any Red Cross—the people who were working, to supplement the company pay, they got all the Red Cross—I exposed that, and there was an investigation that, you know, that supported my charge. They went over and they found that was absolutely true. Nobody believed it, but when I came out with an exposé of what happened—you know, the Red Cross was a sacred cow, you know—and I'd said, you know, that's what the Red Cross was doing there, and that's what everybody was doing—these people were starving to death, literally starving, the people, you know, babies getting extended bellies, and people are hungry. And you know, they'd eaten up everything in the countryside, and we'd better do something about this situation. Then the editorials started coming, said I was a Communist, stirring up trouble, you know. That was stirring up trouble, because I was the one that was—if I hadn't gone there, there wouldn't have been this trouble, you know. So that was the kind or thing we were into.

MOYERS: Tell me about that strike in, I think it was in 1937, in North Lumberton, North Carolina,[77] when you called for the pretty girls, and the American flag, and someone to play the banjo.

HORTON: Oh, well, you see, you—most people when they're doing educational work and organizing, it's so heavy-handed, there's no sense of humor, you know. The working people, you know, they have bread and roses, too, on their mind, and they got—people think self-interest of people is economic self-interest, but there are a lot of other self-interests, you know. Part of it is certainly getting a little pleasure out of the most miserable situation. They have a wonderful sense of humor, they have to have to survive. So if you don't have that, you know, then you don't relate to the people. Now you got to go fishing with them, and drink beer with them, and have fun with them, and so on. One of the things I would do over there, we'd had a massed picket line, around the mill, and the sheriff and the deputy couldn't keep—we had so many people, we'd have a thousand people, they couldn't deal with us very well. So they'd call for the state highway patrol to come in and help. And the governor wouldn't station a highway patrol there for political reasons, or other reasons, but when they'd call for it, they would—they'd come in. Well, I'd helped to organize a newspaper guild in Raleigh while I was over there working, and so I had my confederates there, and the newspaper was right across the street from the highway patrol. So then they'd start out to come to Lumberton, to come down there, then I'd get the call from—one of the newspaper guys would call me. They'd have the—anybody that saw them leave was supposed to call and send word for me, you see, that they were coming. Well, it took about an hour to get there.

MOYERS: For the patrol, you mean.

HORTON: Patrol to get there. And they'd call them, and we'd have a picket line, wouldn't let anybody get anywhere near that mill, real militant picket line, and tough, you know, and the time the troops got there, we'd send practically everybody home, we'd have—we'd keep all the gals around, we'd get some pretty women, and we'd get some guys who played instruments—guitar player[s]—and by the time they got there, there'd be just a few women sitting around, and fellows sitting there picking a guitar, and me sitting under a tree listening to the music, you know, and there'd be nothing going on. And then when they'd drive up with their—they drove up with their masks on, you know, getting ready for warfare with their guns in the cars, and these girls would go over and say, "Hey, Buddy," you know, "how're you doing? You're nice looking, what've you got there?" And they'd start hiding the stuff, they were so embarrassed. We'd pull stuff like that. And then the troops would go back and they'd say, "No, we couldn't—nothing's happening down there."

MOYERS: Just a bunch of pretty girls.

HORTON: Yes, nothing happened. And then the company'd call them, and by the time they got back, we'd have a thousand people back on the picket line. Well, we had to pull things like that all the time.

MOYERS: Was this place, Lumberton, North Carolina, when the four guys came after you with the guns and you made your best organizing speech?

HORTON: Oh, yeah, that's—I had some experiences there, that was very educational to me.

MOYERS: What happened that time?

HORTON: I was trying to get those people to make a decision, because the big thing is to get people to have confidence they can make decisions. I was doing pretty well, so they made all the plans, and committees were set up, and they'd made all the decisions. I just sat with them, and encouraged them to make decisions, but it got pretty rough. And it looked like I was about to lose the strike. And the strike committee got pretty desperate, they weren't so sure of themselves. So they came up to my room one time and said, "We got to talk about plans." And they talked it over and said, "Myles, you got to tell us what to do. We've just gone as far as we can." And I said, "You've got to run this union, so you might as well learn. You learn when it's easy, and you learn when it's rough. And if you don't learn to make tough decisions, you know, I learned, I get the learning experience you don't. I need it less than you do. You need the learning experience. I can get along without it, you know. So you've got to make the decision." They said, "But there's two thousand people involved in this decision." And I said, "Sure, that's why you, you know, it's a rather important decision, but you've got to make it." And one guy says, you know, "You've gotta, you've gotta make this decision." I said, "No, no, I—" And he says, "Now you're not at High-lander running a school, you're running a strike, and there's all these people, you know, and it's a serious business, and you can't just say we've got to learn to do this." So I said, "No, You've gotta make it." So he just pulled—reached in his pocket and pulled out a gun, and he said, "You sonuvabitch, make this decision right now!" *[Laughs.]* I came nearer to going back on my principles of education than I ever did in my life.

MOYERS: But did you stick firm?

HORTON: Yeah, I did. I said, "Well," you know, "You can win this round, but you still won't know how to make decisions after you get through." I admit I was scared, I've usually been scared in situations like that.

MOYERS: You do know fear?

HORTON: Oh yes, I know fear. You didn't survive—I wouldn't have been here today if I didn't know fear. If you don't know fear, it's just like having the sense of touch, so when you burn your finger, you know, it hurts. If you didn't have that, you'd burn your finger off. You know, you wouldn't—or you put your hand in the buzz saw, you wouldn't know it but you'd be looking off when you cut it off. If you don't know fear, in this kind of business, when you're playing on the cutting edge of social change, and conflict situations, where there—you know, where the sides are lined up, and there's violence all the time, you better learn to know it.

MOYERS: What about the time the four guys showed up in the street below the hotel?

HORTON: Yeah, that in a sense was another time I was afraid. They had hired these people to kill me.

MOYERS: Who had?

HORTON: The company. And the company was tied in with the power structure in the town. Bill, just to show you how solid they were, one Sunday
every minister in that town prayed that I'd leave town—every church.
Every church.

MOYERS: Didn't you get the message? Or didn't He get the message?

HORTON: Well, He was busy or something, because He never did anything
about it. I didn't leave, but then I—the reason I—then they sent a delegation to see me, and told me I had to leave town. And I—that was
before they got the people to kill me, that was an afterthought. And I
said, "Well, you know, gentlemen," I said, you know, "I can appreciate
your problem." I said, "This town's been nice and quiet, and you've been
living off of these people out in the mill ridges, and now it's changed, and
they're beginning to stand up and I can see why you'd want me to leave
town. But," I said, and I said, you know, "There's a lot of logic on your
side, you know, the majority of the people here would like for me to
leave town. So you put it to a vote, you know, democratic decision, I'd
have to leave town. But," I said, "none of those things are factors in this."
And they were getting ready for some real posh statement, you know,
"Well," I said, "you have to understand my problem. I come from the
mountains, you know, and you know what happens in mountains, you
know, people live back in the mountains and they inbreed, and a lot of
degeneracy takes place, and then people get so they don't have any of
their mental facilities, are impaired. Of course, they believe all that stuff,
you see, so I knew they'd read all this stuff, and I said, "You know, I'm
just so degenerate I haven't got the energy to leave." *[Laughs.]* They
were fit to be tied. They stormed out of that room. They were really crazy.

MOYERS: Then they put out a contract.

HORTON: Then they put out a contract, and these people came and—

MOYERS: How many of them?

HORTON: Four. And the—my hotel was across from the courthouse, and the
sheriff's office was right across from—on the side next to me, where I
could see the sheriff all the time, and he could see my room. The sheriff
left town, all the police left town, they closed the post office, they closed
the stores—everybody left town in the middle of Wednesday afternoon.
And nobody had ever left those posts before in the history of that town.
And I kind of walked down the street, I didn't pay much attention to it,
but I noticed everything was so quiet. And I looked over at the courthouse, and everything was quiet—usually there was a hubbub around
there. So I went up to my room, you know, kind of wondering about why
all this quietness was around. Nobody was seeing anybody around the
hotel. Pretty soon this car came up, and they stopped outside my window. And I was sitting looking, because, you know, I was a little appre-
hensive, I didn't know about what. And the Klan had tried to run me

out before that, so I was kind of, you know, had that on my mind. So I looked out the window, and these fellows were sitting in that car, and then I knew. They had guns, and I knew what was happening. The town had cleared out, and they was going to—So I thought, well, this is it, Horton, you know. You got to think fast, and keep your calm. So I leaned out the window, and I said, "Hey, what are you fellows doing?" They looked up and, you know, they were going to come up, they didn't expect me to see them. And they didn't say anything. And I said, "Well, I understand you're supposed to kill me." You know. Well, they looked a little confused, and I knew, and I said, "You know, I've been trying to learn how to be a organizer, you know, get some practice organizing, and the more experience I have, the better I'll be, you know," and I said, "this is probably the last chance I'll have to learn anything, maybe I'll just practice a little on you, you know, don't you want me to organize you? My last efforts to organize." They laughed, they thought that was funny. One guy took a big swig of beer, and they laughed and pointed up to me and waved their guns, and said, "Organize us?" And I says, "Yeah, you've got to be organized." They said, "We're against it, we don't have anything to do with organization, that's for, you know, you're a trouble-maker, you're a Communist, you're—" I said, "No, no, no," I said, "I'll organize you, you need to be organized." And I said, "You don't understand. Now, you're coming up here to kill me and you [are] gonna kill me, but each of you thinks, you know, that you won't be killed. Now some of you are going to be killed, because I'm going to—" And I went over, and a Holiness preacher had brought me a big old gun, and I just put it in the drawer, I never even picked it up. And he said, "You've got to keep this," and he gave me a blessing and he told me to keep that gun.

MOYERS: A Holiness preacher.

HORTON: Yeah, he was a worker in the plant. Good one. And so I remembered that gun, and so I went over and got that gun, and I sat there with that gun in my hand, and I said, "Now, you come up here, the first person comes through the door, I'm going to kill him. And maybe the second person, I'm going to kill him. Now the third person and the fourth person are going to kill me. That's the way it's going to be, you see," I said. "You've never thought about the two of you who are going to be dead in a few minutes, you just thought about me being dead. That right?" You know, and they started looking at each other because they hadn't thought about it that way. And I said to the guy in the front, "You know, you're going to be dead in a few minutes, you got a family, what are they going to think, you come back home in a box? Well, how about you in the backseat, you look tough, maybe they'll put you in front, you know, and you'll be dead. Are you ready for this, you know, you guys ready to die? Now, let's see, which two of you going to be dead, now. You got to get organized, so you can decide among yourselves who are going to be dead. So, that's why you need to organize." And I never will forget the feeling I felt, like I see I was really getting through to them, you know. So I was sitting there with that gun, and I had the greatest, greatest desire to try to twirl it, like you do in the movies? And I knew damn well if I did it I'd throw it out the window. *[Laughs.]* But I wanted so much to sit there while they were making up their minds, to twist that pistol around my finger, but I knew, I figured I'd lose it so I'd better not try then. That was going too far. So I sat there holding on to it, scared to death.

MOYERS: Could you have shot the damned thing?

HORTON: I never even thought about it. I figured I'd talk my way out of it, not shoot my way out of it. I never even looked at the gun to see how you—done it that way. Because I was gambling on talking, you know. And sure enough they started looking, and they took some more beer, and they talked, and looked at it. I just kept holding that gun, and I'd say, "Okay, you guys, you got it together? Who's going to be dead, hey, you in the front." I just kept individualizing them, you see. I said, "Maybe I'd shoot you in the head, or maybe the heart. I guess I could shoot you in the heart, you know, or blow your guts out. Now, you know, you're spread out, you're a fat man, the guts spread out up here in the hallway, now that'd be nice, you know." I just kept on being nasty to them. They drove away. They drove away. And I just sunk back in.

Illustrations

Horton, 1940s.

Horton (*with pipe*) at Highlander with labor group, c. 1940

Zilphia and Myles Horton,
date unknown.

Horton, 1940s.

Horton, 1940s.

Horton, Eleanor Roosevelt, and James Stokely, late 1950s.

Horton with Calvin Brewer, 1950s.

Aimee and Myles Horton, 1964.

Esau Jenkins, Charles Gomillion, and Horton

Horton, early 1950s.

Horton, 1950s.

Esau Jenkins and Horton, 1950s.

Billboard showing Martin Luther King Jr. attending a meeting at Highlander, Labor Day weekend, 1957.

Horton, 1960s.

Paolo Freire, *left,* and Horton, *right,* 1987. Person in background unidentified

Horton, *left,* and Freire, *right,* 1987.

Horton, 1970s.

T-shirt honoring Horton, 1987.

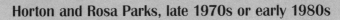
Horton and Rosa Parks, late 1970s or early 1980s

Horton, late 1970s or early 1980s.

Horton, 1984.

Section III

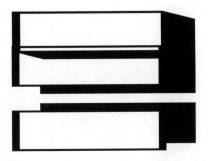

The Civil Rights Movement

We Must Understand People as They Are

[1957]

The following is a speech that was delivered at the Annual Meeting of the National Conference of Catholic Charities in Kansas City, Missouri, on September 14, 1957. The title has been taken from internal references in the speech and encapsulates the main thrust of this address—beginning where people are—especially in relation to the civil rights movement in which, in 1957, Highlander was heavily involved.

Perhaps our experiences at the Highlander Folk School in Tennessee may throw some light on the problem being faced by agencies working with southerners who are moving to northern cities. It took many years for us to create a climate in which Negroes felt accepted enough to relax and learn. For example, a Negro carpenter from South Carolina came to Highlander for a workshop several years ago and on his return told his daughter, a public school teacher, that she should enroll. She insisted her father had been taken in by whites and that his report of full acceptance as a person could not be true. He prevailed upon her to enroll, but she came prepared to return home the same day. On her return she added her testimony to that of her father and tried to interest her younger sister. A year later her sister and her husband came to Highlander. The teacher's story to her neighbors of what impressed her is enlightening.

For the first time in my life I found myself in a place where the brotherhood of man was lived instead of just preached—where discrimination in relation to our living at Highlander was never discussed because it didn't exist. We lived together in a dormitory where we shared a common bathroom and there was a voluntary exchange of such personal possessions as bathing suits, bathing caps, toothpaste, soap, etc. Nobody seemed to remember or care who owned what. The reason I mention *how* we lived at Highlander is because to a Negro in the South the sense of personal dignity and respect which goes with these simple acts is more meaningful than a hundred sermons or a dozen interracial meetings.

During the workshop sessions everyone was comfortable and at ease.

A sincere desire to work with Negroes from the South is a good starting place for whites but is not enough. Repeated demonstrations and consistent practices are necessary.

Highlander is located in the southern mountains and in the early years of the school we found that having staff members with a mountain background was important if we were to deal with problems of the area. Today we find that Negro staff members are even more important if we are to deal with public school integration and other problems of segregation.

When Negro students come to Highlander they are concerned about the status of our Negro teachers. Are they policy makers or subordinates? They are not impressed with token representation.

The creation of the proper climate for learning is conducive to working with any group of people who feel that they are not fully accepted. The first step is to parallel voiced principles with visible practices.

At Highlander we learned that we must start with these natural situations in which we find people and make this the basis for introducing new values.

Values, however, cannot be set by us for the people. On the other hand, we should not leave people alone to educate themselves. We must work with the people in setting goals.

New values are seldom accepted until they can be fitted into one established way of thinking and doing and can be justified among one's associates. What people think of themselves and what their neighbors think of them is more important than what we think.

But first we must understand people as they are. Let me read you a statement: "Higher status is thought of in terms of such material results as a new car and flashy clothes." This sounds like a description of southern Negroes in one of your cities, doesn't it? But it is a description of white people from the southern mountains who have moved to Cincinnati. There is nothing unusual about this reaction and it could well apply to Negroes. When people do not feel accepted they have to compensate in some form that gives them status with their own group. With apologies to Thorstein Veblen, this might be called the "law of conspicuous compensation."[1]

People's values differ, but not absolutely, and the problems of migrants from the South have much in common. However, recent developments increase the intensity of the problem in working with the Negro. His timetable has been accelerated. Hope and despair are mixed. Both sides of this picture were presented at Highlander recently. Let me read the *Nashville Banner*'s comment on two addresses:

Aubrey Williams,[2] veteran of the New Deal wars,[3] sees the danger of armed rebellion unless the Deep South modifies its segregation stand. On the other hand, the Reverend Martin Luther King, leader of the Montgomery, Alabama, bus boycott, believes America is on the threshold of its most thriving period in race relations.

To meet his challenge we must enlist the support of volunteers and not try to do the job ourselves. We have discovered that volunteer leadership can best be developed and motivated at short residential workshops for recognized and potential community leaders.

Citizenship Schools

[1961]

The following text is a transcript of a talk given by Horton at the Experimental Citizenship School Workshop, February 19–21, 1961, at Highlander. Months after this speech, in which Horton describes the history, philosophy, and future course of the Citizenship Schools, responsibility for this important educational program was turned over to the Southern Christian Leadership Conference.

This is a kind of farewell session for me, and I want to tell you why.

Six or seven years ago, we began what might be called a "pilot" program on the Sea Islands,[4] in an effort to find a way of carrying on an educational plan or concept that would make sense in terms of objectives at Highlander, and also in terms of the situation itself. Now, six years later, that period of testing is over. The project in which we experienced, and learned, and in which we are sure of ourselves, is now being replaced by a program which will take the Citizenship School idea all over the South. There are people in foreign countries, too, who are interested, and recently I've been asked to send our program to India. In other words, you people have been part of a project that is giving the world something different.

I'd like to show you what I think has happened, because I believe you'll understand then why I say this really is a beginning of a new stage in the history of Highlander Folk School.

First, I want to say that the idea out of which all this grew, in terms of philosophy, is related to more than small specifics, such as making out a check, or voting, or even reading and writing. It means much more than these things. In fact many programs have tried to teach the specifics, and millions of dollars have been spent on them over years and years. And yet very little has happened. But the Citizenship School represents something that *has* happened, and I want to tell you what I think it is, and why it has happened this way.

As I said before, many programs of education and human betterment have done over and over again the same things we do, and in better ways. So it isn't the doing of these things that makes the Citizenship School different and better. It's something else.

Now what is this difference? Let me tell you what I think. Suppose we make this circle down here represent what *is* in our lives. The situation down here somewhere is what we have to start with, because we have to start from where we are. Most programs do that. And it means they start with something specific that will help people do what they need to do at once. It may be teaching them how to write a check, to make a motion in a business meeting, or registering to vote. It may be teaching them to read and write. But that's where most of the programs stop—down at the "is" circle, so that the person learning never gets much away from where he is. There's no pull to anything farther along.

But the truth is that in themselves these small things have no value at all—they are negative, and in fact they may even produce a disservice. So often the specifics I've talked about are the very things that hold people tighter to themselves. For instance, a man might learn to read and write simply in order to feather his own nest. Or he might learn to make a motion in a business meeting in order to manipulate the meeting. (The best crooks are sometimes the ones to make motions.) Or someone might learn to write a check in order to forge one. If these specifics are learned for selfish purpose only, then they are better not learned.

Now in our Citizenship Schools, of course, we must start, as everybody else does, with the *is*. We have started there, and we have taught and learned those specifics, as they do in other schools.

But we have discovered that there was a magnetic pull up in the direction of what *ought to be*—human brotherhood, dignity, and democracy. We have kept our eyes firmly on the *ought to be*, and it seems to me that in our schools we have succeeded in making a pattern of procedure so that all the things that are needed down here—the specifics in the "is" circle—begin to move together in the direction of what *ought to be*, and this is the difference. This is the magnetic pull.

In other words, you yourselves as teachers and leaders, with your eyes on the *ought to be*, and keeping it in your own minds, have incorporated in everything you have done the values that lead people to look in the direction of the right goals. I think this attitude had made the difference in our schools.

Now if my idea is true, then the *teachers* are the ones who will really make the difference! They can make the program go round and round inside this circle of what *is*, without getting very far—or they can make the program lead up and away in a given direction. I think that this is where the genius of our program lies. We start with what and where we are, but we have our minds set on what we're after, and we know the direction in which we want to move. The idea is to help other people keep moving in the same way, in that direction.

Take for instance an old man who has never learned to read and write, and who wouldn't want to go into an ordinary school where he would be treated as a kid. What happens to him in the Citizenship School? Well, of course the teacher must start with where the man *is*. But at the same time he is thought of always in terms of what he *can become*. And because the teacher thinks of him that way, this man can think of himself that way too.

The difference is in the teacher's attitude toward him. It isn't a fixed or negative attitude. It is in terms of what can be and will be.

Take this young lady. She's younger than I (unfortunately) and she lacks certain information which I have learned. Now if I think of her simply as limited, compared with me, in knowledge, then my attitude will be negative —patronizing. This won't help her much. But if I think if her in terms of what she can become, why I have a concept of her that staggers the imagination! I can't even make the boundaries to her possibilities! There is no limit to the admiration and appreciation I can have for her in terms of what she can and will be!

That is the way I feel about our classes. I think they really are different from the kind that are being carried on in Chattanooga on the radio, where teachers teach segregated classes and the people are taught to read. (But the teachers don't talk about anything significant because if they did they might get into trouble.) Of course some of these people are going to learn to read. But I don't think the relationship of the teacher to the people can possibly produce the kinds of results we are achieving in the Citizenship Schools, because we are getting results not only in terms of reading and writing but in terms of intelligent first-class citizens—hundreds and hundreds of them— simply because we began by assuming that they *could* be citizens.

Now all this may sound far-fetched to you. You might not express it in the same words. But if I have observed correctly, this is what really is different in our schools. The difference is not the method—although methods should be constantly improved and we should learn the best ways there are of doing the mechanics, too. But even the best method will take you round and round in a circle if you don't have a goal, and that must be in your minds from the beginning. The goal—and I think it is brotherhood, democracy, a kind of world in which we need to live—must be constantly in view —and when this is so then we really have a different kind of teaching, not in terms of mechanics, but in terms of philosophy, which means a different kind of program.

That is it. And to me it is worth all the years of experimenting, refining, and observing, to discover and define it. And what does this mean to you, as teachers? Well, we all have different ways of saying things, but I believe I am safe in believing that you teachers are persons who have confidence in the people you teach, and have been able to actualize your best ideals in terms of these people. You have been able to see them become the persons you believed they could be.

I want to posit for you that this belief, this confidence you have in people is what makes you good teachers, as we understand the term. And this, I think, is a new idea, a new concept of teaching, realized in a new combination and relationship of ideas, goals, and methods, and the interaction between them. As I have said, the six years in which you have carried on and been a part of an educational experiment are over. Now we are taking this experience, which is you, and we are setting out to make the experience available to the whole South, to anybody who wants it. You people on the Sea Islands have made a contribution. You are offering a new educational concept to people. And you are going to be asked to go along with your gift, and help to see that it is understood and carried out. Today you are here to do just that—to pass on your idea to these others here, who are starting out.

The first stage is past. We are trying to set up a program whereby Mrs. Clark can feed into the stream of southern life other people trained like you to do this very thing.[5] We are at the place where we can multiply the idea and spread it far and wide. In a year's time we should have a hundred schools in operation. Next year we should have two hundred more. Instead of our going out from Highlander to work with programs in the field we have worked out a procedure by which people can come here, be trained, and then go out and teach as you are teaching.

We have people here connected with a number of organizations—the Southern Christian Leadership Conference, the Savannah Voters Crusade,[6] the Madison County Voters League.[7] These organizations want to be instrumental in supplying this kind of training to their people. This means that there is official interest on the part of organizations who want to take Esau's idea,[8] which Septima set in motion, which Bernice worked with[9]—to people all over the South.

Of course when you make a contribution, you want to keep it as pure as you can. You must take care that your great idea isn't watered down to the conventional one of simply teaching people to do little things, unrelated to each other and without any large purpose. You must keep that large purpose in mind, hold onto the "ideal that staggers the imagination"—the purpose so large that you can't fully realize it yourself, but have to keep growing to reach it—that you can't fully believe or understand is true. But you must keep remembering that it becomes true if you keep looking, and following that way.

Like every other good, broad, sound idea, this one is capable of growth in its own stances, and we have an example of an adaptation made as late as last month—an aspect of our training which we hadn't actually thought of before. It grew out of a workshop for college students we had here, when Judy Gregory, a student from the University of Virginia, offered a new direction to the nonviolent protest. She said that in addition to protest, there should be the giving of useful service. She said it isn't enough just to be able to go into a store and drink a cup of coffee. We should do that of course, and we want the parks and schools desegregated too. But in addition to demanding rights (which ought to be demanded) she said we should declare at the same time that we're willing to go further and do something ourselves, to make the world better. She reminded us that we have been so concerned about demands for rights that we haven't taken time to look at the other side of the coin and she insisted that the demanding, and the willingness to do something positive, go hand in hand. Well, we took this idea of Judy's and passed it on to Lane College.[10] They took it up, and today we have some people here from a college group that is interested not only in protesting, and demanding rights, but also in going out to be of service—these young people are going to teach in Citizenship Schools. This suggestion was made, and went from in front of this fireplace in a workshop session, and in two months it will have been tried out. If it works, perhaps Mr. Porter and these three students will be pioneers in a new idea that will spread to other colleges. You see how it grows and spreads on its own momentum.

And here is another of those suggestions that suddenly appear, and find their place in the big concept of the Citizenship School idea. Less than two weeks ago Lewis Jones was in my house.[11] I told him about the Southern Christian Leadership program, and I said that if they took up the idea and spread it through their communities, they would need to find a lot of new teachers. I said I knew our experience would be helpful, but they would have to work faster than we had been able to. Lewis got up and walked back and forth in front of the fireplace (a lot of things happen in front of fireplaces here) and finally said, "I've got an uncle down in Texas. He's a retired school teacher, and he would like nothing better than to teach in one of these schools." And then he said, "I've got an aunt, too." Lewis has enough relatives to staff schools all over the South. And who are they? They're retired people who have had professional training—religious educators, ministers, teachers. And this will be a golden opportunity for them to make themselves useful.

So this workshop represents a whole story—people, program, and ideas. Here in this room we have college students who are ready to be teachers. We have the suggestion of finding teachers at the other end of the age spectrum. We have people who are from the organizations which want to help spread our idea. We have people who know and are the program, and we have people who are already beginning to carry it to other places. You people will come up with other ideas that we haven't thought about before —maybe better ones.

But what I'm trying to say is that once you got a dream pinned down to where you know what you're reaching for, you can let your mind flow and make it come true. The only thing you have to do is start with people where they are, and then, instead of going around in the same circles over and over, let everything you do and say lead in a worthwhile direction. And try always to be imaginative and creative as you think of the resources.

That is about all there is to it.

I started out by saying that this is in a sense a farewell for me, because in the past I've been interested in this program as a pilot project. But this is the beginning of a new association. Now Mrs. Clark is working with Bernice, and they will take the idea and spread it throughout the South. And you people who are starting out now, with their help, will begin embroidering, refining, and adapting it, as we move into a new stage of activity.

You will be pioneers in the second stage, that enlarge and makes available the idea for wider use. You represent the people who will launch the idea. You have the great South ahead, the open sky above, and in an age when millions of dollars are being spent for rockets and space ships, this idea which you jointly will launch can be of more value, can be more earthshaking, more significant to human welfare than all the rockets at Cape Canaveral.

It's a Miracle—I Still Don't Believe It

[1966]

This interview originally appeared in the May 1966 issue of Phi Delta Kappan. *The original prefatory material indicates that the interview was taped the previous June at the then-new Highlander Research and Education Center in Knoxville, Tennessee, and that in it Horton "describes educational methods he has developed to enable spurned and exploited minorities to attack their problems successfully."*

PHI DELTA KAPPAN: There is disagreement among Student Nonviolent Coordinating Committee and Southern Christian Leadership Conference people with regard to the future of nonviolence in the civil rights movement.[12] What attitude do you take? Do you take a position?

MYLES HORTON: I have an answer I have been using for years. At Highlander we discuss all kinds of philosophies and try to understand them, but we don't necessarily take a position on the things we discuss or present. However, on this question there is a definite answer. Education per se is nonviolent. It is a means of helping people to understand, of enabling people to change their own minds voluntarily on the basis of information and illumination. Our whole approach to life is an educational approach. We can't beat things into people's heads, so in that sense we predate the nonviolent advocacy. We go no further than that because we don't want to alienate or cut off the opportunity of working with people who hold different points of view.

PHI DELTA KAPPAN: So you set yourself certain limited goals and try to reach them by any means at hand. For example, right now in Mississippi the object is to get Negroes to understand the issues and register to vote. Is that correct?

HORTON: Yes. The current civil rights movement with which Highlander has been associated from the very beginning through its students and educational services started out as a protest. The bus boycott in Montgomery was the first. One of our students, Mrs. Rosa Parks, was the person whose refusal to give a white man her seat precipitated that movement.[13] The Negro demands were minimal, for fixed seating on a bus. So it started out just as a request for decent treatment. Then the nonviolent methodology evolved.

Negroes have historically been both violent and nonviolent. Sometimes they use force and sometimes—for the most part—nonviolence. Their first demands in the current movement, you know, were just to eat at a greasy-spoon hamburger joint, or get into a movie. But that wasn't what they really wanted. These were just symbols of wanting a little dignity. The student leaders were influenced primarily by Martin Luther King and people like the Reverend James Lawson, who has been conducting workshops in Nashville.[14] But the first meeting of the sit-inners, which later became the SNCC, was at Highlander, and I remember the discussion very well. In fact, I have some written records of it. On tape I have a speech I made to them at the time. I said, "I am convinced that these spontaneous student protests mark the beginning of a sustained effort which will lead to fuller participation by Negroes in all phases of economic and political life." My observation then was that 15 or 20 percent of the students espoused nonviolence philosophically and for the rest of them it was a matter of going along with what seemed to be the best procedure.

So to say the SNCC movement is a nonviolent movement is both accurate and inaccurate. It started out with a kind of pragmatic commitment to nonviolence as a tactic, which it has pretty well carried over to this day. Now the difference is that you get people saying openly that they don't believe in nonviolence or saying that if they can't win nonviolently they'll use violence. Really, it's not a great shift in the thinking in terms of convictions.

PHI DELTA KAPPAN: What you said about the sit-ins reminds me vividly of a self-deprecating little talk you once gave at the Spring Conference in Chicago.[15] You had been trying to help workshop groups to clarify their thinking and all of a sudden they spontaneously came up with the notion of the sit-in as a way to achieve their goals. You took no credit for the idea, but after all it was people who were at Highlander who developed the tactic.

HORTON: Well, one way to look at it is the way our enemies look at it, which is one-sided but does throw some light on the matter. They point out that not only was Rosa Parks a student at Highlander but that a majority of the leaders of the sit-ins had been at workshops at Highlander. All of this is factually true. What I was saying at the Spring Conference and what I would still say is that it didn't occur to us to tell Rosa Parks what to do or to work out the strategy. But we did say to these people, "You should have dignity and you should command respect and you're going to have to organize to get it. Now just how you go about it we don't know." The things we talked about were very close both to the SCLC (which has a citizenship school program we've worked out and given them for their educational arm) and to the Council of Federated Organizations (COFO),[16] SNCC, and the Mississippi Freedom Democratic party,[17] their programs are evolved from their own thinking and they quite often are first articulated at Highlander workshops. The 1964 Summer Program in Mississippi,[18] for example, was planned at a Highlander workshop in Greenville the previous November. Certainly, it wasn't anything we take credit for. The truth of the matter is that the workshop was run entirely with a staff of Mississippi people, so it was our workshop only in the sense that we financed and organized it and put it together. The ideas didn't come from us. They came from the COFO staff, and the workshop staff was selected by Robert Moses.[19]

PHI DELTA KAPPAN: Yes, but you're the catalyst. I think that's what we'd have to say. The enzyme that brings these elements together and produces novelty.

HORTON: Sometimes they ask questions, you know. But the creativity of this movement, I say, couldn't come from the brain of a white man.

PHI DELTA KAPPAN: Maybe that's right. There were two very important points made at this Spring Conference I mentioned a moment ago. One of them was, "Here is the fellow, more than anyone else, who is responsible for the civil rights movement in the South." The other was "He's the only white man the Negroes fully trust."

HORTON: Well, Rosa Parks made that statement at Montgomery on the radio. My wife heard it, asked me about it on the telephone, and wrote me about it.[20] I joined the easy last part of the [Selma-Montgomery] march like so many other lazy people did, and marched in from the edge of town into the capital, Montgomery.[21] And on the way in there was this big billboard with a picture of Martin Luther King "at a Communist training school." Rosa Parks was one of the speakers in Montgomery. She was introduced by King as "the mother of the current civil rights movement." She commented on this picture and said the story was going around that Dr. King is a Communist because he's been at what's called a Communist training school. She said that King had not been a student, although he was a speaker there and she heard him. She said she had been a student there and she wanted everybody to know it, and wanted them to know what kind of school it was. She made the statement that's been picked up and used in some articles around the country: "Myles Horton is the first white man I ever trusted and he taught me to trust white people." This maybe has some significance: that those of us who are white can somehow win the confidence of Negroes to the place that they trust some whites. And if they trust some whites they have hopes that they can trust others. Which is a minor contribution to make; I don't want to belittle it. But once having done that, then the creativity comes maybe from the feeling of security or hope or strength that grows out of it.

PHI DELTA KAPPAN: I know that your workshops often start with a discussion of the self-image of the people who attend them. I'm wondering if you devote a good deal of time to trying to change that self-image. How is it done? Can you do it in a couple of weeks? Can you really instill some hope?

HORTON: There's more to it than you suggest. This is a controversial point in education. My position is that whatever Highlander has been able to do in changing people and helping them achieve a certain feeling of dignity comes from the fact that we deal with people who come with problems. We don't justify our existence on the basis of what happens in a week or month at Highlander. The educational process has started long before they come, and continues after they leave. What we do at a typical workshop is say, "What are your problems, how do you see yourself, what do you want to do, what do you want to be?" If the workshop is three weeks, we'll take a week, maybe, to state and analyze their problems. We find a few central problems and spend a week discussing them with the help of consultants, audiovisual aids, etc.

PHI DELTA KAPPAN: Do you have all of these people together, the consultants and students? There are no separate sessions?

HORTON: Yes we always sit together. We try to work with twenty-five to thirty people at a time. If there are more we divide them into groups. Now, during the second period we have these people talk about themselves and their problems. Then we throw light on these problems by using information and also by using their own experience, which they've never looked at before in the way we put it together. We add something to it for recombining, but a lot of it is drawn right out of the people. There might be some sound research that throws light on a problem which we can bring into the picture, or there might be the experience of somebody else, or it might be something written in a book, you know. Or something very stimulating in a movie. We use a lot of audiovisuals. We tape the people's discussions so they can hear them played back, and also so we'll have a record.

PHI DELTA KAPPAN: This is almost like the Communist "self-criticism" procedure, isn't it?

HORTON: Well, there is a lot of criticism, a lot of informal discussion. People who've never been willing to air their problems before do it here. They talk about how they've failed.

PHI DELTA KAPPAN: What are their problems, typically?

HORTON: Well, mostly their inability to achieve what they want to achieve. And largely among the Negroes it's because of the white domination which doesn't allow them opportunities. This is usually the complaint. Also, they quite often say, "Well, we can't get our own people together."

There's just as much criticism of their own people as of the opposition. They seldom find anything wrong with themselves—at first, you see. Then we have to encourage them to be more critical. "Maybe you can learn from this person who has succeeded," we say. "Maybe he has done it this way and maybe you can learn from this experience and maybe the reason you have been failing is that you dominate everything—you want to run the show. You're used to doing it." Preachers are usually that way, you know. You finally work through this. Then you're feeding in information and suggesting alternate approaches at the same time you're discussing it. That's the second part of a Highlander workshop.

The third part comes when we ask, and this is very important: "What are you going to do when you get back home? With what you have brought here, with what you have learned?" Inevitably their thinking will have changed. They have new ideas and new ways of looking at he situation back home. They have been stimulated by something they've read or seen or heard and have a picture of their problem quite different from that they had when they came. Some talk about what they're going to do when they get back. With a new perspective, this third and final period has several facets. One is just thinking through and putting together what they want to do—articulating it. Another thing is, they've made a commitment to other people who like themselves have brought problems. They've said things in the presence of other people and their plans are recorded on tape. We encourage them by saying, "You've brought these problems here. We've been a sort of catalyst in a process that makes a little bulge in your education. Now are you going to keep on learning? You can learn more after you get back home than you did here because you've learned to look at your problems in a different way. Highlander will continue to relate to you in terms of this process when you get back. So you're not going back alone. We'll work with you if you get in trouble."

So when we are asked why we claim to change people's ways of doing things in a week or two, we say we don't say that, you see. The length of the formal workshop period may be just a week, but you have to think of the total educational process. But if a workshop is well done—and we don't always do it well—not only information and new thinking but hope and a feeling of competence are produced. This is probably as important as anything else—the feeling that you can do something worthwhile.

PHI DELTA KAPPAN: Do you have to overcome a lot of self-pity?

HORTON: Only self-pity and intolerance for other people like themselves. The white man is a devil, but the devil is their poor neighbor who won't cooperate with them or get off their back. You see, they are almost on an equal footing. In most of the workshops this kind of feeling is present. So you have to produce a feeling that people can rise above that somehow. Another way of saying it is that we try to give people a sense of their own dignity by listening to what they're saying or even what they're thinking. You know, sometimes people can communicate without saying things.

I remember something Dr. Fred Patterson said shortly after he resigned as president of Tuskegee[22] to head the Phelps-Stokes Foundation.[23] He came to Highlander to observe a workshop. Afterward he said it was so foreign to anything he had ever known that after two or three days he thought, "Myles has scraped the bottom of the barrel just to get together a hodge-podge of people. He's got Ph.D.s, he's got illiterates, he's got educated Negroes and ignorant white people. It's an impossible situation." He said, "I was just about to make up my mind that this thing was no good when it began to dawn on me what was happening. I wished this was what Tuskegee had been doing all through the years."

He said, "Why you put me, as a college president, on the same level of respect with this white sharecropper from West Tennessee who couldn't read. You did it by making me see that he had learned some things while I was going to school and running a college and didn't have time to learn, and by making him understand that even though I was a college president maybe I had learned some things he needed to know. Then for the first time I understood what Highlander was." Patterson said, "I felt that you were really treating me with respect and not using me."

I think he put his finger on something. It's an atmosphere, a climate, you create.

PHI DELTA KAPPAN: You have a real touch if you can produce that kind of climate.

HORTON: This is what we try to do. I'll show you before you leave some little poems that the students left on the walls and little things people say about Highlander after they have been here a week and begin to see what I'm talking about.

PHI DELTA KAPPAN: I want to know how the white sharecropper came to be here.

HORTON: Well, he was interested, strangely enough, in desegregation. Of course that was five or six years ago when we were trying to get people together to talk about integration in schools and communities as result of the Supreme Court decision.[24] We had these contacts through some work we'd been doing with the Farmers Union cooperatives.[25]

PHI DELTA KAPPAN: You get people here worth all kinds of motives, I guess, through different channels.

HORTON: You see we have to watch ourselves. We assume certain people are interested in certain things. That's because we think they're supposed to be interested.

PHI DELTA KAPPAN: "White sharecropper." That's supposed to identify someone. But he's still an individual first.

IT'S A MIRACLE—I STILL DON'T BELIEVE IT   **153**

HORTON: He was interested in this problem. He wanted to come, and he went back to his community, had Negroes in his home, and was really a local leader—still is a leader.

Part of our methodology is to learn not to be surprised or shocked at anything anybody says or thinks. You know, you just sit and you try to draw a person out and understand. Maybe people are shocked but I'm not shocked, because I'm interested. We approach everybody the same way and this gives people a feeling of ease. The people that we work with sense it. And they begin to pick it up. But at first they think, "Why don't you say something?" I'm listening, you see, and I don't have anything to say. Some other students say, "We can't say that. That's not the way our government runs," or "That's not the way people think." I say, "Now wait a minute. That's a man talking about what he thinks. He can say anything he wants to here. We want to hear him out and see what and how he thinks. You can say what you think but let him say what he thinks." You don't have to put people in little boxes, you know. It doesn't take long to get this spirit around.

PHI DELTA KAPPAN: I'm reminded of the remark that is attributed to Malcolm Knowles [professor of adult education, Boston University], who regards Highlander as one of the truly unique adult education institutions of our time.[26]

HORTON: He's been a supporter of Highlander all along. When we had trouble with the state he came out with very strong letters of protest and endorsement and a detailed defense of Highlander. Malcolm has understood that we do get educational results. So many people in formal education have difficulty grasping anything outside of their own way of doing things.

PHI DELTA KAPPAN: Yes, they say, "What are your standards of admission?" This sort of thing. Let me start a new line of questioning. I understand that you are now interested in slum problems and particularly in the rural slums of Appalachia. What progress have you made?

HORTON: We don't know how to touch it.

PHI DELTA KAPPAN: You're just feeling your way at this point?

HORTON: Up to now we've been busy—since organization of the labor unions in the thirties—with people who were already conscious of their needs and problems could easily be made conscious of them. In the early days before the 1954 Supreme Court decision we had to work pretty hard to reach Negroes. But by having Negroes staff members we were able to get a start. Now, with the Appalachia program, we're right back where we were from 1932 to 1935 during the depression, trying to find ways to approach the problem, without any movement, any apparent spark to the thing, any way of getting hold particularly of the poor whites. We are feeling our way along. It is very challenging and exciting to me.

Years ago we organized and developed what was credited with being one of the most effective literacy citizenship programs in the South. We got more people to learn to read and write and to vote than other agencies, according to a government adult education official. We worked out all the technicalities and set up teacher training programs. Then I completely lost interest and didn't have anything to do with it for a year or so, until we got the bright idea of peddling the program to other organizations. Then I got interested in it again. Dr. Martin Luther King decided he wanted to use the Citizenship Schools for the Southern Christian Leadership Conference, so I spoke to him about getting the staff, materials, and money. We helped get his first grant for the Citizenship Schools. That was kind of fun, getting the program over into the hands of somebody else. But once I get a program developed it's not terribly exciting to me.

When you asked me about the civil rights movement I said it isn't that it's less interesting than it was in its first two years when we were getting the civil rights people to run their own workshops. But there are a hundred workshops going today. It's really beginning to go. Now what we need to do is to keep getting new ideas and giving a little help, a little encouragement. When you do this it does not take a lot of creative time and energy, because you know what you are doing and why.

Now this Appalachia thing: I'd be willing to bet you that five years from now I won't know much more than I do now. I think there will be a lot of activity; a lot of things will happen. But we'll be lucky if in five years we have a program that will produce important results. To do this you have to dig deep and tap creative forces of the people in Appalachia. You must have something basic enough to provide a common denominator for use in other like situations. This doesn't come from thinking alone; it comes from experimenting, taking old ideas and evolving new ones. Finally, you may get something that is so simple that you ask, "Why didn't that occur to us before?" You don't think of these simple things. You think of the complicated ones.

Let me give you an illustration of what I mean. The secretary and bookkeeper here is a mountain gal, a wonderful woman whose father was bushwhacked—shot down—and Miss Mack has a salty way of talking and thinking. We get a lot of harassing phone calls from the Klan and Birchers.[27] One day somebody asked, "How many mulattos have you got running around over there?" Mack replied, "How many have you lost?"

You couldn't accuse me of making this story up. If I could make up a story like that I'd be a millionaire. It's the same with educational ideas. It took me several years to get my first simple, usable idea. *[Here Horton described his early work for the Presbyterian Church, his study at Union Theological Seminary and at the University of Chicago, and his year in Denmark examining and teaching in the folk schools.]*[28] It came almost like intuition through all this rational business I was working so hard at. And I thought, "What you must do is go back and get a simple place and move in there and let the program grow out of the people's needs. You can't know in advance. You can go to school all your life and you'll still never figure it out because you're trying to get an answer that can only come from the people in the life situation." I came back to Tennessee in 1932 and I have just been following this intuition ever since. Now I am egotistical enough to want to try it in Appalachia. It will take time to get close to the people I grew up with.

PHI DELTA KAPPAN: Do you think all this federal money is going to help or hinder you?

HORTON: I don't think it's going to help do what I want to do. I'm not against money; in fact, I think there needs to be a lot more money. But I don't think that this amount of money, the top-down way it is being spent, will necessarily help very much. Poverty is too basic a problem to be solved with this amount of money and this approach.

PHI DELTA KAPPAN: A much harder thing to get will be ideas, I suppose. I have some preconceived ideas, such as the notion that the best thing to do is close up shop and get these people of Appalachia out into other areas.

HORTON: Let the people have something to say about it. Let's not assume we can think through this thing. I am a little discouraged about all the agencies that have been working in this area. I've been working with them, I've been on their boards, a consultant; I've taught for them, so I'm not saying "them"; I'm saying "us." We say people are apathetic; people don't think; they have been spiritually killed by relief; they have been underemployed so long that all the intelligent ones have left. We make all these judgments. Some of them may be right; I'm not saying they're wrong. But I'm saying I don't think we have any right to make such judgments and then to act on them. We've got to get behind the judgments somehow and listen to the people themselves.

Now, when I get away from speculating like this and get out and try to do something, or when I meet with the little group here in this room—twenty-five or thirty people who are really sweating this thing out—and they ask me, "Okay, now quit the speculating and say what to do"—I'll have to admit I don't know what to do.

I've been up against that before. But I found out what to do from the people. This will be the hardest thing I've ever tackled—much more difficult than working with the unions or civil rights movement. I'd just like to give it a try.

PHI DELTA KAPPAN: How do you explain your own motivation in this? You are very different from, say, a reformer like Saul Alinsky.[29]

HORTON: Motivation is something I've never been able to figure out for myself or anyone. People say to me, "They beat you up, they burn you out, they call you every kind of name. Why don't you leave? Why don't you get a job somewhere else?" Well, it's hard to answer. And the only answer I have is that I was born here and I want to stay here and help as best I can.

PHI DELTA KAPPAN: Oh, come on. You really enjoy this conflict situation.

HORTON: No, I really don't enjoy it, but I don't mind it. It's worth it. It bothers me, but I don't take it too seriously.[30]

PHI DELTA KAPPAN: Did you make any effort to find out who burned you out these different times?

HORTON: Oh yes. In fact, I know. The fire marshal told me the Klan burned us out in the Smoky Mountains. He knew the people who did it. But he said that he couldn't get any witnesses to testify in court. He said they brag about it; they laugh about it. But you couldn't convict them.

PHI DELTA KAPPAN: Because they'd be sitting in judgment of themselves?

HORTON: For the same reason you can't convict the sheriff of Neshoba County, Mississippi.[31] When the courts decide to get you they are not an instrument of justice but an instrument of the status quo. There's nothing you can do. A Department of Justice official who read all the court records and did a lot of work on the Highlander Folk School case told me that he was absolutely convinced that this case was planned from the very beginning by representatives from the attorney generals' offices in three or four southern states in such a way that there would be no way we could appeal. The whole thing was planned from the beginning to use the courts to close Highlander and confiscate our property.[32]

PHI DELTA KAPPAN: Did you ever have anyone take a good portrait photograph of yourself?

HORTON: The picture of me I'm really the proudest of was the big photo on the front page of the *Nashville Tennessean* during the Highlander Folk School trial when I was sitting in the courtroom laughing. I was just sitting there and I was kind of bored with all this procedure. I told the judge if he wanted to get information about Highlander I'd tell him so he wouldn't have to call all those state witnesses. Finally, he found that my information was usually more reliable than the stories being told by the state's witnesses, most of whom had court records. But all that time I was sitting there and I knew they were going to close us down. All these officials from the Deep South were meeting every night with Tennessee officials so I knew it was the end.

I said to myself, "They think of an institution as a building and a charter and that they'll close us down." It's very easy to find some way to do that. I was looking around the room full of people who had come in to testify for me. When the trial started I horrified our lawyer by telling him we wouldn't subpoena anybody. He said, "How are you going to get any witnesses?" I said, "Just announce to the press that anybody who wants to volunteer as a witness can be a witness." But he said we couldn't do it that way. I said, "Sure you can—you'll have a whole courthouse full."

Well, we had sixty people from the University of the South alone, including twenty-five professors.[33] That was the nearest university. We had people from all over the United States and two from Europe. People just flooded in there. We couldn't use all of them. The number of Highlander volunteers with Ph.D.s was about equal to state's witnesses with criminal records. So they were sitting there in the room and a lot of our former students were sitting there. I got to thinking of all the people all over the South who would form little Highlanders in their own communities; you know how these things get going. I was sitting there smiling and I have a way of just blanking out when I get bored. The judge banged his gavel and said, "Order in the courtroom. What are you laughing about?" I didn't realize I was laughing. But the TV cameras caught it.

So I told him. "You're having a trial about buildings and some paraphernalia. I just realized how powerless the courts are to deal with something like Highlander, because it's in the minds and hearts of people and there's really nothing you can do. And I was thinking about how amusing it was to spend all this state money on a trial."

PHI DELTA KAPPAN: I particularly want a copy of that picture.

HORTON: Later on we were having a little private session with the judge and our lawyer said, "Now, look, judge, all you're going to do is have another Scopes Trial, a disgraceful thing to Tennessee.[34] What do you think Horton is going to do when you close Highlander down?" And the judge said, "I think I know now that Mr. Horton will go out and start another school. I'm just going to do my duty and close it. He doesn't take this seriously because a building isn't important to him. He started out with nothing and worked for nothing all his life and will start over."

PHI DELTA KAPPAN: Were you reimbursed?

HORTON: No. They even took my home and my mother's home.

PHI DELTA KAPPAN: I thought I read that the school sold for about a third of what it was worth.

HORTON: But that went to the state. We got nothing.

PHI DELTA KAPPAN: But you were able to get a charter for the Highlander Center?

HORTON: Yes, and we took the identical board and rechartered. We stated in our application for a new charter that the purpose was to take over the program of the Highlander Folk School.

PHI DELTA KAPPAN: Didn't you have any difficulty?

HORTON: Oh, sure we did. The state secretary's office hesitated and we threatened to sue them. Under Tennessee law if you apply for a charter it's mandatory that they give it unless they can prove that you have some illegal purpose or ulterior motive.

PHI DELTA KAPPAN: Didn't they prove you a bad character?

HORTON: No! Listen here, I've got to educate you. This is something I've learned. A corporation is a new person, a new-born babe. So when they hesitated we said, "What do you mean you aren't going to give us a charter? There can be nothing ulterior in this corporation. It doesn't exist. It's just a figment of the imagination. It's legally pure and has never done anything because it has never existed."

They said, "Yes, but it's all the *same* person." So I said, "No, no—read your law. A new person is a new-born babe. And if you don't approve it by four tomorrow, we will sue the state." I've learned a lot of law in this process.

They sent it over to our attorney's office by messenger.

PHI DELTA KAPPAN: Surely it must have been kind of impressive to the people of Tennessee to see the kind of support you got merely from making an announcement in the press.

HORTON: We gained contributors. We didn't lose a single board member. We didn't lose any public support.

PHI DELTA KAPPAN: Have you ever been written up in *Time* or the other national news magazines?

HORTON: Oh, every once in a while, usually when there is something sensational. Education is not of any great news value.

PHI DELTA KAPPAN: There has to be some conflict for education to be mentioned.

HORTON: The thing that excites me about my job doesn't excite the press. I minimize these things that most people get excited about because to me the important thing is just the excitement, the creativity of working with people and seeing things happen, to put together things that work and get people moving to think for themselves. This to me is challenging and rewarding and I still look at it in a kind of amazement, like it's a miracle every time it happens. I still don't believe it.

The Place of Whites in the Civil Rights Movement

[1967]

This speech, taken from Horton's prepared text, was given at an April 26–29, 1967, Amherst College Conference on "The Negro: Assimilation in a Democratic Culture." Other lecturers included Whitney Young Jr., executive director, National Urban League; Kenneth Clark, professor of psychology, City College, City University of New York; Ivanhoe Donaldson, director of the New York Office of the Student

Nonviolent Coordinating Committee (SNCC); and Lawrence Levine, professor of American history, University of California, Berkeley. In this talk, Horton argues that "the role of concerned whites is to help strengthen Negro leadership—not seek to share leadership," building on themes touched on ten years earlier in "We Must Understand People as They Are."

It is an honor to take part in the Amherst College Conference on the Negro and Civil Rights. What I have to say about the civil rights movement and the white man's role is colored by personal values and experience which is limited to the South. I do not speak as a neutral.

Unfortunately, my experience does not include activities in the colleges where there is so much healthy ferment. I was recently reminded of this gap in my education when Paul Goodman remarked, "Students 'dig' you, but you don't 'dig' them." Be that as it may, I would like to share some of my impressions.

The civil rights movement is not the result of a master plan. Mrs. Rosa Parks,[35] a Negro seamstress, was arrested in Montgomery, Alabama, in 1955 for refusing to give up her bus seat to a white man. The first protest meeting was called by Mr. E. D. Nixon,[36] a Pullman-porter and union organizer. Both were local NAACP officials.[37] Mrs. Parks reacted, Mr. Nixon acted, and Rev. Martin Luther King emerged as the leader of the Montgomery Improvement Association,[38] bringing something old, the Southern Negro's religion, and something new, passive resistance.

The only demand at first was for fixed seating on the white man's bus. But the violent resistance helped the Negro understand the racist nature of white society. By 1957, when the Southern Christian Leadership Conference was formed, Negroes were no longer satisfied with a place on the white man's bus. There was a growing awareness that human dignity was structured out of white-dominated society.

Three years later, the Student Nonviolent Coordinating Committee emerged as a protest against the humiliating denial of service at dime-store lunch counters.[39] The students' only demand at first was for a seat at the white man's lunch counter. But they were beaten and jailed into a realization that they wanted more out of life than white society had to offer.

Both these southern-born civil rights organizations have functioned more as vanguards of a social movement, committed to social change, than as conventional organizations with fixed structure and well-established programs. And unlike the older civil rights organizations in which whites played a leading role, SCLC and SNCC were formed entirely by Negroes. SCLC has never shared basic policy making with whites and SNCC has recently returned to its original position of having control in the hands of Negroes. Both are Negro-led if not Negro-fed.

During the past ten years, the civil rights movement, spearheaded by SCLC and SNCC, has uncovered seeds of freedom buried deep in the collective memory of the Negro. A spirit of hope and of human dignity has been awakened and brought to life. Southern Negroes are today drawing on their inner resources as never before in my memory. There are beginnings of political, economic, and educational programs in which seeds of future society are being quietly sown.

I will not detail the more familiar voter registration campaigns and campaigns to elect Negroes to county and municipal offices (some successful), but give examples that show the range of less well-publicized activities. These unheralded activities of the movement include:

—A Negro printing press publishing its third volume of movement poetry.[40]

—The Free Southern Theater, barnstorming the Deep South, giving free shows, mostly for Negroes who have never seen live actors.

—The Georgia Folk Festival and the Atlanta Penny Festival, which presents Negro history through drama and song; the Southern Student Organizing Committee tours of integrated folk-singing teams.

—The SNCC Photographic Department.

—SCLC's Operation Bread Basket, which has won thousands of new and better jobs and stimulated Negro-owned businesses.

—The Southwest Alabama Co-operative Association.

—Strike City, Mississippi, where sixty persons ejected from plantations are now living in houses which they helped construct.

—The Poor People's Corporation has developed seventeen Mississippi cooperatives.

—The Liberty House Co-operative provides for the marketing of goods produced by the cooperatives.

A *Wall Street Journal* article, "Dixie Negroes Start Co-ops to Break Their Dependence on Whites," observes that: "Seldom has a more unlikely business venture got off the ground."

Most of the educational activities go unrecorded because they are carried on by nonprofessional teachers, without supervision or coordination, in the most unlikely places and manners. Some workshops are in taverns and stores, others in homes and churches (most schools are off limits for education). Movement people, working for the most part independently, bring together their neighbors to talk about politics and welfare, and the cooperatives and credit unions. They discuss the government Poverty Program and Negro history and the war.[41]

In Tennessee's Fayette and Haywood Counties, educational programs are being built around the nine succeeding candidates to local offices in the recent elections. Even though three thousand adults who "have gone on to teach tens of thousands in their home towns" have been trained by SCLC as Citizenship School teachers, there are few reports.

There has been little reporting from the movement people who have participated in scores of Highlander workshops on Freedom Schools,[42] Voter Registration, Campaigning for Negro Candidates, and others. But we learn, incidentally, of creative educational activities being carried on throughout the South. This new breed of movement educators feel responsible only to the people they teach, who in turn, become teachers of their neighbors. Some, however, approach education in a more formal fashion. The Sunflower County Mississippi Improvement Association is trying to establish a fund for a voter registration and political education staff. They are also planning to run Negro candidates for mayor and other local offices and start a Negro supermarket.

The Child Development Group of Mississippi illustrates the spread of leadership and local initiative. Hundreds of educationally deprived Negroes ran the program, and when the grant for the Head Start schools ran out, the poor continued teaching without pay until it was renewed.[43] They made maximum participation of the poor feasible.

Here are some excerpts from a Mississippi County report of a movement worker:

> We are planning a leadership conference for community leaders. A Political Handbook has been drawn up for the county and we hope to begin political education classes in each of the five beats soon. We also plan to continue having voter registration drives. In terms of candidates for the 1967 elections, we plan to run candidates in three out of five for offices of supervisors, justices of peace, a constable, and to run a black candidate for sheriff.
>
> In keeping with the concept of Black Power, several black-owned, operated, and controlled businesses have been established in Clay County on a cooperative basis. Presently, there are three cooperatives set up under the auspices of the Poor People's Corporation and we are working on a cooperative insurance fund for Negro industrial workers who get fired.[44]
>
> Two more communities are interested in setting up co-ops, but the PPC isn't ready to find any more groups because of their lack of funds. It might be pointed out here that all of these groups have been important to the political programs and activities we have engaged in. Number One, it gives us a strong basis of operation in the community and it seems that people are more responsive to political programs and activities in communities where those groups exist.
>
> We decided it might be profitable to open a restaurant and presented the idea to the MFDP executive committee,[45] who went for

the idea and we went to work immediately, taking Sheetrock and scraps of wood to remodel the MFDP Center that was previously used for meetings. What the restaurants will offer that other places don't offer is mostly color-different music and different food.

The decentralizing and vitality of the movement is underlined by the four hundred requests for financial assistance reported by the Southern Regional Council in an article by Pat Watters in the winter 1967 issue of *New South:*[46]

Is it over, then, fading away, giving up the movement and all it promised? Certainly, if one considered only the organizations, the answer would be a qualified yes, for the time, apparently. But the organizations were ever a thin representation of the more basic element of the movement, which is the people. The effect of what has been happening to the movement was described this way by a Southern Regional Council staff member: "It used to be that you could go to a civil rights headquarters in almost any part of any Southern state, and find out who the leaders and active people in any community might be. Now, there aren't as many headquarters. The leaders and the people are still active—maybe the people in five houses at the end of some little dirt road in some little town in the Black Belt. It's just more difficult to find out who they are these days."

One of the strong indications that the people are, indeed, still active is in the number of requests for funds received during the past year by the Voter Education Project[47]—more than four hundred for more than a million dollars.

It would seem that the movement people are beginning to understand the nature of the thick white wall standing between them and the opportunity. There is a realization that the reversal of "separate but equal" doctrine did little to reverse the separate and unequal practices for the Negroes in the South or automated into ghettos where they are suspended between their rural background and the TV world off-limits to them.

Many of the movements' strategies have reverted to the thinking behind A. Philip Randolph's proposed March on Washington in 1941:[48] "We shall not call upon our white friends to march with us," he said. "There are some things Negroes must do alone. This is our fight and we must see it through. If it costs money to finance a March on Washington, let Negroes pay for it."

They are beginning to realize that their resources can be converted into economic and political power only by the establishment of parallel institutions in all areas where they are excluded.

Stokely Carmichael points out that:[49] "Traditionally, for each new [ethnic] group, the route to social and political integration in America's pluralistic society has been through the organization of their own institutions with which to represent their communal needs within the larger society." (In *Massachusetts Review,* Autumn 1966.)

This traditional request for peaceful coexistence, side by side but retaining the Negro's identity, was widely condemned and Carmichael was accused by even some Negro leaders of encouraging the white backlash. But the following editorial in the March 1967 issue of the *United Mine Workers Journal* sets forth another point of view. Justine McCarthy writes:

> When you come right down to cases, the so-called "white backlash" does not exist.
>
> The reason we say there is no such thing is simply that whatever anti-Negro prejudice has been publicized recently was always there. Anti-Negro prejudice in America is a sickness that has plagued our society for nearly as long as the nation is old.
>
> It's much easier to be prejudiced against someone if you can identify him by the color of his skin.
>
> We don't think the fight of American Negroes is essentially any different than the fight of working people of all races in the 1930s. Working people in the nation's mass production industries wanted essentially one thing when John L. Lewis led their organizing drives in the '30s.[50] They wanted a sense of dignity as human beings and not to be just cogs in the machine.
>
> That's what America's Negroes are fighting for today: A sense of dignity as human beings. That, of course, is essentially what Stokely Carmichael is saying when he chants "Black Power." He's saying to Negroes: "You must have a sense of dignity as human beings." Unfortunately, perhaps, Brother Carmichael is stepping on a lot of toes and bringing to the surface a lot of hostility that was already there anyway.
>
> Responsible Negro leaders are opposed to the "Black Power" slogan if it leads to violence. But, let's be honest, the violence up to recently has all been on the other side. The violence that robs Negro Americans of their human dignity is the white violence of race hatred, of black ghettos, of "keep them in their place," of lynching and beatings, and constant insults and low pay and lousy jobs and all the other degrading ways that white America has forced on its Negro citizens.
>
> The whites of this nation had better start applying the chant "We Shall Overcome" to themselves. Because if they don't overcome their prejudices, we're all in for some terrible times blacks and whites.

Unlike Editor McCarthy, some whites are disturbed. They see Black Power as racism in reverse. What gave rise to the Black Power slogan and the National Committee of Negro Churchmen statement that: "Powerlessness breeds a race of beggars. We are now faced with a situation where conscience-less power meets powerless conscience"?[51]

The civil rights movement started as a revolt against injustices, and the first demands were based on individual aspiration for status in middle-class society. Viewed from the vantage point of a Black Belt cotton chopper, white folks seem to have about everything that could be reasonably hoped for. The practices, not the values, were challenged. But it became apparent that what gains that were made seldom, if ever, applied to the hard core poor.

"Millions of urban poor," a U.S. Bureau of Labor Statistics points out, "are employed in occupations in industries where earnings are low and many, because of lack of education or skill, are limited to menial jobs with substandard wages."

In the American big cities where most of the Negroes are gathered, more than half live in poverty areas, and those in nonpoverty areas are not much better off economically. In fact, another study points out that over the last twenty years, the Negro's economic status has worsened in relation to that of the whites.

There is criticism of the movements' change from protests of injustices to demands for jobs. But it should be remembered that economic opportunity is being demanded now in the context of the freedom struggles that preceded. Economic demands are not a substitute for, but basic to freedom. Not only should there be freedom to a job with adequate pay, but freedom to say "no" to the polluted mainstream of American life, and freedom to self-definition, Stokely Carmichael might add, freedom to buy any house you can pay for, freedom of movement for Negroes is denied in the name of property rights.

When "white" and "property" are combined with "law and order," we have a sacred trinity that only heretics dare question.

Passing from the economic, another source of confusion is the apparent rejection of whites, especially by SNCC.

Julius Lester of SNCC's Photographic Department writes:[52] "At one time, black people desperately wanted to be American, to communicate with whites, to live in the Beloved Community. Now, that is irrelevant. They know that it can't be until whites want it to be. It is obvious now that whites don't want it. If the white man interprets that to mean hatred, it is only a reflection of his own fears and anxiety and black people leave him to deal with it. There is too much to do to waste time and energy hating white people."

It may be some comfort to latecomers to the civil rights movement to learn that SNCC started out with a healthy skepticism regarding whites in policy-making positions. "Negro college students," I wrote in May 1960, "are excluding white youth from inner circles of their demonstration movement because they fear the whites will take over the leadership and in some instances don't trust them" *(Social Southern School News).*

It is fortunate that the civil rights movement started out as a non-violent movement. But as parts of the movement begin to take other forms, some, including friendly critics, protest. Negroes alone are expected to remain nonviolent under all circumstances. Other minority groups have been praised for defending themselves and for fighting against their oppressors.

Too often, whites have a fixed concept of what a Negro civil rights leader should be and say. All men are not made in our white image, except for color. Negroes do not necessarily accept the white hierarchy of values.

Here, we are up against a real problem. We think by setting up a hypothesis and casting about for various bits of information that [we] will prove or disprove it. Despite our rational pretenses, we tend to look for examples or illustrations that will document what we already believe. About the only illustrations that will document what we already believe. About the only illustrations we can see are the ones we are looking for.

There is a mountain saying that "before you criticize a person, you should walk a mile in his shoes." But seldom are poor people's shoes available or comfortable enough to wear.

At a meeting of the student demonstrators, Guy Carawan,[53] music director at Highlander, asked for new lines to "We Shall Overcome." I suggested, "The Truth Shall Make Us Free," mindful of the fact that the truths then held by the protesting students were not necessarily the ultimate truths. Truth is not easily come by, and often hidden from those of us who are color-blind and insulated from the smell of poverty. My experience has been that it is in the lives of the poor, their frustrations and dreams, that more of the truths that will make all of us free are to be discovered. Most of us have not yet learned that democracy can be set in motion by the most unlikely people.

We do not need to concern ourselves with the summer soldiers looking for a way out or those who say "whoever eats my bread, sings my song," but with the sincerely perplexed white.

In some quarters, liberal whites, viewed at first with skepticism, are now often considered the enemy. Even the completely involved white movement worker has been downgraded. Welcomed for a time, partially to get national attention, the attention he got proved to the Negro that the nation only cared for whites. He is constantly reminded that the dedicated and courageous white civil rights workers who sacrificed their lives are honored and remembered, but that the nation does not even know the number and only a few of the names of the Negro martyrs.

In the *Dark Ghetto: Dilemmas of Social Power,* Dr. Kenneth Clark warned us when he wrote: "The white liberal must be prepared, in this turbulent period of transition, to accept the fact that even his closest Negro friends will feel some hostility towards him for while the white liberal can delude himself into believing himself color blind, the Negro of insight and sensitivity cannot."

The white liberals must cross a long bridge. The entrance is crowded, but only the few who make it all the way can be trusted not to turn back. The time for testing was not during the exciting and rewarding days when the movement was in its glory, but now when tough-minded thinking and hard work is called for.

The question is can we support civil rights leaders who are stumbling along a new path to freedom, their own path rather than the white man's super highways? Are we willing to pay the emotional and social costs of pioneering? Negroes have borne these costs for three generations, nursing hope for peacefully securing justice and attaining freedom from restrictions. Now our turn has come to pay with accrued interest.

The Negro has two problems: he is poor and he is black. But the rest of the poor in America share with the Negro the problems of poverty and black and white together must form an alliance. The role of the white is not only to support Negro organizations, but to help create an economic and political situation where full participation and adequate income is the accepted way of life for all Americans.

Whites must support and carry on educational and organizational programs in the white communities where racism must be attacked at its source. In addition, concerned whites should select for support some of the economic, educational, and political programs and organizations being set up by movement people. Offshoots of the movement include educational and economic activities in Appalachia and with poor whites in our great cities. These activities provide additional opportunities for white participation.

The peace offensive led by Dr. Martin Luther King is another related cause that deserves support and invites white participation. The dove of peace may be black!

As for me, I have found no reason to change my position stated in 1960 when I had the privilege of being the first white speaker at the Nashville mass meetings growing out of the student demonstrations, and expressed the hope that the Negroes would not stop in their march to freedom until the white man was also free. I said, "I am part of the civil rights movement because I am not free," and that "the role of the concerned whites is to help strengthen Negro leadership, not seek to share leadership. Whites who have had their time and failed should play second fiddle and let the Negroes call the tune."

The Negroes are in the vanguard. They are still the action. But the struggle for human freedom is for every man who knows that he is not free.

Walking toward Real Freedom

[1967]

This interview with Donald Stephens, Hassie Easlic, Ethel Clyde, and Harry Davidson was conducted in New York in May 1967; there is no indication of the purpose or occasion of the interview. The title is taken from internal references within the text and reflects one of the ongoing themes of Horton's thought, especially in this period. Horton touches on many issues, including the history of the civil rights movement, Citizenship Schools, and the Black Power movement. He also makes explicit connections between his and Highlander's work with the civil rights movement and their emerging work in Appalachia and on Appalachian issues.

MYLES HORTON: In the thirties or late forties, Carl Rowan,[54] who is a columnist for a number of papers and was with the U.S. Information service, had written a book on his trip through the South. He spent quite a bit of time in Charleston and had interviewed Mrs. Septima Clark,[55] who, at the time, had not come on the Highlander staff. She had been fired from her job in the public schools because of her association with Highlander and some civil rights activities. In that book he made the statement that you evidently like—I certainly do. He said the only three white southerners who could be trusted by the Negroes were Aubrey Williams,[56] Judge Waring,[57] and Myles Horton. He bought that book and autographed it for me, and I have that in my collection. Since then, there are more white southerners you could put on that list, but I guess that was one of the first lists made.

Incidentally, when I was speaking at Amherst last week on the symposium of the Negro and the civil rights,[58] during the question and answer period, suddenly somebody asked me why I thought Negroes did not want to get in the mainstream of life? Why, I said, that the mainstream of American life was too polluted for nice people to get into, that they need to change. Some student in the American Studies Seminar asked me why the Negroes were different, why I thought they might add something to, instead of pouring into, the melting pot. Suddenly, in the middle of that conversation, I said, "Why should I be answering that question. Here, you have Whitney Young,[59] Kenneth Clark,[60] and Ivanhoe Donaldson,[61] all these folks, and I'm a white man." And Kenneth said, "Go ahead, say something, you've earned the right. Go ahead." And Whitney said, "Yes, he's one of the few white southerners who can speak for us, go ahead, you can talk as well as we can." And one of the professors said, "Well, that's quite an honor for a white southerner to have one of these people say that."

But getting back to the South—more recently, things have happened. During the heyday of the civil rights movement when the big marches were on in Birmingham, Selma,[62] and the Washington March,[63] a lot of liberal whites joined in and quite a few of them were southerners. But now, people are getting tired, the excitement is over. People thought it would be over in a couple of years. They thought they would be getting back to business as usual. Now that it's a long, hard fight, a lot of people are dropping out. A lot of liberals are deciding that the wrong people are doing the wrong thing at the wrong time or at the right time, but all the things that are required of people, that the right person does the right thing at the right time, just doesn't satisfy most white liberals, they find too many problems. So there are a lot of people drawing back and finding alibis. They use the Black Power slogan as one of the reasons for withdrawing support of the civil rights movement. But what's actually happened is that, because the Negroes did stand up and demand that they be treated as equals and not play second fiddle to white liberals, they have won the respect of a lot of white people, in the South particularly, that never had it before—real respect. There is less dropping away from the support of the civil rights movement among the white supporters in the South than in the country as a whole. Because most people in the South, as few as they are, who took an active part, knew what they were doing. They knew the prices they had to pay, they knew it was a long fight, they weren't just summer soldiers getting involved and thought it was easy while it was nice. They were in it for keeps. So, naturally, they don't get scared away so readily when the chips are down and you have to really start work.

We picked up a large number of white supporters relative to the Freedom Call Rowan made. We have a sizable list of people. Now the question is whether those whites can be capable of finding a relationship to the movement that can be sustained over a period of time. That's the problem, because the civil rights movement is shifting very rapidly toward what it was before Rosa Parks sparked the civil rights movement by refusing to give her seat to a white man.[64] If you should go back before that time, if you had said the Negro should build up their businesses and consolidate their political power, people would say, why, that's kind of conservative. There is nothing very challenging about that. That is what they have been saying all along, that's nothing new. They are right. But in the context of the civil rights struggle, having already said, "We want to be treated as humans, we want equality," in the context of the fight for full freedom, then, to do this takes on a new meaning. It isn't the same as it would have been before, because before they were doing it as second-rate citizens, and now they are trying to do it as first-class citizens on the basis of equality. So there is a tremendous difference in what's happening today, when the followers of Stokely Carmichael,[65] who go around yelling "Black Power," spend all their time trying to build up Negro business, Negro cooperatives or Negro restaurants in Mississippi or Alabama or trying to get Negroes elected. Just yesterday, we got a report from Sunflower County, Mississippi, where the people are working night and day to try and get some Negroes elected to the newest level of jobs, as well as in the municipal set up where there are poor counties. So, they are actually taking the concept of Negro power and they are trying to do with it what they should be doing with it and what was considered before the civil rights movement started as a conservative sort of thing. It's not anymore because they mean business, this is the exciting thing, to me, that's happening in the civil rights movement, the fact that people are getting their feet on the ground in a context that means every step they take they are walking toward real freedom because they are no longer doing it in an inferior sort of way, like "We'll settle for this." No, this is just the beginning.

HASSIE EASLIC: They want to make a salary. Is that what they are working for, in the context of this society as it is?

HORTON: Well, actually, that's a good question. That's a very good question to ask because the answer is not quite that. No, the Negroes in Mississippi and Alabama, just to use two places with which we have some familiarity, know they have been excluded from all the regular processes of government, of economic opportunity. Every time they knocked at the door they were told to go around to the back door and wait. And every time they tried to say "But we have a right to vote," they were told all kinds of reasons people couldn't vote. They were deprived both economically and politically, there's no question about that. So that is why it is so hard to set up what they call parallel structures, such as the Freedom Democratic Party,[66] the Black Panther Party in Lowndes County,[67] the Freedom School,[68] and community centers. Incidentally, there may be a hundred community centers developed as a result of this kind of thinking that are now run by Negroes. These are some examples. But only within the last year have they started building, with one or two exceptions (except the Poor People's Corporation,[69] which stimulated the growth of Negro cooperatives a couple or three years which now has thirteen, I think). There has been not much centered on economic life until last year. Now, let's take one county—Clay County, Mississippi, for example. They are working independently now, but the young Negroes still think of themselves as being part of SNCC, I guess. But they get no financial support, that kind of thing. They work with the Freedom Democratic Party, freedom schools, they have a community center, and their last report they were talking about setting up a Negro restaurant. They turned the Freedom Democratic Party headquarters into a restaurant—a Negro-owned restaurant.

There is a little factory where the Negroes have been trying to organize a union. They expect to be fired so they are trying to set up a cooperative insurance program for these Negroes that fully expect to get fired. They have two cooperatives in that county already and they are working on a third. They are running four people for office in that county. They have an educational program. They have a handbook of political activities which describes all the offices and how they are run, what they are supposed to do. They have political action workshops. They had a workshop on how the Negroes can get elected to office. This is all done, mostly, with money raised there locally. This is something most people don't know is happening. This is all done under the name of Black Power. This is what they have said Black Power means to them. The movement is far from being dead. It is very much alive.

[Text omitted]

Getting back to the things that I'm more interested in right now, talking about history more than anything else. I was trying to make a transition not just for myself, because I was already a native mountaineer, but for the people who wanted to work with us. And I found the biggest problem we had was that everybody wanted to do the things that they ended up doing in Mississippi. So they came flocking into the mountains and many of the organizations were struggling with that. The Southern Conference Education Fund,[70] among others, tried to do something with that problem. They took these people. Highlander ran workshops for them. We tried to straighten them out, tried to get them to understand some of the problems that were different, and after a year of that, we ran a little program ourselves. Ethel, you helped with this. Thorsten, Sam Clark, John Chater—all these people are now very active in the poverty programs. But they went up in the Highlander program of the summer people, and we came to the conclusion two years ago that that was not an answer. When I say "we" I mean Highlander. Other people went ahead doing it. The SCEF went ahead having volunteers. The Council of the Southern Mountains with headquarters in Berea started a program of Appalachian volunteers where they brought 1,500 people into the mountains in summer.[71] But we said no. That is not the way to do it and we're not going to be a part of that. We are going to try to find something that will work. So, we started working, rather quietly, with people who were in the mountains for the minimum of a year, in the hopes that they would stay on longer, or people who were natives. We just quit working with all the summer people, all the volunteers. That meant that we didn't have anybody to work with. We had hundreds of people we could have worked with, but refused to work with and nobody to work with that we wanted to work with.

That's when I settled down into my business of going back and living in the mountains and talking with the people and trying to find out what is going on and see if I could find some people. At first, I didn't. I didn't find anybody. No takers. But that's never discouraged me. I've been able to start a number of programs like the Citizenship School program. It takes time, but if it's a good program and a good idea, you will make up for your lost time later on. If it is not a good program, you are just wasting time with it anyway. So time is relative. I ran across one group in the mountains that I was able to tie to. The Appalachian Volunteers had a permanent staff of people who were there to supervise these hundreds of people that came in the summer.[72] And these people were partly people from Appalachia, partly outsiders who were committed to working there. I found that they were really getting out in the community and building some organizations of the poor around them. I started working with them as a hope. I tried to find others who were really active in getting organizations of the poor started, but I couldn't find anybody. Church groups talked about it, other groups planned for it, other groups thought they were doing it. But when it really came to somebody that could say here is a group of people that are organized and speak for themselves, they were very hard to find. There are only a half a dozen groups like that. We had an experimental program last year, right before Christmas. Now this may sound very simple and very elemental, but to me this is the way things seem to me to work.

I asked people—anybody, SCEF, religious groups, Appalachian Volunteers—anybody who had some poor people they were working with to pick some what I call grassroots leaders. That is, people who have not quite emerged as leaders, though they are not members of a political clique or have already got jobs supervising the poverty program or with a union or superintendent of a Sunday school, but somebody who hasn't quite gotten so involved. I had to spend a month trying to get these people to understand who I was talking about. But I finally got it through their heads the kind of people I wanted. They brought twenty-five people to Highlander from two counties. It was an experimental program. Wise County, Virginia, and Harlan County, Kentucky, the old coal county, part Negro and part white. There are quite a few Negroes in Appalachia. So, we sat down and talked about problems, what they should do and how they should go about doing something about it. As a result of that five-day workshop (they were there five days and we had a hard time keeping them that long; none of them had ever lived with Negroes. No whites had ever lived with Negroes; no Negroes had ever lived with whites before, and that is something Highlander has done

THE CIVIL RIGHTS MOVEMENT

since '32), they went back and they started doing things. They started running their own little workshops. They started organizing their communities. They started going to other communities and neighboring states and helping people. What they were doing isn't world shaking, but what they are doing they are doing themselves.

Well, as a result of that one experimental workshop, we have been asked to run four others and now we are booked up. We can run as many as we have the money to run. And they feed back into the communities and more poor people's organizations got going as a result of it. So that is a line of approach that we are interested in following for the time being. In the meantime, I have been seeing if I can get my contacts reestablished with the mountain organizations like the Council of the Southern Mountains. This is the old established organization. I went on their board at the last meeting. I resigned about ten years ago because I was so disgusted with them. But now they are coming alive. They asked me to help with their program. They want me to do educational work for them. It's hopeful. There is another organization that is just getting started in the mountains called Committee on Appalachian Development.[73] It is built around a fellow called Harry Caudill, who is the author of *Night Comes to the Cumberlands*.[74] It's about strip-mining and what has happened in the mountains. Harry is a lawyer, a member of the state legislature, and a very brilliant writer and a real crusader. We have put together an organization made up primarily of professional people, some retired government engineers, some business people, some people who are still active in the professions. The purpose is good. This organization has authorized the formation of a poor people's congress to be held this summer. Two or three thousand people brought together in Appalachia should really stir things up. We are having a planning session for that at Highlander the eleventh of next month. You will be very interested in how we do in this. We have only poor people's organizations sending delegates to plan what they want to talk about. We are going to let them plan the program. Now this does two things: it makes them have to do some thinking about what they would like to see in Appalachia, and also it makes them show up at the meetings, you see, and it will also lay a basis for those of us who aren't as close to the problems as they are to learn from them. Now these people are sending delegates. Then at the end of that, after they decide what they want to do, then we can say any organization that is in Appalachia—I mentioned a couple, SCEF, the Southern Mountain Project,[75] newly formed church groups down there—and we are saying to these organizations, the Friends, that work in Appalachia, now, if you really mean business as they all say they do, and I think all do, then you help do what these people want to do. Quit peddling your own programs and do what representatives from twenty-five poor people's organizations want to do and see what happens. Well, of course they all committed themselves very readily to this approach. And that is where we are with this thing. So we have got a lot of things that really are moving. Now, this thing is getting too big for Highlander. We run on a budget of $125,000 a year for all staff. We run about three or four programs. We deal with people directly. Then we deal indirectly with all these other organizations. We don't want this thing built to be around Highlander. We want Highlander to stay in the background because we function better developing people to feed into these organizations and take leads.

Some friends of mine at Antioch College and Goddard College[76] (Goddard is a little college in Vermont. Do you know Goddard? Did you ever hear of this one? It is one of the liberal colleges. It was started about thirty years ago by a fellow named Tim Pitkin,[77] a Vermonter, one of the followers of John Dewey, I guess is about the easiest way to describe him. It is sort of remarkable. I think it is one of the best colleges in the country) have gotten together a group of experimental colleges, about ten in the United States, and they have decided that they want to do something other than just run their colleges. They want to experiment with real education. They have decided, among other things, to start a college in Appalachia. Now this college is unique. It has two purposes. One, it is kind of like Highlander. It deals with the situation realistically. Two, to provide a place for their students to go and study for a year and learn from real situations where the teachers can also learn something. It is something needed. We never had quite this kind of thing before, you see. Now, I'm interested in it for two reasons. One is that it gets more people working in Appalachia at a time when we need more people.

Highlander cannot do the things that I'm already involved in myself. I've got more things started right now than Highlander can take care of, than I want Highlander to take care of. I think it is good to have a lot of different people working. I work with a wide range of people, so-called leftists like SCEF and so-called conservatives like the Glenmary Sisters,[78] a Catholic group down there. I work with all of them. They all come to Highlander. But I like to stimulate other people to do the kind of thing they want to do. This group will have access to funds that Highlander will never have. It doesn't want to have it actually. They can get government money for a faculty program or a student program down there. They can get money into the area and we need ways to get money into the area. But they can also bring some vitality in terms of educational ideas that we are in need of. We can do the kind of thing that, you know—you were talking about getting people to the place where they think of something more than just making a go of business or voting or something. It is this kind of education that they are concerned about. A real liberal education, really an education that makes people free in the broad sense. The trouble about these people is they deal with foundations and the

THE CIVIL RIGHTS MOVEMENT

government very actively. Of necessity. Now I've pushed them. I've told them that the timetable they were working on, getting done in two or three years, that they probably wouldn't even be welcome. You know, we would kind of run them out. We kind of kidded them about waiting so long to deal with it that we didn't need them. The truth about the matter is they are needed anytime, but they are needed right now very badly because if they can get in on the ground floor of what we are doing now and make their unique contribution, to get involved, to get accepted, in this transition period, then we have got something. For example, if SCEF gets going on their program they can have more people than Highlander could ever think of having. *[Illegible text omitted]*

None of these programs are really going in the South in any big way. We are just beginning to get to the people, starting to get them organized. I talked about the part of organizing the poor in Appalachia. How you could actually get these people organized, get them turned out to learn more about how to run their organizations, go back and run their organizations, and this summer build up this Appalachian People's Congress.[79] This is an example of what I am talking about. Up to now, there hasn't been any test of whether or not you can do anything. Whether Highlander can do anything, whether they can do anything at all, because there hasn't been any way to see, to make the efforts. I've been trying to help them get this going.

We went out there to Hellier, Kentucky, to Marrow Bone Hollow on Boar Bottom Creek. There was a story about Hellier in *Life* magazine about five years ago. It said it's the gateway to Hell, it's impoverished. Well, we found a building. I say "we." I got some of the local people down there to do this that I knew that they didn't know at Goddard. They found an abandoned school building, huge, oh, it was as big as this hotel. Three stories, it's gutted, it's a shell, solid brick, but just a shell, right in the middle of Hellier. The local people heard about this and they got terribly excited about it. They wanted to help. They wanted to have a school down there. They want these people to come. I was talking to Tim Pitkin. I went on up to Goddard when I was in New England to talk to him about this. They have slowed down with their funds. They can't get moving until fall. Since we stirred up interest in this building, people heard about it. It is up for sale. Four thousand dollars. Somebody is going to tear it down and use the bricks, that is what they are going to use it for. So, I'm on a crusade to try to find some way, not for Highlander because I don't want this to have anything to do with Highlander. I don't want Highlander to touch this. My relationship with this will be through my connection with the Council of the Southern Mountains, some of these organizations and with a relationship like they have with Berea or Highlander or with anybody else, but it is not a Highlander project. I have been very much interested in getting this group going, and I am trying to find a way to get four thousand dollars to buy that building. Not for Highlander, but for Goddard to buy, get a new program going. Once they get that building, they can get foundation grants and government grants through their college. And the local people can come and help build this.

So, this is the kind of thing I am interested in promoting. Of course, I have got to keep Highlander going, too. My main job is to try to raise money to keep Highlander eating and we have a hard time paying our bills. But there are times when you look at the overall picture and it seems more important to get something different started. Something new started than to continue plugging away on your own program. Because, for what I have in mind, this organization can do something better than Highlander can ever do because Highlander is branded. We have always been integrated and people say we are Communists and we have trouble with people because we are interracial and because we believe in freedom of speech and because we have SCLC meetings there, SNCC meetings there, you all know all those things that we do all the time. I want this to be completely separated. This is just my way of saying that things are really happening in Appalachia and if we can really push. Now, I am going to get back and spend practically all of my time running workshops for these organizations. SCEF will have some people to send, and the Appalachian Volunteers still have people to send and work on this committee to set up this People's Congress in the summer. Now, this may be the biggest thing that is going to happen in Appalachia. So we are going to move kind of fast.

This is the way it looks to me, Don, and I am just as much a part of the civil rights movement doing this as I would if I was right down in Mississippi on a picket line. In fact, I have never been on a picket line. I don't function on picket lines, I function in a background capacity. So that is about my story. There is one other thing that has nothing to do with this, but I think has to come. I have to get it in, and that is that I think that before Appalachia can be anything, we have got to redefine jobs to mean that people can do what they want to do where they live and get paid for it. To have a whole new definition of what a job is so people don't have to work to make profits for somebody else. So they don't have to work for some federal agency. There should be new types of jobs that don't create any money for anybody, but keep people occupied. They have to deal with the social services, adult education, recreation, and I'm not excluding that from that nonproductive work, like rebuilding the countryside and cleaning up towns for which there is no money, but which needs to be done. But it seems to me the whole concept of jobs should be changed so people can start staying where they are. The ghettos might be out this summer, probably in Harlem, practically every Negro ghetto in America is liable to explode, and we have to change our thinking. We first must find a way for people to live where they are or we'll never solve city problems. So I don't feel that you can separate the city problems from the rural problems. I don't feel a bit isolated from the main problems of America by working where I am and trying to do something in Appalachia. I think I am helping you people right here as much as those there, although that is my aim. My aim is to help people wherever they are. I just happen to be there. But I see no contradictions. My work with the civil rights movement and my work which deals with urban problems and with the whole problem of world peace. I think this is the way it works.

A Faith Venture

[1968]

The following text is taken from a transcript of Horton's talk with the Friends World Institute on April 8, 1968. Only the speech, with its title taken from internal references in the text, has been included; the question-and-answer period has been omitted. As he did in "Walking toward Real Freedom," Horton here continues to make linkages between the issues in the civil rights movement and the issues then current in Appalachia.

One of my friends, a minister, wrote me one time that Highlander was a faith venture. I suppose it is. But our faith is not [in] a method, or any kind of educational approach, but in people themselves. We've tried all kinds of educational techniques throughout the years to see if we could figure out what would be most helpful and have discovered for ourselves that the best way to go about educating people is to bring them together in an informal residential setting where they can relax and be encouraged to start thinking and talking among themselves. Out of this kind of interchange among peers —people who understood and are not intimidated by each other—we found a lot of learning would come.

We have felt that people, especially poor adults, who had been denied opportunities for full development had a capacity that was untapped and if you could find someway to get people turned on and give them confidence that they had something to say about their own lives, they would come up with some creative answers and activities.

Knowing that there is some information that poor people have been denied—and we don't hesitate like some educational theorists—[we] do not say here [are] some facts or here [are] some ideas, when such information is requested. I've never had any kind of experience that made me feel I would intimidate a student by telling something I knew or believed. I never felt like I could indoctrinate anybody because I was always very happy if anybody would listen to anything I had to say.

We tried to work out an educational program where there is very little difference between teachers and students. Highlander people learn together and share ideas. The staff may have more formal information and are more articulate. On the other hand, the so-called students probably have deeper insights into human relationships, they have a better understanding of how to deal with people, like themselves. Our job is to believe in them and give them responsibility, and encourage them to do their own thinking.

Some observers have tried to isolate a Highlander methodology or technique. Techniques are something you use and discard. It's just like having a car that no longer works. You don't say I am committed to this car, education car. We can get committed to these things and say that we have to fit ourselves to our methodology. I take the same position about institutions of all kinds. I'm saying let's minimize our loyalty to institutions that do not serve the needs of people.

Today I see the possibility of a grassroots, bottoms-up coalition. As long as our whole focus was on civil rights, we couldn't construct a broad base because we only tried to right a wrong. We were trying to carry justice where there was injustice, to deal with the sickness of society. We weren't trying to re-create society, to build. Important as it was, it was restrictive. That is why I am so delighted now with the possibilities of working with other poor minority groups.

This development ties into something that is important to me. The kind of society that I would like to see would be what we call pluralistic society where instead of putting everybody in the melting pot and have everybody look alike, we would have everybody's cultural values expanded on and encouraged, aiming for a great variety. A customary example is a symphony. I would rather use a jazz band. Symphonies for the most part are made up of people who have been trained to play in a specific manner; originally a jazz band was made up of musicians who just started playing for fun, for enjoyment, for entertainment. They had a wonderful time playing solo and developed their own style, their own way of doing and own way of being. When they learned that they could have more fun if they got with other musicians who were equally individualistic and worked out some way of playing together, we had early jazz. I grew up hearing very early jazz, played by roustabouts on the riverboats. I heard that wonderful, wonderful jazz that seemed to be discordant but wasn't quite. Everybody would take his turn doing his piece, doing his thing as you call it. If you notice, the trumpet player will play and then somebody else will play but everybody supports everybody doing his thing.

This is the kind of society I would like to see. That is why I am for Black Power. I would like to see Negroes get together as an ethnic group, as a cultural group, and do their thing their own way and develop their own style. I would like to see the Mexican Americans do the same thing. I would like to see the people in Appalachia do the same thing.

Then I think they would get to the place where it would be kind of interesting if they got together. But they get together on their own basis. They don't have to give up anything to get together. They get together because everybody profits by their getting together.

They all have more fun playing together. But they still play their own tunes, they have their own style, they do it their own way, but somehow there is something there that unifies.

Now to me that is the kind of society I would like to see, a rich society, and it means you have got to give people a style before they can come in, but still have their own way of doing and being. That is what Stokely Carmichael has been trying to say when he said that we don't want integration.[80] What he really means and what he has said very specifically on at least two occasions is that he doesn't want integration the way the white man offered it, integration into his society as second-class citizens. If people like Stokely could say we come in our own way, playing our own tune, our own style, and you accept us as we are and we accept you as you are, then and only then would integration have any meaning.

This is the kind of society I am talking about. Up to now, the civil rights movement has provided that kind of base. It always has. It's the most creative thing we have had. But it has not been what I am talking about now and it is something you young people can join in and support, but it couldn't be your thing. Let's take the best values of middle-class society. Let's get the best values of everything and recast them and try to pull things together so everybody is an equal to everybody else in their own way.

Equality doesn't require conformity or agreement. Out of this kind of thing would come a social structure, wouldn't it? It would become an arrangement like the jazz players have of playing together. That would be my idea of how a government, or an establishment, or an institution, should provide for this kind of thing.

I'm not against structures. I said a while ago that we have outgrown the shell and we've got to grow us a new shell. I would rather have a soft shell that can be expanded but that is difficult to conceive of because people can't write books about it and talk about it, or analyze it. But this is more my kind of thinking and why I'm interested and that's why I think I saw an embryo.

The people planning the Poor People's Campaign in Washington have just a touch of this.[81] It may suggest something to this country that we can move on and establish what we could have done at the beginning of this country. We could have had a full society with things to start with.

Over here at the Cherokee Reservation not far from here they are trying to find Cherokee teachers, teachers to teach Cherokee to the children. They are having a hard time because twenty years ago they wouldn't allow them to teach Cherokee in the schools and now they have discovered that they would like to get this group to learn Cherokee and they don't have anybody that knows how to teach it. If they had left them alone, they would all be speaking Cherokee. This is what I complain about in our society.

This to me is going to give some of you people a chance to get in on a new basis. Because I don't think you will want to disassociate yourself from this kind of thing. Just like I don't see why you should be so excited about associating yourself with what we have. It makes education terribly exciting. I don't know how we are going to put this together in terms of educational programs, but it has its possibilities.

Racism, Education, and Social Change

[Early 1970s]

The following is an excerpt from an undated interview, probably from the early 1970s, with Morris Mitchell.[82] In it, Horton engages the interrelationship of racism, education, and social change and explains at length what he calls "unconscious racism." The title is taken from internal references within the text.

HORTON: A lot of people who have never known they are racists have more problems getting rid of racism than some of us who grew up knowing that we were racist. I grew up knowing that Negroes were different and different meant inferior. Not different in the fact that we had a different kind of values, but different that we were not alike. Consequently, when I examined my relationship with Negroes, I examined it from a background of knowing Negroes the best a white person can know a Negro.

An advantage and disadvantage of being in and working in the South is that I can work with Negroes as an equal. I have all these advantages. I can look at myself and know the changes which are necessary. I suppose that makes it easier for me to know how to see my unconscious racism.

Whereas these people who are from the National Student Association, liberal groups, liberal political groups, these people think of themselves as being liberated, or radical. They never examined their racism which showed itself to me in their assuming that all the structures that white people hold so dear, parliamentary law, majority votes, what I call procedure sort of claptrap, should be held dear by Negroes also. When they started cutting up qualifications for representatives at the Democratic Party convention in Chicago they thought that you had to have that.[83] You have to elect people in a democratic way by parliamentary law. This is the way it is done.

Negroes have never mastered that way, their churches don't act that way. The civil rights movement taught white people not to act that way.

In the mountains poor people got together and they don't have any Robert's Rules of Order, don't have any procedure. They get together and talk. None of the poor people, Negroes or whites, fit these categories.

I say this is unconscious racism. The assumption that what white people do is the right thing to do and therefore anybody else who is going to function in society is going to have come in and act that way. They are going to have to do things that way. I have tried in vain to get them to get people to decide how they wanted to be represented. They couldn't, just couldn't understand what I was talking about.

AUDIENCE QUESTION: They ask you to bring people up there?

HORTON: Yes, and I said these people will not qualify. I just got a letter from *[illegible]* Brooks. He was at the receptionist desk signing people in. I stood around there and watched, Negroes particularly, come up.

"Well where are your credentials?"

Negroes would say, "Well, we didn't send anything in."

"You mean you didn't send in a list of members? How many delegates do you have? You have to go to the credential committee."

Some poor white guy would come up from Appalachia, "Somebody sent me the money, said for me to come up here. Said for me to get all the people I can and come on up here."

"Well, which people belong to which organization? Go to the credential committee."

They had more people going to the credential committee than they had in the meeting. They got some poor people and some Negroes there. What finally happened was that the white people got fed up with the whole thing. They are not as advanced in their own organizational thinking as Negroes. They went out on the town or sat around and went to sleep. But the Negroes got together and set up the convention. The newspapers didn't know any of this. If they thought anything at all, they thought a bunch of Negroes here, a bunch of whites there. They didn't know why.

I will give you another example of this racism. They hired a special parliamentarian to work out some laws to make it democratic. He had a student background and could do this. He boiled the thing down to nineteen, rewritten.

"O my goodness," I said, "that is too much. People are not going to pay attention."

He said, "Well how much? This is what is left."

I said, "Well this is a different kind of thing. At least the people I am interested in are not going."

He said, "Well, how long do you think?"

I said, "Oh, about one-half page triple spaced. So that people can use it."

He said, "That wouldn't be enough."

I said, "They are not going to use any of it anyway. They are not going to pay any attention."

He said, "You cannot have a convention without rules. You cannot have a convention without these things."

I said, "I guess you cannot have a convention with Negroes, the ones you have asked to come. They are not about to play your game."

Nobody got the idea. There was one or two people kind of nodding, but they didn't say anything. This to me is unconscious racism. It is the feeling that the way we do things is the way it should be done. When you say that you want to work with people, you say that you want to work with them on our terms. This is what we are saying to Negroes. As always, integration means you come in on our terms, you eat our food, you follow our procedures, you be like us, and that is integration. That is what we have told the Negroes. They are not about to have anything to do with us.

Now the Negroes at this convention did just what Negroes are going to do at all conventions. I wish people in Appalachia would do this. I wish they would say, "First we have got to get our ways of doing things worked out among ourselves. Then we can force whites to meet with us on our own terms, or not meet with us at all. I think that is what Black Power is. I think it is an effort to be themselves, to work out their own machinery. I don't know anybody in the Black Power movement who doesn't know, although, he won't say so, who doesn't know that a tenth of the population cannot basically change society here without cooperation of allies.

Now what you are saying is that essentially white folks are so hung up on this business of parliamentary procedure, of coalitions and trying to fit Negroes in. The Negroes are saying, "We are not even going to talk about coalitions. We are just going to run our own affairs for a while and there is no point in talking about coalitions."

When they get to the place where they feel secure enough to talk about coalitions, but the kind of coalitions they would like to be in. In the meantime they will talk about integration, but the kind of integration they decide they want to be a part of. So right now it is a kind of consolidation, and thinking period; power to Negroes who believe that way. As a result of this they are already getting some Negroes in office. As soon as they get the office they immediately have to start facing these other problems, but they know that trying to get business set up, trying to get cooperatives set up, for example, as soon as you start selling something on an outside market you have to deal with it. They know that this is going to lead, if Black Power is successful, to this kind of relationship. They ain't talking about it now. They are right not to talk about it because all we can do is say, "This is the way it has to be done."

This is what I call unconscious racism. I think that it probably is just as dangerous as conscious racism. I think in that sense we haven't made a tremendous lot of progress. I don't think the white folks in this country have made many gains, but I think Negroes, and a sprinkling of poor people in Appalachia, are beginning to think for themselves.

I am not naive enough to believe that the little tapping at the door by the poor, black or white, is going to get anybody to open the door and say come in the front room and sit down at the table. You can have this half.

We are building up in the minds of some of our disadvantaged people the idea that they are going to have something to say. Now the ground is being taken out today. I have just heard a report from Washington on the fate of the poverty program. It looks like the politicians are going to take over the poverty program.[84] They are watching these poverty programs. They will select the teachers who are going to train the people. They will select the people who are going to run the programs and maybe people like me have just about got our two cents worth in, in terms of trying to influence people, the training of people in the poverty program. Something is happening. Not because of what people like me have done but for reasons that seem a little bit confused. The poor work and hold organizations that participated in having something to say about their own lives.

I don't think that anybody really meant it. I thought so at the time. I said so at the time. I simply took advantage of it and told people what they said and show[ed] it to them. Push in there and demand the right to do something.

[Text omitted]

What Is Liberating Education?

[1979]

This interview with Bingham Graves first appeared in the May 1979 issue of Radical Teacher. *The original prefatory material gives a good indication of the content of the interview.*

For Myles Horton, education is integrally related to peoples' struggles against oppression. The Highlander School is devoted to this concept and so stands in contrast to schools of formal and traditional education.

In this conversation, Myles compares three literacy programs: (1) schools set up in northeast Brazil among peasants by Paulo Freire,[85] author of *Pedagogy of the Oppressed,* who was ousted from the country for his work; (2) the national Literacy Campaign of Cuba in 1961, which brought down the illiteracy rate from 23.6 to 3.9 percent in one year; and (3) the Citizenship School started on the Sea Islands of South Carolina in 1954 to teach reading and writing to black people so that they could pass the literacy requirement for voter registration, a Highlander program which was eventually adopted by SCLC and spread across the South.

These three programs were uncommonly successful, not only in proliferating spontaneously and in teaching large numbers of adults to read and write, but also because they enlisted the vitality of the people involved to begin to struggle for more control over their lives.

BINGHAM GRAVES: How are the Citizenship Schools which Highlander helped start related to Freire's literacy schools and the Cuban literacy campaign?

MYLES HORTON: I think that all three programs were based on the feeling that for people to be really free they must have the power to make decisions about their lives, so that they can acquire knowledge as tools to change society. The people that conceived all the programs held a radical philosophy: the system was bad and had to be changed. They all had a revolutionary purpose.

The black people in South Carolina had to read not only to be able to register to vote, but to be free—to keep up with what was going on, to find out about how they were oppressed, and to learn about what black people were doing in other parts of the South and the world. So, it was necessary for them to be literate in order to be free, just like in Cuba.

In Cuba, they identified literacy with freedom—to empower the people to be free and to govern themselves. That was a nationally held idea. José Marti, who was kind of patron saint of the revolutionary nationalists, said that illiterates can't be free.[86] So they said, we will drop everything in terms of education until we see that nobody else is illiterate.

The same was true in Brazil in the schools of Paulo Freire. If the peasants who were being exploited weren't literate, then their growth was very limited.

All these programs were based on the democratic principle of faith in the people; i.e., trust in the people's ability to govern themselves and make decisions about their lives. The underlying purpose was the same: to empower people. That was the common denominator.

GRAVES: The Citizenship Schools were a part of the civil rights movement, so is it a question of "chicken and the egg" as to whether people were responding to the schools or to the "movement"?

HORTON: First of all, it wasn't part of a movement, but it was part of a little effort. The literacy program in South Carolina began ten years before the civil rights movement. There were pockets of struggle for the right to vote and against the oppression that was going on. Esau Jenkins, a bus driver on one of the Sea Islands, was a leader of one of those groups.[87] The idea to start a school to teach people to read and write so they could register to vote was developed by him as he talked to his people everyday. He couldn't find anybody in South Carolina to help him set up a school, so we at Highlander tried to devise a program that would meet the needs that he explained to us.

We couldn't have started a Citizenship School just anywhere. It could be started only where some people wanted to vote, to do something about their situation; and that place was Johns Island.

GRAVES: So you didn't try to sell the program?

HORTON: No, if people weren't ready for it, you couldn't do it. It isn't a kind of mass education gimmick that you can plunk down anywhere and it works. That's why they couldn't get people to come to those state-financed literacy programs. It wasn't that people wanted to read and write because it was a good thing. They wanted to read for a purpose. That's why so many programs don't work; they are based on the thought that everybody if given a chance would learn to read and write. It's obviously not true.

GRAVES: You have said that the Citizenship Schools were built on the experiential knowledge of the people. What does that mean?

HORTON: Its basic concept—you must start where people are. That means their perception of where they are, not yours. You must find out from them what they know, what they are interested in. You need to know what they do in their spare time, how they work in groups—say, churches, schools, communities. Otherwise, you would proceed with a program that didn't tie into where they were. I spent months going to visit in the homes of the people in the Sea Islands, to see what their perception of themselves was. Then you ask yourself: how do you start from where they are and build a process that moves step by step, situation by situation, experience by experience, to where they want to be.

You must trust people's ability to move in the direction that will give them more freedom, more justice, a more creative life. In the case of the Citizenship School, the basis was their everyday experiences and their ambition, their goal, which was voter registration. The content comes from what the people want to learn.

GRAVES: Freire talks about the use of loaded words to teach reading.

HORTON: The peasants were learning more than the words; they were learning what the words mean under an oppressive system. They were dynamite words, because of Freire's interpretation, his use of them. For example, the word "plow" has a social meaning: why a peasant has to plow and the boss doesn't; why people in the city don't plow. Not just how a plow works and what it looks like. He chose words that had a struggle element, a growth element. He wouldn't have done that if he had not been a social radical. His goal was to change society, and without that content these programs would not have spread like they did.

The content has to be what the people are interested in, otherwise they won't have motivation that will enable them to go through the laborious and painful process of learning to read and write. It's very difficult for someone who hasn't had this experience to understand what torture it is for an old woman or man who has never held a pencil, to learn to from a word or to learn to read. They get frustrated and discouraged, so they have to have strong motivation to get through it.

GRAVES: How do you give people this motivation?

HORTON: You don't give people motivation. You give them experiences that stimulate their motivation—motivation is from within. They learn that they can do things that they never thought they could do before other than read and write. They can talk about their problems with someone that they never knew before. That's a very important learning experience—a step in the right direction from being self-centered and toward having confidence not only in yourself but in other people, your peers. As they see that, they can begin to see how they can link up with other groups that have the same problems—another community, another state, and eventually other people in the world. So you are empowering people to broaden their horizons to a place where they can grow.

Segregationists used to say in the days of the civil rights movement that if you give black people an inch, they'll take a mile. Well, I always said that I disagreed; I thought if you gave them an inch, they'd take a thousand miles—and should. Once you get a taste of freedom, a taste of learning, you want more and more of it. That keeps the motivation going, even to the point that people will sacrifice their lives.

On the other hand, you can destroy this motivation if you do things for people instead of allowing them to do things for themselves, to start from where they are. If somebody said they would like to get an ax to chop down a tree, that being as far as their horizon went, then you should get them an ax. You shouldn't say, "I'll chop down the tree for you since I know how to use this ax." You empower the person to do it himself, so he can use that ax for other things. He doesn't have to know that he'll use it for more things to start with.

If you do it for him, then he'll never get that experience, and you'll have to do the next thing, and then the next thing. That's the way you control people—by denying them access to knowledge and understanding. You empower people by giving them understanding of how to do things and access to knowledge. Before long, people will be chopping down a forest.

GRAVES: Is that why Freire was kicked out of Brazil?[88]

HORTON: Well, not because he had a mechanical method for teaching people how to read and write; nobody would kick you out for that. The government knew that his programs were successful and people started organizing and making demands; they began to change, to act as groups and get these ideas. It was his very success that alerted the government to what he was up to. He was a troublemaker; he was stirring up the peasants. They kicked him out because he was getting results.

Just like our people in the Citizenship Schools. They started to register to vote, to throw their weight around, getting into demonstrations and making demands. That's where the opposition to our program came from—not because we were successfully teaching people to read and write.

GRAVES: Would you say that the content of most literacy programs doesn't provide this growth element?

HORTON: The concept of most programs has to do with training people to be employees, to be exploited for moneymaking purposes, or to train people to be the managers, to exploit people. The ordinary schools want the future productive workers to learn discipline, to learn authority, to accept regimentation; it's a training ground for what they are going to do later in life.

But the three programs we are discussing were liberating programs; instead of teaching people to take orders and to respect the experts, they were doing the opposite. They were teaching people to make decisions, to act on those decisions, and to learn how to work with other people to achieve their goals and to challenge an exploitative system.

These are fundamentally different concepts: one is to make people free, the other is to make slaves out of them. One is to liberate people and the other is to make sure they are useful to the system. Many people are trying to adopt Freire's educational system, but it cannot be reduced to a mere methodology; to make his system work you must have a radical philosophy.

GRAVES: Formal educators might say these literacy programs cannot be viewed as "successful adult education" because they aren't strictly adult education, because they are attached to people who are struggling for something else.

HORTON: Well, the answer to that is that they aren't succeeding in educating people. When we started the Citizenship School program, there was federal and state money for literacy work, and for ten years prior to that time those budgets were never more than half spent. They had teachers on the payroll who couldn't find students. They didn't know how to deal with people.

If their programs worked, we could wipe out illiteracy in this country. The program in Cuba worked. Why didn't it work here? The answer is very simple: it was a different kind of conceptual framework in which the operation takes place. So, what is so sacred about an educational system that doesn't work?

People say the schools are failing. The powers that be in this country aren't worried about that, as long as they are being provided with enough laborers, enough managerial people to serve their needs. From the educator's point of view the schools aren't successful, but from the capitalist's point of view they are successful—in turning out enough nuts and bolts to fit their specifications. When they need more, they'll get concerned about the schools.

GRAVES: In Cuba, the literacy campaign followed the revolution. What then was the liberation struggle to which that campaign was related?

HORTON: Simultaneous to that campaign, the people were being told in many ways that they had to become involved in building a new kind of society and in defending it. They no longer simply worked a little piece of land for somebody. They had to take responsibility for defense, productive work, increasing production.

It changed their self-concept, enabled them to talk about things that they never had a right to discuss before—to plan things, come up with ideas. They needed to be literate in order to read the paper, posters, speeches, which gave information. The country went heavily into education.

They said anybody who can read and write can teach somebody else to read and write. They used seventh-grade kids on up. All kinds of people were teaching. It was the equivalent of peer education on a country-wide basis.

You see, the purpose of education is to serve whatever system it's a part of. In Cuba, the educational system is to make socialist men and women. In America, it's to make capitalist people. Since the system is different the education takes different forms.

GRAVES: In your experience, what is the effect on people who are changed, who stand up and face struggle but are defeated?

HORTON: That's a good question. Of course, there's always some good that comes out of a situation where people learn to fight, learn to take up for themselves, stand up. Struggle, per se, is educational. People learn they can struggle and not get killed. They learn they can struggle and still eat. They feel better because they have stood up for their right and engaged themselves with self-respect. It's a powerful consciousness-raising educational process; that shouldn't be underestimated. If you only try to do the things where you win, then you'll never try to do anything worth doing.

You never win wars all at once; you win and lose battles. You have to win the battles in order to win the war, but a battle is not a war. Most people only have a limited goal unless somebody else helps them analyze their experiences, interpret them, tie them to the past and to the future. That's the role of an educator.

The Adventures of a Radical Hillbilly, Part 2

[1983]

The following is the second part of Bill Moyers's 1981 PBS interview with Horton, which appeared in print in the summer 1982 issue of Appalachian Journal. *For the original prefatory material, see "The Adventures of a Radical Hillbilly, Part 1," in section II. In this far-ranging interview, Horton recalls his and Highlander's involvement in the civil rights movement and once again establishes the connection to issues and initiatives in the Appalachian region.*

MYLES HORTON: One of the ideas that we had at the beginning of Highlander was that we had to use cultural activities as part of the program, because people need not just intellectual discussion, or even—

BILL MOYERS: Politics—

HORTON: Action—learning from action and doing it, but they also need something to, you know, to cultivate the spirit and soul. And it's obvious that drama and dance and music and things like that would contribute —and art, different kinds. Well, we were really fortunate in that when Zilphia,[89] my wife, came to Highlander, she was a trained musician, from Arkansas, and you know, had a background of—a miner's background, her father was a coal miner. But she also had, you know, musical training. But the musical training, but, you know, was a classical kind you get in a—you know, going to college and so on. So she—but she soon, you know, started singing labor songs and folk songs and learned to play the guitar and accordion—she played the piano—and used her music to help fit into the program. The same time she was doing it, she was a good teacher. She was a very good teacher, like in training shop stewards on how to take up grievances, and the Highlander way of doing it, not just technically, but in rallying the people behind you. And she'd use drama as part of her way of teaching, so she developed a drama program along with the music program. So she had two kinds of programs going.

MOYERS: Do you remember that song that John Hancock of the tenant farmers taught Zilphia?[90] Called "No More Mournin'"?

HORTON: Yeah. Yeah. Yeah, that's a beautiful song. I was teaching in a school for sharecroppers, tenant farmers out in Little Rock, Arkansas, in a school that Claude Williams ran.[91] And the police were, you know, harassing us, because we had some whites and blacks together there. And every time the police would come, why, I would sit down in the audience like a white person being entertained, and the blacks would start leading singing. And John Hancock was the—became the star, because he could always make up songs if we'd run out of songs. And that's the part—I brought that back to Zilphia. I collected that.

MOYERS: Do you remember that song?

HORTON: Yeah, I can't remember the words now, but I remember the—

MOYERS: No more mourning / No more mourning / No more mourning after awhile / And before—

HORTON: Before I'll be a slave / I'll be buried in my grave / And go home—

MOYERS: Leadbelly was here, too, wasn't he?[92] He wrote a song that was going to be used to raise money for Highlander, that became a classic.

HORTON: Yeah.

MOYERS: You remember that one?

HORTON: Yeah, Leadbelly was never at Highlander. He always wanted to come to Highlander, but he did three or four benefit concerts for Highlander.

MOYERS: But he did write that song.

HORTON: Oh yeah, he did a lot of songs, a lot of music. Zilphia used to play with him, they'd play together. He said she's the only white woman could play, you know, black music, that he ever saw. And he'd get her to play with him anytime she was around. She'd get on the piano and play with him.

MOYERS: "Bourgeois Blues" was—

HORTON: And she'd—he'd sung the—We were at a party, a fund-raising party, in New York, and—well, that was back when we had respectable sort of sponsors like Mrs. Roosevelt and all the big people in—

MOYERS: Eleanor Roosevelt?

HORTON: Eleanor Roosevelt. Well, she was at Highlander twice; she was a great supporter of Highlander. But at that time she helped us, used her influence to get a name—a bunch of name people together there, and Leadbelly was the performer at that place. And when we were getting ready to put on a program, Zilphia and Leadbelly were back playing backstage—playing, just having fun, and he said he wanted to try this song out on her. He'd just been working on it, but he tried to get it done for that occasion, he wanted to use it for that occasion, but he hadn't finished it. And—so she liked it so well, she said go ahead and use it anyway. She persuaded him to sing it even though he wasn't quite satisfied with it. So that was the beginning of "Bourgeois Blues"—that was the first time it was ever sung.

MOYERS: There is a story that a couple of striking tobacco workers from Charleston, South Carolina, brought your wife, Zilphia, a song which she and Pete Seeger then turned into what has become one of the most famous hymns of the civil rights movement, "We Shall Overcome." Is that a true story?

HORTON: Well, it's almost. There was a strike of tobacco workers, working in the tobacco plant in Charleston, South Carolina,[93] and we always encouraged students to bring songs that they had written or used on a picket line, and just like Guy [Carawan] does today,[94] we still do the same thing here now. And that song was a kind of rough-hewn song that they'd gotten from a black hymnal; the blacks had sung it, and the white people had picked it up—they had tried to make a strike song out of it. And it was a song that Zilphia said wasn't singable; it was too hard to sing. So she sat down at the piano like she always did with people like that, and they worked out the music so it'd be simpler. She used to say there was singable songs, and then there was songs like "The Star-Spangled Banner," which nobody should sing. You know, she thought songs should be easy to sing. So that was revised, and that became a very popular song that week. People liked it after they had simplified it a little bit.

For ten years it was just a Highlander song, and then the labor movement started using it a little bit more, and then it died down, and just kind of stayed in the Highlander domain. And then Guy Carawan, who is in charge of music here now, taught that song, which is a black peoples' song, to a lot of his people in SNCC,[95] and later on did it for the Southern Christian Leadership Conference, and it kind of—the song came back to the people where it originated from, and then it became a popular song again in the civil rights movement, and now as you know it's sung around the world. It's everywhere.

MOYERS: How do you assess its impact on our times?

HORTON: Oh Lord, it's no—there's no one song that I know of that is still, you know, you see the Irish scrapping, you see people in Chile, they use it in Chile, it was used in Cuba, it's used in, it's sung in China, all the schools sing it in China—it's used everywhere. I don't know of any song of that kind that is so widespread.

MOYERS: Well, it symbolized, didn't it, your own transformation from the union movement to civil rights?

HORTON: Yeah. Some people had tried to describe Highlander, they said Highlander was just a series of different schools, you know, it was a community school, we were poverty, you know, a depression school, we were an industrial union school, a CIO school, we were a farmer labor school, we were a civil rights school, we were Appalachian—that's one way to describe it, because you have to, you know, break things up to describe them. But to me, it's very inaccurate. Highlander has just been one school all the way through, we were just doing the same thing with different groups of people. We try to empower people. We're using these different periods of interest in the South to—as a means of educating people to take more control of their own lives. And although the subject matter differs, the approach differs, the purpose is the same. We use the same methods that I described earlier, and the same purpose—the purpose is to help people become so empowered that they can begin to have something to do with their lives. And you can't do it with large numbers of people.

MOYERS: Is that why you've stayed small and—

HORTON: Yeah. Well, see, the reason is—I knew that intellectually, and I said Highlander is—I never want to be big, because I always want to deal with twenty or thirty people at a time, because that seems to be the maximum you can deal with effectively. And I don't want to have a lot of branches, I just want to be small. And whatever influence you have, developing people with a multiplication influence. They multiply, that's where you get your, you know, your two cents' worth—you multiply people, you deal with leaders who multiply themselves. Then you have an outreach. You don't do mass education, so you don't need to deal with a lot of people at a time, because that's not the way you get your Brownie points built up. It's how many people are influenced. That's done best by taking the people who can multiply themselves.

MOYERS: I'll tell you something that in looking back over your life has helped me. And it's what you discovered about how much conflict is in the lives of poor people, and how often only conflict is the way they can resolve their problems. You know, well-educated middle—

HORTON: That's a very hard thing to explain to my nonviolent, pacifist friends. They say, you know, of course you'd always advise against violence. And I say, no, I said, Highlander—the people that Highlander deals with live a life of violence, and this violence takes a lot of forms. Not just the physical violence, but the violence of starvation, the violence of depriving people of education, the violence of being—you know, of oppression of various kinds. All those are forms of violence. So you have to choose a lesser violence always, never between—Our choice at Highlander was seldom between violence and nonviolence—it was between the lesser forms of violence. We had a discussion some of us, some young people that came down from the East during the big summer in Mississippi,[96] you know, in—when was it, '64, '65?

MOYERS: '64.

HORTON: '64. And we were down at Greenwood, Mississippi, and they were talking about, maybe we'd better talk to the police, maybe—after all, they're not all bad, and we, some of us could talk to the police. And I remember these kids were just a bunch of them from Yale, just had come down. And they were going to talk to the police. So one of these black guys said, no, no, no. And finally this white guy said to this guy, "Why is it that you don't want to talk to the police?" He says, "When they sees this black head, they hits it." Now, see that's what blacks have known all the time, and people don't know. They just hit them because they're black. Kill them, because they're black.

MOYERS: But the point I want to get at, because I think it's essential to you, is that when middle-class, upper-class, well-intentioned, liberal people rule out conflict as a way of poor people solving their problems, they leave those poor people powerless, don't they?

HORTON: No, they support the status quo. What they're doing is reinforcing the situation, firming up the situation as it is, and not allowing for any change, and the condition of those people will get worse. It'll continue to get worse, because if you don't struggle against oppression, oppression moves in on you. So what they're doing, they're accelerating the rate of oppression on people by not understanding it has to be a struggle. A struggle is not only, in my point of view, the moral thing to do, but it's a great learning experience. People—the greatest education comes from action, and the greatest action is struggle for justice. So if you deny people the opportunity to become empowered and educated, deny people the right to be free, you know, to be people, and they all do it in the name of law and order.

MOYERS: Have you ever taught violence?

HORTON: I haven't used violence since I was fourteen years old. See, I don't —neither practice nor advocate violence. But I know that in a class-structured society, violence exists, and the victims are the poor. And I'm not going to stand back, and when they try to devise ways of doing things, and not try to help them work out their own ways of doing it. And I'm also sure in my own mind that there are times come when you've exhausted every avenue of change in revolutionary situation, if the people won't get off your back and won't give you leeway to grow, you've got to push them off. And that's violence.

MOYERS: Well, I think it's important to point out, as I understand your teachings, that conflict is a form of violence without necessarily being ultimately violent against the person. That you believe that organizers, workers, should bring conflict into the lives of the workplace, in order to force the companies to change their ways. That you thought that blacks should confront white society and the power structure and bring conflict. And my point earlier was that most people want to look the other way.

HORTON: Yeah. You see that conflict is already there, you don't bring that conflict. The conflict is there, is hushed up from both sides. Blacks are afraid to do anything about it, because they're afraid to get killed. Whites don't want to do it, because they don't want to change the structure, they want to do it by having meetings another hundred years, you know, praying another hundred years. So nobody wants to do it. So you take a situation like that, with the people you're working with, you say, "Look, this conflict is there, you've lived with it a long time, the violence is operating in various ways. So, you know, let's look at it, and maybe by expanding that area of violence or interpreting that area of violence, we can confront the situation in such a way that we'll begin to resolve it." Now we don't try to resolve a situation at the lower level of accommodation, you know, to lower—we try to resolve it at the higher level, of justice. So when we talk about using conflict, we don't use it to settle something, we use it to cause the—a real banging of the forces, so you come out resolving it at a higher level. Like in the civil rights movement, we weren't interested in settling for having some kind of peaceful relationship with blacks and whites, until blacks got, you know, their rights, and I knew as a white southerner that the quickest way to educate white southerners was not to talk to them, not to deal with them, but for the blacks to stand up and demand to be treated equally. Then you would educate white southerners to respect them as equals. Fastest way. So that was our philosophy.

MOYERS: Rosa Parks was at a workshop at Highlander a couple of months before she went back to Montgomery and sat down on that bus and refused to get up and give her seat to a white man.[97] Now she introduced conflict in a situation that heretofore had had conflict repressed for her, but not present for the white.

HORTON: Yeah, yeah. And the conflict was there all along. She just refused to accept the situation, and that brought the conflict which was there to the surface. And then when they brought the police officers, she still, you know, accelerated the conflict by not—by making them take her to jail. So she set the thing up, set the conflict where it could be seen, and it made it possible for E. D. Nixon,[98] the black organizer down there, the Pullman porter organizer, to organize the boycott, and to get King involved—he's the one that got King into that situation.[99] King didn't want to get in it. He first went to Abernathy,[100] who had the biggest church. You see, Abernathy didn't want to do it, so he went to King because he had the smallest church. If you had the big church—or are you going to take one that didn't have any competition? So Martin was picked simply because he was a new minister there and low on the totem pole. And Martin said, "Well, we'll think it over, we'll let you know tomorrow. And Coretta and I, you know, we've decided we weren't going to get involved in anything,"[101] and he's really building up to go and take over his father's church,[102] you know, these black people own these churches, like farms.

MOYERS: That was his destiny.

HORTON: And it was all planned for him, and he knew that. I met Martin when he was a junior in college.[103] And when I met him, his father had told me, Martin's going to take this church one day.

MOYERS: So he didn't want to get off into that—

HORTON: He didn't want to get off into this—

MOYERS: Maelstrom.

HORTON: And he said, well, let you know tomorrow. Nixon went back, sent out the announcements that it was going to be in Martin's church. So he called Martin the next day and said, "Well, King, what have you decided to do?" And Martin said, "Well, we've thought about it and we're going to do it." And he said, "It's a good thing, because the announcements have been out for about four hours."

MOYERS: Was it a coincidence that the trigger of all this, Rosa Parks on the bus, happened two months after she was at Highlander? Was that just a coincidence?

HORTON: No, not according to Rosa. Now I never tried to tell what happened at Highlander, just let the people it happens to, tell. Rosa said that the connection between those two things was that at Highlander it was the first time in her life she had met white people she could trust, fully trust. And what Rosa—Rosa had known some wonderful white people who were full of social equality and—but, what she was saying was she had never been in a place where you could demonstrate by everything that happened that you believed in full social equality. You know, that Highlander was—anywhere you went, you know, it was—everybody was equal. There was no, you know, there was no way—I always said we were too small and too poor to discriminate. We didn't have any facilities for discrimination. There was no way we could have done it if we wanted to, you know. So you know, Rosa just saw a total way of living she'd never seen before, she just couldn't believe that that would, you know, happen. She didn't go back with any plans or anything, she went back with a different spirit.

MOYERS: How did that come about, that you were able to integrate Highlander, because the laws of Tennessee were against it, the churches were against it, the political, the local political leaders were against it, everyone was against it. How—what was the technique for integrating it?

HORTON: Well, you know, a little expansion of the your-home-is-your-castle idea. This is one place that we were going to do what we pleased, in terms of the way we were going to work, and there's certain principles that you just don't question. I grew up in the South knowing all these interracial people who were—who would talk about social equality but would never eat together. They keep talking themselves into more distance. So they were getting further apart the more they talked, there were fewer people'd do it—they had a few blacks that would meet with the whites and talk, and a few whites that'd meet with the blacks and talk, and the rest of the people got burned out, they weren't getting anywhere. But that was the interracial thing in the South. And I learned, you know, when I was in college, to dislike that heartily, and I said, you can do it—you act, and then the planning and thinking comes. First, if I ever get a chance, I want to act, and let the talk come later. I'm not going to talk first thing—you talk yourself out of it. But if you could set up a situation where people act, then the action would change their hearts. So that's the reverse of what most people have to do.

MOYERS: Because many of those union organizers you had here were often members of the Klan.

HORTON: Well, the head of—the educational director, which was the head of the Reuther campaign, when Reuther ran for, you know, against R. J. Thomas for the presidency,[104] was a former Klan official, according to him, he told me himself, that he was elected to that job because he was a Klan official, and Reuther figured there were more Klan people in the union in the South than there were non-Klan people. We worked with Joe, we worked with him, you know, we'd work with people, knowing all the time they were that kind of people. And they objected to blacks at Highlander; in fact, they tried to have a workshop at Highlander without any blacks, and I wouldn't let them—I told them they had to leave. And they said, well, you know, we've paid you, we reserved this place a week ago, we got all this stuff. I said, I don't care what you've done, if this black guy came up and he heard about it, and he came up and—I said, he's going to stay or nobody stays. And a lot of these people that didn't know me—from outside the South, you know, they said, huh, you know, nobody can tell us what to do, we're powerful, you know, that sort of thing. But people of the South that I'd worked with, they told them, you know, that I meant what I said, and that they'd be—they'd leave when I told them they'd leave. And they said, who is this guy that can tell us we have to leave? And this guy that was the head—that used to be the Klansman who was, you know, who was instrumental in helping set that up, but knew me, he said, Myles has ways for you to move, and he said, if you don't want some of these mountaineers to come in and shoot your ass out, you better get going when he tells you. He said, he knows what he's talking about, he's got the power. So instead of leaving, they let that black guy stay. See, that's the way you get them used to it. Then those same people started bringing blacks to Highlander. Once you make

THE CIVIL RIGHTS MOVEMENT

them do it some way, then they'll find out it's not so bad, and they'll keep on doing it. It was the UAW after that that set the pattern of unions always bringing blacks to Highlander.[105] But I had to be a little rough on them to start with.

MOYERS: What about that story about the time the white farmers were here?

HORTON: Oh that's the farmers' union. We organized the National Farmers' Union, a very good organization, a liberal organization of farmers.[106] We organized the families into cooperatives and so on. And we ran a workshop of people from Alabama and up here in east Tennessee, and all around down in west Tennessee, which is the, you know, a real racist part of the country. And we had some black people in that workshop. Black farmers. So we were milling around outside and these white farmers said, what are these black people here for, what they doing here? And I said, I don't know, I said, you know we have a lot of different sections here, different kinds of people come—union people come, church people come, all kinds of people come. These are farmers, these are farmers' union people, we don't have anybody here but farmers' union. I said, some people get mixed up, probably they just thought this was a workshop on NAACP or something else, but maybe, I don't know.[107] I said, I'd like to know myself. So I said, you go out there, you two guys go there and you go find out if they're farmers, go ask them if they're farmers.

MOYERS: The two white guys go out and ask.

HORTON: Yes, so the black guys said they were members of the farmers' union. We don't want them, you tell me, you know, you come back and tell me, we'll run them off, you know, if they're not farmers or farmers' union members. So they can't think of anything else to say, so they go and ask them. Of course, yeah, we're members of the farmers' union, and so on, and so on, and so on. I see these fellows scratching their heads and the mountain guy looks at the farmers and looking back at me. They came up here just two counties—Greene County, a couple of counties from here—came back and I said, what'd they say—do they belong here, are they farmers? The fellow goes, Yeah, and I said, Good, I'm relieved, and I said, I thought we were going to have to send them away. And I just turned and walked off. Then they had the discussion among themselves— they had to deal with all that problem. I wouldn't argue with them, wouldn't do anything with them. I just left that with them. And then they had to internalize that, you see, and deal with it. Then they said, well, farmers, you know, we won't run them off, then we have to be nice to them and so on, so they came in and ate with them and it was all over.

MOYERS: What does that say about it, what does that say to you?

HORTON: You have to do things like that all the time.

MOYERS: What does that say about identity and how we shape our perceptions of people? They didn't want them to come as blacks, but they were welcome as farmers?

HORTON: Well, they couldn't deal with the problem I posed for them, people not being welcome if they were farmers, not having a right if they were farmers. It put them in a different category. They weren't blacks, they were farmers. We do that all the time, you help people perceive things differently. You enable them to break out of their encrustation of thinking and perceive things a different way.

MOYERS: Did you find that your efforts in organizing workers and in trying to solve some of the other problems were running into racism everywhere you—

HORTON: Yeah, you see, racism is a barrier. You could go so far—you could get people organized, but—and you could integrate unions, but then when you tried to relate to the larger community or go beyond just the more practical unionism, you get into politics for example, then you found that racism always was a barrier. Then we said we were going to have to remove that barrier. It wasn't—it was a negative kind of way of approaching it, the barrier was in the way of democracy, you see, so you had to get rid of it. So we were trying to devise programs, worthwhile ways for people to learn to work together at that time. Before the '54 decision, we had anticipated that decision by setting up a workshop four months in advance to discuss the Supreme Court decision on schools, and there hadn't been any decision.[108] It was a gamble, and they passed a law months before the workshop, and recruiting had already been done, everything had been done in advance. You know, we took chances, we kind of pushed the—pushed it as far as we could—we gambled, to try to promote interest in that kind of thing. So we were sure that there was a groundswell. We had been working in South Carolina in what we called a Citizenship School,[109] schools for training, teaching blacks to learn enough—reading that they could pass the—to qualify to vote in South Carolina you had to read part of the Constitution. And we developed a very successful program there that has eventually spread all over the South, and that was under way at that time. And we had students, college students, black and white, coming to Highlander for three- to four-day Easter weekends, and out of that group about 80 percent of the people who were in on the formation of SNCC came.

MOYERS: The Student Nonviolent Coordinating Committee.

HORTON: Coordinating Committee. John Lewis,[110] Julian Bond,[111] and the Bevels,[112] and all those people had been at Highlander before. John Lewis says that he'd been to all kinds of church gatherings and things like that, and Highlander was the first time he ever ate with white people. So they had that background. So we'd been laying some groundwork, in the hopes that something would happen.

MOYERS: But when they were, when they were getting workshops on direct action, voter education, didn't you start coming under sustained attack from Alabama, Tennessee—

HORTON: Oh yeah, that's when—people in Tennessee, even though they opposed Highlander, didn't initiate those things. The first step taken against Highlander was initiated—was a state investigation of Highlander initiated by the Attorney General in Arkansas, who came over and asked that they investigate Highlander because Highlander was training a lot of people, you know, there were a lot of people from Arkansas that were coming to Highlander, and they were coming back to Arkansas and raising cain.[113] That was the first outside pressure. Then later on the governor of Georgia[114] sent an agent to a workshop where Martin Luther King spoke.[115] They used that meeting, they took pictures of that meeting, and they had billboards all over the South—Martin Luther King at a Communist training school.[116]

MOYERS: Who took pictures?

HORTON: The agent from the governor of Georgia. And they claimed that they circulated over two million copies of that propaganda against Highlander.

MOYERS: Showing Martin Luther King at a Communist meeting.

HORTON: Communist training school, they said, and it was Martin speaking at that meeting. And that was before Martin was known very well, you know, he was with the Montgomery Improvement Association then, and—but we thought something was going to come of that, but most people didn't think much was going to come of it.[117]

MOYERS: Wasn't there a trial?

HORTON: Well, as a result of this exposé so-called, of Highlander, they told the people of Tennessee, you know, the governor, you've got to find a way to put those people out of business—it's not just a Tennessee matter.[118] And that led to the trial—that was the impetus that led to the trial. So they finally—they finally had a raid on the school.

MOYERS: Literally? I mean, the police came in?[119]

HORTON: Well, there was vigilantes, police, and we didn't know who was who, there was about twenty people came in, armed people. We'd been having a—there was a group of—a choir from one of the Montgomery churches there on a kind of weekend sort of program, and they were high-school-aged kids, and they were there. They were looking at a movie that George Mitchell made, called *The Face of the South.* And they raided them while the lights were off for looking at this movie. And they came in with their guns flashing around and they demanded "Turn on the lights." And nobody would turn on the lights, and it was while the darkness—it was still dark, that those kids started singing "We Shall Overcome." And that night they added, "We are not afraid." It became one of the permanent verses. That was the night that was invented by those high-school-aged kids from Montgomery. And they said, like at the vigilantes, we're not afraid, we're not afraid. That became one of the lines of the song. But they hauled Septima Clark, Guy Carawan, and some other people off to jail—I wasn't there at the time. I was away. They hauled them in to jail and kept them overnight—just to set up a trial.

MOYERS: What did they charge them with?

HORTON: They charged them with having liquor and serving liquor, and Septima Clark with running it,[120] she's antiliquor, a religious leader, you know, and Guy doesn't drink, and they were serving Kool-Aid to those kids, that was the drink that was—

MOYERS: Wasn't there some beer, too?

HORTON: No, no, what we had done in previous years, when labor people were there, since we lived two miles out in the country and the black and white people couldn't go uptown and drink beer, because it was illegal, you know, to be served beer in town, we would get a case of beer and put it in the cooler and put a cigar box there and everybody would put in a quarter at that time, and when you ran out, somebody would take the box and go get another case of beer and put it in the cooler. So later on the judge ruled that was selling beer without a license. For example, if there were three people in a room and one of them goes out and buys three cans of beer and two people give him a quarter apiece, legally that's selling beer. So he—that's the illustration he himself used, the judge used. So he said that according to my testimony, which nobody could ever question, he said I was the most reliable witness in the trial, that we did that. I explained the process, I explained just what we did, and he said it was on the basis of my explanation that he found us guilty of selling beer, because there wasn't any beer at that time.

MOYERS: Anything to try to bring a charge against you, a case against you, to close you down.

HORTON: They had eighteen charges against us—one charge that we were running an integrated school, to which we pled guilty, proudly, and said we always had and we always were going to keep on doing it. So we were guilty of that, but they also got the charges for selling liquor without a license, and they charged me with operating a school for personal gain—not personally, I was never in court, you know, as Myles Horton, but I was—as Highlander. I was operating a school for personal gain. They testified that I had never taken personal gain, but there's no limit to what people could take. We had a system then, pretty much as it is now, people get paid on the basis of the size of their family, and it's still true today. And if there's a problem—somebody gets sick, or a child gets sick or something—and they need more money, well, you know, that's all the money that people have, so the school will provide it. So they said, is there a top on how much you can provide? And I said, no, we never discussed that, if there was a top on it, because we didn't have it. And the top wasn't, because people would only take what they needed. And because nobody wanted to spend time raising money—everybody wanted to run the program. So I said it's not a problem, and he said, is there no legal requirement? *[inaudible]* so I said, there's no legal, we're talking about any of it, it's all just understood. So he says, on the basis of that, then you could, you know, take some money, and he says, what Horton *[inaudible]*.[121] He hadn't cut it yet, but he's getting ready to cut it. And I was convicted on anticipation on his part of me cuttin' the melon later on. That was his—

MOYERS: What does it make you feel like, when the whole apparatus of the state as well as the whole weight of public opinion, are turned against you, and you're hounded and intimidated, harassed—

HORTON: Ah, you know, it's not that clear-cut. There was never a time when we didn't have friends. We had—at that time, we had the labor movement, a tremendous lot of support from the labor movement, who opposed all this. We had the *Nashville Tennessean* editorially supported us. We had the *Chattanooga Times,* the mother of the *New York Times,* supporting Highlander. So we weren't completely alone. And we gradually won over papers in Memphis and other places. So it was a raw deal. What I used to do, I'd take advantage of those hearings and try to educate the people of Tennessee, because it was all covered by radio and TV news. It was a big thing in Tennessee. So I'd use that as public education. And of course the enemy stayed enemies. You don't win them over. But you make friends. And during the trial—to give an idea of the kind of support we had—the *Chattanooga Times* which covered the trial said that every witness the state had, without a single exception, had been convicted and had served time. Every witness. And he said Highlander didn't have any witnesses like that. And he said, in fact, Horton refused to subpoena any witnesses—I said if there aren't enough volunteers to testify for Highlander after all these years, we don't need support. Over two hundred people signed up to testify. So the papers tell those stories. So, you know, the Cranache people we had to get educated. We were never all alone.

MOYERS: What are you doing right now?

HORTON: Right now we're in a kind of a, I guess, kind of a transition period, in a way. We've been working for the last ten years or more in Appalachia trying to help get a lot of spirit in Appalachia. When we first started we decided the civil rights movement, you know, was—had plenty of leadership. Hundreds and hundreds of people had been to Highlander and thousands had been to citizenship schools that came out of Highlander. And plenty of leadership developed out of the civil rights movement. So we said, "Look, you don't need Highlander. You can write your own program." We set up a program for the Southern Christian Leadership Conference. I was an adviser to SNCC on educational programs. So, you know, you've got all you need out of Highlander. They didn't agree with that, but we said, you know, "You had it and we don't. You can do your own program. We'll give you our blessing, but we're not going to do it." We're going to come back where we started—in the mountains—and start working with our own people, because they're behind. And we're going to try to get some consciousness of what happened in Appalachia built up. We started out in the mid-'60s and we had a very hard time getting people together to play music. Now you can't keep 'em away, you know. We have to keep—

MOYERS: Mountain people?

HORTON: Yeah. And we'd get people together to talk about activities of different kinds. Half a dozen peoples' organizations in Appalachia, none of them working together, the spirit was low. But since then, we've come a long way in Appalachia—there's maybe fifty organizations which now are combined into Appalachian Alliance,[122] which is something we've always felt it was important to get people together instead of competing and we work together. We just completed a land study—

MOYERS: What did it show?

HORTON: Which is a part of the Appalachian Alliance, that, I don't know, that practically three-fourths of the land in Appalachia is absentee owned. Those people pay one-third the taxes on their land that the local people pay, which means there's no tax base for schools, health, roads, or anything.

MOYERS: Well, give me an inventory of the problems that are faced in Appalachia. I thought there had been a War on Poverty,[123] an Appalachian Regional Commission.[124] I thought all of that had been—

HORTON: Well, when the War on Poverty was announced, and I don't have to explain that to you, I was asked if I thought that was a good thing. And I said, yes, but I'd like to qualify it. And they said, but do you think that's going to be a good program to get people out of poverty? And I said, no, I don't think it will deal with poverty, although that's the subject. But I think a lot of people will get experiences out of that that will enable them to do things on their own later on, and they'll find out that something can't come down from on high that will solve their problems for them. So there'd be a lot of good learning that would take place. And I was asked, well, what is Highlander's role? I said, wait a little bit 'til people start getting disillusioned. And then start trying to help people analyze their experiences so they can build on it to take things in their own hands to start doing things for themselves, and bring pressure on the government to do sounder jobs. So that was my analysis when it was first announced. And that's what the program at Highlander was, to try to, you know, salvage from the people that learned something, you know, out of that, some capabilities of doing things.

MOYERS: Is there a lot of disillusionment in Appalachia?

HORTON: Oh, yes, Appalachia has been the guinea pig of the country. All— you know, anybody that wants to try out an idea, they try it out in this region. And we've been missionaried to death, starting back with the religious missionaries, you know, who were going to bring down the New England culture to us mountain folks, teach us how to use some manners —along with a lot of good solid education, they should be credited with that. Then there were the political, you know, missionaries come in, then the economic people come in to save the South by buying up the land and developing industry. Now the—then the War on Poverty missionaries that came in, and now we're getting the multinational people coming in. So we've always been—somebody has always been coming in and going to save the region. And they always take more out than they bring in. And that's why we think people have to, you know, take control of their own organizations and their own lives.

MOYERS: Well, how are you going to do that? I mean, if—

HORTON: Well, we're making a little headway in the sense that the Appalachian Alliance has a voice. I mean, Appalachia never had a voice before. There's a structure for a voice.

MOYERS: Who are these people in it—

HORTON: There are about fifty peoples' organizations in the region, practically all the organizations in the region are run by people there now. They've learned to work together. We've got a lot of Appalachian study programs going, in fact all the universities—there was a time when there weren't any, about ten years ago.

MOYERS: What about the economic realities?

HORTON: Now, you see, the thing that we've been trying to get people to understand is, that this wave of people living on the land, getting back and retreating into the past is not—is not going to help Appalachia. Appalachia is tied into the—through the multinationals—with the rest of the world. We're part of the world. So one thing Highlander's into is bringing people from—Appalachia is kind of a Third World country. Get the Third World people together, you know.

MOYERS: To do what, because if three-fourths of the land is owned by absentee owners, how in the devil are you going to bring pressure against them? What do you want them to do?

HORTON: Well, you know, they don't have to stay that way. You know, if you get enough people power built up, you can do things to those big chunks of land.

MOYERS: Now you're sounding like a Utopian again.

HORTON: Oh, no, I'm just saying you can—I'm talking about some direct action, moving in and occupying some of them, you know, really have a showdown and force the issue so people would begin to understand that you can't have a—Appalachia is rich in resources, it's poor in people. Because all the richness goes out, and, you know, we've got to find a way to take back some of the richness that belongs to the people.

MOYERS: Haven't you been in jail enough? I mean—

HORTON: Well, about a dozen times, maybe.

MOYERS: But isn't that enough?

HORTON: Well, I'm not trying to—I don't want to go to jail. I never did want to go to jail.

MOYERS: But I mean, if you start urging people to occupy absentee-owned land, you start telling them to take it back, you're going to wind up in jail or worse.

HORTON: Well, you know, we did that in our American revolution. We started taking over British-owned land right and left, remember? That's how we got this country going. There's a good American tradition. Of course, you're right about the law and order people—they don't understand that, but they can be educated. I know—I'm serious, I think somehow the people have got to take back the sources of their wealth, and I don't think we're ready for that, I don't think the people understand that, but I think they got to quit trying to escape, you know, hide out, and stand up and say we demand our rights.

MOYERS: Who are the losers in Appalachia, and who are the winners?

HORTON: Well, the win—the people who are already in Appalachia who are the winners, are the agents for the absentee-owned companies, you know, and the people who work for them, in terms of economic welfare. The losers, of course, are the people back in the hollows who have no tax base to support their schools and their communities.

MOYERS: So the issue's still, as it was twenty years ago, poverty?

HORTON: Sure, it's poverty.

MOYERS: But isn't it—

HORTON: It's relative poverty. Poverty is a relative thing, you know. People say, you know, capitalism is a wonderful thing—look how much better it was now than when—to be when you were growing up. And I say, is the gap between the rich and the poor wider? And the important thing is the lack of distribution of the wealth, and the use of the wealth. Not the wealth— we don't have people starving, as they were doing when Highlander started, not many, anyway. But the rich are getting richer, and poor are getting poorer, relative to each other, you know. The blacks, as a result of the civil rights movement, the middle-class blacks prospered. And it's misleading to talk about blacks prospering, because the majority of working-class blacks are worse off in relation to working-class whites, than they were before the civil rights movement. Those problems haven't been dealt with. The problems of poverty haven't been dealt with.

MOYERS: Powerlessness.

HORTON: And they've got to have power in the hands of those people. Now one way to get at this, I guess there are two theories of how you have revolution—and that's what I'm talking about. One is that people are desperate, and out of desperation they act. I think that leads to fascism. I don't think that's—you know, I think people who are desperate are going to follow any leader that comes along. In fact, it's kind of the desperate people who voted for Reagan. A lot of desperate people voted for Reagan, saying he must—he'll have a gimmick. That hat fooled them. I understand that up in Canada, I read a columnist that said, Reagan was all hat and no cattle. All style and no substance.

MOYERS: And you think people like that?

HORTON: And I think a lot of poor people, a lot of union people, voted for him thinking he's going to—they were fooled by that hat, you know? They thought, you know, he's going to do something. People still have to think somebody's going to save them—somebody's going to come on a white horse to save them. Now what we've been trying to do is get people to understand that's not the way to salvation—they've got to save themselves. And if you're going to do it, not out of desperation, then you've got to do it on the basis of rising expectations. We say to the people, you deserve more than you have. You deserve part of the good things of this life. You deserve the right to, you know, the opportunity to be more creative, you deserve the opportunity to have a higher standard of living, you deserve the right to, you know, to health as well as theoretical education. You know, we keep saying that you deserve those as human beings, and the system should deliver those to you. If it doesn't, change the system until it does. We still are letting people make decisions for us, instead of people learning to make decisions for them. But when people at the bottom learn to make decisions, there's enough of us, you know, that we can begin to bring pressure. Now that situation hasn't developed in Appalachia because the lines aren't as clear-cut. Everybody's got relatives on both sides. And knows somebody on both sides—has neighbors on both sides. You know, the black and white cases were clear-cut in the South, you know. There wasn't any problem about understanding, you know, who you were. It was legally enforced racism, in other words, it was more clear-cut, and when the blacks started finding out that, they could go to jail and still survive. They'd been saying if you're doing anything we don't like, we'll put you in jail, and so they backed off. They found they could go to jail and even die, you know, the people, when they—when no longer were the whites able to say, we'll put you in jail or we'll kill you, and stop the movement, then the blacks took off. But they had a clear-cut issue, clear-cut issue, and they had some white friends, you know, all along.

MOYERS: Are you saying that democracy is not working very well, as you see it?

HORTON: No, democracy is not working at all in Appalachia, not at all.

MOYERS: How do you define democracy?

HORTON: Democracy, to me, is where people have a way to control many facets of their lives—political, economic, social, cultural—and in so far as they are minimized, democracy is denied.

MOYERS: Some would respond that, well, if you've got a good job and you're making a good income, you've got disposable income, then you have some control over your life.

HORTON: Most of the people in Appalachia go hunting jobs all over the world. Most of the people go out all over the United States. We have more people going out of the state to find jobs, out of the region to find jobs, than any other part of the country, because there's not jobs in the region. People—that's an outlet, you see, so they can escape that way. In the depression they come back home, but there's too many escape valves that they—it's hard to get people to get some consensus on what to do. I think, you know, that we've got to learn that, you know, if you don't have the strength, you know, you don't have the people, you don't have the power to deal with the big United States government, which of course is subject to the multinationals. The United States government doesn't run the show, you know, they are run.

MOYERS: So they are still—

HORTON: You've got to be realistic and know that you've got to be big enough to tackle this problem before you can—you've got to get allies. That means we've got to cut across all kinds of racial and religious and national grounds.

MOYERS: So there is still an agenda for an old radical, with the kind of—

HORTON: Oh, boy. I think the interesting thing to me is that we're just beginning a little bit to get people to understand this.

MOYERS: You know, as you talk, there's a paradox. You were active in union organizing and, in time, the unions began to Red-bait you. The AFL—[125]

HORTON: They got conservative and bureaucratic.

MOYERS: Well, in time, northern liberals turned against you because they were afraid of the Communist associations. In—

HORTON: They were a little afraid that some of this civil rights business would get in their towns and affect their housing.

MOYERS: And then in 1969, after all the battles that you'd helped to win, you went to Chicago and there you were the only white face in a sea of black faces, and everybody joined hands to express solidarity, and you held out your hands, and no black would take them.

HORTON: They were singing "We Shall Overcome" and nobody would touch my hands.

MOYERS: What does all that say to you?

HORTON: It says that these blacks know that where there's a racist society—most whites are racist to them, and they could not possibly have known that I'm any different from any other white. I understand that fully well. It bothered me that we hadn't made enough inroads that they would think there might be exceptions to whites, but it didn't bother me personally. I wasn't hurt personally.

MOYERS: It doesn't bother you that, in time after time, the people to whom you've given your life and your energies wind up not appreciating—

HORTON: No, I think you have to be objective, not subjective, about these things. You have to understand the forces at work, and understand that those things happen. I don't take these things personally—I never took these attacks on Highlander, these investigations, the court trials, the confiscation of our property, even the beatings I never took personally, although it was my bones that were cracking. But I mean I never thought of it as them—that Myles Horton, you know, me, what I know me to be, was what they were after. You know, I was a symbol. I represented something that they hated. I represented something that was challenging their whole way of life, and that's what I represented to the blacks in Chicago when no one would take my hand and sing "We Shall Overcome." I represented, you know, that picture. And when the Klan over here at Marysville beat me up, I represented, you know, bringing blacks into their homes, not—So I try to keep a little objective about this thing.

MOYERS: How do you see yourself, Myles Horton?

HORTON: I'm an instrument, you know. That's why I don't take these things personally.

MOYERS: An instrument of what?

HORTON: Well, I'm an instrument of—I tried to be an instrument—at Highlander I try to make, you know, I tried to make Highlander an instrument of empowering people, a way to get people to understand that they can be creative and imaginative. They don't have to put up with this system the way it is. They can create a new one to—that would be more humane. And they've got to not be so subservient to technology which is moving in and dominating their lives. You know I think you've got to use yourself and use Highlander, to help do this, you don't have a program— I don't have a program—Myles Horton is trying to do this, Highlander's trying to do this—we, here we are, we're trying to use our facilities and what little we know and how we work to help empower people. You were talking earlier about education, how you educate, you know, and I was talking about the kind of structural things that you could put your finger on. But really, the way you educate is by example. You educate by your own life, what you are. I can—I'm interested in people learning how to learn. Now, the only way I can help is to share my enthusiasm and my ability to learn myself. If I quit learning I can't share. I try to get people to feel, you know, be human. I think you have to love people to do these things. I tried to do this. If I don't love people, I can't help people learn to love. I can't do anything other than I'm doing myself.

MOYERS: How can you love somebody that's beating you on the head? How can you love the man who won't take your hand when you hold it out in solidarity?

HORTON: It's humanity, you know, that you love. I don't—I didn't feel sorry for those people, you know, I'm not a good guy like Martin Luther King was, in loving all these people, you know, and thinking you could save them. I don't think I can save them by loving them, but I think I can survive and understand who they are, and they're unlovable, so I can't love them. But I don't have to hate them. I don't have to think it's personally directed at me. I mean I just don't bother with them.

MOYERS: You don't have to let them—

HORTON: No, you see, I think you should have some good healthy enemies. I'm just as proud of my enemies as I am of my friends.

MOYERS: Who are your enemies?

HORTON: Well, the people that are enemies are people who are racists, bigots, who don't believe in people living decent lives, they're people who think poor people ought to stay poor, they're law and order people who think structures come before people—I've got a lot of people that believe in things that I don't believe in. I don't want their friendship.

MOYERS: You've got some healthy enemies.

HORTON: Yeah, I think you should measure yourself partly by your enemies as well as your friends.

MOYERS: Do you still believe—

HORTON: I'm not a good guy, you know, saying I love all these people personally. They're not lovable.

MOYERS: Do you believe, with your old friend Reinhold Niebuhr, that it is possible to establish justice in a sinful world?

HORTON: I think you can work for justice in a sinful world, and you can always have the hope, and sometimes the proof, that you can make headway, you know, in terms of justice in a sinful world. We could—the industrial union movement before it got conservative was making headway; the civil rights movement—that was making headway. You see, I've had some experiences of—it makes you realize things can happen in dealing with justice and injustice. I don't think there will ever come a time when there aren't problems. I don't envision a time when everything is perfect. I don't—I think, I like to envision a time when there's more good than evil, which is not too—there's more evil than good today in this society. I'd like to envision a time when people are—more people are freer in more areas of their lives. I think all those things are possible. I think you keep pushing. But your sights keep moving, too, you know. There's the old story you climb the mountain, you see another mountain. Now, you know, that doesn't bother me. I've got—you know, people accuse me of never being satisfied. Well, why should a human being be satisfied, you know, he might as well—that's the end.

Section IV

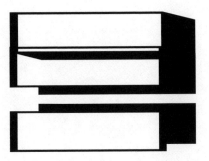

Educational Philosophy

Educational Theory

[1933]

In the following text, taken from notes written in 1933, Horton outlines his theories of mutual adult education and relates them to Highlander's work with the labor movement. This piece, written in the earliest years of Highlander, explicitly calls for education as a means of "bringing about a new social order."

Mutual Education

Our residence group is small. At the beginning of our first term, November 1, 1932, we had only one student, a coal miner's son who, after a few months in a conservative southern college, had come to us hoping that we would help him in facing some of the vital problems of life.[1] Soon others joined our group, both young men and women. However, there have never been more than eight of us. The number of resident students is limited to fifteen, and one of the most valuable features of our school is the mutual education made possible by the living, working, and studying together of a small group of students and teachers. Friends educate each other. A wide variety of experiences is represented by members of the group. Some have hardly been more than a day's travel from home, while others have traveled both in this country and in Europe. The ideas of a middle-aged worker who had participated in a number of radical labor movements were supplemented by economic theories learned from graduate schools of this country and study abroad. Theological seminary graduates discuss religious problems with those who question the value of religion. First attempts at writing are criticized by a visiting teacher whose literary products are published. We are educated not only by this process of sharing experiences and knowledge with one another, but also by taking part in group life. While we do not propose to set up a Utopia, we do strive to live out our ideals in so far as it is possible. This calls for a sympathetic understanding of the aims of the school. Members of the group must be adaptable and, above all, must possess tolerance: tolerance not only for the views of the members of our small group, but for the views of the community of which we are a part. Mutual criticism is practiced and the will of the group respected. There are no privileged individuals: all are treated alike. Students who pay with money or produce are on an equal footing with those [who] pay in labor. Teachers receive no salaries. They have no authority because of their position as teachers. Their wishes receive the same consideration as do the wishes of the other members of the group. Even class attendance is a matter of individual choice, unless the students as a group decide otherwise. Under no circumstances is anyone regularly excused from doing his or her share of the manual labor, such as cleaning houses, washing dishes, building fires, and other necessary work.

Adult Education

Our community program in one way or another touches all ages, but our major emphasis is with people eighteen and above. Especially here in the mountains, there is a crying need for schools where older people can learn about themselves and their world without having to start back in the sixth grade where many of them left off twenty years ago. More than likely the experiences of such adults would place them on a level with college graduates rather than on a level with their own children in the sixth grade. Education is life: consequently life is education. So here at the Highlander Folk School we have men with college degrees, and men of fifty who never finished grammar school, grappling with the same problems.

It is not more education that we are after, but a different kind of education. Now, more than ever before, it should be clear that a conventional college education does not necessarily turn out a product that is socially useful. Our so-called educated class has failed us. The industrial rulers of our country and most of their underlings are college trained men. Wide spread adult education is essential to democracy. There must always be leaders, but they must have an intelligent following. The spreading of knowledge through a large group is a difficult task, but the widespread understanding of the social forces which will enable the masses to assume social control is essential to the welfare of our country. This means that adult education must be cultural rather than vocational.

The disinherited worker must be awakened and enlightened regarding his destiny, not trained to do better work for his industrial masters. Consequently one of our specific aims is to educate labor leaders who will have social vision. The old parties, like the captains of industry who control them, have failed us. The time is ripe for a new step in the development of society. The change from slavery to feudalism was of a radical nature; but perhaps even more revolutionary was the transition from feudalism to capitalism. Now capitalism is breaking down. For a long time socialistic principles have been absorbed by a dying capitalism desperately desiring to live on past its day of usefulness. At present we are neither fish nor fowl. We cannot revive a dying philosophy; it can be artificially stimulated, but eventually it must go the way of slavery and feudalism.

The Highlander Folk School stands for a new day. A shuffling of the old cards cannot satisfy us. We seek aid in building a new social order where human values, not property values, will be supreme. We strike at the roots. Consequently, nothing short of a new economic system based upon production for use and not for profit is our goal. But we teach that a new party of and for the people, such as the Socialist Party, could, by peaceful and constitutional measures, produce the necessary changes. Whether the transition can be made peacefully or not will depend upon the result of the race between social enlightenment and the uncontrolled economic forces that now threaten us with disaster. The burden of the present crisis cannot be shifted to the backs of innocent children. Too long have we escaped our responsibility by leaving our important social problems as a heritage of confusion to the children in whose hands the future lies. Children have been allowed to grow up in a blighting environment produced by the greed of their parents. In our childhood we were always told to get educated so that we could grapple with the problems that our parents were saving for us to solve. But the blighting environment was too much for our ideals. *[Illegible text omitted]* Now we are trying to ward off the problems we have failed to solve. Shall we pass on the ever-increasing burden of unsolved problems to our children, or shall we put an end to this unjust and meaningless process?

The educational psychologists have made it impossible for us to excuse ourselves by saying that adults cannot learn. We of the Highlander Folk School would like to see a world fit for children to be born into—a world where all children could live a full life. That is why we seek not to mirror the times but to enable people to understand direct social and economic forces. In this way a society may result in which the present class distinctions based on economic advantages will be eliminated. In other words, we propose to use education as one of the methods for bringing about a new social order. We are not dogmatists, but we do have a definite direction. The Highlander Folk School is an experiment in purposive adult education.

Goals and methods cannot be separated. But too often Progressive Education, for example, is thought of as only progressive method. As if getting nowhere correctly and in a hurry were a great achievement! Our first step was to choose our goal, and now we are experimenting with the best methods of achieving it. Obviously, working with a life situation requires an entirely different method from that used in teaching an academic subject. Knowledge alone is not enough. We stress the idea that both experience and objective facts such as are learned from books and lectures should be made to stand the test of critical thinking, and that the knowledge thus derived should be utilized in attacking our social and individual problems. Such relating of factual material to life and action based upon the knowledge gained in this way calls for a method which utilizes both intellect and feeling. A creative intellect can give direction, but without emotional warmth there is not sufficient driving power for the attainment of a goal. Consequently, we are seeking a method combining both feeling and intellect.

Special Courses

The idea of having special two weeks' courses for people who could be with us for only a short time was suggested by a middle-aged worker who spent a week with us. He told us that many unemployed, like himself, would be glad of such an opportunity. We announced a two weeks' course and found a number of the unemployed in the mountains and in nearby industrial centers eager to come. However, a week before the course was to begin, the Reconstruction Finance Corporation gave one or two days per week to most of our prospects, and they were unable to attend.[2] Only one student arrived the day the course was to begin. A young woman came in with a heavy basket of peas, onions, and canned goods to pay her expenses. She was from the mountains, but had worked in a hosiery mill in Chattanooga.

The course went through on schedule. The mornings were devoted to class work, and the afternoons to study, work, and recreation. The regular evening classes went on as usual. The special student was given individual attention by teachers and students as well. In this was she able to profit from a program of study pitched on the level of the resident group. We attempted to organize our thinking regarding Socialism, Communism, Fascism, and Capitalism.

Most of the classes were held around the open fire in the big study room, but one interesting class was held in the kitchen. We tried to do all the housework before time for class, and would even postpone class for a few minutes when necessary, but on this occasion the student cook absolutely refused to leave her stove. The class met in the kitchen. There had been an assignment. Each member of the class was to demonstrate to the satisfaction of the other members that they understood a number of economic theories previously discussed. One student used a blackboard, propped over the sink. Another explained the theories by illustrating her points by the use of pots and pans. One analyzed the running of a neighbor's bakery, from whom we sometimes buy bread, and showed how the various theories worked out in everyday life. This proved to be one of our most profitable discussions. A visitor who had dropped in at the beginning of the discussion said that she would never forget the illustration of "surplus value" given by the girl who had come for the two weeks.

"When I was working at the hosiery mill in Chattanooga," the student said, "we were told that our wages must be cut or the mill would have to close down. Of course we took the cut. About two weeks later I read in the paper that the daughter of the mill owner was sailing for Europe for the summer. I suppose it was the surplus value we had produced that payed her way."

This experiment with a special course failed to accomplish its original purpose of reaching the unemployed. Nevertheless, it proved very beneficial to the resident group. So many problems were raised during these two weeks that the group decided to spend the next few weeks following up the lines of thought that were suggested. Time enough has elapsed between the date of this course described and the time of this writing for us to be able to say with some certainty that facts acquired because they are essential to the solving of a problem are more or less permanently added to one's body of usable knowledge.

If education is to be vital it must deal with situations, not subjects. In our classes we can only introduce the student to whatever phase of the problem of life the subject covers. This is fragmentary and not enough. We cannot think without something to think about—a problem. And the problem cannot be artificial. The situational approach gives the problem-solving process a setting of reality. This, in general, is the theory back of this feature of our program—the project.

As educational projects our teachers and students have made a study of labor conditions at the Palmer mines, located about twenty-five miles from the school, and have investigated the Rossville Textile Strike in Georgia. The Wilder Miner's Strike, however, has been the subject of continuous study and investigation.[3] Wilder is situated in the Tennessee mountains about 140 miles away. It has furnished us with discussion material for classes and has given us a life situation about which to write class papers and even articles for the state and labor press.

After a critical examination of the facts which we had gathered by personal investigations we concluded that the strikers were on the side of justice, and set out to help them win their strike. From that time on we were educated by our own experiences. In an effort to create favorable public opinion we learned many things regarding the stand taken by various newspapers, churches, and public officials on such questions. We appealed for funds to help carry on the strike and arranged for Norman Thomas to visit the conflict area.[4] We are following up his visit with a labor Chautauqua in an effort to educate the strikers to see that their fight is part of a greater battle of the workers the world over. One of the strike leaders recently said that our visits helped keep up the morale of the Union men and suggested that we send over students and let the strikers help educate them. Here is mutual education on a broader scale. We learn from the miners and they are helped by us.

Our use of conflict situations vitalizes and makes realistic our educational program. Such a conception of education does not allow for standardization. Examinations are out of the question. At the Highlander Folk School we have neither entrance nor exit exams. The incentive is furnished by the student's desire to gather and organize facts which can be used in facing life's pressing problems.

Individual Problems

We place such value on the learner's experience in the educational process that we insist on each resident student having a community project. This makes our school a kind of community center.

One student has a dramatic club. Plays are given at the regular Saturday evening community meetings. One play, built around a local situation, was written by the director and one of the teachers. A labor play, "What Price Coal," was presented by the club at the end of the term. This project has not only helped the student-director but has been of benefit to those who have taken part in the plays, and has afforded a great deal of pleasure to the community.

A girls' club, chosen as a project by another student, has grown into a music class. She is now giving a number of piano lessons each day. Arrangements have been made with the local schoolteacher for a number of the pupils to take lessons during school hours. Such activities not only contribute to the cultural enrichment of the community, but help make our school a real part of the community life. This work, along with the collection of mountain songs, has been so worthwhile that we have arranged to have the student carry on her work through the summer as a regular part of the school activities.

One boy, especially interested in labor problems, organized and helped carry on a study class for the miners at Palmer.

Larger Task

"You are opening windows so that people can look out upon life," a neighbor said to us one day. We like to think of our work as opening windows not only for our own students and community but for a larger area. We are offering to furnish a weekly feature article to country newspapers at actual cost of paper and postage. This column will be called "The Open Window" and will be filled with articles of a social and cultural nature.

Summer Conferences

We are offering our building while school is not in session for conferences at a minimum cost. Already a writer's conference is scheduled for the last week in May. The Socialist Party training school for the southern states is to be held here in June. Later in the summer a short course will be given by the school for people in the neighboring towns and cities.

People's Needs Make an Educational Program

[1957]

The following talk was given by Horton at the American European Conference on Residential Adult Education at Bergen, The Netherlands, June 1957. Horton emphasizes the need to start where people are in the educational process and argues that this approach involves moving potential barriers to education, including unemployment and segregation.

There is no resident adult school movement in America, but rather a scattered group of independent and unrelated adult schools. This is good, for there is already too much conformity. It is a pleasure to report that pressures for conformity are only beginning to reach the resident adult schools and so far have been unsuccessful.

I speak from my experiences as director of Highlander Folk School, a regional adult school in the southern part of the United States. To discuss our schedule and method of work at Highlander would be somewhat repetitious. I will comment on what appears to be a basic problem of residential adult education, the manner of deciding on program, of selecting educational activities. The method I will talk about is, of course, only one way of selecting subject matter. Whereas in some schools the program is built around certain subjects of interest or around a traditional educational activity or activities, the program at Highlander is arrived at by finding out what problems people are facing.

In terms of overall philosophy, however, there is less diversity than in subject matter. The one unifying factor in residential adult schools is a goal or direction based on value judgments. The more tangible, practical aspects of our residential adult schools are less important than the philosophy and purpose which is of an unfolding nature and is difficult to define.

The educational program, however, should focus on a definable step leading to the goal, or, to put it another way, the point of departure should be a recognized need to be examined in the light of the overall purpose. Such an educational concept enables students to hitch a star to their wagon.

The constantly changing program at Highlander is based on social and economic issues that affect people in our part of the United States. I am extremely interested in Oscar Guermonprez's[5] comparison of Allard Soog at Bakkeveen[6] here in Holland with Highlander in his welcome address. Both started in 1932 and both base their program on meeting needs of individuals as they are related to situations that affect their total lives.

Our first program grew out of the problems of people facing a depression. Later we developed a program to help unorganized workers and farmers and nonvoting citizens. Now we are concerned with problems of desegregation and integration in the public schools.

Perhaps I can explain best what I have in mind by using the blackboard. Up here is our goal—not a blueprint or a clearly defined philosophy but a direction—in our case, a democratic and humanitarian goal which applies to all people regardless of race, religion, or anything else. Without a goal, we would find it difficult to make practical decisions as to program content, methods of teaching, or for that matter the organization of the school itself.

The way people live at a residential adult school is as important as any subject taught. If the setup of the school is in conflict with the goal, I doubt that any worthwhile education takes place.

Down here are the people—men, women. In our part of the South, some white, some dark, some American Indians—copper colored. Education is for people, but people are both individuals and members of their local and world communities. Now what stands between people—all the people—in the South and this goal or direction in which we are trying to move? In the early days of Highlander, unemployment was a barrier that prevented people from reaching their goal. I remember trying to talk with people about democracy, music, and literature only to have them run the discussions to what they were going to eat, how they could provide medical service for their children, how they could have a roof over their heads. So unemployment stood between people down here and the good things of life up here.

Instead of pretending that unemployment didn't exist, we tackled it educationally. Later another barrier stood between the people and their goal: lack of organization among farmers and industrial workers. We sought to use education to help remove that barrier. Still later we had the problem of war which had to be taken into consideration in working out a program. All along we had concerned ourselves with the problem of nonparticipation in government and had tried to help remove that barrier by educating people to the importance of voting. In the last few years we have amplified that program and now we are using education to remove another barrier—the barrier of segregation.

As one barrier is partially removed, we relate a portion of our program to other barriers. Breaking down barriers is not a goal in itself, but is necessary if we are to move in the direction of the goal.

It would seem to me that with a goal and a concept of starting with the problems of people whatever they happen to be we can gear residential adult schools to the lives of people in such a way that they can reevaluate and can face life more intelligently.

Coming back, in closing, to the people, we see them join hands and move a step nearer to their goals.

Crisis Education

[1960]

The following was originally presented as a statement at the Saugeen Seminar, an International Residential Conference, held in Port Elgin, Ontario, August 11–20, 1960. It was then reprinted in the October 1960 issue of Mankind, *from which this text was taken. In this short piece, Horton explains the educational implications of dealing "specifically with the crisis problems of the local community, letting people work out their own problems and learn to do things for themselves."*

For adult educators concerned with social problems, the space age of increased travel and mass communications has important implications. While on the one hand it is now possible for anyone to go out and sample a variety of social action programs, increased literacy also means greater accessibility to knowledge. If one does not go out into the world, reports, research findings and evaluations, suggested models, and pilot projects can be delivered to the front door.

These changes do not diminish the dilemmas of the adult educator. To name a few: he must define from the multiplicity of problems those which have the greatest need for immediate action; he must evaluate many proposed solutions and decide whether this program or that project can be adapted to fit his needs and whether it can be transferred from one place to another or from one country to another. Furthermore, should the methods used be democratic or totalitarian? Confronted by these choices, what are to be his standards for selectivity?

Over the past twenty-five years, Highlander Folk School has been carrying on an educational program in the areas of social, political, and economic problems through residential adult workshops. We have elected to work with problems in a way which would set democracy in action. We have proceeded on the premise that there is a need for each local community to work out processes whereby people can do things for themselves, where they can develop their own leadership to meet their own problems.

Highlander has been working for many years in this area of democratic education through crisis education leadership development. We have found that best results in leadership training are obtained when people want help with solving their own problems or in carrying out an urgently needed program. Then people are challenged by doing something which involves them in a leadership role. Such results are often obtained when there is a crisis situation. People's interest is heightened and they learn faster. Therefore the place to attack a problem is at the point at which the people concerned are aware of it.

For example, the present problems of Negro voting and registration in the South provide a natural issue around which to develop leaders, not only because a crisis situation has been created in most southern communities, but because it involves practically the entire population in a community. Our experience shows that many leaders and potential leaders are ready to act on these problems, provided they can have the opportunity to work out and thus basically understand a definite program of action.

They are doubly encouraged when they are equipped with information, with facts and figures that can be used in involving others. They need practicable, workable information and need to know how to go about doing things in their own communities. Thus, motivated by a challenging goal and equipped with the practical steps, they not only become leaders themselves, but are in a position to develop other leaders.

Crisis education involves making a choice and taking action which will remove the cause of the crisis. This often involves fresh insights and bold new perspectives. Objectivity is essential in analyzing a problem, but personal value judgments and moral decisions determine what is to be done. Resolving a crisis demands dissent; crisis education is always controversial. There is no place for historical romanticisms. In crisis education, theory and practice are often merged, as are means and ends.

This does not undermine the importance of objective scientific method, which must be utilized to research the existing problems. However, it must be blended with folk knowledge and nonacademic concepts in tackling immediate problems. Solutions cannot be apart from the culture of the people concerned.

Our aim has been to deal specifically with the crisis problems of the local community, letting people work out their own problems and learn to do things for themselves. It is this process, not the specific, localized community solution which can be used and applied elsewhere.

A Learning System

[1971]

In this speech, originally given at the Unitarian Universalist Fellowship in Memphis, Tennessee, on November 14, 1971, Horton examines the effects of technology on the educational system. The title comes from internal references within the text and refers to Horton's idea that education "should be a learning system instead of a teaching system." Only the text of the speech has been included; the question-and-answer period has been omitted.

I haven't given much thought to history in some time because I think there are so many pressing problems now that demand attention, that history should be used primarily as a means of preventing mistakes. We haven't learned too much from history except what not to do. One of the things I want to talk about this morning has to do with this business of the pursuit of truth—I would put an "s" there because I think there are many truths and something bad happens when truth is finally discovered and institutionalized. It is quite often used for unhumane purposes. But the pursuit of truth, the struggle for truth, is always liberating. So, I am always more interested in searching out new truths. Like most of you here, my interest, as had been indicated, has been in people. I think occasionally I have lost sight of the fact that just changing people's attitudes, liberating people, is not enough. There are some hard facts that are also truths that people like us seldom bother to take a look at.

Recently I have been more and more impressed in thinking about education for the country and in other countries, especially with a lot of low-income people, with the fact that the technological developments have pretty much taken over education. And most of us who don't bother about things of that kind, who live in a world of ideas, are not aware of what is happening. I know that this applies to me. Just like we had environmental problems all along and almost suddenly we discovered them, we have the encroachment of technological society which we may also discover too late to do much about if we don't wake up. So I would like to talk briefly about how this looks to me and as a basis of discussion—not the truth, but a search for the truth—and then talk about problems of education that result from technology.

I hadn't realized until I started thinking about this a couple of years ago how dominating technology is. I had kind of grown up thinking of technology as an extension of man's arm and something to be used for mankind. I think that is no longer true. I think technology is an independent force aside, apart from man, apart from people, apart from its use and it embodies in its process and dictates expansion. It has a life of its own. Just like in legal terms, a corporation is a person. I think technology is a force outside people that has to be dealt with. Change and extension of technology is inevitable, but human progress is not inevitable. I think we usually reverse that. We usually think human progress is bound to happen, but I don't think it is true at all. I don't think there is any evidence that human progress is inevitable. Change is inevitable, but I [do not] think technology is inevitable. Man is grown into this all-encompassing machine and made a mechanistic device. This is a very dehumanizing process; unless we really think about this and analyze it and mobilize human forces, man is going to move backward as technology moves forward in relation to each other. When that happens, people are going to be ground down and reshaped into kind of flesh-and-blood robots—no longer free spirits. The old concept of survival of the fittest will be mechanistically interpreted as survival of the most efficient robot. If this sounds extreme, I think it could be documented. People are being turned into unthinking robots used by technology and having less and less opportunity to be humane.

I was in discussion the other day with a very interesting person named Everett Reimer who came by Highlander.[7] He has written a book on deschooling. It is entitled *School Is Dead*—something about deschooling. It was published a couple of weeks ago. I asked Everett if he really thought the schools were really dead and he said, "No that was just a publisher's blurb." He knew the schools were alive and thriving and under the complete control of technology. It is an interesting book which I would recommend—I think the correct title is *Deschooling in Society*.[8] While Everett was there, we had a little meeting at Highlander and had a discussion with some people from the University of Tennessee, people interested in free schools and alternative schools structures came in and took part in the discussion. In the process, it was pointed out that a lot of discussion had to be given in all kind[s] of training—we were talking about airline pilots at the time—in dealing with people as human beings. You know the general interest in the country in sensitivity training and all kind of things that help people be human—next day I heard on a television program a statement that 80 percent of the people who were employed in services or in factories or any place where you had to deal with people lost their jobs because they didn't know how to deal with people. Now this is a terrible indictment to society. You have to go to school to be trained to be human, and this is just one measure of what technology has done to us. We have gotten in such a state that being human and dealing with people as human beings is so unnatural that you have to have an educational program for people to train them so they can be human. There is no reason why people can't grow up human if you had a decent society. Why should you ever have to go to school to learn

EDUCATIONAL PHILOSOPHY

to be human, to talk to your neighbors and to deal with people in a humane way? This is just one indication of where we are already because of this mechanistic system. We take these things for granted. We take these courses to learn to be human. We never stop to think why in the hell are you unhuman to start with.

Instead of technology in the past being an extension of man's powers and at man's services, used by man for man, technology is now becoming an extension of technology itself. This independent force is something outside humanity, and it is not helping man; it is helping itself as something independent. Unless technology is turned around and used for humanistic purposes before it is too late, what could have been a blessing—and I think in the beginning was a blessing—will be the kind of ruination of mankind. And I would repeat that it is on us just like pollution is on us and we have breathed bad air so long, it is on us and we don't even know it is around. We kind of think it is inevitable, that this is a junky world of things, a materialistic world where everybody strives for materialistic things, where people are "thinkers." We say, well that's the way it is. It is the way it is, but it does not have to be this way. It seems to me that there are better things for people than this.

Let me talk about education in the light of this. You are not talking about some teacher using some innovations that makes education more effective. Or you are not talking about some alternative school system which is an imitation of the other but has slightly different arrangements or slightly different subject matter. You have to talk in terms of inventing an entirely new educational system to cope with this—a very creative and imaginative kind of education that isn't controlled by technology. And the goal and purpose of education today, whether you believe it or not (and we don't like to believe it if we are in education because we like to deal with other things—a little world we can carve out and say we have something to say in it) is partly tradition. Tradition we have inherited from the past like summer vacations to pick cotton, letting children out in time to go home to milk the cows, all these things that we never stop to examine; teachers getting up and lecturing which was a carryover from the days when people couldn't read and nobody but the clergy in ancient times could read. So, you had to read to people who were illiterate. We don't stop today to ask why do we read to people who can read? Why do we lecture to people who can read? There are a lot of hangovers from the past that have no reason for being. They did have a reason at one time but don't any longer. The whole concept of teaching is an archaic idea. Education should be [a] learning system instead of a teaching system. The whole thing should be turned right around. We are tradition bound with structures and ways of education. We do little gimmicks every once in a while and think we are getting ahead, but it is still about the same stuff. So traditionally education is tied in with the past, not the present. There are a few little paint jobs here and there, but nothing basic. That is one thing about education.

The schools have been co-opted as an instrument of technology, and we didn't even know it happened. Now technology is at the service of capitalism or the system—whatever system you have. Technology in Russia would be at the service of socialism, and here it is at the service of capitalism. In other words, the school is an instrument of the system. Technology is an instrument of the system; the school is the instrument of technology to serve the system. Technology is an instrument of the system; the school is the instrument of technology to serve the system. And the system's interest is what? Money, profit, things. So education that some of us spend our lives working at is a tool, a tool of a tool—not even a first-class tool. It is a tool of technology which is a tool of capitalism. It is a third-rate tool. We know some of the other problems. Teachers who are in education know what is wrong with education better than anyone else—I shouldn't be talking to teachers. It isn't that people don't know, it is that they are caught in a system where they can't do. I have a friend, about ready to retire, who has for years been the head of a midwestern school system, and he said if you set out to invent an educational system that would kill creativity and prevent learning you couldn't have invented a better system for that purpose than the one we have. He has been spending his life, he says, trying to tamper with it and adjust it and he says it is impossible. He says it won't work. It is designed not to work, can't work, there is no way for it to work. This is a professional schoolman. The school people know what the score is. They are robots already.

Part of the traditional inheritance is the old outmoded melting-pot concept. We are going to melt everyone down and have them all look alike, all white middle-class people, going to Sunday school, saluting the flag, buying cars—you know, the good things in life—kind of an elitist—teaching people things instead of helping them learn—transmission of concealed knowledge, most of which belongs in museums for people to go and look at like they look at a dinosaur. We tell kids in education they need to learn all this stuff because it is education. We learned it from somebody; we spent a lot of time learning it and we have to get our money's worth out of that, so we have to teach it to someone else. So we pass on all this congealed knowledge with all the juice squeezed out of it a long time ago and call it education. Transmission of this kind of congealed knowledge, frozen knowledge —some of it is useful but most of it belongs, as I said, in museums. Education is bad enough traditionally, but when it has been subverted by technology, with technology an end in itself, it is even worse because then it is being used—it isn't that we are stupid and don't know that we still have to pick cotton or milk the cows, but it is that we are being used. We are really being used.

Technology has not only taken over education, but it has taken over science. And scientists are being used, too. They are used for technological purposes instead of humane purposes. There is something about technology and science that are the same. They are both valueless. They have no values; they have no system of values. They are amoral. There are no value judgments involved—what works, not what is right. Efficiency has become the god. They have their god, too; what works, that's the end of science, and yet we kind of pretend to say we have something to say about morals and values and influence on people's lives. Way down in there we are allowed to do that so long as that doesn't get back up into the works.

Now what this has done, the schools being an instrument, has increased and accelerated the trend of man whose ultimate role is to increase technology and keep it in repair. Don't ask any questions. Got a machine to keep up, have to build more machines, keep them in repair and keep your mouth shut. Not any kind of values of morals, or right or wrong. Well, where does this leave us since we are moving so rapidly into this technological age with education of the status quo serving agency in terms of humanistic education? Well, it is kind of becoming a sideline, an embellishment. You kind of bootleg it a little. More and more educators are really experts at technicians. In a technological setup, you have things down to small units so you can analyze them, so you can control them, so you can have tests, so you become an authority; you know everything in that little unit, and if life gets in the way you kind of squeeze it out. Schools are pretty much that way, too, you know. The traditional way of dividing up classes—arithmetic, reading, grammar, language, geography, thirty minutes, thirty minutes, thirty minutes, etc.—that serves technological ends much better than it serves educational ends. It has very little to do with education. In fact, it is a handicap to education, but it helps people cut things down to [a] size they can encompass, test, and understand. They can find the traditional system very useful. So they need experts, technicians, specialists, and explicitness. They are insecure with any untried bold ideas where the results are unpredictable or uncontrollable. This is what is wrong with education. We have accepted this technological kind of thinking to where it has got to be something that can be tested or controlled. It has to be small enough, it has to be laid out in such a way that you can know in advance what the results are going to be. And when you talk about people, talk about kids, talk about human beings as the objects of this kind of education, then it is very demeaning—a human being handled like you handle a machine with predictable results, and yet how much of our education is done that way? More and more people are becoming experts and not educators, and they are doing it because of technological thinking. And, of course, that is primarily training; that is not education.

We have got to take over technology. We have got to find a way to make technology man's servant instead of man technology's servant. Instead of allowing it to go on like it is, it could be used to free mankind from drudgery, allow for a higher standard of living, give us more leisure, more quality in life; it could be used for society's interests. If we don't move fast, the spirit of man is going to be enslaved in this process to the place where we are all robots and we think it is wonderful. We think the stinking air is good because that is pure; we think that technology is good because that is the way we have done. I have already indicated how tradition-bound we are, and give us a few more years accepting technology and we will say that is the way the world is. Who ever heard of having a world in which you weren't a robot? What else could there be? If you were not a robot, you might make a mistake. You aren't programmed; who could think for themselves? We are bordering on that now. Well, we have a lot of work to do if we are going to do anything about education in this country, and I have already indicated that I think the only way it can be done is not to close down the schools, junk the schools, or make speeches like I am about it—it is a waste of time—we talk to each other and pat each other on the back and say this is fine, then we go back doing the same things we have been doing. But we have to find some way to involve people—new people—and that gets into the decision-making process.

[The] decision-making process in education today is largely in the hands of men, men who make their living, directly or indirectly, as part of the technological system, to think technologically, who can understand things where the results are predictable, where it can be controlled, who are practical, unimaginative, thing-oriented—and they control the schools. They control the schools because this is a man's world so far and we have gotten us into this mess. Now, I think the only way we are going to get out of it is to find some way to shift the decision making away from men. The first thing we could do is to (since we have quite a supply of women) say, what would happen to women if women got in there. Now this isn't a women's lib plug I am making. I am talking about something else. I think women, because of the nature of our society and because women have been excluded from having an equal role in society, women have not yet become so conditioned by technology that they are freer than men to be imaginative and human and to be creative. I think if women were in the same position men were in and had been in position a long time—I wouldn't know which would be better. I am not saying there is any inherent difference. I am just saying that because of the situation, women have not been so conditioned to think technologically and practically and only say what works so there would be a tendency for them to say, "Let's be human." So I think the first step would be to do that.

Then the next step would be to involve students in decision making. Students today play like they make decisions until they are certified as adults, that is by the time they graduate. They are certified. Then we say to them to go out and make serious decisions. And they have never made a serious decision in their lives. Decisions they have made have been in a conditioned, controlled, playlike decision atmosphere. Then when they get out in the real world, they are supposed to make real decisions. And, of course, they haven't the slightest idea what a real decision is because they have never made one and wouldn't know one if they met it coming down the street. But that is the way we think in terms of education, and that is because the total educational concept is really, in terms of decision making, the playpen. You know, when our kids were little we put them in a playpen. It wasn't a playpen; it was a jail and we put them in a jail to get them out of our hair, and we called it a playpen because we didn't want to be so brutal. Kids knew the difference and we knew the difference. The kids couldn't talk, so we named it a playpen. I remember my son Thorsten kind of broke out in a way one time. Hollis Reed, who used to be down in Memphis—a labor guy from the trainmen—Hollis was there one time and we were sitting talking and drinking beer. Hollis set his beer can down next to the prison (the playpen), and Thorsten reached out for it. He couldn't stand up yet, but Thorsten held himself up with one hand [and] drained the can with another. Now, he was trying to get out of jail.

Well, as people get a little bigger we call it kindergarten. Then we expand it a little bit and put dingles and decorations on it and call it a grammar school. Then we make it real big and pay to get a new paint job and call it a high school. When you get in college, though, there are a lot of bangles and dangles, it is bigger, and there are a lot of jim-cracks; it is still the prison, still the playpen. Just different names as you go along—making the people who do the naming happy. So people grow up in a school system like that. We are the jailers. And we say, play like you are making decisions. Here you can make a decision. Even college people we say that to. Make a decision about what is going to happen in your college—no, not here; not anything having to do with the budget or with teachers or with content of education, but there are some things here you can make decisions about like dating, dormitories, like meetings, speakers. All these unimportant things you can make decisions about. Now go ahead and learn to make decisions, boys and girls. You can't make any mistakes that are going to hurt anything. So the things are delegated to them and nobody wants to bother about them. That is called decision making. Then, as I said, they come out of the playpen certified as adults, ready for the world. They are robots and they are going to stay robots, for they never have had a chance to be anything else. So, I am saying women and students—and where do you start? Kindergarten and right on up. Decision making can start from the very beginning. They can't make any worse mistakes then have been made. There is no way they can invent mistakes that are worse than mistakes that have been made. Can't do any worse. They may not do any better, but they have got to learn to make decisions. Turn schools into learning centers instead of places where you teach people and involve a lot of people in deciding what schools are and you may have a chance.

[Text omitted]

A People's Movement to Liberate Education

[1972]

The following essay was originally printed in Cutting Edge *in 1972. Here Horton argues that the educational system is "locked into and shaped by our economic system" and that the key to changing the educational system is a complete overhaul to the processes by which decisions about education are made.*

What role should schools serve in building or reconstructing a society? Perhaps this is best answered by asking what kind of society do we want. If a democratic society, then the schools must provide models or experiences in decision making through democratic practices. If a totalitarian society is the answer, then the schools will naturally be structured to create dictatorial practices. Unfortunately, the latter model is used in most American schools, with some far-reaching effects.

The educational system is locked into and shaped by our economic system. Furthermore, our educational systems have top-down decision-making processes which ensure bureaucratic control. Nothing short of a powerful and sustained people's movement to liberate education will basically change the situation in schools and in society. In my opinion, the basis for a liberation movement is to be found in our American ideals, which are buried deep in our educational tradition and have been kept alive by lip service, although dishonored in practice. To teach democracy without practicing it in the schools reduces the concept to a hollow shell.

Educators are perhaps more aware of the educational contradictions and inadequacies than are many other segments of society. Unlike some of the poor, for example, who believe schools educate and think of schooling as the best way for their children to move out of poverty, some educators know what the potential for self-realization and democratic practices can be. However, this knowledge is not limited to educators. Many poor people are equally concerned about education and have insights that would enlighten the controversy and deepen the awareness of educators. This is particularly true of minority groups who look at modern schools from a wholly different perspective. For them, schooling is an alien concept or force which impinges upon their way of life as a hindrance or problem to be tolerated and eventually ignored. But peoples' consciousness can be expanded to include genuine involvement in the educational process. Therein lies the potential for change.

Too often, educators with their individualistic orientation continue to believe their pronouncements will be heeded despite their record of under-achievement in bringing about change. The assumption evidently is that the few now in power will eventually do what is right and reasonable. Or per-haps that somehow, somewhere, others will put the theories of educational pundits into practice.

Educators should stop talking primarily to one another and reach out to other people for fresh insights and exchange of ideas. People tend to listen to those who listen to them. What I am suggesting is that educators come out of their enclaves and help build a people's movement to liberate edu-cation made up of bottom-up alliances and coalitions involving all segments of society ready for change.

We, as educators, will have to forgo the convenience of building-bound education and learn to relate to people as well as subject matter. Most of the dynamics for education change are outside institutional walls. When education is restructured to serve the whole man and the whole world, walled-in education will become as archaic as a moat around a castle.

A step in this direction would be to involve people in the educational process from nonacademic walks of life, especially those who do not have academic qualifications. The poor rather than the student of poverty are the poverty experts, just as the Indians, Chicanos, and blacks are the authorities on their problems.

If teachers from kindergarten through graduate school spent half their time in their communities, and people from these communities were brought in to do half their teaching, education would become alive and rel-evant. Furthermore, this fifty-fifty arrangement would open up avenues for alliances essential for the restructuring of education. The process could be accelerated by staffing educational institutions half with professionally trained teachers and half with people already directly involved in their com-munities. This would facilitate mutual learning on the part of both groups.

The key to fundamental change, I believe, is a new decision-making process. It will not be enough to change the content and form of education. All those concerned should be directly and personally involved not only in initiating the original planning but must also be accepted as equals in all deci-sion making. There will need to be great flexibility with provision made for decision making in bits and pieces as well as for overall long-range policy.

The fear of irresponsibility cannot be an excuse. Given bona-fide decision-making power, people not only learn very rapidly to make decisions, but assume responsibility for carrying out the decisions based on their collective judgment. The problem is not the danger of irresponsibility, but that of con-vincing students, minorities, and all voiceless people that they have, by right, the authority and responsibility. The danger is not too much, but too little, participation. People will only learn to make decisions by making them.

In addition to providing a means by which people can make education serve their self-determined needs, an updated decision-making process is educational in its own right. It is a means of accelerating the kind of learning people need if they are to take control of their own lives and govern themselves. The majority of people have so long been accustomed to top-downism that they will have to be reeducated both in theory and in practice as to their rights, opportunities, and responsibilities. The meaning of democratic involvement in decision making and the evolving of new decision-making methods presents a challenging and creative educational concept and should be incorporated into all education at all stages.

Why Don't Reforms Reform?

[1972]

The following was originally presented as a speech at the Unitarian Universalist Fellowship in Memphis, Tennessee. The date has clearly been recorded as December 15; the year is less certain, though it is most probably 1972. The question-and-answer portion of the presentation has been omitted. In this speech, Horton argues that the changes brought about by reforms, rather than total reconceptualization, are never substantive enough.

What I want us to talk about this morning is the pursuit of truth in the service of humanity. It is kind of buried in the middle there. Good folks like us find it very easy to share our privileges and yet most of the world cannot join us. It has always been my feeling that obligations to join the people who are not so privileged is on us, not them. If we are content to take advantage, for enlightenment, human, or whatever purposes we choose to label them, of the privileges that you have, then you are not exercising the freedom you still have in this country to pursue the truth in the interest of humanity.

I want to share my frustrations this morning more than anything else. A friend of mine wrote a book a couple of years ago on Cuba and inscribed it "To Myles Horton, who knows how hard it is to make a revolution." I used to think that it was relatively simple to deal with fundamental change. All you had to do was stop being paternalistic and deal with people as equals. It is not that simple even when we try to have solidarity with groups that are not so privileged. When we do the best we can, using our intelligence, our resources, and our heart, we still find that the changes that are brought about are not enough.

That is why I have been thinking lately of why reforms fail to reform. Some of you people may say I know of examples where reforms worked. I too know of reforms that worked superficially, and I have been a part of reforms that have appeared to work.

The more I think of what has happened in my lifetime as a social activist the more discouraged I get about the methods we have been using and our rather naive acceptance of a series of reforms made by people of goodwill and intelligence who think that society is going to be changed.

The facts are that except for material gain, for things, there is a serious question about social progress. Certainly people are better off in terms of conveniences, gadgets, better of in terms of standards of living in some parts of the world. If we look at the world as a whole as we should, as we must, voluntarily or involuntarily, then we find that even in material ways a few countries have got a disproportionate share of the material things. It is an illusion to think the world has even made material progress.

I think that the haves and the have-nots present the real dilemma as I understand the facts—the rich are getting richer and the poor are getting poorer, relatively. There is something wrong with the world, something wrong with a social organization where that is true. We live in a world of illusion, that is why we tend to gloss over these problems.

There has been a lot written and talked about [regarding] the advances among black people economically, but relative to the advances among non-blacks the gap has gotten wider in the last two years. The distance has increased at a tremendous pace. So if you think in terms of relative advancement you see that we still have not dealt with the problem of the advancement of a group that is constantly on the minds of any of us here in the South. It is an illusion that because some blacks have moved into the middle-class economic brackets there appears to be real progress. The working black and the unemployed black are worse off relative to the whites than ever before.

Now if we take that kind of thinking and apply it to a world situation, the picture is even worse. It isn't a relative problem we are talking about; it is one of hunger, lack of medical care, of survival. I don't think that a case can be made for any genuine progress.

The situation is so confusing because the old way of looking at things is no longer adequate. My understanding of the economic situation was if you owned the means of producing wealth it was yours. You could either live in a decent sort of self-sufficient way, make your living on your farm, your store, your little business without exploiting other people, or if you were in the big-time you could make your living by exploiting other people. That is, hire other people to work for you so that you make profits out of their labor.

It was relatively simple, who owned, who controlled. They controlled education, they controlled the thinking, they controlled the press, they controlled the politicians, and they did that because of ownership, but it is not quite that simple today. The multinational corporations go into a foreign country, raise the money for their operation there from the local people for the most part. They keep control and own it. It is hard to figure out who owns what. In other words, the people who pay for things don't necessarily own them simply because of the manipulations of big business.

It is getting kind of hard to deal with conceptually. You can say to ITT,[9] you need to be broken up and ITT says we don't own anything, there is just a lot of little shareholders, and they will fight this. It is their company. Everybody knows that is not true. Nevertheless, it is a fiction we accept. We accept it all over the world.

It is hard to analyze if you are talking about dealing with the power that we are trying to deal with. Now in the light of that old-fashioned idea of reforms, just simple reforms, good people pecking away here and there, all of that has to be reexamined. It is getting too complicated to deal with in terms of trying to change the school system here, of trying to change the economic system there, or trying to patch up the political system some other place.

We are putting little patches on things that maybe don't even exist except in our mind. The power that runs these things, we don't even deal with them when we try to reform. It may be that complicated. In other words, I am suggesting that we have to do a lot more serious thinking about how we are going to bring about change in the interest of humanity. More thinking than we have done up to now. We have to reexamine a lot of our concepts and not continue to think that by being good people, people of goodwill, people who are trying to change here and there, that we will make progress.

It is as if we were in a barge heading upstream here in the Mississippi River. We have a lot of paddles, windmills, sails, gasoline motors, batteries, all kinds of gimmicks trying to push that barge upstream. We are making progress, doing great inventions and changes in terms of how you hold the paddle. We are preoccupied with all these ways of making progress against the current, of measuring the relative distance we have come from where we started in terms of the current, that we never take time to look across to the shore and find that we still have the same scenery we had when we started.

That is the way reform seems to work. The energy is wasted. Maybe not wasted entirely; we would get swept downstream if we didn't do something. We are certainly not making any real progress. We are just changing the material things that keep us where we are. It is there somewhere that I think that we need to have some very serious discussion.

I am confused. I am very confused about where to go from here. I have a suspicion that we have to think in terms of involving large numbers of people, in terms of something worth carrying on, a sustained battle for a long period of years instead of thinking that we are going to have a quick victory. I seem to think it is in there somewhere, but how to get that going I am not certain about. I am, frankly, at a point where I would like to know what to do.

It seems to me the reason why I am unburdening myself to you is not because I want sympathy; I have gotten along pretty well without that. I think that you, just as I, are concerned about these problems. Maybe if we will struggle with them together we will begin to get somewhere. There are some truths or some paths to truth I think that we can figure out if we will put our minds to it.

Now one of our problems is that we are so content to associate with people like ourselves, because we are in good company, that it blinds us to the insights we might have if we found out about how people live who probably are going to be the ones that are going to have energy and the sustained power to change things. I think that we live sheltered lives. I don't know if anything can be done about this. I think the only way we can pay for that sin is to use our heads and try to think, try to use our intelligence, our resources, our creativity, and our ability to get information to come up with some solutions to these problems.

I think that we are going to have to do something to justify this privileged life we are living. I would hate to think that we are going to force the people who have not to use the only power, the power of violence, to change things. I think those of us who do not like to think of using physical violence, we should assume some responsibility for refusing to do something that would force somebody else to use violence. That is the way it is going to end up if we don't get busy.

If I had some prescriptions here I would dish them out, but what I have is a problem. My experience is that when you have a problem that you cannot solve, instead of talking about it, crying about it, you share it with other people. Maybe together you can get some answers, and that is what I would like to do. You may question my analysis of the situation, fine; I would like to discuss it.

Decision-Making Processes

[1973]

The following text was originally included in the 1973 book Educational Reconstruction: Promise and Challenge, *edited by Nobuo Shimahara. In this essay, Horton examines the history of Highlander in order to highlight the necessity of involving students in decision-making processes that are of real consequence to their education and to their lives. In doing so, he links his work and ideas to those of Paulo Freire.*

Decision making, as a process involving all those whose lives are affected by the decisions being made, will be explored in this chapter against the background of forty years spent in fieldwork and residential adult education. My commitment to a view of the educational process as itself a process of decision making derives from experiences at the Highlander Folk School and the Highlander Research and Education Center, both in Tennessee. From the founding of the Highlander Folk School in 1932 in the mountains of Tennessee to the present moment and our work for an Appalachian Self-Education Program,[10] my colleagues and I have been explicitly concerned with education for fundamental social change. Whether we were working with mountain people in a local community, with industrial unionists at our residential workers' sessions, with members of the National Farmers Union,[11] with civil rights workers in the South, or (as at present) with Appalachian mountain people, our concern has been to relate whatever educational resources we have had at hand to the expressed needs and aspirations of the men and women taking part on our workshops and programs. Because *their* insights and experiences provided the context in which their cooperative learning took place, I have learned as much from them as from the many philosophers and educators who have contributed to the shaping of the "Highlander idea."

My intent here is to discuss some of the implications of this experience for a conception of decision making within American education generally, at this moment of extreme uneasiness, widespread suffering, and gathering discontent. When I turn my attention from some of our vigorous Citizenship Schools and residential workshops to the bureaucratic hierarchies in the public school systems across the nation, I am struck all over again by the persistence of top-down decision making and by the proliferation of minutiae-oriented experts more given to division than vision. I am struck by the way in which the schools, always tending toward service to the status quo, have so easily and smoothly been transformed into agents of American technology and consumerism. In a fearful distortion of the pragmatic test, technological growth is justified not by the way in which it fulfills the needs of human beings, or contributes to their welfare, or assures at least a minimal subsistence at decent levels to the poor, the sick, the excluded, but by the fact that technology "works" to solve the specific technical problems it was invented to solve. Moreover, it appears to "work" best when questions about morality, decency, and humanity are set aside. Efficiency can then become the governing principle. The role of the human being becomes subordinate to technology: he is valued to the degree that he maintains it efficiently, improves it (if he is greatly talented), or keeps it in repair.

This may sound extreme, but if we look at the ways in which the spirit of technology permeates the schools, affects their objectives and curricula, determines the nature of the decision making within and around them, we cannot help recognize the necessity for inventing a radically different education

EDUCATIONAL PHILOSOPHY

system, if we are to make the human being the object of our concern —and make it possible for him to choose his own life. The issue of expertise may be the crucial one. Expertise, as we all know it in our capitalist society, accompanies specialism and a concentration on technique. We need only recall the segmentation of education into units, each one breeding its own kind of specialization, each one in some manner isolated from the others. The model, clearly, is a mechanical system. The guiding principles are explicitness, neatness, and testability. The experts in charge are primarily technicians or management specialists; predictability and control are their watchwords. This is one reason why there is so much implicit emphasis in the schools upon congealed knowledge, knowledge as commodity to be transmitted in discrete plastic-wrapped packages. It is why, no matter what the desires of individual teachers, the humanistic emphasis is made secondary. Open questions, like bold and untried ideas, disturb the managerial mind.

Many teachers, obviously, are not managerial in their orientation; and, if free to engage in what they fundamentally believe "education" to be, they would not spend as much time as they do turning out what can only be considered nuts and bolts produced according to technological specifications. They may *feel* free behind their closed classroom doors; but they are not free because the bureaucratic structure forces them to be preoccupied with rank, status, and vested interest. Again, the decision-making system is most at fault, since it is so much a function of a centralized pattern of bureaucratic control, which inevitably makes the individuals *under* control feel powerless. Few can deny that this kind of system stretches all the way from the offices of the federal government to the state government to the local school boards. Professional educators must either accede to the rules or exert themselves trying to circumvent them, once they realize how such rules interfere with their function as educators. Too often, however, in an effort to preserve professional integrity without too much risk, they set up their own adaptations of bureaucratic authority systems which they proceed to justify with claims of educational expertise. *They* are concerned about individual students, they say; *they* know what is best for them. Once they begin justifying deciding *for* other individuals, they have been co-opted by a system bent on imposing powerlessness upon its component parts. Whether they consciously intend to or not, they have imitated the larger technological model of control and committed themselves to enforcing compliance and conformity upon young people who might as well be in a prison—or, to speak more gently, in a playpen. Feeling penned in, deprived of opportunities to participate in decisions made in their name, in their behalf, and (purportedly) for their "good," most students respond in the only way they can: they concentrate on grades, promotion, and graduate requirements, on what is expected of them. Education falls by the wayside; no one is interested in taking the kind of initiative required for learning how to learn.

Many critics of the school system have pointed to the ways in which compulsory education deprives young people of freedom as well as initiative (too often without their even being aware of it). Separated from the "real" world, living in an artificial atmosphere (like that of a playpen or a Skinerian air-crib),[12] children are permitted just the amount of freedom adults think they can afford to give them at each stage. Safety and convenience are piously used as excuses. The playpen is continually enlarged and redecorated; the children behind the bars are permitted to pretend they are determining the circumstances of their lives, to *play* at making rules and decisions. But the invisible bars of the playpen remain—a dividing line between what is defined as "immaturity" and what we conceive to be adult accountability. In time, many students begin to suspect what is happening. They begin slowly to recognize the unreality involved in maintaining them as helpless children, unless they are so docile and so brainwashed (or so infantile) as to confuse the atmosphere within the school with social reality.

The student revolt of the last decade was partly due to a spreading recognition that young people's decision-making powers were limited to the areas which their elders had decided were relatively meaningless. The adults held firm control of the funds; they decided the shape and scope of the playpens; they decided what education should be for and how the specifications should be designed for the human products they hoped to produce. When young people confronted their own powerlessness and, at the same time, the inequities and brutalities of the system they were expected to serve (and even die for, if necessary), they were outraged. Not only were they being infantilized and demeaned; not only were they being frustrated when it came to free or original self-expression; they were being *used* by people who seldom, if ever, consulted them when decisions were being made. Members of minority groups, similarly, came to realize that they also were being controlled, excluded from decision making, pressed into conformity to the status quo. Learning, in the sense of honest exploration of significant questions, was made next to impossible in too many schools. John Dewey's distinction between "schooling" and "education" was becoming more and more clear.[13] Education, he said, was a far larger concept than schooling; the school was only one of the multiple agencies likely to educate the young. "Education goes on," wrote Joseph K. Hart, "whether and whenever the individual finds himself in a social situation. The reason for this is that life goes on whether schools keep or not, and life is always educative, one way or another" (*Education and the Humane Community* 103).

It was with the fundamental belief that life is not only educative, but is the source of significant problems and programs, that Highlander's approach to education developed over the years. The conceptual framework was always flexible. The purpose was to use education to bring about a new social order and to do so within the context of an emerging social movement, be it unionization, civil rights activities, voter registration, or the struggle against strip

EDUCATIONAL PHILOSOPHY

mining in the mountains. Preconceived programs were never imposed; learning activities were never defined in advance. Services were provided by the Highlander field staff and by people in the local communities. Additional workshops were conducted at the folk school or the research center on issues growing out of developments in the communities, but they were held only on request. A continuum of learning was provided by the combination of residential workshops, ranging from three days to three months, and field programs; and Highlander became part of the learning process before and after. The participants themselves brought the subject matter for discussion into the residential workshops; and whatever educational experiences were enjoyed during the workshops were tested later in the field while the learning process continued among those involved.

The programs, forms, and many of the people have changed, but Residential Adult Education and Field Work, both of which grew out of our early experiences as a community school, have remained central to our work. It is relevant to this general discussion to note that our original community school was influenced by the early folk schools that began emerging in Denmark during a period of intense turmoil in the nineteenth century.[14] The first folk school, established near the German border in 1844, was dedicated to the preservation of the Danish language, then being threatened by a German-speaking upper class. The second school, founded in 1848, espoused the cause of the peasants in their struggles against the landlords and nobility during that period of widespread revolution in Europe. The major impetus for the folk school movement, however, came with the loss of southern Jutland to Germany in 1864: within the next thirteen years, twenty-six folk schools were established, each one emotionally committed to a clearly defined social ideal. Free of government control and unhampered by the need to rank, examine, or certify, they were headed by teachers peculiarly sensitive to injustices and peculiarly hopeful about the future. The inspiration had come from Bishop N. S. F. Grundtvig,[15] who had long "pondered over the problem of how to awaken the people" and decided that the people themselves ought to be the ones to develop free schools for adults. They were therefore "freer in form and more closely connected with the lives of the people than would otherwise have been the case" (Degtrug and Degtrug, *Folk High Schools of Denmark*, 83).

In Denmark in 1932, I could not help but be moved and excited by the examples of free adult education still apparent in Scandinavia; and, when I returned to Monteagle, Tennessee, we set up our own Highlander Folk School for the woodcutters and the people who were unemployed in the Monteagle community in those early depression years. Almost immediately we discovered how rapidly ordinary people could demonstrate their ability to play leadership roles and develop a sense of responsibility to their fellows. All depended, it now seems clear, on their being involved from the start in the making of all necessary decisions with respect to their education.

We learned a great deal about emerging leadership and about the speed with which analytic understanding could develop among individuals concerned to work out plans for the improvement of their own lives.

This learning carried over into the work we did with the unions that grew up in the pre-C.I.O.[16] period in the mountains and surrounding areas. We already knew enough to be confident that the heretofore unrecognized local leaders would grow in understanding if they were set free to learn and to act upon what they learned. Since people engaged in working with structures (like trade unions and schools) tend to identify more readily with the structures than with other people, we made a point of dealing directly with voluntary organizers and the officers of small unions. Later, we decided to concentrate on working with shop stewards as well as the committee members and local officials of the small unions, because they were the ones required to act independently who had a primary allegiance to their fellow workers. Once union leaders go to the payroll of the international union, we thought, their loyalty is likely to go to the bureaucracy rather than to the workers, because the bureaucracy pays their salaries. Our rule of thumb, in consequence, was to deal primarily with those who were answerable to the members of the union concerned, and whose power and tenure rested in the hands of the workers themselves. Eventually, some of these people would enter the bureaucracy, and we hoped (with justification, it turned out) that what they had learned when they were free to learn would carry over into their new activities.

We took the same approach when we began working with the farmer's union. In Greene County, Tennessee, for example, we learned that the local justices of the peace were responsive to the needs of the farmers, whom they accepted as their peers. Even though the justices had official titles, they qualified according to our criteria: they were more responsive to their fellow men than to the demands of the structure or the institution. We involved a number of the local justices of the peace, therefore, in the formation of the farmers' union programs, because they were the recognized community leaders and accountable to the community. (The justices of the peace in the Appalachian coalfields today are quite different. They tend to be beholden to the coal operators and the power structure; and they would not, under any circumstances, be considered as potential participants in Highlander programs. We have repeatedly found that education alone cannot counteract the influence of the establishment on individuals, so we avoid dealing with those who are not free to act on what they themselves think is right).

Perhaps the best illustration of our ongoing approach is the Citizenship School program, since it so clearly evolved out of interaction with a specific group and in obvious relation to an important social movement. The program was developed on Johns Island, on the South Carolina Coast, where 2,700 poor rural blacks worked their own subsistence farms, labored for large plantation owners, or held jobs as domestics in nearby Charleston. Esau Jenkins,[17] a community leader and a native of the island, made his living by operating a bus from Johns Island to Charleston, carrying people to their jobs. At a workshop in 1954, he asked for Highlander's help in preparing the islanders to read the section of the South Carolina Constitution they had to decipher in order to register to vote. He had been trying to teach people to read on his short bus trip to Charleston each day; but the needs were urgent, and he could not meet them all himself. The Highlander staff spent two years meeting with and listening to the people on the island; and some of them (less reluctant than the majority) were persuaded to attend a few Highlander workshops.

The first Citizenship School was held in the back room of a country store under the direction of Mrs. Bernice Robinson, who had insisted that she "couldn't teach" because she had never taught before.[18] For an advisor, she had Mrs. Septima Clark of the Highlander staff.[19] Mrs. Clark was a teacher who had had her first teaching job on Johns Island. She and Mrs. Robinson planned a school with the participants that would meet two evenings a week for three months, and the fourteen adult students provided the curriculum. They wanted to learn how to read the required part of the state constitution; but they also wanted to know how to fill in blanks when they were ordering out of a catalogue, how to fill in money orders, how to keep a record of the hours they worked, etc. Bernice Robinson reported that, in an effort to stretch their minds, she had tacked up the Declaration of Human Rights on the wall and told them she wanted them to be able to read and understand it by the end if the three months. It happened that the enrollment increased during the first two months from fourteen to thirty-seven, and 80 percent of the class succeeded in registering to vote.

During the next two years, the new "first-class" citizens spread the word of their success throughout Johns Island and up and down the coasts of South Carolina and Georgia. Citizenship Schools opened in many places, sometimes initiated by volunteer nonprofessional teachers, sometimes at the request of people who wanted citizenship above all else. The three months' pattern was adopted by each new school, but each one's character and emphasis were determined by the participants. The people seemed to have adopted the Citizenship School program as their own. One volunteer teacher wrote: "People need to feel that they are part of a community, and not only a community, but a country, a state, and a world."

The results were encouraging when the program expanded to answer the needs in other states. Two-thirds of the adult students attending eight schools qualified as registered voters. Convinced that the program could be adapted to many situations, Highlander set up residential workshops to train Citizenship School teachers and replaced the individualized approach originally used. Bernice Robinson agreed to supervise the expanded program and helped develop a weeklong program designed to give volunteer teachers an understanding of the Citizenship School idea along with basic skills and the resources needed to organize and set up their own local schools. Later on, the training workshops facilitated the transfer of the Citizenship School program to the Southern Christian Leadership Conference, which still operates such schools.[20]

It should be noted that from the beginning (and in accord with the Danish folk school tradition), music and singing have played a crucial part in all the programs, including those of the Citizenship Schools. Today, as in the past, Highlander is pioneering music workshops, community musical activities, and—on occasion—the rediscovery of the musical heritage often buried in the Appalachian hollows. Ballads, hymns, folk songs, songs of protest: all these have done much to arouse people to awareness and to the sense of community. Music, in fact, contributes to what Paulo Freire calls the process of "conscientization." As I understand the term, it refers to the kind of learning process which involves the perception on the part of oppressed people of certain cultural, social, economic, and political realities affecting their lives. It also refers to their capacity to transform those realities and to take action against the elements which oppress them.

Paulo Freire developed his program in literacy projects among Brazilian and Chilean peasants; and they have had great relevance for other Latin American people and for various Third World populations as well. In spite of the distinctiveness of his work, there are many connections between what he has done and what Highlander has done among mountain people and disenfranchised blacks. The apparent gap between the plight of the disinherited here (or in Latin America) and the condition of public school students oppressed by bureaucracy seems to be very wide, but the concept of conscientization seems to me to be relevant to all these groups. It is, of course, necessary to avoid sentimentality and the peculiar luxury of paternalistically identifying with the desperately poor, especially those in remote sections of the world. If we are, however, to develop a notion of decision making which is linked to an ideal of social change, it is as important to help American students to perceive their life situation within the bureaucratic system as it is to enable Latin American peasants to understand what conditions oppress them. This kind of understanding may make possible the deconditioning of *any* conditioned individual and, in addition, may make it possible for people of all kinds to become "united by their action and by the reflection on that action and on the world" (Freire, "Cultural Action for Freedom," 46).

Freire's methodology, based as it is on "generative words and themes," can be adapted to be many kinds of educational situations. Our Highlander programs, like Freire's, have focused on real-life situations at the level of the participants' perceptions; and we, too, have worked with words and themes with which people can identify emotionally, and from which new generative words and ideas can be derived to be used for critical examination of the

EDUCATIONAL PHILOSOPHY

participants' lives and the larger world. I need only to refer to what I have already said about playpens and the artificial circumstances fostered in the schools to highlight the significance of a type of pedagogy geared to the existential situations of those affected and involved.

Freire writes, on words occasionally evocative of John Dewey's,

The educator's role is to propose problems about the codified existential situation in order to help the learners arrive at a more and more critical view of their reality. The educator's responsibility, as conceived by this philosophy, is thus greater in every way than that of his colleague whose duty it is to transmit information which the learners memorize. Such an educator can simply repeat what he has read, and often misunderstood, since education for him does not mean an act of knowing. The first type of educator, on the contrary, is a knowing subject, face to face with other knowing subjects. He can never be a mere memorizer, but a person constantly readjusting his knowledge, who calls forth knowledge from his students. (Freire, "Cultural Action for Freedom," 17)

Because the participants are both the subject of and in control of the learning project from beginning to end, the educational process *becomes* a decision-making process on the part of those most deeply affected. Not surprisingly, they are so highly motivated by learning the words that help them discover their true life situations that they become functionally literate in as little as thirteen weeks. According to Freire, however, conscientization does not depend on literacy. It proceeds *along with* the perception that words are connected with real-life situations. Nevertheless, learning to read and write can lead immediately to liberating action, often as in the case of Freire's peasant participants (and Citizenship School participants who often became civil rights activists) in the form of organization against oppressive landlords. Later, conscientization moves to a still higher level when it turns to the future and takes the form of radical denunciation of all dehumanizing structures. Revolutionary action is thus made possible, the kind of action based on the demand for human dignity and illuminated by the dream of a new society. Perhaps most significantly of all, Freire stresses the fact that conscientization must be in response to the emergence of a popular or social movement, to a climate of hope where people are "anxious for freedom."

It may well be that, in the technologically focused school systems of the United States, there is a culture of silence comparable with that existing among the oppressed peasants. This culture, too, may be a result of anti-democratic, bureaucratic structures; and, in attempting to effect radical changes in education, we may be affirming a faith like Freire's—in the intellectual capacities of the voiceless and their potential for building a new society. At Highlander we have had such a faith; indeed, we still nurture it as we work in our "self-education" programs among the Appalachian poor. Why cannot we address ourselves to the problems facing the public schools in the same spirit? Why cannot we think about ways of altering decision making to the end of enabling human beings to become conscious of themselves and *their* real-life situations—to grow, to learn, to change?

If we are to think seriously about liberating people to cope with their own lives, we must refuse to limit the educational process to what can go on only in schools. The bars must come down; the doors must fly open; nonacademic life—*real* life—must be encompassed by education. Multiple approaches must be invented, each one considered educative in its own right. We must stop studying people, stop deciding for them, no matter how young they are. We must stop thinking mainly in terms of the system, since, in truth, education can never be reduced to or confined within a system. There are already vast resources outside the traditional institutions. Experimental research is not necessary to uncover the multiple alternatives to "school" learning, alternatives ranging from conventional volunteer activities to experimentation in free schools, university programs, and the diverse communes which now exist. Other important alternatives are the educational activities created as a part of the civil rights movement, the programs invented by various ethnic and minority groups, the learning achieved by prisoners in their cells and in prison libraries. There are, as well, the legitimately educational approaches devised in and for the labor movement, the peace movement, the women's liberation movement, and other great social movements of deep concern to many people. Of course, some of the activists involved can be brought into classrooms to share their experiences and insights; but this, it seems to me, is of relatively little importance. I do not believe that the existing system can be fundamentally changed simply by introducing representatives of the outside world.

I need to point only to the use of paraprofessionals in large urban systems to indicate what I mean. The very term suggests that the system itself is being cautiously extended to include a few people without the traditional certification. My observations have taught me that, once they are brought into the system, the juice of life is squeezed from them. Instead of being enabled to develop new educational approaches on their own or to make use of their own experiences in setting up creative learning centers, they are cut off from their peers and made to serve as agents of the experts in charge. Inevitably they take on the coloration of professionalism and become more and more cautious the longer they work with those they think of as superiors. They begin to resemble some of the union leaders mentioned above; their loyalty is offered mainly to the structure or the system; they cease to feel accountable to either the children or the community.

They receive certain benefits, of course, from being fitted into the academic structure; but they themselves could learn far more and make a greater difference to the world if they were helped, instead, to learn how to develop and maintain their own educational programs in the community to which they belong. This is only a single example of the radical thinking required to extend and enrich education—to remove it, in other words, from the grip of the status quo. Most of those involved with schools find it almost impossible to conceive of expanding education in this fashion, or of providing multiple educational experiences (some of them not yet imagined) for people of all ages, outside as well as inside the school. I have spoken earlier of the ways in which education tends to be segmented and divided into testable units. Once those in the system agree to consider it in that fashion, they become next to incapable of reconceiving the learning process. They become incapable of imagining how to free educational resources, how to redeploy personnel, how to equip nonprofessionals to work toward increased awareness by using life experiences they share with their own peers. Some research has been carried on with regard to what is called peer teaching, but ordinarily the term has meant a process of children teaching their classmates (or children one year younger than they) segments of prescribed subject matter. There is no question but that the one who teaches benefits a great deal, sometimes even more than the one who is tutored or taught. Too few people, however, have thought of peer teaching outside the boundaries of the school. They have seldom thought, for example, of the poor teaching the poor or of enlisting professionals from fields other than education or people from various walks of life (from the arts, the crafts, even from the assembly lines) to come and serve as part-time teachers in situations geared to full participation—yes, and decision making —by all of those involved. We need only imagine for a moment how much, say, a successful lawyer or concert pianist would learn, if asked to teach some of his contemporaries who happened to live in a slum. This would be peer teaching in a new dimension, with persons learning from persons, with expertise entirely reconceived. But, as I have said, it would only be truly meaningful if it were related in some manner to a social or political movement.

The folk school idea may still have relevance. Today, most Danish folk school students come from urban areas. Because each school is free to define its purpose (as long as it remains within the nonrestrictive folk school pattern), the social, economic, and political problems important to the students become the core of the subject matter that is taught. Highlander, as I have suggested, has also been shaped by the needs and the questions of the people for whom education services were provided. It seems to me that when we think of extending education beyond the confines of city schools, we can think similarly of educative environments—in this case, the particular urban community itself. As in the case of Highlander, we can treat the community, be it slum or suburb or "downtown," as more than a chance environment. Why can it not be treated as a consciously experienced set of conditions and surroundings, where people can come to understand the nature of society by examining the conflict situations and the crises thrust upon *them,* in their own personal lives? If this were the orientation, the part-time teachers would not and could not be visiting "experts," assigned to transmit bits of some commodity called knowledge. They would be enablers, much like Freire's researchers, or like our own Citizenship School teachers. Those participating as learners would bring with them the experimental material, the backgrounds, the problems worthy of investigation. The responsibility of the teacher, part-time or full-time, would be to promote understanding of the learners' lives, sensitivity to injustices, future thinking about a better world.

Now I am entirely aware that mere criticism of existing structures and advocacy, no matter how eloquent, are not likely to change the structures and practices which now exist. It is not only that they have been codified and in some measure sanctified by time; they are almost fatally affected by our society's preoccupation with practicality and efficiency. I have already spoken of the ways in which the schools are dominated by technological advance. More and more observers are considering technology, in fact, to be an independent force, dictating an inevitable and constant expansion. If this is the case, enormous creative effort will be required to prevent the transformation of persons into robots treated as means to technological ends. Great human power will have to be mobilized to make sure that educational development is guided by such traditional principles as justice and freedom, by humanistic and personalistic concerns.

This is why I do not believe that far-reaching changes can be effected by introducing innovations and reforms into the existing system. A radically different system must be invented by people from all walks of life. A radically new climate must be created in which all kinds of people are challenged to cope with real problems and inequities. The forms of the new education that is necessary are difficult to visualize from our present perspective; bold experiments will be essential on every level, the kinds of experiments that can take place only when much that has been taken for granted is deliberately *un*learned.

As I have been suggesting, I believe our only hope lies in democratizing the decision-making process. This means departing from past practices, particularly those which have involved handing down decisions from above and embodying them in the educational structure. No longer can the implementations designed by those at the top of a decision-making hierarchy be accepted as in some manner God-given. No longer can people accede to a veto of their expressed will. If they are to ensure that that will is embodied in practice, they must be involved from the very beginning in a reconstruction of the entire educational process. This demands a guarantee that they participate in crucial, not only peripheral, matters; it means that they must participate in the decision-making process itself and not in a merely supportive or advisory capacity. It means, focally, that they be taken seriously as persons with a *right* to participate in any and all decisions which affect, even tangentially, their lives.

When I say "people," I mean individuals from all segments of society, working together to put the expertise of professionals to what those affected know to be social use. Only with such involvement can power for real change be generated. Only with such involvement can people make sure that power comes from the bottom, percolating upward instead of dripping delicately downward to where the people exist and have their being. Only in this way can the rich resources in this country be utilized; the resources of personal experience and awareness in the ghettos, on Indian reservations, in Appalachia, as well as in the central cities, on Main Streets, on the prairies, on the coasts. If the decision-making process is reconceived, all sorts of resources will suddenly become available—resources far more important, far more valuable than either expertise or cash.

The problem becomes one of overcoming powerlessness and moving people to act in concert. We are all aware that most people are unlikely to act, except out of desperation, until they sense that some desired change is actually possible and until they are able to imagine a channel through which the desired change can be brought about. I need only summon up the memory of the Montgomery bus boycott, which did so much to launch the civil rights struggle in the South, or Highlander's Citizenship School program, which equipped so many people to vote and to challenge the status quo. In both cases, most of the people who eventually participated were originally convinced that things could not be significantly changed. Brought up in a political system of delegated authority, they were similarly convinced that most of those elected to represent their interests seldom did. In one idiom or other, they were inclined to say fatalistically, "You can't fight City Hall." Very much the same situation exists with respect to the schools. Most people, persuaded of their ineffectuality, simply accept traditional patterns of education. They fatalistically accede to the claims of the system's success in turning our products certified as marketable—even if they themselves have not been so certified and never expect to be. They cannot even imagine the existence of a system committed to liberating individuals to live their lives productively and joyfully. The obsolete structures looming over them seem indestructible, even though there are visible cracks in the walls. And the reason for this is that they have no access (or think they have no access) to the decision-making processes.

Self-confidence is needed; learning is needed. It seems to me that learning and decision making are inseparable. People learn from making decisions, and making decisions helps them learn. The motivation for decision making, like the motivation for learning, comes through genuine involvement in an undertaking considered worthy of the effort and possible to achieve. If adults who have never participated in decision-making processes are to be involved, it should be understood that adult learning and school learning differ markedly. Adult learning comes largely from experience; it is mainly (at least until conscientization begins) firsthand. Most adults, no matter what the class to which they belong, have little confidence in academically formulated solutions to what they know to be really tough problems. It is also important to confront the fact that, because of their need to earn a living and their other responsibilities, adults cannot spend great amounts of time in new learning at any given period. Moreover, because they have had so few opportunities in their adult lives to test their learning capacities, they are likely to feel deeply inadequate—especially if they belong to the group so questionably described as "disadvantaged." It would be, in consequence, absurd to expose them to a traditionally academic approach, especially one that does not take their competence and their experiences into account.

Most adults seem to learn best in small, informal discussion groups or workshops where there is no teacher and all are on an equal basis. If assistance is needed and requested, it is provided, and only then. At Highlander, we frequently recruited people for workshops on the basis that they had problems in their community and had expressed the desire to talk with other people who had similar problems. Staff members would be available to help, for example, with techniques of keeping discussions properly focused or with bits of factual information. Not long ago, we sponsored a communications workshop because a participant in an earlier workshop on community organization had started a community newspaper and needed some information on how to maintain it. A welfare rights group, at the same time, needed information on preparing pamphlets to be used as educational tools; some people involved in fighting strip mining wanted to find out about the way newsletters could disseminate information about campaigns such as theirs. In each case, decisions had to be made, decisions of moment to those participating. In each case, significant learning proceeded *in the process of shared decision making*. The participants themselves, in effect, were inventing alternate channels for their own education. We have seen this happen frequently in the last decade among minority groups in their various struggles. The civil rights movement in the South demanded precisely the kind of learning made possible by democratic decision making of the type described. Every time people decided to ride a Freedom Bus,[21] or to sit in at a lunch counter, or to march down a highway, individual leaning and conscientization takes place. If they had not, there would have been little determination, little staying power and (probably) insufficient courage. The people would not have developed the sense of potency and worth necessary for sustained militant action. And this, again, is part of the point.

If we can begin thinking of alternative educational structures in connection with the democratization of decision-making processes, we will find ourselves conceiving of lifetime education; because there is no longer any rational reason for limiting the period in which individuals are given opportunities to learn. We may find, in fact, that the ordinary divisions (childhood/youth/adulthood/old age) are meaningless. For many adolescents, dropping out of school may turn out to be more advantageous than staying in school. Since it will soon be impossible to prepare in advance for living in a rapidly changing world, or even for making a living, it will no longer be tenable to divide education into a period of preparation and a period of "adult" or continuing education. Decisions will have to be made at every stage; educational services and facilities should therefore be available at every stage; educational services and facilities should therefore be available to the one desirous of using them, no matter how old or young he happens to be. It follows from this, of course, that continuing or adult education should be integrated into the over-all educational system—when and if that system is reconceived, opened outward, and fundamentally remade.

We should have learned by now that fundamental restructuring will not occur in response to outcries against the inadequacies of the present system or according to elite blueprints for change. Advocacy alone, while titillating and intellectually stimulating, has never brought about radical change. It has an important role to play only when coupled with a dynamic process of transferring decision-making powers to the population most immediately concerned. This will not happen until the critics' insights merge with the insights and aspirations of people from many walks of life into some common purpose. It will not take place until the walls between the ivory tower theoreticians and practitioners are broken down once and for all, and until we confront the fact that education cannot be humanized until theory fertilizes purposeful action and action puts theory to the test. This is a familiar challenge to educators, I realize, but, unfortunately, far too few have ever dared take the radical steps necessary. They have gone on believing that innovations and reforms within the system would suffice to bring on the desired change.

One way for well-meaning educators to stimulate interest in democratic decision making might be to open up a public debate on a redefinition of educational goals. This, in itself, would be a test of the practitioners' commitment; since, as we have seen, the bureaucracy has long since made them defenders of vested interests, and among those interests has certainly been the determination of goals. If they dared, however, they might propose for public consideration the formulation of a Bill of Education Rights, which might include the right to free speech, the right to equal education opportunity regardless of color, religion, or sex, the right of minority groups to develop educational programs of their own. Like the original Bill of Rights, this bill would not be treated as a statement of fact, prescription, or ultimate principle. It would simply be the first stage of an ongoing search for the kinds of principles which serve as lodestars, or what John Dewey used to call "ideal possibilities." They would provide a sense of direction and standards by which we might test the educational activities we undertake. This does not mean, of course, that our goals can or should be finalized at any stage. If decision making is at last democratized, there will always be fresh insights arising out of the discussion and interchange; there will always be new experiences being articulated, new visions being made clear. Nevertheless, if energies are not to be dissipated in endless, circular movement, some formulation of overall purpose is required. The desire ought to be to spiral upward in our endeavors aiming toward our imagined better state.

Quite naturally, organized special interest groups stand in the way—and will stand more firmly in the way the more clearly the people define their purposes, because those purposes cannot but be at odds with technological aims. We must be aware of the fact that one of the methods special interest groups have of protecting themselves is the method of bureaucratic decision making or keeping people under control. Therefore, redoubled efforts should be made in diverse communities to free up as many policy-making bodies as possible and to open them to groups of teachers, students, and representatives of the public at large.

The decentralized boards of education in the cities may well have opened up new opportunities for effecting community participation in policy-making and, at length, community control. The opposition first aroused among the public and the teaching profession was complex and emotional, particularly in the case of the Ocean Hill–Brownsville Demonstration District in New York.[22] Vested interests seemed to be at stake, along with the merit system, the power of the teachers' union, and the authority of New York's Board of Education. Some of the hostility, however, was undoubtedly due to a lack of confidence in the ability of neighborhood people to figure out what the educational needs of the children were. It was assumed in many places that they would choose curricula and methodologies which would not work, or that they would politicize the schools to such an extent that learning could no longer take place. As it turned out, of course, the critics were quite wrong; and where the community control has been seriously attempted, it has usually proved viable. Certainly it is a step in the right direction; but it must be supplemented by a range of hitherto unfamiliar decision-making methods— methods which involve all those affected by the decisions being made.

Education, I have been suggesting, is too important to be left in the hands of institutions and experts. Decision making must not only be decentralized; it must be pluralistic, with various decisions being made on many levels, with varying degrees of intensity, some temporary and others long range. We might call this a multichanneled approach to decision making, since all sorts of new channels will have to be invented as involvement increases. Efficiency will definitely not be the objective, nor will neatness or speed. But, given bona fide decision-making powers, the people (as we have learned at Highlander) will rapidly learn to make responsible and socially useful decisions. Moreover they will be quite willing to assume responsibility for carrying out the decisions based on their collective judgment. The problem is not the danger of irresponsibility or inefficiency, but the problem of convincing students, minorities, and other disenchanted people that their involvement will have meaning and their ideas will be respected. We have continually to keep in mind how systemically they have been excluded, how powerless they have been made to feel.

The majority of people in every community, in fact, have been so accustomed to top-downism and deferring to experts that they require theoretical and practical reeducation as to their rights, opportunities, and responsibilities. Concerned and creative educators—*radical* educators—will have to devise a range of imaginative opportunities which will permit people totally inexperienced in decision making to become involved and, by becoming involved, to learn. In addition to providing a means by which people can make education serve their needs as they perceive them and promote their aspirations as they define them, the decision-making process being proposed is educational in its own right. It is a means of accelerating the kind of learning people need if they are to take control of their own lives and govern themselves in all their relationships.

There are many educational leaders, it seems to me, who know on some level what education ought to be. They are, frequently, being frustrated by their inability to achieve what they envision; and they are slow to recognize that what is required is involvement of other concerned people on the community level. Without allies, educators will continue to talk to each other in what will finally become nothing more than an academic cloister. The thrust on their part should be to maximize the development of all the human resources at hand, to create atmospheres where spontaneous growth can take place—beginning where all new growth begins, at the roots. If they are to be democratic leaders, they must commit themselves to unleashing human forces and working to free those forces for a focus on the achievement of mutually accepted goals.

Theoretical preparation, no matter how excellent, does not equip the educator for work with community people. There must be a recognition of the fact that a mastery of data or skill in conceptualization is no substitute for the learning which comes out of actual experiences with human beings outside of academic walls. I would like to propose a mode of ensuring this type of learning through an adaptation of the work-study plan which has worked so well for many college students in Antioch College, for instance, and other schools.[23] The educator's official responsibilities, I think, should keep him in the classroom and office for half of his work time and in the community for the rest of his time. He should function in the community, not as an observer or researcher, but as educator, functioning somewhat as Freire's people did, as some of Highlander's workshop staff people have worked. It can hardly be denied that an effective educator ought to have as much firsthand knowledge as possible about what goes on in the homes, on the streets, and the larger world where those being taught do most of their living and learning. Many schools employ paraprofessionals or street workers to mediate between the neighborhood and the teachers; but this, it seems to me, is not sufficient. For one thing, it wastes the talents of the para-professional by incorporating them into the existing system. For another, it maintains the cloistered arrangements surrounding the teacher. As I view it, the educator—be he a third grade teacher or a college professor—ought to be out there in the community, learning how people of all ages behave and learn outside the classroom. The object of such learning is not just to make him a better classroom teacher. It is to nurture in him a genuine interest in the people of the community, a recognition of them as allies, as supporters, and as people who are worthy and who have potential contri-butions to make, once they are involved.

A third grade teacher, for example, cannot get the insight he needs sim-ply by appealing to the parents of pupils as parents and nothing else. They are not only parents; they are persons with feelings, memories, and under-standing apart from the parental roles. Once a person-to-person relationship is established, rather than a teacher-to-parent relationship, it may become possible for the teacher and the parent to work together in the decision-making efforts that mean learning for both. Otherwise, the presumption too often is that the authority exercised over the children is also being exercised over the parents; and that is not a relationship of equals, of persons respect-ing one another for what each one is and can become.

In sum, I have been suggesting that the only way to effect radical changes in the educational system is for educators to make alliances with as many likeminded people as they can—including community people, students, var-ious ethnic groups, union members, and other teachers—wherever they are and whenever there are issues to be dealt with which make a difference to people's lives. Obviously we have to start on a piecemeal basis, but we should keep in mind that the total system needs remaking. Refusing the technolo-gist's habit of segmenting, we know enough to realize that no single segment can be dealt with separately. The setting of goals, the development of cur-riculum, the making of policy, are not separate undertakings. They are part of a totality, which will be changed to the degree more and more people begin participating in decision making and becoming agents of fundamental change in the educational system and society at large.

We have learned from the folk schools in this country and abroad, from Paulo Freire and others like him, and from the great popular movements of this century that people become motivated when they are personally involved in processes relating directly to them and their own life situations. We have learned that they become energetic and committed when these processes relate to their hopes and aspirations, when they are free to par-ticipate in the determination of goals. We need to make possible the full and active participation of men and women who have not been completely con-ditioned by technological controls. We need social guerillas who, in the name of humanism, will once and for all break the restricting molds.

Democratic Involvement in Decision Making and Action

[1976]

In the following speech, given at the Public Relations Conference in Brainerd, Minnesota, October 13, 1976, Horton examines the important links between democratic decision making, education, and social change and argues that it is through bottom-up education, in which decisions are made by the people themselves, that "powerless people empower each other and become collectively involved."

Good public relations for a service program must be based on the democratic involvement of the people for whom the program is designed. They are numerous, speak in many voices to many people, and can be the most convincing advocates. People are most active in programs when they have a genuine part in planning and running them. There are a number of approaches to democratic involvement. I would like to mention three: decision making, action research, and adult education for social change.

Decision Making

If people are to participate in other than peripheral matters, or in a supportive or advisory capacity, they need to be involved from the beginning. Only then will they be convinced they are being taken seriously. This involvement cannot be limited in any way and the scope of the involvement must be all-inclusive. It must encompass purpose, structure, and process. When decisions are made that affect people's lives, they have a right to participate. But often they do not have and are not given that opportunity.

The involvement of all segments of society is a necessity, as well as a right, for it is from the people that the power for change will be generated. *[Illegible text omitted]* But for this to occur there has to be a change. The drip-down process of decision making needs to be replaced by a percolator process where the power and energy comes from the bottom.

When I worked with labor unions in the '30s and '40s, I came to the conclusion that what was needed was a percolator system. Here ideas come from the bottom, go to the top and get structure, and then go back for revitalizing and testing by workers who generate new ideas. The percolator system has a lot of vitality. Did you ever watch a coffee percolator work? It really goes up down, up down. I believe the percolator system is much more effective than the drip system where everything comes down from the top.

If we are to have a democratic society, people must find or invent new channels through which decisions can be made. Many alternative channels will have to be opened up. Already some minority groups are beginning to use a variety of channels for decision making, several of which have proved to be quite effective. A few of these mechanisms have roots in history, such as the right to petition, but others are new and sometimes startling. Decision making will be effective by whatever form the voice of the people takes provided it is powerful and persistent enough.

Decision making must be decentralized with all kinds of decisions being made on all kinds of levels, with varying degrees of intensity, some temporary and others long-ranged. In addition, if participation is to be significantly increased, opportunities must be provided that will enable people with little or no experience in decision making to become involved. People can only learn to make decisions by making them.

Fear of irresponsibility and mistakes cannot be used as an excuse for caution. Given bona-fide decision-making powers, people will not only learn rapidly to make socially useful decisions, but will assume responsibility for carrying out the decisions based on their collective judgment. The problem is not the danger or irresponsibility or that wrong decisions will be made, but to convince people heretofore ignored or excluded that their involvement will have meaning and that their ideas will be respected. The danger is not too much, but too little participation.

The majority of people have been accustomed to accept top-downism and deferring to officials and experts. They will have to be reeducated both in theory and practice to their rights, opportunities, and responsibilities.

Action Research

I would like to say a word about a special type of involvement some of us will be discussing during the next two or three days—action research. It is not the research done by professionals or certified experts, but by groups of community people. The kind of research I have in mind is described in a booklet published by the Institute of Responsive Education.[24] To paraphrase: research becomes a form of action when it is done by people who themselves must act. It provides a means of organizing large numbers of people and building a base of mass support for given problems. It is a way for community people to define problems, collect the facts, and act collectively.

One form action research could take would be for people over a period of time to clarify and define their problems at informal community gatherings or house meetings. Then a committee could turn the central issue into researchable questions and come up with a hypothesis or some answers they want to test out.

EDUCATIONAL PHILOSOPHY

The research tools to be developed should be ones which involve the largest number of people; for example, personal interviews. I recall members of a Tennessee Farmers Union Cooperative doing interviews with dairy farmers by phone and personal visits and gathering for potluck supper to tabulate and analyze their findings. The farm family researchers had spent three months finding out what they wanted to know and during that period their membership almost doubled.

Adult Education for Social Change

When people come for a Highlander workshop the first thing we do after taking it easy and getting rested for awhile, is to have them tell what is on their minds and what they are doing in their community. What is it they want help on? This is where we get our workshop curriculum—the subject matter.

For example, we had a group from Bigstone Gap, Virginia. Some said they wanted a factory that would employ poor people. A woman who lived back in the mountains said she couldn't get enough people together to do anything in such a small community. How could she combine it with another community across the ridge and organize a PTA? That was her problem and, she thought, her solution. Just like the other people thought the factory would be their solution. Some of them wanted roads. They talked about their crooked politicians and the treatment they got from the welfare office. They talked about not being able to get people out to meetings. You might say those are not very important problems. But those were the problems they thought they had, and they were important because they were their problems.

Our job is to build on what they identify as their own problems and to do this in their own language. We get them to share experiences and [we] introduce information only if specifically requested to do so. We might say, "Here is an experience that somebody else had and this is what happened." We might ask if anyone had any similar experiences. We get them to talk about their experiences. The information most usable comes from their peers, somebody like themselves whose experience can be duplicated.

If you start this way and don't get away from people's problems and keep asking them for answers, they will begin to see that after all, there are related problems they hadn't been aware of before. They may start talking about other situations and may conclude that what they originally thought was a big problem is no longer important to them.

Over the years, problems brought to Highlander may sound [a lot] alike, but they are not. The context is different, the situation is different, the people are different. If you start where they are, and stay within the group experience, or extensions of their experience, they go home and continue to work on the problems. They go back and keep on learning. But if you cut off that root from what they conceive their problem to be, their understanding cannot grow.

The learning process is already in motion when people come to Highlander. If we build on their experience and concern, the learning speeds up. They talk to each other before going to sleep. When they eat they talk to somebody across the table. And when they get in their cars to go home, they are still talking about their problems and what they have learned.

When we started labor union leadership training, the workers got to the place, through their own experience, of realizing that they needed help in setting up committees, conducting meetings, involving others in political and community action. To deal with these problems they had to get information. They had to find out what the laws were because the laws affected what they could and could not do. They also had to know something about how you get along with others because they needed allies. They needed to get cooperation from farmers, middle-class people, and church people. We have ideas too. But we know that people won't even consider our ideas as alternatives until we have worked with them in terms of their ideas and needs.

At one of our Appalachian weekend workshops, one group said that their main problem was to get people out to meetings. So we had a little discussion and helped them figure out how they could have bigger meetings. They worked out ways to double and triple attendance. The group was then asked, "What's going to happen when you have three times as many turning out?" For the first time they analyzed their situations and goals and finally decided it wouldn't make a great deal of difference. They concluded they didn't want to have big meetings after all. It took us two or three hours to get them to the place where they figured out what they really wanted to accomplish. But once they saw it, they acted on it and with great success.

Let me describe briefly another example of how this process can work when a group of people decide to solve a local problem. Several years ago some West Virginia welfare recipients approached Highlander with the request for a workshop on community organizing. These people were from Boone County, a rural coal mining area in the southern part of the state. They wanted a meeting to talk about community education, and how to organize people into a welfare rights organization. They recruited people, arranged transportation, and drove over fifty miles in one day to our residential center in Tennessee.

The workshop began on Friday night and ended on Sunday. Within that span of time the group developed a strategy to build a welfare rights organization in Boone County. More importantly, they decided that an educational program was essential in order to explain to members their legal rights and to understand the intricacies of welfare law in their state. Who would be the teachers? Welfare recipients themselves. They reasoned that they knew the problems best and that they could be the best teachers of their own people. Lawyers were found who were willing to help interpret

EDUCATIONAL PHILOSOPHY

laws. University students and Vistas were found who could help supply transportation, research, and public relations skills.[25] Church organizations supplied funds and some technical assistance.

These recipients, most with little or no formal education, in a very short period of time developed and ran an educational program which dealt with constitutional rights, welfare law, and organizing skills. Out of this small beginning there developed a statewide group which eventually became a force state legislators grew to fear. When new welfare laws were proposed for West Virginia, members of this group marched on the legislature, demanded to be heard, and quickly proved that they knew more about the laws than did the lawmakers.

Today the organization is still expanding, still growing, both in membership and in understanding of how education can be used as a potent force for social change. Occasionally members of the group request another workshop at Highlander. We look forward to it with eagerness because they always end up teaching us more than we teach them.

Just before and during the civil rights period, black leaders and a few sympathetic whites met at Highlander workshops to exchange experiences and to make plans.[26] In some workshops rather detailed plans for integrating schools and other public facilities were worked out and published. Each participant before leaving told what his or her plans were in returning home. I recall that Rosa Parks (who sparked the civil rights movement) had no specific plan when she left Highlander and that was just a couple of months before she refused to move on that bus in Montgomery.[27] They drew strength from knowing that they were few but not alone, and formed lasting friendships. These contacts enabled them to work together later on a Southwide basis.

Highlander is part of the before and after learning process. The subject matter for discussion is brought into the residential workshops by the participants, and the educational experience at Highlander is taken back for testing and used, as the learning process continues. In one study that was made of Highlander programs the following observation was made: "Although each program represents a distinct and differing response to the educational needs of a given group at a given time, the data reveal important common elements with regard to the kinds of people who participated in the programs and the way in which the programs were developed. Highlander students, whatever their backgrounds, came from groups actively seeking solutions to their problems" (A. Horton, *The Highlander Folk School,* 313).

Who Comes to Highlander

Highlander has looked for emerging community organizations and leaders, men and women who are involved in doing something for other people, as well as for themselves. Highlander's concept of emerging leaders was evolved from learning experiences starting in the thirties when the woodcutters and unemployed in the Monteagle community demonstrated their ability to play leadership roles and to develop a sense of responsibility to their peers. They also demonstrated rapid growth in understanding, analysis, and planning.

This learning was carried over into our work with the pre-CIO period when unions were developing in the mountains and surrounding areas.[28] We had confidence that the unrecognized local leaders could grow in understanding and, furthermore, that they were free to learn and act on what they learned. People caught up in whatever structures that were around tended to identify more with the structures than with the people. Consequently, we dealt primarily with voluntary organizers and officers of small unions. As the labor union program developed, we decided to limit our activities primarily to shop stewards, committee members, and local officials of smaller unions who could act independently and whose loyalty was to the workers.

When union leaders were put on the international union's payroll, we theorized that their loyalty would be to the bureaucracy rather than to the workers, since the bureaucracy was in a position to decide whether or not they would be paid. Our rule of thumb was to deal with people who were responsible to the members of the union and whose tenure in office and power rested in their hands. We knew that many of these people would eventually become part of the bureaucracy, but hopefully they would carry into their new activities some of the things they had learned when they were free to learn. That proved to be sound.

When we started working with the farmers' union, we carried over the same approach. The criterion was whether the people were responsive to their peers or to some structure. In Greene County, Tennessee, we learned that the local justices of peace were responsive to the farmers' needs, the needs of their peers, even though they held an official title. Consequently, we involved a number of the local justices of peace who were the recognized community leaders in the formation of the farmers' union programs there.

Early civil rights workshops were made up of black people we had worked with in the unions as well as farmers, ministers, owners of black businesses (such as beauticians and undertakers), and a few courageous teachers. These people were relatively free from white control and domination.

The labels people carry, their titles, are not important. What is important is their relationship to their peers. When we conceptualize emerging leaders, the important criterion is loyalty to one's peers. It has been our experience that education is not a powerful enough method to counteract the influence of the establishment on people they control. We try to deal with people who are willing to take a chance, who are willing to act on what they think is right and should be done.

As I have pointed out, Highlander had chosen to relate primarily to workers and farmers, the poor, and victims of discrimination. We have used education as we believe it functions most effectively, that is from the bottom up, to help powerless people empower each other and become collectively involved.

I am looking forward to your reactions to what I have said and to hearing your views. We should all profit by sharing our experiences and hopes.

Highlander's Educational Program

[1977]

The following interview was originally printed as a six-part series in the Ryegrass Working Papers, *the newsletter of the Ryegrass School in Uniontown, Washington. The following text reprints parts 1, 2, and 4, sections that focus on education for action, education versus organizing, and the necessity for coalition building. The original prefatory material is included below.*

In this issue, we introduce the first segment of a lengthy interview with Myles Horton, cofounder and past director of the Highlander Research and Education Center, New Market, Tennessee. It was taped by Bill Olson in September 1977 at the Highlander. It is our intention to share this interview not only as a perspective of recent American social history, but more importantly as a description of the process and potential of this type of organization.

Part I

BILL OLSON: For our school in Washington we're trying to wrestle with the question of whether we want to be an organizing program or a school. Or do we want to be a little of both? Now, one of the questions is the difficulty in organizing over a large geographical area and the probability that if Ryegrass School were to get into really heavy organizing work that probably it would be necessary to focus on a single community or pair of communities. We're looking at a three-state or maybe four-state area: part of Montana, Idaho, Washington, and Oregon. So I am wondering if the size of the area affects the kind of activity we can successfully work in.

MYLES HORTON: Well, I've always taken a position that Highlander was not in the business of organizing, or even of training organizers, but in education for action, and trying to help develop people who would become activists. Highlander, itself, would not be a part of that organization because we'd want to work with people on many, many fronts.

"Utah" Phillips gave me a little pin last time I saw him.[29] It says, "One Battle, Many Fronts." And I appreciate it because that's the way I felt about things. The one battle is to have a revolution in this country and change society, but there are many fronts for dealing with it. Instead of saying, "We are going to be an organizer of something," like Alinsky was an organizer,[30] we say, "Our job is to help people who hopefully will become organizers." But since there's no one way to organize, we don't try to train organizers. We try to develop their thinking ability to analyze, to understand problems so that they can develop into organizers.

A tremendous lot of people who have been to Highlander have been organizers. But we didn't tell them, "One, two, three. This is the way you organize." We tried to help them understand how to analyze their problem, how to deal with the situation, and tried to get them committed philosophically to dealing with these problems. The advantage to our approach is that we don't get tied up in a given organizing campaign on a limited basis.

Organizing is a full-time job. I've organized unions, co-ops, political groups, and other things. And when I start to organize, I've got to concentrate on that organizing. I can't be free to deal with a dozen different people in a dozen different situations, trying to help them think through their situation. Now, if Highlander became just an organizing institution, and if we were going to do a credible job, then we'd really have to exclude everything else. So we avoid tying ourselves down to any one group.

That doesn't mean at times we haven't been identified very closely with the CIO,[31] civil rights movement, and more recently with Appalachia, trying to help develop leadership and get people working together in an alliance. But we haven't said, "This is our job." We work through and with other people. Highlander is not organizing something. We do education that supports organization. That is a very important distinction.

OLSON: How much of your success, then, depended on a certain level of activity already existing in the South or in the mountains or wherever you've been working?

HORTON: Well, we have had two, what I would call "movement type" periods at Highlander. One the industrial union movement and the other the civil rights movement. I'm talking about big movement activities. And now we are hopefully on the fringe of something in Appalachia. In none of those instances were there activities when we started on that program.

We started in '32 trying to promote and work with an industrial union movement. There was none in '32. The AF of L was at a very low ebb.[32] The Communist trade unions had been liquidated.[33] There was nothing organizationally to build on. We started working with the people to organize and strike. And then by '35, the CIO was formed.

EDUCATIONAL PHILOSOPHY

Now we didn't form the CIO, but since we had been working with the people in the South who were trying to do something, the people who were promoting the CIO asked for us to help, because we were the only people that had any contacts. So if we hadn't done that and hadn't had those contacts, they wouldn't have asked us to run the educational programs and recommend organizers because they wouldn't have known us. We wouldn't have had any credibility. We anticipated that; therefore, we were part of it. And Highlander was, later on, the official CIO educational training center in the South.[34]

We started working on civil rights problems specifically—we always said everything should be integrated, but I mean we said, "This is a problem we've got to deal with"—in the early fifties. We started developing programs. When the civil rights movement came along, the people who became the leaders of the civil rights movement had already been to Highlander. Most of the people that started SNCC had been at Highlander.[35] Rosa Parks, who started the thing off, had been here.[36] We had been working with Fred Shuttlesworth, who was one of the leaders at Birmingham.[37] We had been working with all the people who later became leaders. So they just continued to work with Highlander. They weren't going to start working with somebody else who had jumped on the bandwagon after it got started, because they didn't know them, didn't feel comfortable with them.

We thought there was a potential in development of Appalachia. And we thought that could be encouraged, and Highlander could play a role in encouraging it. We couldn't create it; just like we didn't create the civil rights movement; we didn't create the CIO. We were anticipating. We said, "If it comes, we want to get in on the ground floor. We want to be a part of it, and we can help promote it." When we first started working with the Appalachian program, you couldn't get ten people together to do much of anything. Most organizations in Appalachia were antiquated and were against any kind of thing we believed in. They were institutionally related things, establishment-oriented. And now, things are happening in Appalachia. And Highlander knows the people because a lot of them—just like a lot of the people who became part of the civil rights movement—have been at Highlander.

They're exploratory and want to do something, and if you offer a program to help stimulate them, they're going to come to it. Then they're going to become the leaders. And when they become the leaders, they'll still come back to Highlander, because they know that's where they're comfortable. That's where they got help in their development, so that's where they're going to try to continue to get help. If you wait until a situation is ready-made, you couldn't be a part of it. So it's primarily a problem of analyzing and deciding first what should be. Second, is there a potential for this thing to happen? And you make an analysis. Sometimes you're right; sometimes you're wrong. I think we've been right on the three things I've mentioned.

In Grundy County, where Highlander used to be located, we organized the county politically.[38] First, we organized unions, started out having discussions and study groups, and then we got co-ops. Then we put together a county political organization, and we had our independent labor ticket, and we won eleven out of twelve offices in the county the first time we tried. But we had done all the work in advance. And we found that the state wouldn't have anything to do with that county. They cut off all the funds, wouldn't pay the sheriff, wouldn't pay anybody. So we realized that the laws don't affect people like us if you happen to win. They only affect the "right" people. Then we said, "Well, the county's too small a unit. We'll have to work on a state basis."

We were, I guess, a little bit overenthusiastic by our experience and success and the idea that other people were beginning to like it around the mountains. We decided that it might be possible to put together a state coalition of labor, farmers, and liberals, and do something politically. And we were able to persuade people that it was a good idea. Labor was very much interested in getting support of farmers and other people, because in Tennessee, at that time, more people were in rural areas than in industrial areas. It's different now. But labor said, "Sure, it's a great idea. We'll support you for that." They gave us money and backing. Railroad Trainmen, Teamsters, CIO, AF of L. And it was the fact that we had delivered. We had showed it could be done in a county.

Well, we needed farmers. So we got the National Farmers' Union interested.[39] And for about five years we organized farmers' unions and farmers' cooperatives as part of a Highlander program, ran the program for them. And we needed the farmers to make the coalition, so we went out to organize them. And we succeeded in organizing several thousand farm families in Tennessee and running educational programs. And we had meetings with labor and religious people, civil libertarians, and all the good people. But the time wasn't right. We hadn't analyzed correctly. And the war came along. It probably would have worked if it hadn't been for the war.

Well, that's an example of analysis that wasn't right. I don't mean to say a lot of education didn't go on. We organized dozens of co-ops, and we got a lot of people working together, and we had farmers supporting unions, and we got a lot of middle-class people involved. So some good came of it, but our goal wasn't achieved because our analysis was wrong.

You don't wait 'til it happens; you've got to try to figure it out in advance, and start plugging away in a small way. If it happens, if your analysis is right, you're okay; if it isn't, it doesn't happen as much. I don't know any other way to deal with it.

OLSON: Is there anything else you think I should know about Highlander?

HORTON: No, I think if you've got your direction straight, got your philosophy straight about what your long-range aims are. Maybe you won't ever achieve them. But that's where you're moving. That's your lodestar. That's the most important single thing: to know what direction in which to move. Otherwise you go around in circles. You've got to have long-range goals to give you basic direction.

The other thing is that you've got to know is this goal worth spending your time on. And you've got to somehow get yourself in the frame of mind where you say, "I know what I believe. But I'm going to have to deal with people, and I'm going to have to find out from them who they are and where they are—their perception of themselves, not your perception of what they are, but what their perceptions of themselves are."

Then you've got to start working with them, moving them by giving them learning experiences in the direction you want to go. But if you don't start where they are, then you go off and leave them. They don't move. You just go by yourself. So they're just the opposite ends of poles. One is where you want to go, and the other is where the people are, and you've got to hitch them together. People learn from their experiences, and everything is an extension of the experiences they have. So if you don't start with experiences they have, you can't make an extension of it. You know, the hard thing for me when Highlander first started—and this is pretty well documented in a doctoral dissertation that my wife, Aimee, wrote—is the unlearning we had to do at the beginning.[40] I insisted on getting that in. If you just pretend you always knew these things and didn't go through some learning experiences, then people wouldn't learn much from you. We were pretty academic, in spite of the fact that some of us had been working with people. And we were trying to apply academic learning to nonacademic people. And we had to start learning from the people where they were so we could move with them, instead of moving off by ourselves.

That's about the hardest part, learning to hitch onto the people where they are, yet at the same time, move them in the direction toward your goal. They're not going to learn what you say; they're going to learn from what they experience. And you've got to figure ways to give people learning experiences. The early days of Highlander, when we first started working with unions, we tried to give them experiences, instead of just talking to them. We didn't talk about co-ops, they ran one. They organized themselves into a Highlander local union, and they ran a union. We could help them understand how to do things, but they were doing them. We'd start with their problems, always. It wasn't that we were interested in helping them solve that particular problem. We were interested in them learning how to solve problems.

So if you start with what they have, instead of some theoretical something, then it ties right into their experience, and then you expand that experience. If you ever break that contact, then you go off and leave people. Somebody asked me one time, "Who really runs Highlander? Is it the contributors? Is it the board? Is it the staff?" And I said, "Well, I never thought about that much. But I guess the people that run Highlander are the people we work with. They determine what we do and how fast we go." They really run Highlander in the sense that if we're working with a group of people, we stay with them. We have solidarity with them on their level. That doesn't mean that we don't have ideas of our own that we contribute. But we contribute by giving them experiences through which they can learn.

Part II

OLSON: I was watching the Brown Lung videotape today, and what I was struck by was that the people from Highlander just kept their mouths shut and listened to the talk of the people who were involved.[41] I also noticed that when they did speak, they spoke only to summarize what was going on and maybe move it just a little further. And once they broke over a little barrier or moved a step further, then the people in the audience just took it up.

HORTON: Yeah, that's right. Well, that's a very important thing because you're not just a convener, you're an educator. You are part of the group, too. You share your experiences when they're appropriate. Or you bring in somebody else's experiences when it's appropriate. Let's say you get a group of people together, and they've pooled their knowledge. Maybe for the first time, they're learning to trust each other enough to learn from each other—peer learning is a powerful tool. Sometimes, because you've had more experience, you see something in their discussion that they don't see. So you highlight that.

That's why you've got to have a goal yourself, or you wouldn't know which way to move people. We want them to learn to work together. We want them to learn to learn from each other. We want them to learn that they need more people to work with them, more and more strength. We want them to learn that they need to analyze their situation. They're not used to analyzing their experiences, contemplating what they know and expanding it, and thinking about it. You do it just by contributing to the discussion in such a way that you kind of move them along. And then, when people get to the place where they don't have within their experience the information they need, and you have that or have access to it, you share it with them.

You don't say, "You do this." You say, "Here's some information to consider." If it ties in, they'll take it and ask for more. But you can't move beyond an extension of their experiences. You can extend it, but you can't break that; they've got to perceive it as being an extension of their experience, related to their experiences. But anything you can do to broaden that is educationally sound. We don't accept this idea that it's detrimental to make any contribution to people's thinking.

We think that if you're going to be an educator, you've got a responsibility to make a contribution if you can make it in such a way that it makes sense to them. Any contribution—I don't care how radical it is or different it is from their experiences—if it relates, you can share it with them. Part of the idea is to stretch their thinking, not to solve problems, but help them learn to analyze and think, to expand their horizons and create more problems. And know that once they solve that one, that's just a step to other, bigger problems.

I think that's where we differ from people who are into organizing. Organizing, quite often, has a specific, limited goal. And the job of the organizer is to accomplish that goal. Well, we don't think that's very important. We think in achieving a goal, you're supposed to learn that there are other goals, not that it's a dead end. And that's why we shied away from organizing. Because it's always a very limited thing, to get it done the quickest, most efficient way, to achieve a given end. Well, that doesn't help people develop their thinking. That's not education. I don't mean to say that no education comes out, but a limited amount of education only.

On the other hand, you can take a specific thing and use it as a basis for helping people. So you don't minimize it; you don't say it's not important. Somebody comes here with a very specific thing they want to do. Well, we try to help them figure out how to do that. We don't say, "That's not important." Or, "That's not what Highlander is all about." That's what Highlander is about, helping them deal with their problems in such a way that they learn from those problems how to analyze and think. So we would struggle with them to help them solve that problem, and then in the process of doing that, nine times out of ten, they'd decide that's not what they want to do. They realize that's a very limited thing. Now, an organizer would say, "I'll get that done. That's it." That's why we say we don't do organizing; we do education.

I used to have a lot of discussions with Alinsky. I knew him before he got into this organizing, and we were very close. But we finally came to the conclusion that we had different approaches. I think he was the best organizer in America. I respect him for his organizing. He did more with organizing than most people do in terms of broadening it out and making it educational. But there came a point when he would achieve his goal, but I wouldn't be satisfied with that. I would use that as an educational base. He contracted to achieve those goals, and he would do it. And there was never any confusion. He was always very popular and very clear-cut and very charismatic. It was easier for him to explain organizing than it is for me to explain education. It's easier to do organizing than it is to do education. He would help me in meetings and forums. Sometimes he'd say, "Oh, Myles can't explain. Let me explain." And sometimes he'd do a very brilliant job of it. I'd just sit back and let him do it. So I think you have to make that distinction if you're going to do education. Or if you're going to do organizing. Either way, you've got to make that distinction.

OLSON: When a group focuses on organizing rather than on education, what kind of problems can it run into?

HORTON: Well, sometimes you get the impression that those groups are under pressure to achieve a specific goal without involving people in the process, except formally. Sometimes the people vote on things and approve them, but actually, the thinking and analysis and work is done by the organizers, which doesn't give the people a learning experience.

One young organizer was here recently, and he raised the question about how he had to organize under pressure and didn't have time to educate people as much as he would like to. He came to Highlander to discuss some of these educational ideas. And I said, "Well, why is that done?" And he said, "Well, one thing is we are in competition with other organizations for funds. We have to organize that way to get the funds, because if they can organize faster than we can, then they get the funds." There are pressures if you have to deliver, have to produce. It's shortcut. But, you can justify that.

If you're not interested in a radical educational program, then you can justify achieving specific aims that benefit people yet at the same time don't involve people in the process. They don't learn anything, but they get something. I'm not against getting things for people. They get it. They have it. And it's good for them.

I think they can be good at organizing and training people to organize. And as Saul Alinsky used to say, "You can't set up an organization without some people learning something." I agree with that. I'm just not an organizer. I've organized unions and a lot of things, but I always try to work in a little education. I think you have to make a choice as to whether you're going to be an organizer and do some specific things or do education.

There are a lot of combinations where they work together, but when the crunch comes, you've got to make a decision as to whether you want to achieve an organization or you want to develop people's thinking. I can think of two experiences having to do with organization where people have decided that what they set out to do, they didn't want to do. From an organizing point of view, that's a bad record, you see, because you didn't achieve what you set out to do.

Right over here in a neighboring county in the forties, we were working with the farmers, when we were trying to put together that coalition. The University of Tennessee had a man in extension who was just trying to organize co-ops. Whether they succeeded or failed, he got credit and promotion for organizing them. And he told the farmers they should have a dairy co-op. We had a farmers' union over there and they asked us to help. And we said, "Okay, if you want a dairy co-op, we'll help you get organized." And they said, "Organize it." We said, "No, no, you've got to organize it. We'll help you, but you organize it." And they said, "Okay." And we said, "Let's get some facts. How many people will be in it? How much milk is there?" and so on. They said, "The university will send out a questionnaire." And we said, "No, no, you talk to the people or telephone them or something. Have personal contact."

We wanted them to get to know each other and work together. They got all the facts together: found how many cows there were, how much milk there was. They did all the work. And we said, "Okay, now is that enough for a successful dairy co-op? Is that enough volume to make an efficient production unit?" And they said they didn't know. We said we didn't either, but I said, "I have a friend in the farmer's union who runs a dairy co-op, and we can ask him." So we asked him and he gave them the facts and figures.

When this guy from the university extension found out about it, he raised hell because we had killed his idea of having a diary co-op. But the people learned a lot in the process. They saved themselves a lot of money and a lot of headaches, because they learned the facts. They made an analysis themselves. Well, that's not a very good organizing job; it's a good educational job.

Another instance happened in the labor unions. Years ago, we were asked to come over here to Knoxville.[42] (We were in Monteagle then.) They had a big textile mill strike, and they wanted some classes while they were on a long strike to learn about unions. We got a bunch of volunteers, people who lived in Knoxville, and we set up classes. In the morning, people worked in offices and businesses, and so we set up the classes at six o'clock in the morning. We had other classes at night, so people could work and could teach those classes. They had about six picket posts, and we had two classes a day at each picket post. We staffed the whole thing and planned the whole thing.

In the process of those classes, they wanted to discuss how the contract worked and what the demands were. And they came to the conclusion in those classes that the strike was wrong. They'd gotten all excited and struck over something that wasn't in their contract. They were saying, "It's in the contract," and they found it wasn't in the contract. So they were in a kind of quandary, because they were in this big strike and making this demand.

They'd get together in a meeting, and they discussed it; they were getting educated about this strike. So they said, "Well, we can't tell the company we were wrong. We've got a good lot of solidarity here and a lot of spirit. Let's think of something else to ask them." They changed their demand. *[Laughs.]* They didn't go back to work, they just kept the picket line, made another demand and won that one. But they dropped the first demand because they learned they were wrong. It didn't break the union; it didn't break the strike. It made a very strong union because they were intelligent. From an organizing strategy, you would never do such a thing. But we trust people to be intelligent. Well, that's not organizing, that's education. We helped them understand what the whole thing was about. And they were perfectly willing to face the fact and deal with it honestly and openly. And that's education as against organizing.

Part IV

OLSON: Okay, let's talk about something more basic. Do you have discussion groups that actually read Marx? You don't do discussion groups? It's almost all action?

HORTON: This is not a leftist-oriented, philosophical-oriented school. That's where sectarianism comes in—splitting hairs of theoretical discussion. You finally end up like the Weather Underground.[43] You finally get so esoteric and private that you have your own little world. We never go into that. That's all right on a university campus. That's where it belongs. And it never gets off the university campus, except that some people get sixty, and they're still mentally on a university campus. They don't know how to deal with workers, farmers, poor people, Indians, Chicanos, just with themselves.

OLSON: Was that true of the left in the thirties, say of the Communist party?

HORTON: The Communist Party was the only group in America that ever got big enough and strong enough that they had time for anything else. There was a period when the Communist Party had practical programs going all over the United States, where people were at. They had moved beyond theoretical discussion and were making applications. And up until the time Browder made his alliance with Roosevelt, that was true.[44] And there were people who felt the Communist Party had some good ideas and was living up to them and practicing them, and the influence they had was far beyond their members. So the Communist Party had an impact that no leftist group has ever had since. They transcended, got beyond, just college-level discussion groups of intellectuals or would-be intellectuals. And they had a lot of workers involved.

No groups now, as far as I know, have any workers. College people go ahead and get a job in a factory, but I'm talking about a working-class person. And the Communist Party actually did have working-class people. But you have to remember that they were building on the training and development of the Socialist Party[45] and the Wobblies;[46] and they gathered together people that were second-generation radicals who'd gone through there. Since then, everybody has had to start at scratch. They had people like Foster,[47] who was a Debs Socialist who had that experience and had a little orientation, had Wobbly influence. That was a big advantage ain't none of the other leftist parties have ever had.

Then, too, that was the beginning of the Russian revolution which, in contrast to the depression in America, looked perfect. And all the romanticism and excitement of having a socialist country in contrast to a capitalist country in decay, not only won over people to the Communist Party, but got a lot of people who were fellow travelers, who were sympathetic, but didn't belong. And then you had people who were not Communists, but who were committed to the same thing philosophically, who'd be willing to work on a united front basis with the Communists, even though they didn't agree on other things. So that was a different period.

We've never had any body of radicalism since then that anybody knows anything about. You can't find the average person in Knoxville who even knows any of the names of the left groups. It's a very private sort of a thing. And they all look alike. So we don't have any similar comparison.

OLSON: The reason I asked that is because my own personal evolution has been that after a recent failure in a group that I was involved in, I decided that I needed a more theoretical understanding, because I was doing a lot of action without any theoretical perspective. So I set up a study group and we read *Capital.* Our attitude was not to make Marxists of anyone but simply to understand what Marx said, and I've since discovered that Marx had a lot to say that made a lot of sense.

HORTON: Marx, more than any other person, gave me a perspective on analyzing society that's been the basis of Highlander. Highlander is a class-oriented-identified place and always has been. We've always accepted a class analysis of society, and we know where we belong. That one thing has saved a lot of headaches. During the heyday of the sixties, the student protests, when college students thought the revolution was going to come on campuses, we were delighted. We thought they'd learn something from it, although we knew that if you destroyed every university in America, it wouldn't make any difference to the system. But we thought, "That's a good education," so we didn't discourage it; we just tried to point out there'd be a need to go beyond it when we hadn't had a class analysis of society, we would have thought, "Gee, isn't this wonderful?"

OLSON: Yeah, I went through a lot of that in the sixties at the University of New Mexico and at the University of Virginia. In a way, I look at it as rediscovering a past that was blotted out by the McCarthy era and relearning a lot of things that weren't apparent to us. But that gets me to this general question that Bruce and I had worked out regarding what our overall goal should be at the Ryegrass School. I proposed that the general goal should be simply the creation of a level of awareness among the working class that they are the working class. In the Northwest, it isn't always that apparent. People know they're working people, but they don't know what it means.

HORTON: No, the majority of working people don't know they're in the working class. That's because they have no philosophy of it, no analysis.

OLSON: We were thinking our general approach should be to aim at raising their class consciousness, under the assumption that once their class consciousness is raised, once they become aware of the thing and begin to have a grasp of how to deal with it, then the next step's pretty much up to them. Does that make any sense, or is it too theoretical?

HORTON: It won't be too theoretical. Highlander, of course, formulated its philosophy during the depression. And we said our goal was to have a revolution in the United States.

"At that time," somebody said to me, "did you really say that?" And I said, "Yeah. It's in writing; it's in our statements." And they said, "*How'd* you get by with it?"

Well, what they didn't realize was that that wasn't at all a far-out sort of position to take then. There were all kinds of educators, preachers, even some politicians, some labor organizations taking that position. You saw what was happening in the Soviet Union and saw what was happening in the United States, and you could talk openly about needing a revolution, and there weren't many people who would give you a good argument.

So we formed our goal at a different time from now. You wouldn't formulate the goal now. We said, "You can't have a revolution until people support a revolution, so you've got to work with people where they are." That's your goal. Now, you can't move to your goal unless you are going to go by yourself, and I never did see much in being a brigadier general without an army 'cause I ain't about to fight the enemy by myself. So we always say, "Okay, now you have that goal. That's your lodestar. Then the other end of it is you start where the people are—wherever they are, whatever they are—and your job is to develop them in the direction of that goal." So your practical program has to deal with the problems of people as they see their problems, not as you see their problems, in the hope that you can develop them into an understanding of the class nature of society and the need for changing society.

At that time, some of us—I was one—thought we could have a revolution in my lifetime. I said either we'll have a revolution or we'll have a fascism in my lifetime. It looked like that at the time. Well, I come to realize that thanks to Roosevelt and thanks to the Communist Party—in a way, lining up with Roosevelt during the war, they made the capitalist system viable enough that people don't even think of themselves as being working-class people—the timetable has been set back. A more practical goal now would be to get people to understand that they're members of the working class, and that the working class has a historic role and that the change that's going to be brought about can't be brought about without them. I don't mean they are the only ones that can bring about change, but *nobody* can do it if *they're* against it. There's no way you could have a revolution without having a sizable body of working-class people. So you might as well concentrate on building class consciousness. That's an intermediate step, but it's probably as good as we've had since the thirties.

You know, we haven't even had a prerevolutionary stage. When we get people together here at Highlander to talk about their problems as a group for the first time and learn from each other and depend on each other and build some solidarity, I think that's the beginning of a process that could lead to revolution—and without which you can't have a revolution. That's a start. You've got to get people learning to work together instead of working individually. You've got to get rid of individualism as a motivating force and get group solidarity and some cooperative spirit. You've got to get rid of independence as a philosophy of life.

So I am very happy working with people at that stage, because I know that's where they are, and that's the first step. The next step beyond that is to get them into some kind of organization where they function on a permanent, more sustained level. But then, if you stop there, that'll re-entrench the system. You've got to think in terms of pulling these people together into some kind of alliance coalition from the bottom up that will coalesce into a movement. And social movements are not prerevolutionary. But one of the social movements, if we could get enough people educated, then they can begin to envision what could happen if everybody came together. I think those are the stages of development.

So while we started out with a stated, hopeful aim of having a revolution in this country, there never has been a time in which we've got anywhere near a prerevolutionary thing. One of my objections to the time spent in leftist, sectarian groups is that they take away the energy that might be used in building for revolution by talking about one. And spend their time fighting other sectarian groups (which may be a good thing, because they don't bother anybody else). But they aren't making any contribution. They're living in a private little world, and they get it so esoteric and split hairs so much that their privacy's guaranteed forever. They're bright, quite often very bright, very dedicated people, who could be applying that philosophy to building for a revolution instead of isolating themselves.

How People Learn

[1980]

The following are notes from a speech given in May 1980 in California. Unfortunately, the occasion for the speech has not been noted on any of the surviving copies of the notes. The title is an internal reference to Horton's philosophy that "it's more important to concern ourselves with not how we teach, but with how people learn."

Hearing all these things about Highlander—it never sounds to me like Highlander. I read these things. Actually we never set out to do these things and I think probably if we had we'd never have done them. Highlander—if we have a certain amount of recognition, it's that we never worked for it. We had more important things to do. And the important thing was to help people become liberated—you don't liberate people—people have to liberate themselves—but to help them liberate themselves so they could feel confident in developing the power and strength that goes with unity and solidarity with people against injustice and for justice, who have a cause that they believe in. What people did with that, we knew wasn't up to us. We'd have solidarity with them as they achieved more strength in the struggle for freedom, for power that they needed to get justice, but what forms that took we were less concerned with. Our job was trying to help people get going.

Somebody one time asked me why it was that we started educational programs and helped with the developing of leadership of organizations and as soon as they got going we'd turn them over, and start a new program. And I said well in a way we always felt that Highlander's job was to get people going and get out of the way before we got run over. We don't want to hold people back. Too often people who try to help things get going also want to control those groups and limit their growth.

I know education is defined in a lot of ways, but we think of ourselves not as teachers, because teaching has come to mean that people prepare themselves to present a body of information. We think it's more important to concern ourselves with not how we teach, but with how people learn. So our interest is how do people learn. If we can figure out, and insofar as we are able to figure out how people learn, then we can relate to their learning. Now that's different from saying out of our past, or out of our wisdom we've decided that there are certain things that people must learn. We've developed skills in getting that across. That requires a certain amount of understanding of how people learn but primarily only enough to be able to peddle the wares—that's the purpose of understanding people. To us, we don't have a program, we don't do any thinking that isn't based on how people learn.

And we've discovered some things—a lot of us who've been working with this—there's this great similarity, you get together and start talking. We work the same way, use the same ideas, same conceptualization of the process — and I think it's easy to account for that—like the law of gravity and you discover that law of gravity—you don't create it, you discover it, and people who discover it can do things, and people who don't discover it are liable to break their neck.

Now there are laws of learning, it seems to me, you know. And people discover it, and some people don't. If you discover it the same goes whether it's in Brazil or in China or in the Tennessee mountains, the Deep South, you know it's all the same.

And it's based primarily on the fact that people have a potential that is seldom realized, a potential for growth, a potential for love, a potential for knowledge, a potential for wisdom. Those things are only potentials in most people's lives. The potential is there, but it's dormant. And if a program can somehow wake people up, and encourage them by giving them an opportunity to act with this potential, then it's there. I mean you start with it, it's there, it's just finding a way to develop it.

But that takes faith in people; you have to love people to be interested in changing society, it takes caring, you have to care for people, it takes trust in people's ability to do things, to grow—you have to believe that—have to know it's true.

And we know it's true because we've had experiences to document the fact that it's true. Many of you have not, you know, had the privilege of seeing nothing and then something, seeing no vitality and then tremendous vitality, seeing people completely submerged by society and then to see them break that shell and grow. Once you've seen that, and experienced that, then you know you're on the right track, so you don't have any hesitancy about building on that.

Now these sound like generalities, but it's on these elements that Highlanders programs are built. They always are built around starting at the very beginning with people in a situation in which the opportunity for developing their potential is maximized.

There are some schools of people, where people can't be asked to do anything. *[Text omitted]* We reject that totally. We feel that people are completely capable of understanding the most complex ideas that you have, if you understand it well enough to explain it simply.

A Circle of Learners

[1985]

The following text contains several excerpts from an interview with Brenda Bell and John Peters conducted in 1985 for their article "Horton of Highlander," which appeared in Twentieth Century Thinkers in Adult Education. *The title used here is taken from internal references in the text and summarizes the educational philosophy that Horton outlines in this interview.*

BRENDA BELL: Where do you place yourself as an educator, Myles, in the middle of that action and analysis? You as an educator who's working with a person who's moving from action to analysis. How do you fit in as an educator, how do you—

MYLES HORTON: That's a very important question, because you've got a role to play. I think of being in a circle of learners, and I'm one of the people in that circle. And I'm different from anybody else, too. But I'm different in a way—because, well, first of all, because I convened them, therefore I'm different. They've come to Highlander. And my job is twofold: it's one, to be part of the circle of learners, and the other is to facilitate that learning process and help them understand they have experiences worth learning from—which they don't know for the most part, and I know. I know they have those experiences. And I know that unless they build on those experiences, nothing is going to happen. They don't know that, 'cause they've been told by all the authorities that "we'll tell you what to do." "Your ideas are nothing"—you know—"You don't know anything; we'll tell you. You're not an authority; we're the experts." So we have to undo that. That's the role of a person at Highlander, to undo that so they can get to have some confidence in themselves.

And, but in addition to that, in addition to having that role, then you can make a contribution from your own experience once you're accepted as far as that group. By them—as part of the group. Not as somebody in authority, not as an expert telling them what to do. You establish yourself as saying, "Look, let's analyze your experiences—talk about what you know, talk about what you've learned." You give value to them that they haven't had before, and they'll begin to say, "Well, you know . . ."; they begin to appreciate, they begin to articulate, and they begin to accept you as somebody who isn't it trying to dominate them. And then if you're careful, you can make your two cents' worth—out of your own experiences. Part of my experience is reading, and part of my experience is having done it before, and talking to people, and so on, in a way that—an experience that they haven't had, but that's my experience—and it's a legitimate experience to share. As long as I don't bring something into the circle that's alien to the process that's going on there, that's outside the experience of the group.

JOHN PETERS: What is it about authority in that sense that works against—

HORTON: Well, authority is that you know the answers and they don't—your experience is valid and theirs isn't. Authority is that you don't honor people, you don't have any respect for people, you don't respect their experiences—who they are and what they are. It's a matter of "We know, we're going to tell you. We know because somebody—who told us—and somebody, you know, told him—we don't even know where it all started but we're part of that holy line handed down." The laying on of hands, you know, the divine right of authority.

PETERS: What is it about that, though, that inhibits—

HORTON: Well, if you're going to tell people what the answers are to all their problems—you're going to solve all their problems for them—you're saying they aren't capable of solving them themselves, otherwise you wouldn't be doing it. You're demeaning them by playing the role that you are saying they can't play. And you've got to be pretty interested in playing God, you have to say what I know is God's *[illegible]*, you know. And what you know is nothing.

PETERS: And they would naturally resist that.

HORTON: No, no. Oh no, they go to it, they go to it like a duck to water, because that's what they're socialized to do.

PETERS: Then they relinquish their—

HORTON: Oh yeah, one of the problems you have is that people want us to be the experts. It's like, you know, they've been socialized to go to the experts, and they're disappointed when Highlander—when you won't tell them, you know, all the answers. And I just say very simply, "Look, have you ever gotten answers before from the experts?" And they say, "Yeah." "Have you usually found somebody who can tell you what to do?" "Yeah." "And has it worked? If it worked you wouldn't be here, you'd already know what to do." Because you'd go to the guru and they'd tell you what to do. I say, there aren't any such people—we aren't going to play that role. We're going to help you learn how to learn. And how we learn, how anybody learns. And we won't do that, just don't do that. And then they will *[illegible]* to you at first because it's a new experience, a painful experience, because they've never been allowed to trust themselves. It's not something that's welcomed with open arms, you know?

PETERS: You're walking a pretty fine line when you come in as a person who knows some things that they might want to know or think they know, to prove themselves.

HORTON: Yeah.

PETERS: But you can't come in as a person who has information that they know that's prepared and then give it to them as a report. How, then, do you walk that very thin line?

HORTON: Now, getting back to my illustration of the circle: if you're accepted in that circle—and not as an authority, but as somebody who's trying to help solve those problems without dominating it, without trying to tell them the answers, telling them all everything to do—then you can share from your experience things that are relatable, and things that are not outside the experience of the groups so they can incorporate it into their thinking and talking—and it's a welcome contribution. Now that's where you can get your ideas in. You can, if you get used to doing that, you can. You watch the conversation, you watch the discussion, and you ask questions. You got to guide the discussion, to get people thinking along those lines, and you say, "I know—I'd like to share this" with them, and you kind of get them to a place where they discuss. And this little piece of information that you have would be very useful, then you say, "Here's an experience somebody had," or "Here's something I read about," or "Here's something I thought might work or something I did,"—and just throw it in the hopper to be considered along with everything else. You don't say "This is an answer," you say, "something to be considered." And you encourage them to all do the same, too. To do the same thing.

I never had too much of a problem of sharing things that could be used. I have had all kinds of problems sharing things that wasn't any use to them. You know, that I wanted to get off my chest, or I wanted to teach them. That's a waste of your time and theirs. They can't use it.

PETERS: I'm reminded then of the whole notion of dialogue. They're talking about their experiences and yours. Brenda and I were discussing on the way up what dialogue means. I'd like to know what you think it means.

HORTON: I think that any kind of dialogue—if it means anything—if it makes any sense at all—it means that you don't have inferiors and superiors all in the same conversation. You have people who have had different experiences. You have people who know more about one thing and others know more about something else. But you respect each other's experiences and you aren't trying to use that dialogue to hornswoggle people into accepting your views, because you think it's good for people. It's a bottoms-up operation instead of a top-down operation. And it's everybody's on the same level trying to come up together.

Dialogue is impossible if you don't have genuine respect, which I've already said is based on respecting people's experiences. 'Cause that's what a person is. With that, you got to respect—you can share almost any kind of idea you have, so long as it's relevant. It's got to be relevant. What I mean by relevant, it's got to be within the scope of their understanding and experience. It can't be something that's completely off to one side. However valid it is to you.

PETERS: So you're saying that dialogue is one way for a person to check the validity of his experience with another person, and vice versa, so they can build on each other's.

HORTON: And to me, questions are a very essential part of dialogue. I've done workshops and never done anything for a week but ask questions. Never. I found over the years I can get people thinking about anything I thought would be valid, or worth doing, just by asking questions. They try to answer that question, and you ask another question. But that's a form of dialogue. But if they think you're trying to trick them or something, then you can't dialogue. If they think you're the expert, you're the authority, you kill the dialogue.

People think when I talk this way that I mean that everybody has the same level of knowledge about everything—that isn't true at all. But what I'm talking about is something that's happened at Highlander.

Before the civil rights movement, it was [the] president of Tuskeegee Institute,[48] Dr. Patterson,[49] [who had] come to a Highlander workshop on integration of public schools—that was just before the civil rights period, before the '54 decision.[50] And he had some questions about Highlander, but he was with some pretty good friends, so he decided he would come to see for himself. Well, it was a workshop in which we had some people like him: Ph.D.s, college presidents, and different levels of education. Then we had some people who were sharecroppers, some people who couldn't read or write, we had the Gullah people,[51] who we could hardly understand, so we had the whole gang—because the nature of the program was to see if we could pull together some kind of breakthrough approach to involve people in discussing this business of integrating public schools. We weren't trying to get the solutions, we were just trying to get people to talking about it—that was the operating idea.

Then Dr. Patterson made a speech later on in some college, and was telling about his experience and this was written up *[unintelligible]*[52] and he said, you know I thought Myles had scraped the barrel to get somebody, anybody, 'cause I got up there in front of these people who couldn't read or write, all these different kind of people, and I thought, now, he's had a hard time finding enough people to have a workshop, and he's got all these people here who don't have anything in common, and I felt very uncomfortable, you know, he said. I didn't know what was going on for two or three days and then suddenly I was sitting there listening to this white sharecropper from down in West Tennessee, Haywood County, and he was saying things I never dreamed of—never thought of before, about human nature and people, about being with people. My goodness—what kind of psychology is that—what [book is that] in? And I realized that it come out of his experiences. Then I knew what Highlander is about—he knew things I didn't know. While I was learning to be a college president, he was learning to live. When I was learning to be an academician, he was learning how to deal with his neighbors. So he had rich experiences that I was denied. And I was beginning to wonder what I could give to him— I knew what he could give to me.

Now it's that kind—there's a dialogue going on there, and maybe not a word is spoken, but there is an exchange of—

PETERS: Is that what produced meaning? From experience?

HORTON: Well, knowledge—I think experience produces knowledge, and knowledge produces meaning. I think you have to—as I said earlier, just to have an experience—just to *[unintelligible]*[53] happening, which we learn from—analyze—you learn from it, and it becomes knowledge. You got knowledge, and then you got a basis for making judgments and all that thing, you know.

PETERS: If we can get a little picky then: when you analyze the experience, what are you doing?

HORTON: Well, you're trying to help people mine the whole of the stuff in their experiences that are essential. That have some meaning to them in that situation. To them in that situation. It isn't generalized knowledge— it's meaningful to them. It has meaning to them. It doesn't necessarily have any social meaning—doesn't have any universal meaning.

PETERS: Does meaning in the first sense mean for them—refer to its utility?

HORTON: It could be, or it could be satisfaction, but it could be just for that person, just for that person's family.

PETERS: You mean in terms of—

HORTON: A limited sort of meaning. Now, the beauty of working with peers in a group situation is that people learn very fast just [by] analyzing that the things that have meaning to them have meaning to other people, and then you begin to have some knowledge coming out of that, and then new kinds of meaning can be built on that collective. Before you leave, if you gave a good session, they're beginning to move way beyond. They're beginning to extrapolate their experiences by combining and analyzing them, so that they themselves see far beyond where they saw when they came. And out of that grows some real knowledge, knowledge that can be transferred, be shared with other people, *[text omitted]*

PETERS: Once each individual looks critically at his own assumptions, or someone else looks at them, what are they trying to get out of that?

HORTON: Well, you don't try to get everybody. You see, I never—I'm not into everybody doing the same thing, or everybody agreeing. I just try to get enough of the people who move to that stage that they accept the tone of the discussion. And then the discussion, without bringing other people in on it, the analytical level, they get into the group discussion on that level. They might be trying to hide—to protect themselves—to be too awkward or painful to do the things to take part in the discussion.

But if you get a group process going so they—people move a little away from their own personal experience and start to [say], "Well, what can be done?" And it's kind of like a game. They begin to talk among themselves, like they're planning something, you know.

PETERS: What are they doing when they examine it that way?

HORTON: Well, what they're doing is trying to figure out how they can achieve the objective that they came to learn how to achieve. Like they try to organize a strip-mine demonstration, or [unintelligible][54] up where you [unintelligible][55] a union or get a clinic in their community—whatever it is that they're interested in. And that's what they're trying to do. They're not trying to do any educational process, 'cause they're not interested in what we're interested in here. They're interested in solving that problem.

PETERS: So they're looking at the relationship between what they believe to be the case and what they're trying to achieve.

HORTON: Yeah, what they're trying to do, yeah.

PETERS: Are they able in that way to sort out the meaningful experiences from meaningless experiences?

HORTON: Well, then they begin to say, "This will work and this won't; why does this work and why doesn't it?" And then I always say, "Well, that sounds good, does everybody feel it sounds good. But that, you know, you won't know till you try it out, you know. It looks like a good idea to me." I say, "We all seem to think it's a good idea—now let's test it and see if it works."

PETERS: That's part of the action part.

HORTON: Then you [go] back and act again. It comes out of action, and goes back into action. It's only of value if it's of value in action.

PETERS: Do you treat the dialoging as one form of that action?

HORTON: Yeah, all this is action. Action, you know, where action becomes theory is a kind of peak, and as soon as it gets there, it goes down as action. There's only as you approach the peak and start down toward action on the other side is it theory. But if you look at that, you could have a diagram of a triangle, and only the top instances would be theory, but then, in the process I'm talking about, but then if you stand back and look at it, you could cut way down on that pyramid and you could call a lot of these things theory, you see. And formulate it into some kind of a theory, and if you're not careful, you'll freeze some good ideas into a theory to make it rational and kill it, you know.

There's no difference, really, in theory and practice in the academic sense—it's all—thinking about and analyzing your practice had planning other practices, and deciding on a way of doing it that you call a theory. And where to stop it. You're talking about action, and you're going into action, and what you're doing is action, it's an intellectual—it's a group action, you see. It's all action.

[Text omitted]

See, I just—I don't claim that I don't have an influence as—in these sessions. I used to run sessions, you know, I didn't say I didn't have any influence. I just sit here and ask silly questions and chair a meeting, you know. I never claimed—I claim to be an educator. I claim to have something to share. I claim to have a goal. I claim to know what I would like for people to do. But I have sense enough to know that I couldn't get them to do it just because I'd like them to do it. I had to find a way to make them want to do it for their own reasons, and then I share my vision, my ideas with them, and they can take them or leave them. As I said before, if it makes sense to me, then I can imagine they might make sense to other people, you know. And they might be able to universalize on these ideas, just like I've universalized my own experience. I see no reason, if I can universalize on my experience, and understand these things and have concepts of, well, you know, global concepts, or concepts of a just society, who am I? Only I can think that way? I feel that's the height of absurdity. And arrogance.

You know, I think anybody is capable of learning everything I've learned if they'll all go about it and expose themselves and so on. Some of them don't want to learn it, some of them come up for the opposite side of us. That's neither here not there. But my point is, I have no problem sharing my ideas with people. Now imposing on them, you can't do. So you don't waste time doing that.

Notes

Introduction

1. Near the end of *Empowering Education: Critical Teaching for Social Change* (Chicago: University of Chicago Press, 1992), Ira Shor again mentions Horton in a brief, one-page description of how Highlander operates. However, this discussion is merely a functional description and does not address Horton's ideas about education in any detail.

2. Although Freire insists that his pedagogy cannot be reduced to an easily replicable method, that, unfortunately, has often been what has happened. For an excellent discussion of the commodification of Freire's educational ideas and their reduction into a static methodology that eviscerates the political, see Peter McLaren, *Che Guevera, Paulo Freire, and the Pedagogy of Revolution* (Boston: Rowman & Littlefield, 2000).

3. It is important to note here that Freire stresses that educators must remain nonsectarian and not impose their own ideological positions on students. Hence, I see the use of Freire's work to support a specific ideological project as a misreading and a misuse of his work. For a more detailed account of this argument, see my essay "Beginning Where They Are: A Revision of Critical Pedagogy," *Composition Studies* 25, no. 2 (fall 1997): 39–62.

4. For a more detailed account of Horton's childhood and education through to the founding of Highlander, see Myles Horton, Judith Kohl, and Herb Kohl, *The Long Haul: An Autobiography* (New York: Teachers College Press, 1998), 9–95; Myles Horton and Paulo Freire, *We Make the Road by Walking: Conversations on Education and Social Change*, ed. Brenda Bell, John Gaventa, and John Peters (Philadelphia: Temple University Press, 1990); and John Glen, *Highlander: No Ordinary School*, 2d ed. (Knoxville: University of Tennessee Press, 1996), 9–26.

5. For a full description of the significance of Ozone for Horton, see Horton, Kohl, and Kohl, *The Long Haul*, 21–24.

6. Horton was enrolled in one of Niebuhr's seminars at a propitious moment, as the lectures of that particular seminar formed the basis of Niebuhr's *Moral Man and Immoral Society: A Study in Ethics and Politics* (New York: Charles Scribner's, 1932).

7. For the full text of the letter, see Horton, Kohl, and Kohl, *The Long Haul*, 61–62.

8. For a thorough study of Highlander's involvement in the Wilder strike, as well as an exhaustive description of its work in the Labor Movement, see Glen, *Highlander,* 27–153. For a more anecdotal picture of Horton's and Highlander's work as educators with the industrial Labor Movement, see Horton, Kohl, and Kohl, *The Long Haul.*

9. The group was renamed the Congress of Industrial Organizations in 1938; it continued to be referred to as the CIO. See section I, note 5.

10. While Horton did work as an organizer and field representative at times in the late 1930s, most of Highlander's extension work was performed either by or under the supervision of Mary Lawrence. For a detailed account of this work, see Lawrence's *Education Unlimited: A Handbook on Union Education in the South* (Monteagle, Tenn.: Highlander Folk School, 1945), as well as Glen, *Highlander.*

11. For a detailed account of Highlander's split with organized labor, see Glen, *Highlander,* 104–53.

12. For a personal account of Clark's involvement with Highlander and the civil rights movement, see her autobiography, *Echo in My Soul* (New York: Dutton, 1962). See also her *Ready from Within: Septima Clark and the Civil Rights Movement,* ed. Cynthia Stokes Brown (Navarro, Calif.: Wild Trees Press, 1986).

13. For a very good description of the Citizenship Schools, see Carl Tjerandsen's *Education for Citizenship: A Foundation's Experience* (Santa Cruz, Calif.: Emil Schwarzhaupt Foundation, 1980).

14. By focusing on the United Nations and global issues, Highlander sought to link the problems in the rural South to similar problems in the international scene. Similar efforts continue today as Highlander continues to link its work to antipoverty and antiracism work in Latin American countries.

15. See section I, note 7.

Section I. The Idea of Highlander

1. The University of Tennessee in Knoxville.

2. One component of President Lyndon B. Johnson's 1964 War on Poverty, Community Action Programs were federally funded, grassroots initiatives designed to combat the sources of poverty at the local level.

3. Highlander Folk School opened in November 1932. It was originally located on a farm near Monteagle in Grundy County, Tennessee, that was owned by Dr. Lillian Johnson. Johnson, a longtime progressive educator who had been a student of John Dewey, initially allowed Horton and Don West to use the property on a one-year trial basis. Seeing that Highlander had become a part of the community, she deeded the house and forty acres of land to Highlander's directors in October 1935, despite her worries about "its reputation as a den of immoral square dancing and communism" (Glen, *Highlander,* 44). Highlander would remain near Monteagle until the state of Tennessee revoked its charter and confiscated its property in 1961.

4. In July 1933, local bugwood cutters (who became the Cumberland Mountain Workers' League) struck against the Tennessee Products Company of Nashville for higher wages and more accurate measuring procedures. The strike lasted a year and was significant because, as Glen argues, it gave "staff members their first opportunity to respond to a perceived problem within the community and develop a labor organization that could be the basis for broader reforms" (*Highlander*, 34). For more of Horton's take on this strike, see "The Highlander Folk School" and "The Community Folk School" in section II of this volume.

5. In 1937, the Committee for Industrial Organization (renamed the Congress of Industrial Organizations in 1938; merged with the American Federation of Labor in 1955) instigated an organizational drive in the South in which Highlander and its staff were important participants. Highlander hosted annual CIO Southern Schools from 1944 to 1947 and remained affiliated with the CIO until August 1953. For an excellent description of Highlander's involvement with the CIO, see Glen's *Highlander*, 104–27.

6. One of three major organizations (along with National Grange and the Farm Bureau) that represented American farmers in the twentieth century, the National Farmers' Union reflected the interests of small family farms and promoted the improvement of conditions of family farms, as well as support for people attempting to cope in a continually changing world. For a detailed description of Highlander's work with the National Farmers' Union, see Glen, *Highlander*, 128–53.

7. For more of Horton's ideas about the Citizenship Schools, see section III of this volume, especially "Citizenship Schools," and Horton, Kohl, and Kohl, *The Long Haul*. For more on Highlander's involvement in the Citizenship Schools, see Glen, *Highlander*, 185–206. For an excellent first-person account of the Citizenship Schools, see Septima Clark's *Echo in My Soul* and *Ready from Within*. For an overview of the Citizenship Schools, see Tjerandsen, *Education for Citizenship*.

8. In February 1961 the Citizenship Schools program was turned over to the Southern Christian Leadership Conference, a civil rights group founded by Martin Luther King Jr. and others in 1957.

9. The first sit-in was staged by four black students from North Carolina Agricultural and Technical College at the Woolworth lunch counter in Greensboro, North Carolina, on February 1, 1960. On April 1, 1960, Highlander held its seventh annual college workshop, titled "The New Generation Fights for Equality," the focus of which was demonstrations, college students, and the civil rights movement. Two weeks later, sit-in leaders, many of whom had participated in the Highlander workshop, met in Raleigh, North Carolina, to form the Student Nonviolent Coordinating Committee (SNCC).

10. For more on this part of Highlander's history, see Glen, *Highlander*, 207–50; Frank Adams, *Unearthing Seeds of Fire: The Idea of Highlander* (Winston-Salem, N.C.: Jon F. Blair, 1975), 190–204; and Horton, Kohl, and Kohl, *The Long Haul*, 108–12.

11. Part of the 1968 Poor People's Campaign, a multiracial coalition designed to draw attention to the issues of poverty in America, Resurrection City was erected

on the Mall in Washington, D.C., just five weeks after the assassination of Dr. Martin Luther King Jr. A collection of makeshift dwellings for poor people from across the country, Resurrection City was designed to draw attention to the needs of Poor People.

12. An outgrowth of the Council of the Southern Mountains, the Appalachian Volunteers began in 1964 as three Kentucky students working as part-time teachers. Over the next several years, the Appalachian Volunteers, influenced by their involvement with President Lyndon B. Johnson's 1964 War on Poverty, became a major antipoverty organization.

13. See note 5 above.

14. See notes 7 and 8 above.

15. Rosa Parks (b. 1913) was arrested on December 1, 1955, in Montgomery, Alabama, for not giving up her seat on a bus to a white man. Her actions sparked the subsequent Montgomery Bus Boycott. Earlier that year, Parks had attended a workshop on desegregation at Highlander. Of that experience, she said, "That was the first time in my life I had lived in an atmosphere of complete equality with the members of the other race" (Glen, *Highlander,* 162).

16. See note 9 above.

17. In 1938, Highlander and local labor groups, under the umbrella of Labor's Political Conference of Grundy County, successfully campaigned to elect a sheriff, three road commissioners, a county court clerk, and a school superintendent in Grundy County. This apparent victory quickly developed into a crisis in the fall of 1938 as the Works Progress Administration refused to cooperate with these newly elected officials, effectively undermining their authority through the withholding of funds. For a detailed account of the election and its aftermath, see Glen, *Highlander,* 59–63.

18. See note 10 above.

19. Hosea Williams (1926–2000) was a civil rights activist involved in both sit-ins and voter registration in Savannah, Georgia, in the early 1960s. Williams was one of the leaders of the Selma-to-Montgomery protest march on March 7, 1965.

20. Nikolai Frederik Severin Grundtvig (1783–1872) was an important theologian, historian, hymn writer, and educator. His ideas led to the founding of the first folk high schools in Denmark in 1844. Grundtvig argued that Danish education should focus on Danish language, history, and culture and that education should not be only for children but for life. For more, see Grundtvig's *Selected Writings* (Philadelphia: Fortress Press, 1976).

21. In 1934, Highlander attempted to help fifteen men and women establish a food cooperative. In both 1934 and 1935, the Federal Emergency Relief Administration approved grants to this cooperative, but both times the grants were withdrawn because of protests (by people such as John Edgerton, president of the Southern States Industrial Council, a group formed in 1933 to oppose perceived antibusiness

elements of President Franklin Roosevelt's New Deal) that Highlander was communist and taught "anti-American" doctrines.

22. See note 4 above.

23. The Cumberland Mountain Unemployed and Workers' League was formed in July 1934.

24. See note 17 above.

25. Instrumental in the settlement for packinghouse workers of the Austin, Minnesota Hormel Packing Plant strike in 1937, Ralph Helstein (1908–85) actively promoted greater democracy and the participation of women and minorities in the life of the union.

26. See note 6 above.

27. Esau Jenkins (1910–1972) operated a small bus line that transported black workers from Johns Island, South Carolina, to their jobs in Charleston. Convinced that getting the vote would be the most effective means for the residents of Johns Island to change their lives, Jenkins began to teach people on his bus to read and write so that they could pass South Carolina's literacy test for voter registration. In 1954, Jenkins and Septima Clark attended Highlander's workshop on the United Nations where they convinced the staff that a larger literacy program was needed on Johns Island. Over the next two years, Horton, Clark, and Jenkins planned an adult school on Johns Island that would come to be known as a Citizenship School.

28. See note 7 above.

29. The first teacher was Bernice Robinson (1914–94), a black beautician and former Highlander student. Robinson was chosen in part because she had no teaching experience, but she did have experience with the philosophy of Highlander, and in part because she was self-employed and would thus not be in danger of losing her job for teaching other blacks to read and write.

30. Southern Appalachia includes portions of Tennessee, Kentucky, North Carolina, South Carolina, Georgia, West Virginia, and Virginia.

31. A coalition of grassroots organizations such as the Appalachian Coalition, Highlander, the Council of the Southern Mountains, the Jesuit Appalachian Ministry, Save Our Cumberland Mountains, Southern Appalachian Leadership Training, and the Urban Appalachian Council, the Appalachian Alliance was formed in 1977 in response to massive flooding in Central Appalachia that left twenty thousand people homeless. The new organization sought to help individuals gain more democratic control over all aspects of their lives; to help build a unified, grassroots voice for the region; and to change public policy through direct action.

32. The Coal Employment Project was founded in 1977 in response to the consistent pattern of discrimination against women in the coal mining industry.

33. A meeting of popular adult educators from both North America (the North American Alliance for Popular and Adult Education) and Latin America (the Latin

American Council for Adult Education) took place at Highlander March 25–27, 1983. In attendance from Latin America were popular educators Francisco Vio Grossi of Chile, Felix Cadena of Mexico, Ernesto Viacillos from Nicaragua.

34. Mike Clark was director of Highlander from 1972 to 1982.

35. A top aide to Martin Luther King Jr. and vice president of the Southern Christian Leadership Conference, Andrew Young (b. 1932) served a Democrat from Georgia in the House of Representatives from 1973 to 1977 and then as ambassador to the United Nations from 1977 to 1979. From 1982 to 1990, Young served as mayor of Atlanta. For Young's first-person account of the civil rights period, see Eliot Wigginton, *Refuse to Stand Silently By: An Oral History of Grassroots Social Activism in America, 1921–64* (New York: Doubleday, 1992).

36. In 1927, Horton directed a vacation bible school for the Presbyterian Church in Ozone, Tennessee. During his stay there, Horton realized the necessity for a meaningful educational program for the adults of the community in which they could learn to solve their own problems. For the next five years, until the founding of Highlander, Ozone became a reference point for Horton as he attempted to work out his educational ideas. For a more thorough account, see Horton, Kohl, and Kohl, *The Long Haul.*

37. Horton met Mortensen and Møller at a folk dance at a Danish Lutheran church in Chicago in 1931. Begun in 1844, folk high schools derived from the ideas of Bishop Grundtvig.

38. For more on these efforts, see J. F. Kett's *The Pursuit of Knowledge under Difficulties: From Self-Improvement to Adult Education in America, 1750—1990* (Stanford, Calif.: Stanford University Press, 1994).

39. The Living Word was a concept based on Grundtvig's ideas about education for life. Grundtvig felt that Danish education should be based in Danish culture and history and that it should include both reflection and attention to the spiritual. He felt that these educational goals could best be attained through the oral tradition, or words spoken by living human beings—the Living Word—rather than through the study of written texts, which Grundtvig considered "dead."

40. Grundtvig's idea of education for life (*livsupplysing*), based on Danish culture and history and aimed at liberation from cultural oppression, undergirds the concept of Schools for Life.

41. The 1840s in Denmark saw the rise of both the National Liberals, who opposed absolute monarchy, and the Peasant movement. The combined pressures of these groups led to the formation of the National Constitutional Assembly in October 1848 and the signing of Denmark's first constitution in June 1849. For more on the role of the folk schools in this period, see Steven M. Borish's *The Land of the Living: Danish Folk High Schools and Denmark's Nonviolent Path to Modernization* (Nevada City, Calif.: Blue Dolphin Publishing, 1991).

42. Elsinore is located on the northeast coast of Denmark.

43. Esjberg is located on the southwest coast of Denmark.

44. Peter Manniche (1889–1981) founded the International People's College in Elsinore, Denmark, and was a lifelong advocate of international understanding. For more on his ideas, see his *Living Democracy in Denmark* (Copenhagen, Denmark: Greenwood Press, 1952).

45. Lyngby is located just outside Copenhagen.

46. See "Christmas Night, 1931, Copenhagen, Denmark," in section I of this volume.

47. Paul Johannes Tillich (1886–1965), a German American philosopher and theologian, focused his work on the religious and spiritual basis of life. His many books include *The Courage to Be* (New York: Yale Univ. Press, 1952), and *Systematic Theology* (Chicago: Univ. of Chicago Press, 1967).

48. On May 17, 1954, the Supreme Court announced its decision in the case of *Brown v. the Board of Education of Topeka, Kansas*. Its ruling stated that "separate educational facilities are inherently unequal," effectively ending the practice of segregated education in many states.

49. See note 27 above.

50. See notes 7 and 8 above.

51. See note 15 above.

52. Edgar Daniel Nixon (1899–1987) was the head of the Alabama Chapter of the National Association for the Advancement of Colored People at the time of the Montgomery Bus Boycott and played an instrumental role in that action.

53. Virginia Durr (1903–99) was one of the founders of the Southern Conference for Human Welfare, an interracial group of Southern progressives formed to challenge racial segregation and poverty in the South. She was heavily involved throughout the civil rights movement. Clifford Durr (1899–1975) was a prominent civil rights lawyer and activist. Together the Durrs posted bail for Rosa Parks after she was arrested for refusing to give up her seat to a white man on a Montgomery, Alabama, bus in December 1955. For more on Clifford Durr's career as a civil rights lawyer, see John Salmond's *The Conscience of a Lawyer: Clifford J. Durr and American Civil Liberties, 1899–1975* (Tuscaloosa: Univ. of Alabama Press, 1990).

54. See Glen, *Highlander*, 52–53, for a more detailed account.

55. Under pressure from Arkansas Attorney General Bruce Bennett, the Tennessee State Legislature appointed a committee to investigate Highlander. See Glen, *Highlander*, 221–29, for more on this investigation.

56. James Oliver Eastland (1904–86) was first elected to the Senate in 1941 and by 1954 was the ranking Democrat on the Senate Subcommittee on Internal Security. He used his position to attempt to "expose those who promoted racial equality as subversives" so that "he could demolish whatever influence they had in the South and block desegregation of the public schools" (Glen, *Highlander*, 209–10). To these

ends, Eastland investigated both the Southern Conference Educational Fund, an arm of the Southern Conference for Human Welfare, and Highlander, as well as other groups.

57. Horton married Zilphia Mae Johnson (1910–56) on March 6, 1935; they had two children—Thorsten and Charis. An active member of the Highlander staff from 1935 until her sudden death in 1956, Zilphia Horton was especially influential in Highlander's music and drama programs. For a more detailed look at Zilphia Horton's contributions to Highlander, see Vicki K. Carter's essay "The Singing Heart of Highlander Folk School," *New Horizons in Adult Education* 8, no. 2 (spring 1994): 4–24.

58. Members of the CIO food and tobacco workers' union adapted "We Shall Overcome," which originally had been a Baptist hymn, for use of the picket line during a 1945 strike in Charleston, South Carolina.

59. See the Zilphia Horton Folk Music Collection at the Tennessee State Library and Archives in Nashville, Tennessee.

60. Septima Clark (1898–1987), a teacher from Johns Island, South Carolina, first came to Highlander as a workshop participant in 1954. Having been involved in the initial push for what became the citizenship program in Johns Island (see note 27 above), Clark was a natural choice to join the staff of Highlander. She remained until 1961 when she joined the Southern Christian Leadership Conference as Educational Director for the Citizenship School Program that had just been turned over to them by Highlander.

61. The Voting Rights Act of 1965 gave the attorney general of the United States the power to examine states' voting lists and register voters, effectively ending the use of literacy tests by states to exclude black voters.

62. See note 11 above.

63. See note 11 above.

64. For twenty years the residents along Yellow Creek in Middlesburg, Kentucky, had complained about the air and water quality after experiencing abnormally high rates of kidney infections, miscarriages, and other medical problems. Despite these complaints, the State of Kentucky insisted that there were insufficient grounds for it to act against the city. In researching their situation, the Yellow Creek Concerned Citizens discovered in 1981 that about one-quarter of the waste handled by the Middlesburg sewage treatment plant came from the Middlesburg Tanning Company and that there were very high levels of chromium and lead present in the water. A $31 million class-action suit was launched in 1983.

65. Ed Hunter, a member of the Yellow Creek Concerned Citizens.

66. Probably John Gaventa, who later served as director of Highlander from 1989 to 1993.

67. Interviews were originally conducted by Eliot Wigginton and Sue Thrasher for a volume commemorating Highlander's fiftieth anniversary. It was published in 1992 as *Refuse to Stand Silently By: An Oral History of Grassroots Social Activism in America, 1921–1964,* edited by Eliot Wigginton.

68. See note 27 above.

69. Paulo Freire (1921–97) was a Brazilian critical educator who developed ideas of critical consciousness, dialogue, and education as a way of defeating oppression in his work with Brazilian peasants. Freire saw literacy as a way for people to read and write not only the word, but their worlds as well. Freire's many books include *Pedagogy of Freedom: Ethics, Democracy, and Civic Courage* (Boston: Rowman & Littlefield, 1998); *Education for Critical Consciousness,* trans. Myra Bergman Ramos (New York: Seaberry Press, 1973); and *Pedagogy of Hope: Reliving Pedagogy of the Oppressed,* trans. Robert R. Barr (New York: Continuum Publishing, 1994). He also collaborated on a book with Horton entitled *We Make the Road by Walking: Conversations on Education and Social Change,* ed. Brenda Bell, John Gaventa, and John Peters (Philadelphia: Temple University Press, 1990).

70. Primarily a Latin American movement, liberation theology stresses the necessity of the church's involvement in the fight for economic and political justice in an attempt to liberate people from poverty and oppression. It is based on the idea that a better life should be available for people while on this earth and not just in the next life. For more on liberation theology, see Leonardo and Clodovis Boff's *Introducing Liberation Theology* (Maryknoll, N.Y.: Orbis Books, 1987), and Gustavo Gutierrez's *A Theology of Liberation: History, Politics, and Salvation,* trans. Caridad Inda and John Eagleson (Maryknoll, N.Y.: Orbis Books, 1988).

71. Christian socialism is based on the idea that socialism is a direct outcome of Christian ideas and that for it to be successful, it must be based on Christian principles. For more on Christian socialism, see John C. Cort's *Christian Socialism: An Informal History* (Maryknoll, N.Y.: Orbis Books, 1988).

72. See note 5 above.

73. Saul Alinsky (1909–72) was a noted community activist and labor organizer. For more on his ideas, see his books, *Reveille for Radicals* (New York: Vintage Books, 1969) and *Rules for Radicals: A Practical Primer for Realistic Radicals* (New York: Random House, 1971).

74. Horton, Kohl, and Kohl, *The Long Haul.*

75. This is probably a reference to the Tennessee Higher Education Commission.

76. See note 69 above.

77. The Bread Loaf Rural Teachers Network is a national organization sponsored by the Bread Loaf School of English at Middlebury College. The Bread Loaf Rural Teachers Network sponsors summer fellowships for teachers to engage in graduate study and train with technology.

Section II. The Labor Movement

1. League for Industrial Democracy. The LID was formed in 1905 by Socialists including authors Jack London and Upton Sinclair for the purpose of educating young people about socialism and socialist thought.

2. American Federation of Labor. First organized as the Federation of Organized Trades and Labor Unions in 1881, the AFL officially came into existence in 1886. A loose federation of autonomous craft unions, the AFL was opposed to the socialist leanings of other unions and remained largely out of party politics. In 1955, the AFL merged with the Congress of Industrial Organizations.

3. For more on Horton's conception of the Danish Folk High Schools, see "Influences on Highlander Research and Education Center, New Market, Tennessee, USA," in section I of this volume.

4. Reinhold Niebuhr (1892–1971) was a prominent American theologian whose work focused on the interrelationship between religion, individuals, and society. Niebuhr taught at Union Theological Seminary in New York from 1928 to 1960; Horton was one of his students in 1929. A longtime supporter of Highlander, Niebuhr wrote the first fund-raising letter for the school in 1932, which was also signed by Sherwood Eddy, Norman Thomas, Arthur L. Swifts, and George S. Counts. Niebuhr's books include *Moral Man and Immoral Society; Interpretation of Christian Ethics* (New York: Harper, 1935); and *The Nature and Destiny of Man*, 2 vols. (New York: Charles Scribner's, 1941). For accounts of Niebuhr's influence on Horton and involvement with Highlander, see Glen, *Highlander*, 16–22; Horton, Kohl, and Kohl, *The Long Haul*, 46–25; and the introduction to this volume.

5. George S. Counts (1907–74) taught at Teacher's College, Columbia University from 1927 to 1955, where he became known for his work on the social foundations of education and comparative international education, especially for his work on education in the Soviet Union. He served at president of the American Federation of Teachers from 1939 to 1942 and was one of the group of supporters who signed the first fund-raising letter for Highlander (see note 8 above for a full list). Counts's many books include *The Principles of Education* (with J. Crosby Chapman) (Boston: Houghton Mifflin, 1924); *Education and American Civilization* (Westport, Conn.: Greenwood Press, 1974); and *Education and the Foundations of Human Freedom* (Pittsburgh: University of Pittsburgh Press, 1962).

6. Norman Mattoon Thomas (1884–1968) took over the leadership of the American Socialist Party after the death of Eugene Debs in 1926. Thomas was the Socialist Party's nominee for president six times between 1928 and 1948. An active supporter of Highlander, Thomas was one of the signatories to the school's first fund-raising letter (see note 4 above for a full list). His many books include *A Socialist's Faith* (New York: Norton, 1951).

7. Horton probably means Mary Abby Van Kleeck (1883–1972), an American social researcher and reformer whose work as director of the Russell Sage Foundation's

Department of Industrial Studies focused mainly on labor conditions, especially among female factory workers and child laborers, helped bring about legislative reform. Her books include *Mines and Management: A Study of the Collective Agreement between the United Mine Workers of America and the Rocky Mountain Fuel Company* (New York: Russell Sage, 1934) and *Creative America Creative America: Its Resources for Social Security* (New York: Friede, 1936).

8. The Wilder, Tennessee, strike began in the summer of 1932 when two of the area's largest mines announced that they would not renew their contracts with the United Mine Workers of America unless its members took a 20 percent cut in pay. By the summer of 1933, several of the mines had closed permanently and there was little hope for a settlement. The miners and their families were in desperate straits by this time, and in the fall of 1933, efforts were made to secure them alternative employment. The Wilder strike, however, was important for Highlander because it provided a real-life problem around which the school could work in the early period of its existence, as well as providing the school with a high degree of visibility. For a detailed discussion of the Wilder strike, see Glen, *Highlander,* 29–32.

9. See Glen, *Highlander,* 29–32, for more on the violence associated with the Wilder strike.

10. See section I, note 4.

11. See note 2 above.

12. Between 1937 and 1941, Highlander was significantly involved in the educational programs of the southern labor movement. For more on Highlander's educational connections to various unions, see Glen, *Highlander,* 27–153.

13. In 1936, Highlander staff members included Myles Horton, Zilphia Horton, Ralph Tefferteller, James Dombrowski, Elizabeth Hawes, and Ruth Catlin.

14. For a detailed account of this strike and Highlander's involvement with Hosiery Workers unions during this period, see Glen, *Highlander,* 43–44.

15. For more on the first year of Highlander, see Glen, *Highlander,* 23–35, and Horton, Kohl, and Kohl, *The Long Haul,* 58–70.

16. Henry Thomas.

17. See section I, note 4.

18. National Industrial Recovery Act of 1933. The NIRA was designed to aid the nation's recovery during the depression through expenditures on public works. Section 7A of the NIRA was controversial as it made its way through legislative channels because it involved the protection of workers from pressure of antiunion employers and exempted them from having to join company unions.

19. Civilian Conservation Corps. Established in 1933 as part of President Franklin Roosevelt's New Deal, the Civilian Conservation Corps was designed to conserve the natural resources of the country and provide employment and training for rural young men aged seventeen to twenty-three who were out of work because of the depression.

20. Frances Perkins (1882–1965) became the first female member of cabinet in the United States when President Franklin Roosevelt named her secretary of labor in 1933.

21. Federal Emergency Relief Administration. For more information on this cooperative initiative, see section I, note 21.

22. John Emmett Edgerton (1879–1938), a textile manufacturer from Lebanon, Tennessee, served as president of both the National Association of Manufacturers and the Tennessee Manufacturers Association. He was also the founder of the Southern States Industrial Council.

23. Tennessee Valley Authority. A federal corporation created in 1933, the Tennessee Valley Authority was charged with operating the Wilson Dam and developing the Tennessee River and its tributaries in the areas of electricity production, flood control, and navigation.

24. Works Progress Administration. Established in 1935 to take the place of the Federal Emergency Relief Administration, the WPA was designed to put unemployed people to work on public projects during the depression.

25. Founded in 1869 as a secret fraternal order, the Knights of Labor was the first labor organization in Canada or the United States to advocate that all workers should be organized into one union. In 1881, the secret and fraternal nature of the organization was eliminated and in 1917 the Knights of Labor formally dissolved.

26. Probably *Gumbo*, a play written by Highlander students in 1937.

27. In 1938, Highlander staff members included Myles Horton, Zilphia Horton, Ralph Tefferteller, James Dombrowski, William Buttrick, Mary Lawrence, and Claudia Lewis.

28. Probably Mary Lawrence.

29. See note 9 above.

30. On July 12, 1935, a statewide rally of the American Legion was held in Monteagle, Tennessee, the purpose of which was to intimidate Highlander. For more details about the events leading up to this rally, see Glen, *Highlander*, 51–54.

31. Charles Austin Beard (1874–1948) was an American historian who focused on the connections between economic interests and politics, especially in books such as *An Economic Interpretation of the Constitution* (New York: Macmillan, 1956); *Economic Origins of Jeffersonian Democracy* (New York: Macmillan, 1949); and *The Economic Basis of Politics* (New York: Vintage Books, 1957).

32. Mahatma Mohandas Karamchand Gandhi (1869–1948) was a nationalist leader of India who espoused nonviolent resistance and revolution. For more on Gandhi's thought, see his book *An Autobiography: The Story of My Experiments with Truth*.

33. John Dewey (1859–1952) was an influential progressive educator often associated with pragmatism. He asserted the need to begin with students' own experience as a way to create citizens for democracy and to make schools agents of social

reform. His many books include *Experience and Nature* (Chicago: Open Court, 1925); *How We Think* (Boston: D.C. Heath & Co., 1910); *Democracy and Education: An Introduction to the Philosophy of Education* (New York: Free Press, 1997); and *Experience and Education* (New York: Macmillan, 1938).

34. The National Education Association, an association of all levels of teachers, administrators, and other educators, was founded in 1857 as the National Teachers Association. In 1870, it amalgamated with the National Association of School Superintendents and the American Normal School Association to form the National Education Association. The purpose of the NEA is to further the cause of public education.

35. For a more detailed account, see Glen, *Highlander.*

36. All other sources place this number at seventy-five cents per hour.

37. See note 20 above.

38. See section I, note 17.

39. Glen suggests that this was a tricounty effort involving Grundy, Marion, and Franklin Counties. *Highlander,* 60.

40. Cas Walker (1902–98) was the controversial owner of a chain of supermarkets in Knoxville, Tennessee, where he was also a longtime member of city council. He was also the publisher of the *Watchdog* newspaper in Knoxville.

41. The *Watchdog* billed itself as "The All American Paper for the All American City" and was vehemently opposed to Highlander.

42. See section I, note 36.

43. See section I, note 12.

44. In Boone, North Carolina, it is now named Appalachian State University.

45. See section I, note 4.

46. It is unclear as to what Horton is referring in this passage. FCCA most commonly stands for Federal Court Clerks Association or Forestry Conservation Communications Association.

47. *People of the Cumberland* was a 1938 documentary by Elia Kazan, Robert Stebbins, and Eugene Hill.

48. Probably the Richmond Hosiery Mills strike.

49. See section I, note 17.

50. During 1937, Horton worked as a full-time organizer for the Textile Workers Organizing Committee. For a detailed account of this period, see Glen, *Highlander,* 84–92.

51. While Horton worked for the Textile Workers Organizing Committee, other staff members organized an educational program for striking workers of the Amalgamated Clothing Workers of America in La Follette, Tennessee.

52. See section I, note 9.

53. The 1934 Harriman Hosiery Mills strike.

54. See note 23 above.

55. The University of Tennessee at Knoxville.

56. Samuel Marvin Griffin (1907–82) served as governor of Georgia from 1955 to 1959, having previously served as lieutenant governor of Georgia (1948–55).

57. See section I, note 10.

58. This comment is probably a reference to the frequent attacks on Highlander from 1965 to 1968 by the Ku Klux Klan while the school was located in Knoxville. See Glen, *Highlander,* 256–57, for a more detailed account.

59. Sen. James Eastland. See section I, note 56.

60. See section I, note 5.

61. See note 12 above.

62. One of the major English Romantic poets, Percy Bysshe Shelley (1792–1822) is best known for poems such as "Ozymandias," "To the West Wind," and "Adonais," as well as the verse drama *Prometheus Unbound* and critical treatise *A Defence of Poetry.* For more on Shelley's influence on Horton, see Horton, Kohl, and Kohl, *The Long Haul,* 29–31.

63. Horton attended Cumberland Presbyterian College (later Cumberland University) in Lebanon, Tennessee, from 1924 to 1928.

64. The Fourth Amendment concerns protection against unreasonable search and seizure.

65. The Fifth Amendment states that no person shall be compelled to testify against himself or herself.

66. Zilphia. See section I, note 57.

67. Horton's picture appears on the front page of the Sunday, March 21, 1954, edition of the *New York Times.*

68. Ronald Reagan (b. 1911) first came to prominence as a film actor and then, in 1967, as governor of California. He served as president of the United States from 1981 to 1989.

69. See note 4 above.

70. Abram Nightingale was the minister of the Congregational Church in Crossville, Tennessee. Horton credits Nightingale for pushing him to attend Union Theological Seminary in New York. For more, see Horton, Kohl, and Kohl, *The Long Haul,* 31–32.

71. From 1915 to 1928, Niebuhr was the pastor of the Bethel Evangelical Church of Detroit, a post he held until he left for Union Theological Seminary in New York.

72. During 1929–30, a wave of strikes occurred among the textile workers in Elizabethton, Tennessee, over issues of wages and working conditions. For a detailed account of this period of labor history, see *Like a Family: The Making of a Southern Cotton Mill World* by Jacquelyn Dowd Hall et al. (Chapel Hill: Univ. of North Carolina Press, 1987).

73. The Watauga settlement was first established in the early 1770s in the valley between the Great Smoky Mountains on the east and the Cumberland Mountains on the west.

74. See note 8 above.

75. Grundy County, Tennessee.

76. Henry Hollis Horton (1866–1934) was governor of Tennessee from 1927 to 1933.

77. See note 50 above.

Section III. The Civil Rights Movement

1. Thorstein Bunde Veblen (1857–1929) was an American economist and social scientist noted for his investigations of the economic structure of society. He is most famous for his book *The Theory of the Leisure Class: An Economic Study of Institutions* (New York: Modern Library, 1934).

2. Aubrey Williams (1890–1965) was the head of the National Youth Administration, a New Deal program designed to employ urban youth; it was the urban counterpart to the Civilian Conservation Corps. He was later president of the Southern Conference Educational Fund. For more on Williams, see John Salmond's *A Southern Rebel: The Life and Times of Aubrey Williams, 1890–1965* (Chapel Hill: Univ. of North Carolina Press, 1982).

3. See section II, notes 18, 19, and 24.

4. See section I, note 27.

5. Septima Clark. See section I, note 60.

6. The Savannah Voters Crusade of the early 1960s was led by Hosea Williams. See section I, note 19.

7. Probably Madison County, Alabama.

8. Esau Jenkins. See section I, note 27.

9. Bernice Robinson. See section I, note 29.

10. Lane College is located in Jackson, Tennessee.

11. Lewis Wade Jones (1910–79) was a professor of sociology at the Tuskegee Institute in Tuskegee, Alabama.

12. See section I, note 9.

13. See section I, note 15.

14. A United Methodist Minister, James Lawson (b. 1928) was involved in the Southern Christian Leadership Conference from its earliest days, later serving for fourteen years as its president. Lawson was also one of the architects of the strategy of nonviolent resistance.

15. Note in original text: "An annual gathering of educational leaders from all over the U.S. where issues of the day are informally discussed."

16. An umbrella organization of civil rights groups working in Mississippi, the Council of Federated Organizations was organized in 1962 by Robert Moses of the Student Nonviolent Coordinating Committee. The purpose of COFO was to unite the civil rights groups and ensure that they were working toward a common goal.

17. The Mississippi Freedom Democratic Party (MFDP) was formed in 1964 as a challenge to the all-white regular Democratic party in the state of Mississippi. The MFDP sent a delegation of sixty-eight to the Democratic National Convention in Atlantic City in the summer of 1964 and claimed that they wanted to represent all people, unlike the regular Democratic party of Mississippi, which had voted to reject the national party platform in the area of civil rights.

18. The 1964 Mississippi Summer Project or Freedom Summer involved voter registration; Freedom Schools for both elementary and advanced students in subjects such as reading, math, political science, humanities, journalism, and creative writing; a research project into the political and economic life of Mississippi; a White Community Project designed to organize poor whites and help eliminate bigotry; and a Law Student Project designed to launch a series of legal attacks against official forms of segregation and oppression. For a more detailed account, see Len Holt's *The Summer that Didn't End : The Story of the Mississippi Civil Rights Project of 1964* (New York: Morrow, 1965).

19. Robert Moses (b. 1935) became a Freedom Rider in 1961 in an effort to integrate bus service in the South through nonviolent resistance. Moses later became a leader of the Student Nonviolent Coordinating Committee and the main organizer of the 1964 Mississippi Summer Project.

20. Horton married Aimee Isgrig, executive director of the Illinois Commission on Human Relations, in 1961.

21. On March 7, 1965, approximately six hundred civil rights activists marched east out of Selma on U.S. Route 80. Six blocks away, at the Edmund Pettus Bridge, they were attacked by state and local lawmen with billy clubs and tear gas and forced back to Selma. Two days later, Martin Luther King Jr. led a symbolic march to the bridge entrance. King and other civil rights leaders used the courts to ensure that they would be able to hold a third, full-scale march from Selma to Montgomery. On March 21, 1965, 3,200 people set out from Selma. By the time the march reached Montgomery on March 25, the number of marchers had swelled to 25,000. For a more detailed account, see Charles Fager's *Selma, 1965: The March that Changed the South* (Boston: Beacon Press, 1985).

22. Founded as the Normal School for Colored Teachers in Tuskegee, Alabama, the school was known as the Tuskegee Institute from 1937 to 1985. Its name was changed to Tuskegee University in 1985.

23. Established in 1911 by the will of Caroline Phelps Stokes, the Phelps-Stokes fund is a nonprofit foundation whose guiding motto is "Education for Human Development."

24. *Brown* v. *Board of Education,* 1954. See section I, note 48.

25. See section I, note 6.

26. Renowned in the field of adult education, Malcolm S. Knowles (1913–97) wrote *The Modern Practice of Adult Education: Andragogy Versus Pedagogy* (New York: Association Press, 1970). Bracketed information appears in the original.

27. Members of the John Birch Society. The John Birch Society was founded in 1958 to oppose what they saw as the subversive spread of Communism within the United States.

28. Bracketed information appears in the original.

29. See section I, note 73.

30. For a detailed history of attacks on Highlander, see Glen, *Highlander;* Adams, *Unearthing Seeds of Fire;* and Horton, Kohl, and Kohl, *The Long Haul.*

31. On June 21, 1964, three civil rights workers, Andrew Goodman, James Chaney, and Michael Schwerner, were arrested for speeding and then disappeared. On August 4, their bodies were found; James Chaney, an African American, had been severely beaten. In December 1964, nineteen white men, including the sheriff of Neshoba County, were arrested, but the charges were later dropped.

32. See section I, notes 10 and 55.

33. The University of the South is located in Sewanee, Tennessee.

34. In 1925, John T. Scopes (1900–1970), a Dayton, Tennessee, teacher, was accused of violating the Butler Act, a Tennessee law that prohibited teaching the theory of evolution because it contradicted the Bible. Scopes was represented by Clarence Darrow (1857–1938), who argued for the scientific validity of evolution and against the constitutionality of the Butler Act. Scopes was convicted, but the verdict was later overturned on technical grounds by the state supreme court.

35. See section I, note 15.

36. See section I, note 52.

37. National Association for the Advancement of Colored People.

38. In December 1955, the Montgomery Improvement Association was formed to organize the efforts of the Montgomery Bus Boycott and other civil rights activities. Martin Luther King Jr. was selected as president of the organization.

39. See section I, note 9.

40. Probably a reference to Broadside Press, which was founded in 1965 by Dudley Randall (1914–2000). Based in Detroit, Broadside Press published writers such as

Gwendolyn Brooks, Nikki Giovanni, Audre Lorde, Sonia Sanchez, Alice Walker, and LeRoi Jones.

41. President Lyndon B. Johnson's 1964 War on Poverty.

42. See note 18 above.

43. Begun in 1965, Head Start is a federally funded child development program for low-income children and their families.

44. An offshoot of the Mississippi Freedom Democratic Party, the Poor People's Corporation was a network of small manufacturing cooperatives.

45. Mississippi Freedom Democratic Party. See note 17 above.

46. Founded in 1919 as the Commission on Interracial Cooperation, the Southern Regional Council focuses on issues of race, democracy, and civic participation.

47. The Voter Education Project was a program launched in 1962 and run under the auspices of the Southern Regional Council, but coordinated with groups such as the National Association for the Advancement of Colored People, the Congress of Racial Equality, and the Student Nonviolent Coordinating Committee. The Southern Regional Conference ran the Voter Education Project from 1962 to 1969. In 1970, the Voter Education Project became a separate entity and remained so until is was discontinued in 1992.

48. A prominent labor leader, Asa Philip Randolph (1889–1979) organized the Brotherhood of Sleeping Car Porters in 1925, the first union of primarily black workers to be recognized by the American Federation of Labor. Randolph was later one of the organizers of the 1963 March on Washington.

49. Stokely Carmichael (1941–98), later known as Kwame Toure, became a Freedom Rider in 1961, and in 1964 he became a member of the Student Nonviolent Coordinating Committee, of which he became chairman in 1966. He coined the term Black Power and later joined the Black Panther Party, contradicting his earlier stance on nonviolent resistance.

50. John Llewellyn Lewis (1880–1969) was president of the United Mine Workers of America from 1920 to 1960.

51. In July 1966, the National Association of Negro Churchmen issued its statement on Black Power.

52. Julius Lester (b. 1939) was the head of the Photographic Department of the Student Nonviolent Coordinating Committee. He later became a renowned children's author, publishing such books as *To Be a Slave,* which was a Newberry Honor Book in 1969.

53. Guy Carawan (b. 1927) became musical director at Highlander in 1959 and remained in that capacity until 1987. He and Candie Carawan were instrumental in the use of music in the Civil Rights movement; they remain active as consultants to Highlander in the area of music and social change.

54. A renowned African American journalist, Carl Thomas Rowan (1925–2000) is the author of eight books, including *South of Freedom* (New York: Knopf, 1952), the book to which Horton refers here; *Dream Makers, Dream Breakers: The World of Justice Thurgood Marshall* (Boston: Little, Brown, 1993); and *Breaking Barriers: A Memoir* (Boston: Little, Brown, 1991).

55. See section I, note 60.

56. See note 2 above.

57. Appointed United States Judge for the Eastern District of South Carolina in 1941, Julius Waties Waring (1880–1968) went on to hand down several controversial decisions in favor of civil rights, most notably in his decision to effectively strike down the all-white Democratic primary in South Carolina. For a more detailed account of Waring's life and work, see Tinsley E. Yarbrough's *Passion for Justice: J. Waties Waring and Civil Rights* (New York: Oxford University Press, 2002).

58. The conference was called "The Negro: Assimilation in a Democratic Culture" and was held at Amherst College. See "The Place of Whites in the Civil Rights Movement" in this volume for the text of Horton's speech at this conference.

59. Trained in social work at the University of Mississippi, Whitney Moore Young Jr. (1921–71) was in 1961 named director of the National Urban League, a group founded in 1910 to promote economic self-reliance and civil rights for African Americans. In 1963, he helped organize the March on Washington.

60. Kenneth Bancroft Clark (b. 1941) was the first African American to hold a permanent professorship at the City University of New York; he taught there from 1942 to 1975. In 1950, Clark authored a report on racial discrimination that was cited in the 1954 U.S. Supreme Court decision in the case of *Brown* v. *Board of Education*. His books include *Dark Ghetto: Dilemmas of Social Power* (New York: Harper & Row, 1965) and *Pathos of Power* (New York: Harper & Row, 1974).

61. A member of the Student Nonviolent Coordinating Committee, Ivanhoe Donaldson became a principal advisor to Marion Barry from the late 1960s on and, in 1984, an advisor to Jesse Jackson's campaign for the presidency.

62. See note 21 above.

63. The 1963 March on Washington.

64. See section I, note 15.

65. See note 49 above.

66. See note 17 above.

67. Founded in 1966 by Huey Newton and Bobby Seale, the Black Panther Party was a militant black political organization that advocated black self-defense and a radical restructuring of American society to make it more economically, politically, and socially equal.

68. See note 18 above.

69. See note 44 above.

70. The Southern Conference Educational Fund was the educational arm of the Southern Conference for Human Welfare (SCHW) and a strong opponent of segregation in the South. For more on the connections between Highlander and both the SCEF and the SCHW, see Glen, *Highlander,* 207–29.

71. Founded in 1913 as the Conference of Southern Mountain Workers, the Council of the Southern Mountains, though often criticized as conservative throughout its history, began to take positions on issues such as strip mining, welfare, and community control of programs in the 1960s.

72. See section I, note 12.

73. This organization was actually called the Congress for Appalachian Development. Formed in 1966 at a meeting organized by Harry Caudill and E. S. Fraley, the Congress for Appalachian Development was constituted to conserve and develop the natural and human resources of the Appalachian region and to promote Appalachian self-government.

74. Trained as a lawyer, Harry Caudill (1922–90) wrote several books about the extreme poverty and exploitation of the Appalachian region, including *Night Comes to the Cumberlands: A Biography of a Depressed Area* (Boston: Little, Brown, 1963) and *My Land Is Dying* (New York: E. P. Dutton, 1971).

75. I have been unable to find any references to the Southern Mountain Project at either the Highlander archives or in the papers at the State Historical Society of Wisconsin.

76. Antioch and Goddard were two of the self-proclaimed experimental and progressive colleges of the 1920s and 1930s, along with Black Mountain, Sarah Lawrence, Bennington, and Bard.

77. Dr. Royce Stanley ("Tim") Pitkin (1901–86) earned his Ph.D. at Columbia University, where he became very influenced by ideas of progressive education and the Danish Folk High Schools. Pitkin was the founding president of Goddard College, a post he held until 1969.

78. The Glenmary Sisters were founded in Glendale, Ohio, in 1941 by Father William Howard Bishop. The Glenmary Sisters work primarily in the rural South.

79. I have been unable to find any references to the Appalachian People's Congress at either the Highlander archives or in the papers at the State Historical Society of Wisconsin.

80. See note 49 above.

81. See section I, note 11.

82. Dr. Morris Mitchell was the first president of the Friends World Institute (now called the Friends World Program), which was founded in 1965 at the New York yearly meeting of the Society of Friends. Mitchell shared many ideas with Horton, including an emphasis on experiential and problem-solving approaches to education.

83. See note 17 above.

84. President Lyndon B. Johnson's 1964 War on Poverty.

85. See section I, note 69.

86. José Julian Martí (1853–95) was a Cuban writer of both poetry and political prose. His death during a battle with Spanish troops made him a martyr to Cuban hopes of independence.

87. See section I, note 27.

88. Freire was exiled from Brazil in 1964.

89. See section I, note 57.

90. The first rural interracial movement, the Southern Tenant Farmers Union was founded by black and white sharecroppers in Arkansas in 1934.

91. Glen calls Claude Williams "a radical Presbyterian minister" (*Highlander,* 43). Prior to coming to Highlander, Zilphia became one of Williams's followers after her graduation from the College of the Ozarks.

92. Huddie Ledbetter (1885–1949), better known as Leadbelly, was an influential blues and folk singer. Through his association with friends such as Woody Guthrie, Pete Seeger, Brownie McGhee, and Sonny Terry, Leadbelly was often involved in left-wing political causes, writing such political songs as "Bourgeois Blues" and "The Scottsboro Boys."

93. See section I, note 58.

94. See note 53 above.

95. Student Nonviolent Coordinating Committee. See section I, note 9.

96. See note 18 above.

97. See section I, note 15.

98. See section I, note 52.

99. Martin Luther King Jr.

100. Civil rights leader Ralph David Abernathy (1936–90) was Martin Luther King Jr.'s chief aide. In 1951, he became pastor of the First Baptist Church in Montgomery, Alabama, and in 1957 he helped King found the Southern Christian Leadership Conference, becoming its first secretary-treasurer.

101. Civil rights activist Coretta Scott King (b. 1927) was married to Martin Luther King Jr.

102. King served at pastor of the Dexter Avenue Baptist Church in Montgomery, Alabama; his father was pastor of the Ebenezer Baptist Church in Atlanta, Georgia.

103. King did his undergraduate degree at Morehouse College, graduating in 1948. He later attended Crozer Theological Seminary in Pennsylvania, graduating with honors in 1951. He earned a doctorate in theology from Boston University in 1955.

104. William Reuther (1907–70) defeated R. J. Thomas (1900–1967), the incumbent, for the presidency of the United Auto Workers in 1946. The campaign was very close, with many on the left supporting Thomas, who had been president since 1939. For a detailed study of this period in the history of the UAW, see Martin Halpern's *UAW Politics in the Cold War Era* (Albany: State Univ. of New York Press, 1988). The educational director at this time was Jack Zeller, but I have found no record of him being campaign chair for Reuther.

105. United Auto Workers.

106. See section I, note 6.

107. National Association for the Advancement of Colored People.

108. *Brown* v. *Board of Education,* 1954. See section I, note 48.

109. See section I, notes 7, 8, and 27.

110. John Lewis (b. 1940) was chairman of the Student Nonviolent Coordinating Committee from 1963 to 1966. He served as executive director of the Voter Education Project from 1970 to 1976 and was elected to the House of Representatives in 1986.

111. One of the organizers of the Student Nonviolent Coordinating Committee, Julian Bond (b. 1940) began his involvement in the civil rights movement during the 1960 sit-ins in Atlanta. In 1971, Bond became the first president of the Southern Poverty Law Center. He also served four terms in the Georgia House of Representatives and six terms in the Georgia Senate, ending his time in public office in 1986. He is currently chair of the National Association for the Advancement of Colored People.

112. James Bevel (b. 1936) and Diane Nash (b. 1938) were founding members of the Student Nonviolent Coordinating Committee and later staff members of the Southern Christian Leadership Conference, as well as participants in the 1963 March on Washington. They married in 1961.

113. See section I, note 55.

114. Gov. Samuel Marvin Griffin. See section II, note 56.

115. The occasion was actually Highlander's twenty-fifth anniversary.

116. For a detailed account, see Glen, *Highlander,* 217–20.

117. See note 38 above.

118. Frank Goad Clement (1920–69) was governor of Tennessee from 1953 to 1959; Earl Buford Ellington (1907–72) was governor from 1959 to 1963. In 1959, the Tennessee legislature passed a bill that asked Governor Ellington to investigate Highlander. For more, see Glen, *Highlander,* 222–24.

119. For a detailed account, see Glen, *Highlander,* 231–32.

120. See section I, note 60.

121. Bracketed information appears in the original.

122. See section I, note 31.

123. President Lyndon B. Johnson's 1964 War on Poverty.

124. Established in 1965, the Appalachian Regional Commission is a regional economic development agency that represents a partnership between federal, state, and local levels of government. Congress appropriates funds annually for the ARC, to be used to fund highways and area development programs in such areas of community facilities, health, education, housing, and energy. The geographical area with which the ARC concerns itself includes all of West Virginia and parts of twelve other states: Alabama, Georgia, Kentucky, Maryland, Mississippi, New York, North Carolina, Ohio, Pennsylvania, South Carolina, Tennessee, and Virginia.

125. American Federation of Labor. See section II, note 2.

Section IV. Educational Philosophy

1. For more on this first term, see Glen, *Highlander,* 23–36.

2. Formed by the federal government in 1932, the Reconstruction Finance Corporation was an effort to help stimulate the economy during the depression through loans to small business enterprises and the buying and selling of securities. It was hoped that such efforts would encourage both production and employment. The RFC was abolished by Congress in 1957.

3. See section II, note 8.

4. See section II, note 6.

5. Oscar V. L. Guermonprez (1912–77) worked for the Allardsoog Adult Education Center in Bakkeveen from 1934 to 1945 and as team leader at the Adult Education Center in Bergen from 1945 to 1977. In addition, he was the cofounder of the European Bureau for Popular Education.

6. Founded in 1932, Allardsoog was the first Adult Education Center in The Netherlands; it is located in Bakkeveen in the province of Friesland.

7. A critic of universal, mandatory education, Everett Reimer wrote *School Is Dead: An Essay on Alternatives in Education* (Garden City, N.Y.: Doubleday, 1972).

8. *Deschooling Society* is actually a book by Ivan Illich.

9. International Telephone and Telegraph.

10. Modeled on the Citizenship Schools, the Appalachian Self-Education Program was an attempt by Highlander to help poor people provide an educational program for themselves. As Glen writes, "The ASEP would consist of community workshops whose agenda and content would entirely be determined by poor people. Community leaders would learn to be educators rather than organizers" (*Highlander,* 263). For a more detailed description, see Glen, *Highlander,* 263–65.

11. See section I, note 6.

12. American psychologist B. F. Skinner (1904–90) was one of the foremost proponents of behaviorism in which human behavior is seen in terms of response to environmental stimuli. He is the author of many books, including *Walden Two* (New York: Macmillan, 1966) and *Science and Human Behavior* (New York: Macmillan, 1960).

13. See section II, note 33.

14. For more on the development of the Danish Folk High Schools and their historical context, see section I, note 41.

15. See section I, note 20.

16. See section I, note 5.

17. See section I, note 27.

18. See section I, note 29.

19. See section I, note 60.

20. See section I, note 8.

21. Beginning in 1961, Freedom Riders, both black and white, sought to challenge illegal segregation practices in transportation in the South and to point out the injustice of the practice, which was in direct violation of federal law.

22. Controversy surrounded the Ocean Hill–Brownsville District when a large number of white teachers, many of whom were Jewish, were fired in a district with a predominantly African American population. For more on this situation, See Tamar Jacoby's *Someone Else's House: America's Unfinished Struggle for Integration* (New York: Free Press, 1988).

23. See section III, note 76.

24. Parker Palmer's and Elden Jacobsen's *Action Research: A New Style of Politics in Education* (Boston: Institute for Responsive Education, 1974).

25. Founded in 1965, Volunteers in Service to America places individuals with agencies in the community in order to help find long-term solutions to the problems caused by urban and rural poverty.

26. For a more detailed account, see Glen, *Highlander,* 154–84.

27. See section I, note 15.

28. See section I, note 5.

29. Folk singer Bruce "Utah" Phillips (b. 1935) is best known for his union and railroad traveling songs.

30. Saul Alinsky. See section I, note 73.

31. See section I, note 5.

32. American Federation of Labor. See section II, note 2.

33. For more on Highlander's stance on Communist unions, see Glen, *Highlander,* 119–27.

34. See section II, note 12.

35. Student Nonviolent Coordinating Committee. See section I, note 9.

36. See section I, note 15.

37. Regarded by many as one of the most influential leaders of the civil rights movement, Fred Shuttlesworth (b. 1922) founded the Alabama Christian Movement for Human Rights in 1956 and was one of the founders of the Southern Christian Leadership Conference. For more on Shuttlesworth, see Andrew M. Manis's *A Fire You Can't Put Out: The Civil Rights Life of Birmingham's Fred Shuttlesworth.*

38. See section I, note 17.

39. See section I, note 6.

40. See section III, note 20.

41. Olson is likely referring to "Dust in Our Lungs."

42. For more information, see Glen, *Highlander,* 39.

43. Emerging from the Students for a Democratic Society, the Weather Underground Organization, also known as Weatherman, was a radical left organization in the late 1960s and 1970s. For a detailed account, see Ron Jacobs's *The Way the Wind Blew: A History of the Weather Underground* (New York: Verso, 1997).

44. Earl Russell Browder (1891–1973) was secretary-general of the Communist Party from 1930 to 1944 and then president of the Communist Political Association from 1944 to 1945. He was the Communist Party's candidate for president in both 1936 and 1940 and editor in chief of the *Daily Worker* from 1944 to 1945.

45. The Socialist Party of America was founded in 1901 at a unity meeting of the Social Democratic Party, led by Eugene Debs, and the Socialist Labor Party. Debs received almost one million votes for president on the Socialist ticket in both 1912 and 1920.

46. The Wobblies was a nickname for the Industrial Workers of the World, a revolutionary industrial union organized in 1905 by Eugene Debs, William Haywood, Daniel De Leon, and others.

47. In his early days, William Zebulon Foster (1881–1961) was associated with the Socialist Party, the Industrial Workers of the World, and then with the American Federation of Labor. He became one of the leaders of the new American Communist Party in 1920, running for president on the Communist Party Ticket in 1924, 1928, and 1932.

48. See section III, note 22

49. Dr. Frederick Douglas Patterson (1901–88) was president of Tuskegee University from 1935 to 1953. In 1944, Dr. Patterson also founded the United Negro College Fund.

50. See section I, note 48.

51. The Gullah language and culture developed in slave communities on the Sea Islands along the southern coast of the United States, especially near South Carolina. The language, a mixture of Elizabethan English and African languages, flourished because the islands were so isolated; many of them were only accessible by boat until as late as the 1950s.

52. Bracketed material in original text.

53. Bracketed material in original text.

54. Bracketed material in original text.

55. Bracketed material in original text.

Works Cited

Adams, Frank. *Unearthing Seeds of Fire: The Idea of Highlander.* Winston-Salem, N.C.: Jon F. Blair, 1975.

Alinsky, Saul D. *Reveille for Radicals.* 1946. New York: Vintage Books, 1969.

———. *Rules for Radicals: A Practical Primer for Realistic Radicals.* New York: Random House, 1971.

Beard, Charles Austin. *The Economic Basis of Politics.* New York: Vintage Books, 1957.

———. *An Economic Interpretation of the Constitution of the United States.* 1941. New York: Macmillan, 1956.

———. *Economic Origins of Jeffersonian Democracy.* 1915. New York: Macmillan, 1949.

Beard, Charles Austin, and Mary R. Beard. *The Rise of American Civilization.* New York: Macmillan, 1930.

Bell, Brenda, John Gaventa, and John Peters, eds. Introduction to *We Make the Road by Walking: Conversations on Education and Social Change.* Philadelphia: Temple Univ. Press, 1990.

Bell, Brenda, and John Peters. "Horton of Highlander." In *Twentieth-Century Thinkers in Adult Education.* Ed. Peter Jarvis. London: Croom Helm, 1987.

Boff, Leonardo, and Clodovius Boff. *Introducing Liberation Theology.* Maryknoll, N.Y.: Orbis Books, 1987.

Borish, Steven M. *The Land of the Living: Danish Folk High Schools and Denmark's Nonviolent Path to Modernization.* Nevada City, Calif.: Blue Dolphin Publishing, 1991.

Campbell, John C. *The Southern Highlander and His Homeland.* 1921. Lexington: Univ. of Kentucky Press, 1969.

Carter, Vicki K. "The Singing Heart of Highlander Folk School." *New Horizons in Adult Education* 8, no. 2 (spring 1994): 4–24.

Caudill, Harry. *My Land Is Dying.* New York: E. P. Dutton, 1971.

———. *Night Comes to the Cumberlands: A Biography of a Depressed Area.* Boston: Little, Brown, 1963.

Chapman, J. Crosby, and George S. Counts. *Principles of Education*. Boston: Houghton Mifflin, 1924.

Clark, Kenneth Bancroft. *Dark Ghetto: Dilemmas of Social Power*. New York: Harper & Row, 1965.

———. *Pathos of Power*. New York: Harper & Row, 1974.

Clark, Septima Poinsette, with LeGette Blythe. *Echo in My Soul*. New York: Dutton, 1962.

———. *Ready from Within: Septima Clark and the Civil Rights Movement*. Ed. Cynthia Stokes Brown. Navarro, Calif.: Wild Trees Press, 1986.

Cort, John C. *Christian Socialism: An Informal History*. Maryknoll, N.Y.: Orbis Books, 1988.

Counts, George S. *Education and American Civilization*. 1952. Westport, Conn.: Greenwood Press, 1974.

———. *Education and the Foundations of Human Freedom*. Pittsburgh: Univ. of Pittsburgh Press, 1962.

Degtrug, Lund, and Manniche Degtrug. *Folk High Schools of Denmark and the Development of the Farming Community*. Oxford: Oxford Univ. Press, 1926.

Dewey, John. *Democracy and Education: An Introduction to the Philosophy of Education*. 1916. New York: Free Press, 1997.

———. *Experience and Education*. New York: Macmillan, 1938.

———. *Experience and Nature*. Chicago: Open Court, 1925.

———. *How We Think*. Boston: D.C. Heath & Co., 1910.

Dropkin, Ruth, and Arthur Tobier, eds. *The Roots of Open Education in America*. New York: City College Workshop Center for Open Education, 1976.

Fager, Charles E. *Selma, 1965: The March that Changed the South*. Boston: Beacon Press, 1985.

Freire, Paulo. "Cultural Action for Freedom." *Harvard Educational Review* and Center for the Study of Development and Social Change, Monograph Series No. 1, 1970.

———. *Education for Critical Consciousness*. Trans. Myra Bergman Ramos. New York: Seaberry Press, 1973.

———. *Pedagogy of Freedom: Ethics, Democracy, and Civic Courage*. Boston: Rowman & Littlefield, 1998.

———. *Pedagogy of Hope: Reliving Pedagogy of the Oppressed*. Trans. Robert R. Barr. New York: Continuum Publishing, 1994.

———. *Pedagogy of the Oppressed*. Trans. Myra Bergman Ramos. New York: Continuum Publishing, 1970.

Gandhi, Mohatma Mohandas Karamchand. *An Autobiography: The Story of My Experiments with Truth.* Trans. Mahadav Desai. Boston: Beacon Press, 1966.

Glen, John. *Highlander: No Ordinary School.* 2d ed. Knoxville: Univ. of Tennessee Press, 1996.

Grundtvig, N. F. S. *Selected Writings.* Philadelphia: Fortress Press, 1976.

Gutierrez, Gustavo. *A Theology of Liberation: History, Politics, and Salvation.* Trans. Caridad Inda and John Eagleson. Maryknoll, N.Y.: Orbis Books, 1988.

Hall, Jacquelyn Dowd, James Laloudis, Robert Korstad, Mary Murphy, Lu Ann Jones, and Christopher B. Daly. *Like a Family: The Making of a Southern Cotton Mill World.* Chapel Hill: Univ. of North Carolina Press, 1987.

Halpern, Martin. *UAW Politics in the Cold War Era.* Albany: State Univ. of New York Press, 1988.

Hamilton, Alexander, John Jay, and James Madison. *The Federalist Papers.* Ed. Clinton Rossiter. New York: Mentor, 1999.

Hart, Joseph K. *Education and the Humane Community.* New York: Harper and Brothers, 1951.

———. *Light from the North: Danish Folk Schools and Their Meaning for America.* New York: Henry Holt, 1927.

Holt, Len. *The Summer that Didn't End: The Story of the Mississippi Civil Rights Project of 1964.* New York: Morrow, 1965.

Horton, Aimee Isgrig. *The Highlander Folk School: A History of the Development of Its Major Programs, 1932–1961.* Brooklyn, N.Y.: Carlson, 1989.

Horton, Myles. "Influences on Highlander Research and Education Center, New Market, Tennessee, USA." In *Grundtvig's Ideas in North America: Influences and Parallels.* Ed. Danish Institute. Holte, Denmark: Danish Institute, 1983.

Horton, Myles, Judith Kohl, and Herb Kohl. *The Long Haul: An Autobiography.* 1990. New York: Teachers College Press, 1998.

Horton, Myles, and Paulo Freire. *We Make the Road by Walking: Conversations on Education and Social Change.* Ed. Brenda Bell, John Gaventa, and John Peters. Philadelphia: Temple Univ. Press, 1990.

Illich, Ivan. *Deschooling Society.* New York: Harper & Row, 1971.

Jacobs, Dale. "Beginning Where They Are: A Re-vision of Critical Pedagogy." *Composition Studies* 25, no. 2 (fall 1997): 39–62.

Jacobs, Ron. *The Way the Wind Blew: A History of the Weather Underground.* New York: Verso, 1997.

Jacoby, Tamar. *Someone Else's House: America's Unfinished Struggle for Integration.* New York: Free Press, 1988.

Kett, J. F. *The Pursuit of Knowledge under Difficulties: From Self-Improvement to Adult Education in America, 1750–1990.* Stanford, Calif.: Stanford Univ. Press, 1994.

Knowles, Malcolm S. *The Modern Practice of Adult Education: Andragogy versus Pedagogy.* New York: Association Press, 1970.

Lawrence, Mary. *Education Unlimited: A Handbook on Union Education in the South.* Monteagle, Tenn.: Highlander Folk School, 1945.

Lester, Julius. *To Be a Slave.* 1969. New York: Scholastic, 1988.

Lindeman, Eduard. *The Meaning of Adult Education.* New York: New Republic, 1926.

MacKenzie, Lawrence. "A Pedagogy of Respect: Teaching as an Ally of Working-Class College Students." In *Coming to Class: Pedagogy and the Social Class of Teachers.* Ed. Alan Shepard, John McMillan, and Gary Tate. 94–117. Portsmouth, N.H.: Boynton/Cook, 1998.

Manniche, Peter. *Living Democracy in Denmark.* Copenhagen, Denmark: Greenwood Press, 1952.

Mannis, Andrew M. *A Fire You Can't Put Out: The Civil Rights Life of Birmingham's Fred Shuttlesworth.* Tuscaloosa: Univ. of Alabama Press, 1999.

McLaren, Peter. *Che Guevera, Paulo Freire, and the Pedagogy of Revolution.* Boston: Rowman & Littlefield, 2000.

Meyer, Adolphe Erich. *The Development of Education in the Twentieth Century.* New York: Prentice-Hall, 1939.

Niebuhr, Reinhold. *Interpretation of Christian Ethics.* New York: Harper, 1935.

———. *Moral Man and Immoral Society: A Study in Ethics and Politics.* New York: Charles Scribner's, 1932.

———. *The Nature and Destiny of Man.* 2 vols. New York: Charles Scribner's, 1941.

Palmer, Parker, and Elden Jacobsen. *Action Research: A New Style of Politics in Education.* Boston: Institute for Responsive Education, 1974.

People of the Cumberland. Dir. Robert Stebbins and Eugene Hill. Frontier Films, 1937.

Reimer, Everett. *School Is Dead: An Essay on Alternatives in Education.* Garden City, N.Y.: Doubleday, 1972.

Rowan, Carl. *Breaking Barriers: A Memoir.* Boston: Little, Brown, 1991.

———. *Dream Makers, Dream Breakers: The World of Justice Thurgood Marshall.* Boston: Little, Brown, 1993.

———. *South of Freedom.* New York: Knopf, 1952.

Salmond, John. *The Conscience of a Lawyer: Clifford J. Durr and American Civil Liberties, 1899–1975.* Tuscaloosa: Univ. of Alabama Press, 1990.

————. *A Southern Rebel: The Life and Times of Aubrey Williams, 1890–1965.* Chapel Hill: Univ. of North Carolina Press, 1982.

Shimahara, Nobuo, ed. *Educational Reconstruction: Promise and Challenge.* Columbus, Ohio: Merrill, 1973.

Shor, Ira. *Empowering Education: Critical Teaching for Social Change.* Chicago: Univ. of Chicago Press, 1992.

Skinner, B. F. *Science and Human Behavior.* 1953. New York: Macmillan, 1960.

————. *Walden Two.* 1948. New York: Macmillan, 1966.

Sumner, William Graham. *Folkways: A Study of the Sociological Importance of Usages, Manners, Customs, Mores, and Morals.* Boston: Ginn and Co., 1906.

Thomas, Norman Mattoon. *A Socialist's Faith.* New York: Norton, 1951.

————. *War—No Profit, No Glory, No Need.* 1927. New York: Vanguard Press, 1972.

Tillich, Paul. *The Courage to Be.* New York: Yale Univ. Press, 1952.

————. *Systematic Theology.* Chicago: Univ. of Chicago Press, 1967.

Tjerandsen, Paul. *Education for Citizenship: A Foundation's Experience.* Santa Cruz, Calif.: Emil Schwarzhaupt Foundation, 1980.

Van Kleeck, Mary Abby. *Creative America: Its Resources for Social Security.* New York: Friede, 1936.

————. *Mines and Management: A Study of the Collective Agreement between the United Mine Workers of America and the Rocky Mountain Fuel Company.* New York: Russell Sage, 1934.

Veblen, Thorstein. *The Theory of the Leisure Class: An Economic Study of Institutions.* New York: Modern Library, 1934.

Ward, Harry F. *Our Economic Morality and the Ethic of Jesus.* New York: Macmillan, 1929.

Wigginton, Eliot, ed. *Refuse to Stand Silently By: An Oral History of Grassroots Social Activism in America, 1921–1964.* New York: Doubleday, 1992.

Yarbrough, Tinsley. *Passion for Justice: J. Waties Waring and Civil Rights.* New York: Oxford Univ. Press, 2002.

Index

THE MYLES HORTON

READER

was designed and typeset on a Macintosh computer system using QuarkXPress software. The text is set in Times Ten, and display type is set in Britannic. This book was designed and typeset by Bill Adams and manufactured by Thomson-Shore, Inc.